The Future of Difference

The Douglass Series on Women's Lives

and the Meaning of Gender

Edited by
Hester Eisenstein
and Alice Jardine

The Future of Difference

Rutgers University Press

New Brunswick and London

Second printing, 1987
First published in cloth in 1980 by G. K. Hall & Company, Boston, Massachusetts.

British Cataloging-in-Publication Information Available

The editors gratefully acknowledge permission to include the following material: Jessica Benjamin, "The Bonds of Love: Rational Violence and Erotic Domination," *Feminist Studies* 6:1 (Spring 1980): 144–74; Nancy Chodorow, "Gender Relation and Difference in Psychoanalytic Perspective," *Socialist Review*, No. 46, 9:4 (July-August 1979):51–69, © 1979 by Nancy Chodorow; Jane Gallop, "Psychoanalysis in France," *Women and Literature* 7:1 (Winter 1979): 57–63, © 1979 by Janet M. Todd, Editor; Carol Gilligan, "In a Different Voice: Women's Conceptions of Self and of Morality," *Harvard Educational Review* 47:4 (1977): 481–517, © 1977 by the President and Fellows of Harvard College; Audre Lorde, "Poems Are Not a Luxury," *Chrysalis: A Magazine of Women's Culture* 1:3 (1977): 7–9, © 1977 by Audre Lorde; Rachel Blau DuPlessis, "For the Etruscans: Sexual Difference and Artistic Production: The Debate over a Female Aesthetic" © 1979 by Rachel Blau DuPlessis; Naomi Schor, "Pour une thématique restreinte: Ecriture, parole et différence dans *Madame Bovary*," *Littérature* 22 (May 1976): 30–46; and Carolyn G. Heilbrun, "Androgyny and the Psychology of Sex Differences" © 1980 by Carolyn G. Heilbrun. (Note that of the articles reprinted, those by Benjamin and Chodorow were originally prepared for inclusion in this volume.)

The Introduction © 1980 by Hester Eisenstein.

DAUGHTERS (excerpts) © 1977, SISTER/SISTER ® 1978 by Clare Coss, Sondra Segal, Roberta Sklar. All rights, including professional, stock, amateur, motion picture, radio and television broadcasting, and readings, are strictly reserved, and no portion of these plays may be performed without written authorization and/or the payment of a royalty. Inquiries may be addressed to The Women's Experimental Theater, 98 East 7th Street, New York, NY 10009, (212) 886–7785.

Library of Congress Cataloging in Publication Data
Main entry under title:

The Future of difference.

(The Douglass series on women's lives and the meaning of gender)
Reprint. Originally published: New York: Barnard College Women's Center, 1980.
Essays drawn from a conference sponsored by the Barnard College Women's Center and held in New York City, April 29, 1979.
Bibliography: p.
Includes index.
1. Feminism—United States—Congresses. I. Eisenstein, Hester. II. Jardine, Alice. III. Barnard College. Women's Center. IV. Series.
[HQ1403.F88   1984]   305.4′2′0973   84-27715
ISBN 0-8135-1112-7 (pbk.)

Contents

Preface

The essays in this volume are drawn from "The Scholar and The Feminist VI: The Future of Difference," a conference sponsored by the Barnard College Women's Center and held in New York City on April 29, 1979. An annual event, funded by the Helena Rubinstein Foundation, the Scholar and the Feminist conferences have sought to examine urgent current issues—intellectual, political, and social—raised at the points of intersection between the contemporary women's movement and the traditional academy, in an open dialogue between researchers and activists, and among the several disciplines. This is the first of the conferences to be published as a book (papers from three previous ones have appeared as pamphlets) and it inaugurates what it is hoped will be an ongoing series, so that the limited number attending can be expanded to a much wider audience, national and international.

Before turning to the background of "the future of difference," I want to give a brief account of how the Scholar and Feminist conferences are organized, and how they have evolved since 1974. Overall responsibility for administering the conference lies with Jane S. Gould, director of the Barnard Women's Center, and the Center staff; the conceptualization and realization of the theme are the task of the academic coordinator, who works, in a collective process, with a planning committee, made up of Women's Center staff, faculty members and students from Barnard College and Columbia University, and others from the wider New York community. The theme, speakers, and format are chosen after many weeks and sometimes months of debate and discussion.

In the first year, "The Scholar and the Feminist" (Susan Riemer Sacks, academic coordinator) asked the fundamental question, can feminism and scholarship be integrated, and what are the ensuing enrichments and contradictions? The participants presented autobiographical accounts of the impact of feminism on their lives and work as scholars and activists. In 1975, with Women's Studies increasingly making its way into the academy, "Toward New Criteria of Relevance" (Nancy K. Miller) sought to outline how a feminist perspective challenges and alters traditional academic definitions. That is, how does feminism affect both methodology (how research is carried out), and subject matter (what it is that is considered legitimate to do research on)? In 1976 the inquiry focused on the origins of women's oppression, drawing on the perspectives, inter alia, of anthropology and the history of religion. In 1977 an attempt was made to carry the feminist critique of the university into the realm of values: what value system is implied by dominant academic practices, despite the claim of the university to be "value-free," and what kinds of new values does feminist scholarship embody? In 1978 the conference examined some of the new forms and processes to be discerned in the works and experiences of feminist artists and scholars. (See Hester Eisenstein, ed., *The Scholar and The Feminist III: The Search for Origins*, 1976; Mary Brown Parlee, ed., *The Scholar and The Feminist IV: Connecting Theory, Practice and Values*, 1977; and Elizabeth K. Minnich, ed., *The Scholar and The Feminist V: Creating Feminist Works*, 1978; all New York: Barnard College Women's Center, and available from the Center. The editor of each was academic coordinator for that conference.) As this volume goes to press, plans are being completed for the 1980 conference, "Class, Race and Sex—Exploring Contradictions, Affirming Connections" (Amy Swerdlow).

It may be useful to give some details here on the relationship between the 1979 conference and this book, and how we got from one to the other. The day was organized in three parts: a morning panel, introduced and moderated by Alice Jardine, academic coordinator, on "the future of difference," with Nancy Chodorow, Josette Féral, and Monique Wittig; a midday panel, chaired by Domna Stanton, on "difference and language," with Audre Lorde, Sally McConnell-Ginet, and Christiane Makward; and a series of afternoon workshops on a variety of related topics. For the book, Alice and I asked all the participants to write something that was based upon what they had presented at the conference. But of the sessions that day, only the morning panel had consisted of formal papers. All the others had been short oral presentations, followed by discussion. In essence, therefore, we were asking the participants to perform a second, and separate, task. Only three people were unable to contribute to the book (Alice Kessler-Harris and Eleanor Leacock, because of other commitments, and Monique Wittig, because she had promised prior publication of her paper elsewhere, although she provided us with a summary; see below, p. xxi). All the other participants have contributed to the contents of this volume.

Some rewrote their original papers (Nancy Chodorow, Josette Féral, Sally McConnell-Ginet, and Christiane Makward). Some listened to a tape recording of their workshops and then wrote an expanded version of their original presentations, incorporating issues raised in the discussion (Jessica Benjamin, Carolyn G. Burke, Tucker Pamella Farley, Jane Flax, Carolyn G. Heilbrun, Ruth Messinger, Barbara Omolade, and Quandra Prettyman). One contacted all the members of her workshop, collected responses, and then incorporated these into an essay-collage (Rachel Blau DuPlessis). In one case, the editors were able to supply an edited transcript of the discussion, appended to the original presentation (Elizabeth Janeway). (Unfortunately this was not possible for other workshops, given our limited resources.) Other participants contributed materials that had appeared previously elsewhere, but that had been the basis of their presentations at the conference (Carol Gilligan, Audre Lorde); one, in a new translation and with a postscript inspired by the workshop discussion (Naomi Schor); and another, with a new introduction (Jane Gallop). One chapter contains the dramatic excerpts that were performed by the Women's Experimental Theater at the conference, with an introduction (Clare Coss, Roberta Sklar, and Sondra Segal). And one participant chose to include new material, rather than to rework what she said at the conference (Domna Stanton).

As a result of this interesting and varied process of transmutation, the organization of the book differs considerably from the organization of the conference. In addition, many of the chapters include the authors' reflections on the experience of the conference; there are thus echoes and reverberations back and forth among the parts of the book. Meanwhile, Alice was compelled for professional reasons to spend most of the summer and all of the academic year 1979–80 in Paris, making only one flying visit to New York City. Hence it was agreed that I, who was originally to be general editor of the series, would become editor of this volume, as well, while Alice, who could do some pieces of the editing but not oversee the entire task, would become associate editor. The responsibility for the final form of the book (as well as for any errors or omissions) thus rests with me.

My thanks and appreciation go to everyone who helped me in putting this book together: to Jane S. Gould, Janie Kritzman, and Christi Greene of the Barnard College Women's Center for their support, material, and psychological; to Alice Jardine, with whom I worked closely if transatlantically; to all the other contributors to the volume, for their cooperation and hard work; to Irene Finel-Honigman, Nancy K. Miller, Ellin Sarot, and Catharine R. Stimpson for their useful comments on the preface and introduction; to Ellen Doherty, Hedy Floersheimer, and Catherine Franke for editorial and clerical assistance, especially in the final stages;

and to Clive S. Kessler, my husband, for his advice, practical assistance, and wholehearted encouragement.

HESTER EISENSTEIN
New York
March 1980

I would like to express my personal gratitude to the untiring and dedicated Jane S. Gould and Janie Kritzman of the Barnard Women's Center; to the ever-patient and supportive Hester Eisenstein and Nancy K. Miller; and to all the other hardworking and open-minded members of the Conference Planning Committee: Louise Adler, Roberta Bernstein, Mary Jane Ciccarello, Irene Finel-Honigman, Suzanne Hanchett, Elizabeth K. Minnich, Ellen Pollak, Susan R. Sacks, Philippa Strum, and Kathryn B. Yatrakis. All of these people were essential to the process of bringing the conference, and therefore this book, together.

ALICE JARDINE
Paris
March 1980

Post-preface

I welcome the reissuing of *The Future of Difference* in this paperback edition. Thanks to Rutgers University Press the book will now have a much wider audience, although in the three years since its publication it has become something of an underground classic. The issues surrounding women's difference and differences among women are, if anything, more acute now than then, in a time when feminist optimism has been sorely tested by current political realities. I hope that this book's rebirth signals a renewal of strength and energy for those committed to making the world safe for difference.

Hester Eisenstein
Sydney, 1984

Hester Eisenstein

Introduction

The theme of "difference" has been integral to modern feminist thought from at least the time of the publication of Simone de Beauvoir's *The Second Sex*, and in particular since the rebirth of the women's movement in the late 1960s.[1] It is probably too early, in 1980, to attempt the writing of a comprehensive history of recent feminist thought. In any case, it is certainly not my intention to undertake that very considerable task here. But I do want to point to some elements of an analysis of this period, in order to place the essays collected here into a broader context. I want especially to suggest that, in the past decade, there have been significant developments in the attitudes expressed by feminist writers on the subject of difference.

When the "second wave" of the women's movement began to reach the attention of the mass media of the United States, it was portrayed primarily as a threat to the difference between the sexes. To summarize this media caricature of the dangers of feminism: women *are* different from men, and therein lies their charm. Women are "feminine," that is, delicate, emotional, fragile, passive, and dependent. Men are "masculine," that is, rugged, intellectual, strong, active, and independent. And *vive la différence*! If the ideas of the women's movement were to prevail, and women were to emerge from their "proper" place, they would lose their femininity, and begin to think, look, and act exactly like men. If this were to happen, the spice of sexual excitement would vanish, and, with the basis of heterosexual bonding thus destroyed, the family, and soon thereafter society itself, would crumble.

However misconceived and distorted, the media portrait was not entirely fantastic: it had its source in one important current of feminist thinking of the late 1960s and early 1970s, namely, the radical critique of "masculinity" and "femininity" undertaken by Kate Millett, Elizabeth Janeway, and others.[2] According to this critique, these concepts are part of the tool-kit of oppression as practiced by patriarchy. That is, the domination by men of women, as carried out in advanced Western societies, is effected not by force, generally speaking, but through the creation of consent, by means of an elaborate apparatus of social conditioning into appropriate "sex-role" behavior.

Using the concept of sex-role stereotyping, these writers pointed out that biological sex is not coextensive with social gender. Drawing on the findings of researchers into the origins of "core gender identity," they argued that gender is a learned, or acquired, fact of social life, subject to conditioning and reinforcement in the early months of childhood. Further, they pointed to the degree of social pressure exerted throughout the life-cycle to produce behavior considered appropriate to one's gender. The time and energy spent in teaching girls and boys to act like a "lady" or a "man," respectively, belied the notion that these qualities were either inbred or natural.

What was the purpose of seeking to demonstrate that these behavioral stereotypes were theoretically and practically separable from the biological sexes to which they had been attached? Obviously, one of the goals of the women's movement was to remove the obstacles to the full participation of women in all aspects of social life. A primary obstacle appeared to be the belief, and the argument, that women were "different" and were limited by virtue of that difference to the domestic sphere. The requirement that women behave like ladies was a means of artificially *increasing* the differences between men and women, in order to keep women in their place. An important task of feminist thinking, then, was to demonstrate that the differences between women and men had been exaggerated, and that they could be *reduced*. "Male" and "female" qualities, the argument ran, existed potentially in everyone, and needed only to be brought out by new forms of education and family organization.

An extreme example of the argument against difference was the position taken by Shulamith Firestone in 1970 on pregnancy.[3] The most obvious difference between women and men, and the hardest one to argue away, is the mammalian function performed by women as childbearers. Despite our efforts, Firestone held, women would never be entirely the equals of men until we were able to get rid of this difference, as well. She called therefore for the abolition of pregnancy, and for the creation and control by females of a technology that could create test-tube babies outside the womb. Only with this radical erasure of our most radical difference from men could she envision the creation of a "feminist revolution."

Parallel to the impulse to minimize or to abolish the differences between women and men was an attempt to deemphasize the differences among women through the process of consciousness-raising. As women met in small groups and exchanged accounts of life experiences, one of the goals was the achievement of a sense of commonality, despite differences in biographical detail. It was evident to those engaging in this process that some differences had been emphasized, and even created, to keep women separated from one another. Marital status, for example, had long been a source of competitive feelings and of distance between women. Through consciousness-raising, women sought (not always with success) to identify and to develop the qualities that united them, across the boundaries set by social categories: mothers with nonmothers; heterosexual women with lesbians; white women with women of color; and privileged women with poor women. Ultimately, it was thought, the condition and experience of being female would prove to be more important in defining women than the specifics of our differences from one another.

What lay behind these parallel impulses to diminish or to minimize the importance of differences, on the one hand, between women and men, and on the other, among women of all classes, ages, races, and sexual allegiances? I think that they both stemmed from a profound understanding of the political uses of difference. The women's movement had absorbed the lesson of the civil rights movement: "separate," or different, was not "equal." Feminist analysis had revealed that the traditional celebration of women's "difference" from men concealed a conviction of women's inferiority and an intention to keep women relatively powerless. Thus difference from men meant inequality and continued oppression for women. Within the women's movement, to acknowledge or to emphasize differences seemed equally dangerous. It implied the creation of comparisons, of competition and of hierarchies, and, therefore, of insuperable obstacles to unity.

During the early 1970s, then, at least some members of the women's movement shared a belief in what has been called "the mythic power of sisterhood,"[4] that is, the ideological and political conviction that women were more unified by the fact of being female in a patriarchal society than we were divided by specificities of race or class. As the field of Women's Studies, "the academic arm of the women's movement," as Florence Howe has called it,[5] began to develop, some of its practitioners in research and teaching used this same concept, in another form, as a principle of organization. That is, they argued that the commonality or universality of women's experience justified the use of "women" as a category of analysis, as a generic grouping that could legitimately define a field of study. As Juliet Mitchell and others pointed out, although it was not immediately clear what kind of a category this was—were women a class? a caste? a "minority"? a majority?—nonetheless, they were united over time and space by their experience as members of the longest and perhaps most universally oppressed of human groupings.[6]

There was a second element in the argument for establishing Women's Studies as a distinct field of inquiry. This was the argument from exclusion.

The experience of women had simply been omitted from traditional definitions of knowledge. The creation of Women's Studies was necessary, it was held, because women's lives were not included in standard accounts. Or, to put this the other way around, purportedly comprehensive accounts of human experience were rejected on the ground that they did not include female experience, and were therefore both inaccurate and distorted. This justification, it should be noted, rested on an assumption about difference: specifically, that women's lives *were* different from men's, and that it was precisely this difference that required illumination.

Armed with these concepts—the use of women as a legitimate category of analysis, and the prior exclusion of women's experience from the relevant academic disciplines—Women's Studies researchers set out to uncover and to document the worlds of women, and to begin the work of describing and analyzing women's history, psychology, anthropology, and literature, among other areas. This activity represented a considerable shift in emphasis. When feminist writers were rediscovering sex roles and demonstrating their uses in the perpetuation of patriarchy, they had stressed the need to abolish culturally produced differences between women and men as the surest path to equality. Now, far from seeking to minimize women's differences from men, feminist scholars were asserting their importance as a legitimate and even a crucial focus of study.

This focus upon women—what Gerda Lerner has called a "woman-centered analysis"[7]—gradually produced a change in attitude toward the value of women's differences from men. Originally seen as a source of oppression, these were now beginning to appear, on the contrary, as a source of enrichment. Writing in 1976, Jean Baker Miller sought to show that the very psychological qualities evoked by the oppression of women could represent a means of increasing women's strength.[8] To be sure, she argued, women have been taught to be passive. But they have also learned to be nurturing, affiliative, and cooperative—in short, to be endowed with more truly human qualities than are men as currently socialized.

In a similar vein, on the vexed question of reproduction (apparently more a biological than a cultural difference), Adrienne Rich's book on motherhood, published in 1976, provided a striking contrast to the views of Shulamith Firestone in 1970.[9] Rich distinguished between the experience of motherhood, as it might be imagined in a freer society, and the institution of motherhood, by which she meant not the actual mammalian childbearing capacity of women, but its mode of integration into patriarchal structures of power. In this view, the feminist revolution would liberate women, not *from* motherhood, as Firestone had held, but *into* a truly nurturing motherhood, if they chose, perhaps for the first time in history. Rich saw female physiology as a source of strength, not of incapacity, providing women with a richness of experience that might extend potentially to a new human possibility: the healing of the ancient Western (male) split between mind/thought and body/emotion.

As Adrienne Rich's views on female physiology suggest, a woman-centered focus gave rise to some new ideas about maleness and masculinity, too. After all, from this point of view maleness was the difference, or, (to reverse Simone de Beauvoir's terms) men were the Other. Going beyond an initial attention to sex-role socialization, feminist writers such as Dorothy Dinnerstein were taking a second, more profound look at the cultural meanings and implications of "maleness" and "femaleness," and of heterosexuality as a social institution.[10] They were beginning to ask whether "masculinity" was perhaps an outmoded, or even a dangerous, construct. In an extension of this line of thought, the question was raised, by Evelyn Fox Keller, among others, as to whether the very organization of knowledge, the Western concept of science, might be linked to a psychological distortion common to males, and reified in the male-dominated university as the ideal of "objectivity."[11]

A woman-centered perspective produced new views about differences among women, as well. Beginning with a hypothesis about the unity or universality of female experience, feminist scholars soon expanded their horizons, as they uncovered the plethora of differences in women's lives, historically and cross-culturally. Even the original certainty about the universal oppression of women was now up for debate. Using women as a category of analysis, it turned out, was a means of uncovering the variety of female experience, rather than its uniformity, as Michelle Rosaldo has remarked.[12] In this sense, the development of Women's Studies was like a mirror image of the process of consciousness-raising, in which the particularities of each woman's experience are incorporated into a general analysis of how patriarchy operates. Here, a focus on the unity of women's experience gave rise, paradoxically, to an increasing and broadening knowledge of the many important differences in the lives of women, differences that, initially, there had been a reluctance either to emphasize or to explore. In taking this direction, the field of Women's Studies was also responding to changes in the political arena. As the women's movement grew more diverse, it was being forced to confront and to debate issues of difference—most notably those of race and class—as, for example, in discussions and organizing efforts around the issues of abortion and forced sterilization. Thus the discussion and the acknowledgment of differences among women was increasingly a political as well as an academic necessity.

If the schematic view I have been outlining here is accurate, it indicates that the idea of looking at differences and analyzing them from a variety of perspectives had been placed on the feminist agenda in the late 1970s in a way that would have been hard to imagine ten years earlier. What explains this shift in attitude? Part of the answer lies in the logic of a feminist analysis. Before any detailed look at particularities and differences could begin, it was first necessary to establish the validity of seeing women's experience as a generic phenomenon—that is, to establish the reality of patriarchy and of women's oppression within it. But, in addition, I have been suggesting that the move away from the analysis of sex roles under patriarchy, which was the task of earlier feminist writers, and toward a woman-centered perspective, has had a liberating effect. It seems to have created an increased willingness to contemplate the varieties of female experience, and a freedom to look at male experience as different, or even deviant, from what in this view is considered central, or normal. Perhaps, too, the situation of the women's movement politically—in a period of increasing backlash against ideas of progressive social change— has given renewed urgency to the task of understanding differences among women. These, then, were some of the elements in recent feminist thought that lay behind the decision to address the question of "the future of difference."

Following a "prelude" by Alice Jardine, the essays collected here are divided into four thematic parts. In Part I, "Differentiation and the Sexual Politics of Gender," the issue of difference is placed in the context of differentiation, the psychoanalytic term for the process by which children first learn that they are not coextensive with the world. What are the psychological and political repercussions of this process, given that the "object" from which children differentiate themselves is their (female) mother? The writers in this section argue that they are enormous. Continuing the investigation begun in her book on the reproduction of mothering, Nancy Chodorow looks at the process of differentiation as the basis of our concept of difference, in general, and for the formation of gender identity, in particular. Jane Flax explores this issue in relation to its far-reaching implications for the reevaluation of the history of political theory and of Freudian psychology, and then focuses upon a case study of the development of female autonomy in a mother-daughter relationship. Jessica Benjamin examines the relation between the formation of gender identity and what she calls "rational violence," as exercised in heterosexual erotic relationships.

In Part II, "Contemporary Feminist Thought in France: Translating Difference," the notion of difference is examined from the perspective of some French feminist writers and critics. In recent years, work has begun on "translating" the thinking of French feminists into the English-speaking world. Not an easy task! What Domna Stanton calls here "the Franco-

American dis-connection" has many elements: the initial barrier of language; the variety and complexity of French feminisms (only some of which are represented here); and the numerous differences of "discourse," meaning (if I may hazard the translation of such a charged and central term) both a particular use of language and the philosophical presuppositions that this use embodies. Some of these complexities are set forth in the essay by Stanton, who argues that certain voices of feminism in the United States come surprisingly close to the views of such writers as Hélène Cixous, Julia Kristeva, and Luce Irigaray, who are, in various ways, calling for the creation of a specifically women's language and writing. Josette Féral explains why the idea of "difference," in the work of some French writers, has a revolutionary meaning, in that the goal of the feminist enterprise is not to achieve socioeconomic equality with men but to disrupt and subvert Western patriarchal language and thought themselves. But Christiane Makward points to some of the contradictions and difficulties inherent in the position of implicitly accepting a Freudian and patriarchal definition of the "essence" of femaleness. Jane Gallop and Carolyn G. Burke explicate the relation of some French feminist writers to the psychoanalytic tradition, particularly in the work of Jacques Lacan, showing why French feminists have been more receptive than their American sisters to this body of ideas. Like Stanton, Burke suggests a possible link to American feminist writers, who are also "rethinking the maternal."*

Part III, "The Language of Difference: Female and Male in Speech and Literary Production," addresses some of the issues raised by feminists, French and English-speaking alike, about "female" language and aesthetics. What is the relation of language to gender? Do women's speech and writing have a recognizable specificity? These questions are treated here explicitly and implicitly in a variety of forms, including both critical analysis and experimental writing. Audre Lorde evokes the special force of poetry as a source of strength and courage for those seeking to reach "the woman's place of power within each of us." In her essay-collage, Rachel Blau DuPlessis conducts a poetic and critical search for the "lost" language of women: is there a female aesthetic and style, and if so, what are its points of contact and convergence with other moments in literary history and analysis? Sally McConnell-Ginet outlines some of the work already carried out by feminist linguists on the relation between gender

---

*A radically different brand of feminism is espoused by Monique Wittig in the essay she summarizes as follows: "An analysis of the ideology of heterosexuality, from a lesbian perspective, focusing upon the conceptual constructs used in academic discourse; Monique Wittig, "The Straight Mind (La pensée 'straight')," *Questions féministes* 7 (December 1979) and *Feminist Issues* 1, 1 (Summer 1980).

and the use of language, and calls for a more precise and politically sophisticated conception, among feminists, of the role of language in culture. In a complex rereading of *Madame Bovary*, Naomi Schor explores the implications for the interpretation of a text when the male author identifies with, and in some sense speaks for, the female protagonist. She asks the question, Does writing itself have a "sex"? Clare Coss, Sondra Segal, and Roberta Sklar, in the excerpts from their dramatic trilogy, show women exploring their relationships within the family without male intervention or mediation.

In Part IV, "The Naming of Difference: Morality, Power, and Social Change," the question is raised, from a variety of perspectives, as to the relation between the defining of differences and the exercise of power. How do differences among women—black and white; heterosexual and lesbian—get translated into differences of power? Who speaks for the women's movement? Is the "different," that is, heretofore marginal, status of women in public life a source of strength, of a new perspective on morality and ethics, and of an alternative approach to the use of power? And if not, what *is* the ultimate purpose of seeking power for women?

The first two essays examine the relation of black women to feminism. Quandra Prettyman looks at the implicit "tradition of black feminism" in the lives of four women: two nineteenth-century activists and organizers (Sojourner Truth and Frances Ellen Watkins Harper) and two twentieth-century novelists (Nella Larsen and Zora Neale Hurston). Barbara Omolade criticizes white feminists, historical and contemporary, for a false universalism that fails to take into account the experience of black women, from Africa through slavery to the modern black community; she calls for the creation of an independent black feminism.

The next two chapters raise questions about the redefinition of sexuality and gender. They implicitly ask: what would a "postfeminist" gender identity look like? Acknowledging that the concept of androgyny has become so acceptable that it is now suspect to many feminists, Carolyn G. Heilbrun nonetheless calls for a reevaluation of the idea. Pamella Farley demonstrates how "difference" becomes the basis of oppression in her discusion of lesbianism as a social taboo and necessary support of the heterosexual power system.

The final three essays examine the relation of women to morality and power. Using a study of decision-making about pregnancy and abortion, Carol Gilligan argues that women have a special relationship to moral choices. Ruth Messinger draws on her own political experience to analyze the problems and opportunities of women in public life. After outlining the "powers of the weak" exercised by women as traditional outsiders, Elizabeth Janeway discusses with her audience the new kinds of power women can or should be seeking, and the implications of these choices for the long-range goals of the women's movement.

Taken together, these essays may raise more questions than they answer. What is the full range of differences among women and, in particular, among feminists? The issue of differences of class among women is not addressed here, and although the issue of race and ethnicity in relation to feminism is broached, it is by no means fully explored. What are the implications of these and other cross-cultural differences for the eventual realization of the project of a unified women's movement, national and international? Similarly, in relation to male and female differences: what are the consequences, for the theory and practice of feminism, of the fact that the concept of difference seems to be so connected to ideas of "male" and "female," and that these, in turn, are so thoroughly embedded in the language, thought, and cultural organization of the societies that we are attempting to transform?

These questions, in turn, lead to the overall questions that are raised implicitly by the title of this volume. What *is* the future of difference, and what do we want it to be? In some ways, the discussion seems discouraging. As Alice Jardine remarks, concentrating upon difference does not seem to get us beyond the pendulum swing between "same as" and "different from." If, as some of the writers here argue, "maleness" seems irrevocably tied to linearity of thought and rationality, then does "femaleness" have to imply incoherence, or, as Christiane Makward says, "observing an hour of silence," or a lifetime? Is androgyny (or gynandry) an unworthy goal because, as Carolyn Heilbrun points out, it persists in being defined by, and therefore limited to, the very "male"-"female" polarity that we are trying to escape? Does the position of celebrating women as more virtuous than men, because of our experience of oppression, lead us, as Nancy Chodorow warns, into the embrace of a new, nonliberating ideology of the "natural" superiority of women?

Clearly, much more debate and discussion of these issues will have to take place, and these essays are a beginning rather than an end-point. But it may be relevant here to recall the fundamental insight that it is not difference in itself that has been dangerous to women and other oppressed groups, but the political uses to which the idea of difference has been put. The defining of difference has traditionally been linked to the exercise of power, to those who have been in a position to say who is "different," and should therefore be subordinate. I have tried to indicate that, in the recent evolution of feminist thought, a shift to a woman-centered perspective seems to have been accompanied by an increased willingness to contemplate and to examine the meaning of difference and differences. If the naming of differences by the oppressor is replaced with, or at least challenged and contested by, the reclaiming of difference and of individuality by the hitherto oppressed, then a step has been taken along the road to liberation. This, I think, is the process already undertaken by feminists, in this volume and elsewhere.

Notes

1. Tr. H. M. Parshley. New York: Alfred A. Knopf, 1953 (orig. pub. as *Le Deuxième Sexe* [Paris: Gallimard, 1949]).
2. Kate Millett, *Sexual Politics* (New York: Doubleday and Co., Inc., 1970); Elizabeth Janeway, *Man's World, Woman's Place: A Study in Social Mythology* (New York: Dell Publishing, 1971).
3. In *The Dialectic of Sex: The Case for Feminist Revolution* (New York: William Morrow and Co., Inc., 1970), esp. pp. 206 ff.
4. Judith Clavir, "Choosing Either/Or: A Critique of Metaphysical Feminism," *Feminist Studies* 5:2 (Summer 1979): 409.
5. Florence Howe, "Feminism and the Education of Women," in *The Frontiers of Knowledge*, Judith Stiehm, ed. (Los Angeles: Univ. of Southern California Press, 1976), p. 83.
6. Juliet Mitchell, *Women's Estate* (New York: Vintage Books, 1973, orig. pub. 1971), pp. 99 ff.
7. In *The Majority Finds Its Past: Placing Women in History* (New York: Oxford Univ. Press, 1979), p. xxxi.
8. In *Toward a New Psychology of Women* (Boston: Beacon Press, 1976), passim.
9. *Of Woman Born: Motherhood as Experience and Institution* (New York: W. W. Norton & Co., Inc., 1976).
10. *The Mermaid and The Minotaur: Sexual Arrangements and Human Malaise* (New York: Harper & Row, 1976).
11. See Evelyn Fox Keller, "Gender and Science," *Psychoanalysis and Contemporary Thought* 1 (1978): 409–33. But Keller warns feminists against throwing out the baby of true objectivity with the bathwater of masculinist distortions of the scientific method; see her "Feminist Critique of Science: A Forward or Backward Move?" (unpublished paper).
12. In "The Use and Abuse of Anthropology: Reflections on Feminist and Cross-Cultural Understanding," *Signs: Journal of Women in Culture and Society* 5, 3 (Spring 1980): 389–417.

Alice Jardine

Prelude: The Future of Difference

A few words of introduction to the thematics of "the future of difference": each of the previous conferences in this Barnard series has focused in different ways upon the process, product, and function of feminist scholarship. These conferences reflect, in a dramatic way, the phases of consciousness through which we, as feminists, have passed: from an original emphasis on the commonality of the female experience to a recognition that, if we are to give form to a new vision, we must constantly examine *every* cultural presupposition as we explore the possibilities of comprehending, communicating, and ultimately changing our experiences.

Integral to this process of seizing our own self-conception is the theorization process itself. The conference planning committee—whose meetings constituted a kind of conference in themselves—began its discussions with an interrogation of theory. These discussions centered upon two facts: that, as feminist critics, we perceive and conceptualize the world differently from men, *and* that there is a growth of constructive internal debates among feminists, both within and across disciplines, as to why this perception is different.

Now, if there is anything we can all agree upon, it is that women are not men. Or can we? As Nancy Miller put it in one of the many position papers that contributed to the formulation of the conference, that apparently neutral distinction is anything but innocent, in that Western culture has proven to be incapable of thinking not-the-same-as without assigning one of the terms a positive value and the other, a negative. The response to difference on the part of women varies: there are those who exalt it by embracing a certain biology—and a certain eroticism. There are also those who deny it, or, rather, who seek to defuse the power of difference by minimizing biology and emphasizing cultural coding: on some level, these responses are saying, "Woman would be the same as . . . if only." A third strand states, like the first group, that women are indeed different from men, but for feminist reasons they add: women are also *better* than men. This group's reasons would not be biological but sociocultural: as outsiders and nurturers, women do things differently from, and better than, men. At this point it seems impossible to think difference without thinking it aggressively or defensively. But think it we must, because if we don't, it will continue to think us, as it has since Genesis at the very least.

Over and above, or perhaps below, this spectrum of responses to difference, *the* theoretical question persists: Is there a way to think outside the patriarchally determined Same/Other, Subject/Object dichotomies diagnosed as the fact of culture by Simone de Beauvoir thirty years ago, and, in the process, still include women as a presence? In other words, do we want to continue reorganizing the relationship of difference to sameness through a dialectics of valorization, or is there a way to break down the overdetermined metaphors which continue to organize our perceptions of reality?

We are beginning to hear echoes on this side of the Atlantic of certain New French Feminisms which are addressing precisely these questions, but in ways fundamentally different from ours.[1] It is true that I tend to hear French echoes better than others. When Jane Gould asked me to be academic coordinator of the 1979 Barnard conference, I doubt if she realized how important would be the fact that I spend my life walking the tightrope of contradictions between the French and American feminist stances. As Elaine Marks has put it, American feminists emphasize the *oppression* of woman as sexual identity, while French feminists investigate the *repression* of woman as difference and alterity in the signifying practices of the West. To quote Marks, "We raise consciousness by speaking to and working with each other; they explore the unconscious by writing."[2] That is to say, we use words like autonomy and power; they use words like phallocentrism and that word for pleasure which defies translation, *jouissance.*[3] Many American feminists tend to reject the French feminists' writing as impossibly elitist, and as grounded in a philosophical tradition essentially different from ours. The French feminists, on the other hand, often reject American feminism as hopelessly bound up in the very categories of phenomenology they are attempting to explode. As I see it, it is precisely at the sensitive point of contact between American feminist thought—a primarily *ethical* discourse *as prescription for action* and a certain French emphasis on the *human subject's inscription in culture through language*—that we can avoid the neutralization of the question of difference.

One further point: we now know that the inscription of woman into the discursive truth of the dominant order is not subversive to that order. We are becoming more acutely aware of the positions from which we speak and the uses to which our words are put. The positing of difference as a problematic by and for feminists has high epistemological and political stakes. It couldn't have been done even ten years ago. It is perhaps related to a larger historical shift away from Hamlet's founding question, "To be or not to be?''—the anguished "who am I?—toward that fundamentally twentieth-century question, "Who is speaking?" The conference was organized as a space for a multiplicity of voices investigating difference in very different ways. But this multiplicity of voices is also a common voice, which crosses cultural, political, and linguistic boundaries. It is a constantly renewed voice, a strong voice, which, in spite of or perhaps because of difference, will continue to reject the metaphor of woman as a detour on the way to man's truth.

Notes

1. See Elaine Marks and Isabelle de Courtrivon, eds., *New French Feminisms* (Amherst: Univ. of Massachusetts Press, 1979).
2. Elaine Marks, "Women and Literature in France," *Signs: Journal of Women in Culture and Society* 3:4 (Summer 1978): 842.
3. A word for pleasure which has been translated as both "bliss" and "ecstasy"; these terms do not include, however, its sexual reading of "orgasm." Because of the controversy over the correct translation, *jouissance* is rapidly becoming a neologism in English.

Part I
Differentiation and the Sexual Politics of Gender

Nancy Julia Chodorow

Gender, Relation, and Difference in Psychoanalytic Perspective

> I would go so far as to say that even before slavery or class
> domination existed, men built an approach to women that would
> serve one day to introduce differences among us all.
>
> Claude Lévi-Strauss[1]

In both the nineteenth- and twentieth-century women's movements, many feminists have argued that the degendering of society, so that gender and sex no longer determined social existence, would eliminate male dominance. This view assumes that gender differentiating characteristics are acquired. An alternate sexual politics and analysis of sexual inequality has tended toward an essentialist position, posing male-female difference as innate. Not the degendering of society, but its appropriation by women, with women's virtues, is seen as the solution to male dominance. These virtues are uniquely feminine, and usually thought to emerge from women's biology, which is then seen as intrinsically connected to or entailing a particular psyche, a particular social role (such as mothering), a particular body image (more diffuse, holistic, nonphallocentric), or a particular sexuality (not centered on a particular organ; at times, lesbianism). In this view, women are intrinsically better than men and their virtues are not available to men. Proponents of the degendering model have sometimes also held that "female" virtues or qualities—nurturance, for instance—should be spread throughout society and replace aggression and competitiveness; but these virtues are nevertheless seen as acquired, a product of women's development or social location, and acquirable by men, given appropriate development, experience, and social reorganization. (Others who argue for degendering have at times held that women need to acquire certain "male" characteristics and modes of action—autonomy, independence, assertiveness—again, assuming that such characteristics are acquired.)

I am very grateful to Susan Weisskopf, Michelle Z. Rosaldo, Jessica Benjamin, and Sara Ruddick for criticisms and comments on an earlier version of this essay.

This essay evaluates the essentialist view of difference and examines the contribution that psychoanalytic theory can make to understanding the question of sex or gender difference. It asks whether gender is best understood by focusing on differences between men and women and on the uniqueness of each and whether gender difference should be a central organizing concept for feminism. The concept of difference to which I refer here, and which is addressed by other writers in this volume, is abstract and irreducible.[2] It assumes the existence of an essence of gender, so that differences between men and women are seen to establish and define each gender as a unique and absolute category.

I will not discuss differences among women. I think we have something else in mind when we speak of differences in this connection. Differences among women—of class, race, sexual preference, nationality, and ethnicity, between mothers and nonmothers—are all significant for feminist theory and practice, but these remain concrete differences, analyzable in terms of specific categories and modes of understanding. We can see how they are socially situated and how they grow from particular social relations and organization; how they may contain physiological elements (race and sexual preference, for example) yet only gain a specific meaning in particular historical contexts and social formations.

I suggest that gender difference is not absolute, abstract, or irreducible; it does not involve an essence of gender. Gender differences, and the experience of difference, like differences among women, are socially and psychologically created and situated. In adition, I want to suggest a relational notion of difference. Difference and gender difference do not exist as things in themselves; they are created relationally, that is, in relationship. We cannot understand difference apart from this relational construction.

The issues I consider here are relevant both to feminist theory and to particular strands of feminist politics. In contrast to the beginning of the contemporary women's movement, there is now a widespread view that gender differences are essential, that women are fundamentally different from men, and that these differences must be recognized, theorized, and maintained. This finds some political counterpart in notions that women's special nature guarantees the emergence of a good society after the feminist revolution and legitimates female dominance, if not an exclusively female society. My conclusions lead me to reject those currents of contemporary feminism that would found a politics on essentialist conceptions of the feminine.

There is also a preoccupation among some women with psychological separateness and autonomy, with individuality as a necessary women's goal. This preoccupation grows out of many women's feelings of not having distinct autonomy as separate selves, in comparison, say, to men.

This finds some political counterpart in equal rights arguments, ultimately based on notions of women exclusively as individuals rather than as part of a collectivity or social group. I suggest that we need to situate such a goal in an understanding of psychological development and to indicate the relationship between our culture's individualism and gender differentiation.

Psychoanalysis clarifies for us many of the issues involved in questions of difference, by providing a developmental history of the emergence of separateness, differentiation, and the perception of difference in early childhood. Thus it provides a particularly useful arena in which to see the relational and situated construction of difference, and of gender difference. Moreover, psychoanalysis gives an account of these issues from a general psychological perspective, as well as with specific relation to the question of gender. In this context, I will discuss two aspects of the general subject of separateness, differentiation, and perceptions of difference and their emergence. First, I will consider how separation-individuation occurs relationally in the first "me"—"not-me" division, in the development of the "I," or self. I will suggest that we have to understand this separation-individuation in relation to other aspects of development, that it has particular implications for women, and that differentiation is not synonymous with difference or separateness. Second, I will talk about the ways that difference and gender difference are created distinctly, in different relational contexts, for girls and boys, and, hence, for women and men. The argument here advances a reading of psychoanalysis that stresses the relational ego. It contrasts with certain prevalent (Lacan-influenced) feminist readings of psychoanalysis, in particular with the views advanced by French theorists of difference like Luce Irigaray and with the Freudian orthodoxy of Juliet Mitchell.

Differentiation

Psychoanalysis talks of the process of "differentiation" or "separation-individuation."[3] A child of either gender is born originally with what is called a "narcissistic relation to reality": cognitively and libidinally it experiences itself as merged and continuous with the world in general, and with its mother or caretaker in particular. Differentiation, or separation-individuation, means coming to perceive a demarcation between the self and the object world, coming to perceive the subject/self as distinct, or separate from, the object/other. An essential early task of infantile development, it involves the development of ego boundaries (a sense of personal psychological division from the rest of the world) and of a body ego (a sense of the permanence of one's physical separateness and the predictable boundedness of one's own body, of a distinction between inside and outside).

This differentiation requires physiological maturation (for instance, the ability to perceive object constancy), but such maturation is not enough. Differentiation happens *in relation to* the mother, or to the child's primary caretaker. It develops through experiences of the mother's departure and return, and through frustration, which emphasizes the child's separateness and the fact that it doesn't control all its own experiences and gratifications. Some of these experiences and gratifications come from within, some from without. If it were not for these frustrations, these disruptions of the experience of primary oneness, total holding, and gratification, the child would not need to begin to perceive the other, the "outer world," as separate, rather than as an extension of itself. Developing separateness thus involves, in particular, perceiving the mother or primary caretaker as separate and "not-me," where once these were an undifferentiated symbiotic unity.

Separateness, then, is not simply given from birth, nor does it emerge from the individual alone. Rather, separateness is defined relationally; differentiation occurs in relationship: *"I"* am *"not-you"*. Moreover, *"you,"* or the other, is also distinguished. The child learns to see the *particularity* of the mother or primary caretaker in contrast to the rest of the world. Thus, as the self is differentiated from the object world, the object world is itself differentiated into its component parts.

Now, from a psychoanalytic perspective, learning to distinguish me and not-me is necessary for a person to grow into a functioning human being. It is also inevitable, since experiences of departure, of discontinuity in handling, feeding, where one sleeps, how one is picked up and by whom, of less than total relational and physical gratification, are unavoidable. But for our understanding of "difference" in this connection, the concept of differentiation and the processes that characterize it need elaboration.

First, in most psychoanalytic formulations, and in prevalent understandings of development, the mother, or the outside world, is depicted simply as the other, not-me, one who does or does not fulfill an expectation. This perception arises originally from the infant's cognitive inability to differentiate self and world; the infant does not distinguish between its desires for love and satisfaction and those of its primary love object and object of identification. The self here is the infant or growing child, and psychoanalytic accounts take the viewpoint of this child.

However, adequate separation, or differentiation, involves not merely perceiving the separateness, or otherness, of the other. It involves perceiving the person's subjectivity and selfhood as well. Differentiation, separation, and disruption of the narcissistic relation to reality are developed through learning that the mother is a separate being with separate interests and activities that do not always coincide with just what the infant wants at the time. They involve the ability to experience and perceive the object/ other (the mother) in aspects apart from its sole relation to the ability to gratify the infant's/subject's needs and wants; they involve seeing the object as separate from the self *and* from the self's needs.[4] The infant must change here from a "relationship to a subjectively conceived object to a relationship to an object objectively perceived."[5]

In infantile development this change requires cognitive sophistication, the growing ability to integrate various images and experiences of the mother that comes with the development of ego capacities. But these capacities are not enough. The ability to perceive the other as a self, finally, requires an emotional shift and a form of emotional growth. The adult self not only experiences the other as distinct and separate. It also does not experience the other solely in terms of its own needs for gratification and its own desires.

This interpretation implies that true differentiation, true separateness, cannot be simply a perception and experience of self-other, of presence-absence. It must precisely involve two selves, two presences, two subjects. Recognizing the other as a subject is possible only to the extent that one is not dominated by felt need and one's own exclusive subjectivity. Such recognition permits appreciation and perception of many aspects of the other person, of her or his existence apart from the child's/the self's. Thus, how we understand differentiation—only from the viewpoint of the infant as a self, or from the viewpoint of two interacting selves—has consequences for what we think of as a mature self. If the mature self grows only out of the infant as a self, the other need never be accorded her or his own selfhood.

The view that adequate separation-individuation, or differentiation, involves not simply perceiving the otherness of the other, but her or his selfhood/subjectivity as well, has important consequences, not only for an understanding of the development of selfhood, but also for perceptions of women. Hence, it seems to me absolutely essential to a feminist appropriation of psychoanalytic conceptions of differentiation. Since women, as mothers, are the primary caretakers of infants, if the child (or the psychoanalytic account) only takes the viewpoint of the infant as a (developing) self, then the *mother* will be perceived (or depicted) only as an object. But, from a feminist perspective, perceiving the particularity of the mother must involve according the mother her own selfhood. This is a necessary part of the developmental process, though it is also often resisted and experienced only conflictually and partially. Throughout life, perceptions of the mother fluctuate between perceiving her particularity and selfhood and perceiving her as a narcissistic extension, a not-separate other whose sole reason for existence is to gratify one's own wants and needs.

Few accounts recognize the import of this particular stance toward the mother. Alice Balint's marvelous proto-feminist account is the best I know of the infantile origins of adult perceptions of mother as object:

> Most men (and women)—even when otherwise quite normal and capable of an "adult," altruistic form of love which acknowledges the interests of the partner—retain towards their own mothers this naive egoistic attitude throughout their lives. For all of us it remains self-evident that the interests of mother and child are identical, and it is the generally acknowledged measure of the goodness or badness of the mother how far she really feels this identity of interests.[6]

Now, these perceptions, as a product of infantile development, are somewhat inevitable as long as women have nearly exclusive maternal responsibilities, and they are one major reason why I advocate equal parenting as a necessary basis of sexual equality. But I think that, even within the ongoing context of women's mothering, as women we can and must liberate ourselves from such perceptions in our personal emotional lives as much as possible, and certainly in our theorizing and politics.[7]

A second elaboration of psychoanalytic accounts of differentiation concerns the affective or emotional distinction between differentiation or separation-individuation, and *difference*. Difference and differentiation are, of course, related to and feed into one another; it is in some sense true that cognitive or linguistic distinction, or division, must imply difference. However, it is possible to be separate, to be differentiated, without caring about or emphasizing difference, without turning the cognitive fact into an emotional, moral, or political one. In fact, assimilating difference to differentiation is defensive and reactive, a reaction to not feeling separate enough. Such assimilation involves arbitrary boundary creation and an assertion of hyperseparateness to reinforce a lack of security in a person's sense of self as a separate person. But one can be separate from and similar to someone at the same time. For example, one can recognize another's subjectivity and humanity as one recognizes one's own, seeing the *commonality* of both as active subjects. Or a woman can recognize her similarity, commonality, even continuity, with her mother, because she has developed enough of an unproblematic sense of separate self. At the same time, the other side of being able to experience separateness and commonality, of recognizing the other's subjectivity, is the ability to recognize differences with a small "d," differences that are produced and situated historically—for instance, the kinds of meaningful differences among women that I mentioned earlier.

The distinction between differentiation/separateness and difference relates to a third consideration, even more significant to our assessment of difference and gender difference. Following Mahler, much psychoanalytic theory has centered its account of early infant development on separation-individuation, on the creation of the separate self, on the "me"–"not-me" distinction. Yet there are other ways of looking at the development of self, other important and fundamental aspects to the self: "me"–"not-me" is not all there is to "me." Separation, the "me"–"not-me" division, looms larger, both in our psychological life and theoretically, to the extent that these other aspects of the self are not developed either in individual lives or in theoretical accounts.

Object-relations theory shows that in the development of self the primary task is not the development of ego boundaries and a body ego.[8] Along with the earliest development of its sense of separateness, the infant constructs an internal set of unconscious, affectively loaded representations of others in relation to its self, and an internal sense of self in relationship emerges. Images of felt good and bad aspects of the mother or primary caretaker, caretaking experiences, and the mothering relationship become part of the self, of a relational ego structure, through unconscious mental processes that appropriate and incorporate these images. With maturation, these early images and fragments of perceived experience become put together into a self. As externality and internality are established, therefore, what comes to be internal includes what originally were aspects of the other and the relation to the other. (Similarly, what is experienced as external may include what was originally part of the developing self's experience.) Externality and internality, then, do not follow easily observable physiological boundaries but are constituted by psychological and emotional processes as well.

These unconscious early internalizations that affect and constitute the internal quality of selfhood may remain more or less fragmented, or they may develop a quality of wholeness. A sense of continuity of experience and the opportunity to integrate a complex of (at least somewhat) complementary and consistent images enables the "I" to emerge as a continuous being with an identity. This more internal sense of self, or of "I," is not dependent on separateness or difference from an other. A "true self," or "central self," emerges through the experience of continuity that the mother or caretaker helps to provide, by protecting the infant from having continually to react to and ward off environmental intrusions and from being continually in need.

The integration of a "true self" that feels alive and whole involves a particular set of internalized feelings about others in relation to the self. These include developing a sense that one is able to affect others and one's environment (a sense that one has not been inhibited by overanticipation of all one's needs), a sense that one has been accorded one's own feelings and a spontaneity about these feelings (a sense that one's feelings or needs have not been projected onto one), and a sense that there is a fit between one's feelings and needs and those of the mother or caretaker. These feelings all give the self a sense of agency and authenticity.

This sense of agency, then, is fostered by caretakers who do not project experiences or feelings onto the child and who do not let the environment impinge indiscriminately. It is evoked by empathic caretakers who understand and validate the infant as a self in its own right, and the infant's experience as real. Thus, the sense of agency, which is one basis of the inner sense of continuity and wholeness, grows out of the nature of the parent-infant relationship.

Another important aspect of internalized feelings about others in relation to the self concerns a certain wholeness that develops through an internal sense of relationship with another.[9] The "thereness" of the primary parenting person grows into an internal sense of the presence of another who is caring and affirming. The self comes into being here first through feeling confidently alone in the presence of its mother, and then through this presence's becoming internalized. Part of its self becomes a good internal mother. This suggests that the central core of self is, internally, a relational ego, a sense of self-in-good-relationship. The presence or absence of others, their sameness or difference, does not then become an issue touching the infant's very existence. A "capacity to be alone," a relational rather than a reactive autonomy, develops because of a sense of the ongoing presence of another.

These several senses of agency, of a true self that does not develop reactively, of a relational self or ego core, and of an internal continuity of being, are fundamental to an unproblematic sense of self, and provide the basis of both autonomy and spontaneity. The strength, or wholeness, of the self, in this view, does not depend only or even centrally on its degree of separateness, although the extent of confident distinctness certainly affects and is part of the sense of self. The more secure the central self, or ego core, the less one has to define one's self through separateness from others. Separateness becomes, then, a more rigid, defensive, rather fragile, secondary criterion of the strength of the self and of the "success" of individuation.

This view suggests that no one has a separateness consisting only of "me"–"not-me" distinctions. Part of myself is always that which I have taken in; we are all to some degree incorporations and extensions of others. Separateness from the mother, defining oneself as apart from her (and from other women), is not the only or final goal for women's ego strength and autonomy, even if many women must also attain some sense of reliable separateness. In the process of differentiation, leading to a genuine autonomy, people maintain contact with those with whom they had their earliest relationships: indeed this contact is part of who we are. "I am" is not definition through negation, is not "who I am not." Developing a sense of confident separateness must be a part of all children's development. But once this confident separateness is established, one's relational self can become more central to one's life. *Differentiation is not distinctness and separateness, but a particular way of being connected to others.* This connection to others, based on early incorporations, in turn enables us to feel that empathy and confidence that are basic to the recognition of the other as a self.

What does all this have to do with male-female difference and male dominance? Before turning to the question of gender difference, I want to reiterate what we as feminists learn from the general inquiry into "differentiation." First, we learn that we can only think of differentiation and the emergence of the self relationally. Differentiation occurs, and separation emerges, in relationship; they are not givens. Second, we learn that to single out separation as the core of a notion of self and of the process of differentiation may well be inadequate; it is certainly not the only way to discuss the emergence of self or what constitutes a strong self. Differentiation includes the internalization of aspects of the primary caretaker and of the caretaking relationship.

Finally, we learn that essential, important attitudes toward mothers and expectations of mother—attitudes and expectations that enter into experiences of women more generally—emerge in the earliest differentiation of self. These attitudes and expectations arise during the emergence of separateness. Given that differentiation and separation are developmentally problematic, and given that women are primary caretakers, the mother, who is a woman, becomes and remains for children of both genders the other, or object. She is not accorded autonomy or selfness on her side. Such attitudes arise also from the gender-specific character of the early, emotionally charged self and object images that affect the development of self and the sense of autonomy and spontaneity. They are internalizations of feelings about the self in relation to the *mother,* who is then often experienced as either overwhelming or overdenying. These attitudes are often unconscious and always have a basis in unconscious, emotionally charged feelings and conflicts. A precipitate of the early relationship to the mother and of an unconscious sense of self, they may be more fundamental and determining of psychic life than more conscious and explicit attitudes to "sex differences" or "gender differences" themselves.

This inquiry suggests a psychoanalytic grounding for goals of emotional psychic life other than autonomy and separateness. It suggests, instead, an individuality that emphasizes our connectedness with, rather than our separation from, one another. Feelings of inadequate separateness, the fear of merger, are indeed issues for women, because of the ongoing sense of oneness and primary identification with our mothers (and children). A transformed organization of parenting would help women to resolve these issues. However, autonomy, spontaneity, and a sense of agency need not be based on self-other distinctions, on the individual as individual. They can be based on the fundamental interconnectedness, not synonymous with merger, that grows out of our earliest unconscious developmental experience, and that enables the creation of a nonreactive separateness.[10]

Gender Differences in the Creation of Difference

I turn now to the question of gender differences. We are not born with perceptions of gender differences; these emerge developmentally. In the traditional psychoanalytic view, however, when sexual difference is first seen it has self-evident value. A girl perceives her lack of a penis, knows instantly that she wants one, and subsequently defines herself and her mother as lacking, inadequate, castrated; a boy instantly knows having a penis is better, and fears the loss of his own.[11] This traditional account violates a fundamental rule of psychoanalytic interpretation. When the analyst finds trauma, shock, strong fears, or conflict, it is a signal to look for the roots of such feelings.[12] Because of his inability to focus on the preoedipal years and the relationship of mother to child, Freud could not follow his own rule here.

Clinical and theoretical writings since Freud suggest another interpretation of the emergence of perceptions of gender difference. This view reverses the perception of which gender experiences greater trauma, and retains only the claim that gender identity and the sense of masculinity and femininity develop differently for men and women.[13] These accounts suggest that core gender identity and masculinity are conflictual for men, and are bound up with the masculine sense of self in a way that core gender identity and femininity are not for women. "Core gender identity" here refers to a cognitive sense of gendered self, the sense that one is male or female. It is established in the first two years concomitantly with the development of the sense of self. Later evaluations of the desirability of one's gender and of the activities and modes of behavior associated with it, or of one's own sense of adequacy at fulfilling gender role expectations, are built upon this fundamental gender identity. They do not create or change it.

Most people develop an unambiguous core gender identity, a sense that they are female or male. But because women mother, the sense of maleness in men differs from the sense of femaleness in women. Maleness is more conflictual and more problematic. Underlying, or built into, core male gender identity is an early, nonverbal, unconscious, almost somatic sense of primary oneness with the mother, an underlying sense of femaleness that continually, usually unnoticeably, but sometimes insistently, challenges and undermines the sense of maleness. Thus, because of a primary oneness and identification with his mother, a primary femaleness, a boy's and a man's core gender identity itself—the seemingly unproblematic cognitive sense of being male—is an issue. A boy must learn his gender identity as being not-female, or not-mother. Subsequently, again because of the primacy of the mother in early life and because of the absence of concrete, real, available male figures of identification and love who are as salient for him as female figures, learning what it is to be masculine comes to mean learning to be not-feminine, or not-womanly.

Because of early-developed, conflictual core gender identity problems, and later problems of adequate masculinity, it becomes important to men to have a clear sense of gender difference, of what is masculine and what is feminine, and to maintain rigid boundaries between these. Researchers find, for example, that fathers sex-type children more than mothers. They treat sons and daughters more differently and enforce gender role expectations more vigorously than mothers do.[14] Boys and men come to deny the feminine identification within themselves and those feelings they experience as feminine: feelings of dependence, relational needs, emotions generally. They come to emphasize differences, not commonalities or continuities, between themselves and women, especially in situations that evoke anxiety, because these commonalities and continuities threaten to challenge gender difference or to remind boys and men consciously of their potentially feminine attributes.

These conflicts concerning core gender identity interact with and build upon particular ways that boys experience the processes of differentiation and the formation of the self.[15] Both sexes establish separateness in relation to their mother, and internalizations in the development of self take in aspects of the mother as well. But because the mother is a woman, these experiences differ by gender. Though children of both sexes are originally part of herself, a mother unconsciously and often consciously experiences her son as more of an "other" than her daughter. Reciprocally, a son's male core gender identity develops away from his mother. The male's self, as a result, becomes based on a more fixed "me"–"not-me" distinction. Separateness and difference as a component of differentiation become more salient. By contrast, the female's self is less separate and involves a less fixed "me"–"not-me" distinction, creating the difficulties with a sense of separateness and autonomy that I mentioned above.

At the same time, core gender identity for a girl is not problematic in the sense that it is for boys. It is built upon, and does not contradict, her primary sense of oneness and identification with her mother and is assumed easily along with her developing sense of self. Girls grow up with a sense of continuity and similarity to their mother, a relational connection to the world. For them, difference is not originally problematic or fundamental to their psychological being or identity. They do not define themselves as "not-men," or "not-male," but as "I, who am female." Girls and women may have problems with their sense of continuity and similarity, if it is too strong and they have no sense of a separate self. However, these problems are not the inevitable products of having a sense of continuity and similarity, since, as I argue here, selfhood does *not* depend only on the strength and impermeability of ego boundaries. Nor are these problems bound up with questions of gender; rather, they are bound up with questions of self.

In the development of gender identification for girls it is not the existence of core gender identity, the unquestioned knowledge that one is female, that is problematic. Rather, it is the later-developed conflicts concerning this identity, and the identifications, learning, and cognitive choices that it implies. The difficulties that girls have in establishing a "feminine" identity do not stem from the inaccessibility and negative definition of this identity, or its assumption by denial (as in the case of boys). They arise from identification with a negatively valued gender category, and an ambivalently experienced maternal figure, whose mothering and femininity, often conflictual for the mother herself, are accessible, but devalued. Conflicts here arise from questions of relative power, and social and cultural value, even as female identification and the assumption of core gender identity are straightforward. I would argue that these conflicts come later in development, and are less pervasively determining of psychological life for women than are masculine conflicts around core gender identity and gender difference.

Men's and women's understanding of difference, and gender difference, must thus be understood in the relational context in which these are created. They stem from the respective relation of boys and girls to their mother, who is their primary caretaker, love object, and object of identification, and who is a woman in a sexually and gender-organized world. This relational context contrasts profoundly for girls and boys in a way that makes difference, and gender difference, central for males—one of the earliest, most basic male developmental issues—and not central for females. It gives men a psychological investment in difference that women do not have.

According to psychoanalytic accounts since Freud, it is very clear that males are "not females" in earliest development. Core gender identity and the sense of masculinity are defined more negatively, in terms of that which is not female or not-mother, than positively. By contrast, females do not develop as "not-males." Female core gender identity and the sense of femininity are defined positively, as that which is female, or like mother. Difference from males is not so salient. An alternative way to put this is to suggest that, developmentally, the maternal identification represents and is experienced as generically human for children of both genders.[16]

But, because men have power and cultural hegemony in our society, a notable thing happens. Men use and have used this hegemony to appropriate and transform these experiences. Both in everyday life and in theoretical and intellectual formulations, men have come to define maleness as that which is basically human, and to define women as not-men. This transformation is first learned in, and helps to constitute, the Oedipal transition—the cultural, affective, and sexual learnings of the meaning and valuation of sex differences.[17] Because Freud was not attentive to preoedipal development (and because of his sexism), he took this meaning and valuation as a self-evident given, rather than a developmental and cultural product.

We must remember that this transformed interpretation of difference, an interpretation learned in the Oedipal transition, is produced by means of male cultural hegemony and power. Men have the means to institutionalize their unconscious defenses against repressed yet strongly experienced developmental conflicts. This interpretation of difference is imposed on earlier developmental processes; it is not the deepest, unconscious root of either the female or the male sense of gendered self. In fact, the primary sense of gendered self that emerges in earliest development constantly challenges and threatens men, and gives a certain potential psychological security, even liberation, to women. The transformed interpretation of difference is not inevitable, given other parenting arrangements and other arrangements of power between the sexes. It is especially insofar as women's lives and self-definition become oriented to men that difference becomes more salient for us, as does differential evaluation of the sexes. Insofar as women's lives and self-definition become more oriented toward themselves, differences from men become less salient.[18]

Evaluating Difference

What are the implications of this inquiry into psychoanalytic understandings of differentiation and gender difference for our understanding of difference, and for our evaluation of the view that difference is central to feminist theory? My investigation suggests that our own sense of differentiation, of separateness from others, as well as our psychological and cultural experience and interpretation of gender or sexual difference, are created through psychological, social, and cultural processes, and through relational experiences. We can only understand gender difference, and human distinctness and separation, relationally and situationally.[19] They are part of a system of asymmetrical social relationships embedded in inequalities of power, in which we grow up as selves, and as women and men. Our experience and perception of gender are processual; they are produced developmentally and in our daily social and cultural lives.

Difference is psychologically salient for men in a way that it is not for women, because of gender differences in early formative developmental processes and the particular unconscious conflicts and defenses these produce. This salience, in turn, has been transmuted into a conscious cultural preoccupation with gender difference. It has also become intertwined with and has helped to produce more general cultural notions, particularly, that individualism, separateness, and distance from others are desirable and requisite to autonomy and human fulfillment.[20] Throughout these processes, it is women, as mothers, who become the objects apart from which separateness, difference, and autonomy are defined.

It is crucial for us feminists to recognize that the ideologies of difference, which define us as women and as men, as well as inequality itself, are produced, socially, psychologically, and culturally, by people living in and creating their social, psychological, and cultural worlds. Women participate in the creation of these worlds and ideologies, even if our ultimate power and access to cultural hegemony are less than those of men. To speak of difference as a final, irreducible concept and to focus on gender differences as central is to reify them and to deny the reality of those *processes* which create the meaning and significance of gender. To see men and women as qualitatively different kinds of people, rather than seeing gender as processual, reflexive, and constructed, is to reify and deny *relations* of gender, to see gender differences as permanent rather than as created and situated.

We certainly need to understand how difference comes to be important, how it is produced as salient, and how it reproduces sexual inequality. But we should not appropriate differentiation and separation, or difference, for ourselves and take it as a given. Feminist theories and feminist inquiry based on the notion of essential difference, or focused on demonstrating difference, are doing feminism a disservice. They ultimately rely on the defensively constructed masculine models of gender that are presented to us as our cultural heritage, rather than creating feminist understandings of gender and difference that grow from our own politics, theorizing, and experience.

Notes

1. From *The Elementary Structures of Kinship*, quoted in Adrienne Rich, *On Lies, Secrets and Silence* (New York: W. W. Norton & Co., 1979), p. 84.
2. See, for example, Alice Jardine, "Prelude: The Future of Difference," this volume; Josette Féral, "The Powers of Difference," this volume; "Women's Exile: Interview with Luce Irigaray," *Ideology and Consciousness* 1 (1977): 57–76; and Monique Plaza, " 'Phallomorphic Power' and the 'Psychology of Woman,' " *Ideology and Consciousness* 4 (1978): 4–36.
3. The work of Margaret S. Mahler, *On Human Symbiosis and the Vicissitudes of Individuation* (New York: International Universities Press, 1968), is para-digmatic. For a more extended discussion of the earliest development of the self along lines suggested here, see Nancy Chodorow, *The Reproduction of Mothering: Psychoanalysis and the Sociology of Gender* (Berkeley: Univ. of California Press, 1978), chs. 4 and 5.
4. Ernest G. Schachtel, "The Development of Focal Attention and the Emergence of Reality" (1954), in *Metamorphosis* (New York: Basic Books, 1959), provides the best discussion I know of this process.
5. D. W. Winnicott, "The Theory of the Parent-Infant Relationship" (1960), in *The Maturational Processes and the Facilitating Environment* (New York: International Universities Press, 1965).
6. Alice Balint, "Love for the Mother and Mother Love" (1939), in Michael Balint, ed., *Primary Love and Psycho-Analytic Technique* (New York: Liveright Publishing, 1965), p. 97.
7. The new feminist/feminine blame-the-mother literature is one contemporary manifestation of failure in such a task. See esp. Nancy Friday, *My Mother/My Self* (New York: Dell Publishing, 1977). Of course, this is not to ignore or pass over the fact that men have been past masters of such perceptions of women.
8. In what follows, I am drawing particularly on the work of D. W. Winnicott and Michael Balint. See Winnicott, *The Maturational Processes*, and *Playing and Reality* (New York: Basic Books, 1971); and Balint, *Primary Love*, and *The Basic Fault: Therapeutic Aspects of Regression* (London: Tavistock Publications, 1968). See also W. R. D. Fairbairn, *An Object Relations Theory of the Personality* (New York: Basic Books, 1952), and Hans Loewald, "Internalization, Separation, Mourning and the Superego," *Psychoanalytic Quarterly* 31 (1962): 483–504.
9. See Winnicott, "The Capacity to Be Alone" (1958), in *The Maturational Processes*.
10. My interpretation here of differentiation, the self, and the goals of psychic life contrasts with the traditional Freudian view, which stresses ego and superego autonomy. For an excellent discussion of questions of ego autonomy and psychic structure, see Jessica Benjamin, "The End of Internalization: Adorno's Social Psychology," *Telos* 32 (1977): 42–64.
11. See Sigmund Freud, "The Dissolution of the Oedipus Complex" (1924), in *Standard Edition of the Complete Psychological Works* (SE) (London: The

Hogarth Press), vol. 19, pp. 172–79; "Some Psychical Consequences of the Anatomical Distinction between the Sexes" (1925), SE, vol. 19, pp. 243–58; and "Femininity" (1933), in *New Introductory Lectures on Psychoanalysis*, SE, vol. 22, pp. 112–35.

12. See Roy Schafer, "Problems in Freud's Psychology of Women," *Journal of the American Psychoanalytic Association* 22 (1974): 459–85.

13. See Robert Stoller, "Facts and Fancies: An Examination of Freud's Concept of Bisexuality," in Jean Strouse, ed., *Women and Analysis* (New York: Grossman Publishers, 1974), and other Stoller writings.

14. For reviews of the social psychological literature on this point, see Miriam Johnson, "Sex Role Learning in the Nuclear Family," in *Child Development* 34 (1963): 319–34; Johnson, "Fathers, Mothers and Sex-Typing," *Sociological Inquiry* 45 (1975): 15–26; and Eleanor Maccoby and Carol Jacklin, *The Psychology of Sex Differences* (Stanford: Stanford Univ. Press, 1974).

15. For further discussion, see Chodorow, *Reproduction of Mothering*, ch. 5.

16. Johnson, "Fathers, Mothers," makes this suggestion, and suggests further that the father's masculinity introduces gender difference.

17. See Juliet Mitchell, *Psychoanalysis and Feminism* (New York: Pantheon Books, 1974).

18. I have not dealt in this essay with the male and female body, and I would like to say a few words about these before concluding, since they clearly have relevance for the question of gender difference. We live an embodied life; we live with those genital and reproductive organs and capacities, those hormones and chromosomes, that locate us physiologically as male or female. But, to turn to psychoanalysis once again, I think it is fair to say that Freud's earliest discovery showed that there is nothing self-evident about this biology. How anyone understands, fantasizes about, symbolizes, internally represents, or feels about her or his physiology is a product of development and experience in the family and not a direct product of this biology itself. These feelings, moreover, may be shaped by completely nonbiological considerations. Nonbiological considerations also shape perceptions of anatomical "sex differences" and the psychological development of these differences into forms of sexual object choice, mode, or aim; into femininity or masculinity as defined by psychoanalysis; into activity or passivity; into one's choice of the organ of erotic pleasure; and so forth. We cannot know what children would make of their bodies in a nongender or nonsexually organized world, what kind of sexual structuration or gender identities would develop. But it is not obvious that there would be major significance to biological sex differences, to gender difference, or to different sexualities. There might be a multiplicity of sexual organizations, identities, and practices, and perhaps even of genders themselves. Bodies would be bodies (I don't think we want to deny people their bodily experience). But particular bodily attributes would not necessarily be so determining of who we are, what we do, how we are perceived, and who are our sexual partners.

19. See Barrie Thorne, "Gender . . . How Is It Best Conceptualized?" (paper presented at the Annual Meeting of the American Sociological Association, San Francisco, August 1978).

20. For a discussion of these general cultural preoccupations and their psychological origins, see Evelyn Fox Keller, "Gender and Science," *Psychoanalysis and Contemporary Thought* 1 (1978): 409–33.

Jane Flax

Mother-Daughter Relationships: Psychodynamics, Politics, and Philosophy

Introduction: An Autobiographical Note

This essay is a work-in-progress. It represents, in part, a return to my intellectual roots, which are in political theory and philosophy. I am beginning to explore the implications of the analysis of mother-daughter relationships for the study of philosphical problems. If we take it seriously, feminism forces us to revise radically the treatment of these problems, their nature, causes, and solutions. It is a truly revolutionary theory.

As an undergraduate I became interested in the problem of objectivity, on two levels. One is the relation between subject and object, the other, the broader epistemological question of the status of our knowledge and the accounts of it. How can we be certain that what we claim to be real and true is really real and true? What counts as reality and truth, and why? Are there any grounds for certainty about these questions?

I can see now that in part I was concerned with these issues because they were a very abstract and intellectualized, hence safe, approach to some of the difficulties arising out of my particular family relations. I can also see that I am not the only one who attempts to resolve inter- and intrapersonal problems in this manner. My own experience does have a political and social dimension, as feminism maintains. However, this perspective was not available to me in the late 1960s and early 1970s, since feminism was only beginning to reemerge as an active movement.

My dissertation was on the relation between politics and epistemology. I studied the history of philosophy in order to understand the emergence of modern empiricism and its impact on political science, especially in its claim to develop a "science" of politics. More generally I investigated the hegemony of the empiricist notion of science both as the only true form of knowledge and as the correct method for acquiring true knowledge. I attempted to link these developments to changes in the political realm, particularly the emergence of technical rationality as a basis for the claim to power, and the necessity for certain social arrangements, especially bureaucracy, the rule of experts, and the depoliticization of what was formerly or potentially public.

I discovered that philosophy is riddled with dualisms. In empiricism and many forms of rationalism, the subject is considered totally different, in substance and process, from the object. On this premise, the question becomes, how can the subject and object have any relation to each other? All power is given to reason and to the "right" use of it to guarantee knowledge, but the subject is isolated, since the world is either posited as its product or as unknowable in itself. The subject becomes estranged from nature and from its own passions. Ontology (being) is separated from epistemology, and this is eventually elevated by Kant into a formal principle of philosophy. Epistemology emerges as a separate and specialized branch of philosophy.

Despite these developments, it still seems to me that knowledge is the product of human beings, for whom knowing is only one form of activity. The history and life situation of the knower cannot be completely different in kind from the form and content of the knowledge that this subject produces. Therefore, for me, it seemed that epistemology inevitably opens onto ontology, a suspicion confirmed by the study of dialectics, especially in Hegel and Marx, and of phenomenology (almost in spite of itself), especially in Husserl and Merleau-Ponty.

In the process of studying these problems, I became interested in critical theory, especially the work of Horkheimer, Adorno, Marcuse, and Habermas. Although steeped in the Enlightenment and German idealist traditions and riddled with internal contradictions, critical theory does grapple with these issues.[1] My study of critical theory and my involvement in the women's liberation movement led me to the study of psychoanalysis. Critical theory turned to Freud when the events predicted by Marxist theory did not occur, and especially after the "failure" of the German working class to seize power in Germany before World War II. Critical theorists argued that the success of fascism and other forms of authoritarianism could not be explained without an analysis of individual psychological structure and its interplay with and formation through social forces, such as the family and the dominance of the commodity form in capitalism.

Similarly, it seemed to me that aspects of my experience within the women's liberation movement could not be explained by the available political and social theories, including Marxism, and the analysis that posited conscious, quasi-intentional "sex-role stereotyping." I found especially puzzling the intensity of certain consciousness-raising sessions, the avoidance within feminism of subjects like sexuality and mothering, and the painful and personal character of what were characterized as "purely political" splits within the movement (gay/straight, Marxist/ radical feminist, academic/nonacademic, etc.).

With a group of women in New Haven, I helped establish a women's counseling service. Under the supervision of a psychiatric social worker, we received training in basic techniques and theory. The service was intended for women who had immediate problems or decisions to make (divorce, or going back to work, for example) and as a referral service to sympathetic therapists and agencies.

I decided I would like more training in analytic psychotherapy. Counseling seemed too rationally and cognitively oriented to account for and deal with the intensity and persistence of the phenomena that puzzled me. I found a position teaching and working (including doing psychotherapy) in an experimental program at a state university. The supervision provided by psychologists and a psychiatrist enabled me to develop a deeper understanding of the process of psychoanalytic psychotherapy. Now, although I teach political theory full time, I have a small private practice. The patients I have worked with are all very disturbed. Most of them are borderline psychotics who lack a core self. This clinical experience has affected the issues and theory I focus on in this essay.

In what follows, I first outline what I believe is lacking, from a feminist viewpoint, in Freud's theory of psychological development because of his omission of a full account of the preoedipal period. I then trace the absence of this "repressed" preoedipal stage, and the theoretical consequences of this for philosophy and political theory, in Descartes and in the "state of nature" as depicted in Hobbes and Locke. Finally I give a case-study from one of my own therapy patients to illustrate the kind of psychopolitical analysis of patriarchal structures that I believe feminism must begin to undertake.

The Contribution of Psychoanalysis to Feminism

Psychoanalysis provides essential insights into the problem of differentiation. In the therapeutic process and in psychoanalytic theory the abstract subject-object problem recurs on an individual and concrete level, above all, in the transference relationship central to psychoanalysis. The systematic use and exploration of transference (and countertransference) phenomena, and the focus on unconscious processes distinguish psychoanalysis from any other form of therapy. Since gender identity develops originally and most deeply through preverbal and nonrational experience, an understanding of unconscious processes is crucial for feminist theory.

Differentiation is a central issue for women because of the special character of the mother-daughter relationship. My work differs from

Nancy Chodorow's on this point, since I believe that the development of women's core identity is threatened and impeded by an inability to differentiate from the mother. I see as a central problematic in female development the very continuity of identity with the mother that she discusses in her essay (see Chodorow, this volume). This leads us to differences on the importance of the issue of autonomy for women as well. I have developed these ideas elsewhere[2] and will return to them below in an analysis of a patient's dream.

But I want to speculate here on the implications of recent feminist psychoanalytic theory for the more abstract philosophical issues mentioned earlier. This rich clinical and theoretical material can illuminate what have been seen as problems within thought or as characteristics of an abstract and unchangeable human nature. Like all other apparently abstract or universal problems, these problems have their roots in social existence, especially patterns of child-rearing.

Reading Dinnerstein is a profound, transformative experience, because she opens the path for these speculations.[3] In addition, I, like Chodorow,[4] have found object-relations theory to be the most useful and suggestive form of psychoanalytic theory because it analyzes humans as they develop in and through social relations, and stresses the centrality of preoedipal experience.[5] For reasons I will discuss, feminism compels us to investigate the most primitive roots of human beings and of society. In this investigation the concerns and insights of feminism and psychoanalysis meet, engage, and mutually enrich each other.

The Contribution of Feminism to Psychoanalysis

According to Freud, individual development recapitulates social development. The reverse is also true. Yet Freud could never provide an adequate account of either process or of their interaction. In part, his difficulties arise out of an inability to reconcile his biological determinism with an account of psychological development in and through social relations.[6] The notion of the Oedipus complex as the central event in the history both of human culture and of the individual reveals these difficulties. The Oedipus complex is meant to show the irreconcilability in principle between instinct and culture. What Freud's account of the Oedipus complex shows, in fact, is the *interaction* of instinct and culture, and the need for an integration of social and political factors into his theory. Freud argues:

> It may be presumed . . . that in the case of men a childhood recollection of the affection shown them by their mother and

others of the female sex who looked after them when they were children contributes powerfully to directing their choice towards women; on the other hand their early experience of being deterred by their father from sexual activity and their competitive relation with him deflect them from their own sex. Both of these two factors apply equally to girls, whose sexual activity is particularly subject to the watchful guardianship of their mother. They thus acquire a hostile relation to their own sex which influences their object-choice decisively in what is regarded as the normal direction.[7]

Freud assumes here that women look after small children. This is taken for granted and seems to require neither comment nor analysis. Freud also ignores an important way in which these "two factors" do *not* apply equally to girls: for them, their mother is both original love object and "guardian" of their sexual activity. Many questions remain unanswered in Freud's account of the Oedipal situation and its resolution. Where is the father's presence in the girl's experience? What does it mean that the girl's first love object is of her own (not the opposite) gender and that she must develop a hostile attitude toward this first object? Why does the father deter the boy from sexual activity? Why does the mother assume a "watchful guardianship" over the girl? Why does the boy have a "competitive" relationship with his father? Why is the girl's hostility toward her own sex so intense, while the boy's is not, despite his father's prohibitions? What about the boy's hostility toward and contempt for women?

These questions imply that the child's choice of object and attitudes toward his/her own gender take place within a context partially determined by factors that are neither biological nor intrapsychic and intrafamilial. This statement by Freud makes the problems more evident:

Psycho-analytic research is most decidedly opposed to any attempt at separating off homosexuals from the rest of mankind as a group of special character. By studying sexual excitations other than those that are manifestly displayed, it has found that all human beings are capable of making a homosexual object-choice and have in fact made one in their unconscious. Indeed, libidinal attachments to persons of the same sex play no less a part as factors in normal mental life, and a greater part as a motive force for illness, than do similar attachments to the opposite sex. On the contrary, psychoanalysis considers that a choice of an object independently of its sex—freedom to range equally over male and female objects—as it is found in childhood, in primitive states of society and early periods of history, is the original basis from which, as a result of restriction in one direction or the other, both the normal and the inverted types develop. Thus from the point of view of psychoanalysis the exclusive sexual interest felt by men for women is also a problem that needs elucidating and is not a self-evident fact based upon an attraction that is ultimately of a chemical nature.[8]

Not until late in his life did Freud begin to explore the exclusive sexual interest felt by *women* for men as a problem requiring elucidation. For a full analysis of this problem, it is necessary to investigate how power and power relations enter into and help shape the character of childhood development for both boy and girl, and what functions the restrictions of object-choice and sexuality in general serve for different aspects of society.[9] One place to begin is with an investigation of the forces that shape the parents' attitude and behavior, conscious and unconscious, toward the child. These include not only their personal histories, but more general social factors: class; competition—an attribute of social relations under capitalism; and patriarchy, rooted in male control over the allocation of women. Freud himself admitted that he could not fully imagine what course psychological development would take were the family (i.e., the patriarchal family) to disappear.[10]

From a feminist viewpoint, there is an even more fundamental flaw in Freud's account. It consigns to preculture and hence to nature, in its appearance as instinct operating in the id, the entire preoedipal period, the very period when the mother is powerful in the life of the infant and which is especially central to the psychological development of women. Freud's comments on the preoedipal period and the psychology of women are, as he himself admits, "incomplete and fragmentary."[11] Even granting this (something his followers unfortunately did not always do), Freud's analysis is inadequate for a number of reasons: (1) He is unable to grasp fully the character of early infantile experience. This difficulty stems in part from his lack of direct clinical experience with children. (2) His analysis of the preoedipal period is still heavily influenced by what Freud thinks is to follow, i.e., the girl's discovery of her "castration," and the boy's discovery of his mother's "castration" and his fear of being castrated by the father. (3) He does not explore the mother's role in depth. In his account, she appears primarily as an object for the child. (4) He does not analyze closely the impact of this period on the boy, so that Freud can make the naive statement, "A mother is only brought unlimited satisfaction by her relation to a son; this is altogether the most perfect, the most free from ambivalence of all human relationships."[12]

As this astonishing statement shows, the focus on the Oedipal period introduces distortions into the account of individual psychological development. Freud had intimations of this when he discovered the "Minoan" (preoedipal) ruins underlying the Greek ones, significantly, in the context of discussing female psychology.[13] This realization was never fully integrated into his psychological theory or into most subsequent psychoanalytic theory.

The omission of the preoedipal period distorts Freud's metapsychology as well. As Monique Wittig has pointed out, Freud's account of civilization is of a struggle among men after women are dominated.[14] He cannot give an account of this domination or analyze its psychological and social consequences for women, men, and the character of culture. The original act of domination is thus relegated to nature, even though it shapes all that is to follow. It is significant that *Civilization and Its Discontents* begins with Freud discussing his inability to grasp a certain "oceanic" feeling (about which Romain Rolland had written him). This oceanic feeling seems to capture the affect of the early period of symbiotic unity between mother and child. Freud's difficulties in grasping this state and including it within his theory does, indeed, recapitulate social development. Earliest infantile experiences are repressed, not only by the individual in the process of maturation, but also in the collective memory and accounts of our history as well.

Toward a Feminist Analysis of Philosophy: The Return of the Repressed

We can see this repression and its consequences not only in individual psychological development and in Freud's account of it, but in philosophy and political theory and in the actual social relations they reflect. I can only outline these effects here. The repression of early infantile experience is reflected in and provides the grounding for our relationship with nature.[15] This is true, as well, of our political life, especially the separation of public and private, the obsession with power and domination, and the consequent impoverishment both of political life and of theories about it. The repression of our passions and their transformation into something dangerous and shameful, the inability to achieve true reciprocity and cooperative relations with others, and the translation of difference into inferiority and superiority can also be traced in part to this individual and collective act of repression and denial.

Descartes's philosophy is especially interesting when read from a feminist viewpoint. His philosophy is important not only in itself, but also because it defined the problematics for much of modern Western philosophy. Descartes's philosophy can be read as a desperate attempt to escape from the body, sexuality, and the wiles of the unconscious. Experientially the first body we escape from (physically, and then emotionally) is that of our mother. As Dinnerstein points out, our relation with our own body is mediated through our continuing ambivalence about separating and differentiating from her.

In the *Discourse on Method,* the problem of the "cogito" ("I think, therefore I am") emerges in relation to the problem of distinguishing reality from a dream.[16] For Descartes the solution to the problem of certainty and the confusion generated by the senses is a radical reduction of consciousness to pure ego, to that which thinks. The ego is emptied of all content, since in principle there is nothing it can know a priori about its life situation or history, all of that having been cast into doubt.

Consider the assumptions and implications contained within this statement:

> The very fact that I thought of doubting the truth of other
> things, it followed very evidently and very certainly that I existed
> while on the other hand, if I had only ceased to think, although
> all the rest of what I had ever imagined had been true, I would
> have had no reason to believe that I existed; I thereby concluded
> that I was a substance, of which the whole essence or nature
> consists in thinking, and which in order to exist, needs no place
> and depends on no material thing; so that this "I," that is to say,
> the mind by which I am what I am, is entirely distinct from the
> body, even that it is easier to know than the body, and moreover,
> that even if the body were not, it would not cease to be all that it
> is.[17]

My essence and the only thing of which I can be certain is thought. This self needs "no place and depends on no material thing," including (one presumes) other human beings. It is thus completely self-constituting and self-sustaining. The self is created and maintained by thought. This view of the self entails a denial of the body and any interaction between body and self (except somehow through the pineal gland). Social relations are not necessary for the development of the self. The self, it appears, is a static substance. Although it may think new thoughts, it is not transformed by them. One presumes that it comes into the world whole and complete and, like a perpetual motion machine, clicks into operation. It is noteworthy that the one thing Descartes does not throw into doubt and that, in fact, guarantees the success of his whole enterprise is the existence of God. The patriarchal father is not to be questioned by any of his sons.

What Descartes's ego contemplates is the material world, a material world also emptied of particularity and subjective content. Thought contemplates nature not as experienced—how this particular orange tastes or smells, for example—but nature as mathematics. Only when nature is reduced to extension and motion can it be known with certainty. Nature cannot be known in its full concreteness, but only as the abstract object of an abstract "cogito." Any knowledge not built on the foundations of mathematics is like the "moral writings of the ancient pagans," "the most proud and magnificent palaces, built on nothing but sand and mud."[18]

Underlying the concern for certainty is a desire for control, control both of nature and of the body. Descartes was convinced that

> . . . it is possible to arrive at knowledge which is most useful in life and that instead of the speculative philosophy taught in the schools, a practical philosophy can be found by which, knowing the power and the effects of fire, water, air, the stars, the heavens, and all the other bodies which surround us as distinctly as we know the various trades of our craftsmen, we might put them in the same way to all the uses for which they are appropriate and thereby make ourselves, as it were, masters and possessors of nature.[19]

The purpose of science is to capture the power of nature and hence to make it one's own, thus compensating for the weakness of mortal flesh. Such a science might even overcome death, that reminder of the materiality of life, of the dependence on the body.

> We could free ourselves of an infinity of illnesses, both of the body and of the mind, and even perhaps also of the decline of age, if we know enough about their causes and about all the remedies which nature has provided us.[20]

There is a deep irony in Descartes's philosophy. The self, which is constituted by thought and created by an act of thought, by the separation of mind and body, is driven to master nature, because the self cannot ultimately deny its material character or dependence on nature. Despite Descartes's claim, the body reasserts itself, at least at the moment of death. In order to become fully the substance it is, the cogito must master nature and possess its secrets, "the remedies nature has provided us," so that the self will never "cease to be all that it is," that is, die. The desire to know is inextricably intermeshed with the desire to dominate. Nature is posited as pure otherness which must be conquered to be possessed and transformed into useful objects.

The posture of Descartes's cogito replicates that of a child under two in its relation to a caretaker (usually the mother and/or other females). The child originally believes that it and its mother are one person, a symbiotic unity.[21] However, due to frustrations in having its needs met and internal psychological pressures (primarily a growing desire for autonomy), it begins to realize that its mother is a separate person, an other. This discovery is accompanied by panic, for the child is still dependent on the mother and can sense its dependency. At the same time, the child is exhilarated, for the possibility of autonomy and overcoming the state of powerlessness requires separation. One reaction and defense to the discovery of separateness is narcissism, in which the outside world is seen purely as an object for the self and as a creation of the self. Through "good enough" social relations,[22] this stage is transformed into a genuine reciprocity in which separateness and mutuality (interdependence) exist simultaneously. However, denial of separateness, of the individual integrity of the object (mother), will lead to the adoption of narcissism as a permanent character structure.[23] This is precisely the type of solipsistic, isolated self with delusions of omnipotence that Descartes's cogito displays.

Why Are There No Women and Children in the State of Nature?

A parallel denial of early infantile experience, especially of primary relatedness to and dependence on the caretaker, can be seen in political theory. The notion of a "state of nature," as conceptualized, with variations, by Hobbes and Locke, is particularly relevant for feminist analysis, although many of their underlying assumptions are shared by other theorists. It is noteworthy that both Hobbes and Locke assume that "man" is a solitary creature by nature and that dependence, or indeed any social interaction, inevitably leads to power struggles and ultimately either to domination or submission.

I would like to point out several features of the state of nature. First is the persistent image of a solitary creature, roaming over a vast empty space. This is similar to an under-two-year-old child's experience of the world when the mother leaves it. In Hobbes, and, to a lesser degree, Locke, the state of nature is marked by the prevalence of anxiety and insecurity. Significantly, the anxiety is centered on the fear of wounds to the body and deprivation of needed and desired objects. This parallels the paranoid aspect of the separation process.[24] "Natural man" attributes this fear to an external "bad object"—to fear of aggression from other persons who will not respect his autonomy. In this view, aggression and separateness are viewed as innate to human nature, rather than as problems with social roots.

It is only possible to view people in this way if an early period of nurturance and dependence has been unsatisfactory and/or denied and repressed. The "state of nature" seems to be primarily populated by adult, single males, whose behavior is taken as constitutive of human nature and experience as a whole. Hobbes is clearly puzzled about how to fit the family into his state of nature. There are only a few fragments about the family, in which he offers an almost radical feminist account.[25] In the state of nature, men and women are equal (in ability to do harm to others). Children owe obedience to both parents, but if there is a conflict, children should obey the mother, for parentage can only be ascertained with certainty for the female. However, since men make the laws, once civil society exists, men dominate women.[26]

Hobbes's mechanistic model of human behavior does not include the female. That is, it excludes the traits culturally attributed to females—sociability, nurturance, and concern for dependent and helpless persons. Humans are said to be motivated only by passions, especially fear and the wish to have no impediments to the gratification of desire, which is insatiable and asocial. Given these premises, the state of war inevitably follows. The parallels between Hobbes's and Freud's assumptions, especially as to the character of fundamental instincts and their social consequences, are striking and would be worth developing further.

Women and children exist, but it is not clear how they fit into this system. Similar statements could be made about Locke, although he denies that absolute patriarchal power exists in the state of nature (for political reasons, as a defense of the assertion that there is no "divine right" of kings).[27] Despite this, the inhabitants of his state of nature also appear primarily to be unattached male adults. The account of child-rearing in the state of nature is focused on the problem of equality, rights, and reason. The implications for his theory of a period of human dependence are not explored. Although Locke is interested in education, these concerns did not seem to have an effect on his first premises. The family is discussed in terms of rights and the particular nature of the "contract" between husband and wife. Since it is a pre-rational state, childhood has no implications for political or civil society, which is occupied by rational adults. It seems to have no implications for the character of adulthood, either, since adulthood is equated with the ability to exercise reason.

In conclusion, then, philosophy and political theory reflect the fundamental division of the world according to gender. The work that only women do (child-rearing) and the qualities it demands—relatedness, sociability, nurturance, and concern for others—are not seen as part of human nature or the human condition, since the concepts of self and human nature reflect male experience after the preoedipal period. The period when women are powerful in their children's lives is repressed, on both a social and an individual level. Only thus is it possible to deny the most fundamental proof of human bonding, the sociability and interdependence which characterize early infantile experience.

This denial is an essential element of patriarchy, since, as Chodorow shows, male identity is created out of a rejection of the mother, including the female parts of the male self. The female represents all that is not civilized and not rational. In turn, this denial becomes a justification for relegating women to the private sphere and devaluing what women are allowed to do and be (see, for example, Aristotle's discussion of the family as the realm of freedom).[28] Not only is individual psychological development distorted, but these distortions are elevated into abstract theories of human nature, the character of politics, and of the self which reflect, it is claimed, unchangeable and inevitable aspects of human existence.

The Politics of the Unconscious: A Case Study

Precisely because human experience begins with and through a relation with a woman or women (and not men), it has different consequences for women and men. Under patriarchy, primary differentiation occurs according to and through engendering, but the two socially produced genders have very different qualities. This differentiation contributes to the reproduction of patriarchy. I want to discuss here the psychological consequences for women in our society of developing in and through patriarchal social relations. I will do this by analyzing a dream reported by one of my therapy patients. This dream is an example not only of typically female conflicts, present in a compressed form, but of the interaction of personal history with more general social and political dynamics. The careful use of the most traditional psychoanalytic procedures, from a feminist perspective, indicates the need to go beyond their usual boundaries.

K., a female, age twenty-five, reported the following dream: she is upstairs in her parents' house, packing books to take with her. She is moving out of the house, and her books are her most important possession. Downstairs, her mother is singing "Michelle," a Beatles love song, into a microphone. Around the room are amplifiers, speakers, and other sound equipment. Outside this room, in the doorway, sitting in an armchair and reading a paper with his back to the mother, is the father. The patient knows that as soon as the mother has finished the song, she (the mother) intends to kill herself. The patient runs downstairs and picks up a rifle—the weapon with which her mother intends to shoot herself. However, she is unable to smash the rifle, even by jumping on it, because it is encased in some sort of plastic. The dream ends at this point.

K. is from an upwardly mobile, working-class family. Her father is a plumber who, after much struggle, developed sufficient clientele to move his family out of an apartment in a midwestern city to a suburban house. K.'s parents identify with their Middle European ancestry; their parents were immigrants with whom they retained strong ties of loyalty and duty.

K. has one brother, several years older than she, who became violent as a child. After he attempted to set fire to wooden apartment stairs, he was sent to a special school for emotionally disturbed children when K. was early school age and remained there for the rest of K.'s childhood. K. was not informed of the reasons for his disappearance (although the family visited him once a week) and feared that she, too, would be sent away. The parents would assert the "American" and "normal" character of their family by going bowling on Sunday with the brother.

K.'s father appears to her to be extremely controlling, controlled, and irrational. He would sort through the garbage to be certain that nothing he wanted was thrown out. He would fly into uncontrollable, unpredictable rages and would punish his children with severe strappings. This behavior would alternate with a remote, perfectionistic, demanding one.

K.'s mother was an alcoholic for much of K.'s childhood. Her behavior ranged from drunken rejection of her children, to an occasional, genuine regard for their needs, to displays of affectionate but overly invested support. When K. was six, her mother chased her down the hall with a knife for requesting a hot lunch, like that prepared by the other children's mothers. When K. was eleven, she was raped by her grandfather (her mother's father) the night of the wake for his wife. The circumstances strongly imply K.'s mother's complicity in the rape. Many years later she told her daughter that she, too, had been raped by the same man. The need to deny her unconscious knowledge (or belief in) her mother's complicity in and compliance with her father's and grandfather's behavior, to avoid seeing her mother as a bad object, was one of the most powerful aspects of K.'s psychodynamics.

K. was in her early twenties when she came to therapy, and her presenting symptoms were paranoia, extreme anxiety, and an inability to concentrate so severe that she had to drop out of college despite her high intelligence. She lacked many of the reality testing skills and the ability to organize experience characteristic of a fairly well-developed ego. Her core self was underdeveloped, frozen in a state of panic and terror, and she was unable to form trusting relations with others. Her personal relations were marked by intense dependency and idealization, alternating with states of rage (usually unacknowledged and perceived as threatening both to herself and the object). Separation-individuation had not been successfully completed, owing in part to the narcissistic behavior of the mother. She harbored a deep desire to return to the symbiotic state with a "good mother" but had to deny this wish (despite acting it out both with her therapist and boyfriend) out of fear of her own rage and (perceived) powerlessness. She was diagnosed as a borderline personality tending, especially under stress or fear of abandonment, to disintegrate into psychosis.

The dream was built both out of her history of social relations and out of an actual event. K. had been visiting her parents and was sorting through her books, deciding which ones to keep and take with her, and which ones to sell. The mother suggested that K. should allow her father to look through the books she intended to sell to see if there were any he wanted. This suggestion provoked an intense argument between the two and threw K. into such a state of anxiety (and unacknowledged rage) that she called her therapist long distance. Books and reading had always been her means of escape from the family into a world of order, rules, and regularity. They represented autonomy and freedom from the intrusions of her father and grandfather and the demands of her mother. Now her mother was trying to intervene even there and, worse, to introduce the father's presence as well, thus repeating from the patient's viewpoint both her role in the rape and her complicity in the father's behavior.

The symbolism and content of the dream throw light not only on this particular woman's psychodynamics, but on what Rubin calls the "sex-gender" system as a whole.[29] Upstairs, symbolically in the more rational part of the mind, the ego or reason, K. is packing her books, also the symbol of autonomy, order, and reason, and her means of escaping the craziness of the family dynamics which lie below in the unconscious. The books are an ambivalent symbol because they are identified with the male. Note the symmetry with the father reading his newspaper (a chronicle of the external, primarily male world of events). His back is turned to the mother, who is singing her desperate song of love. The mother is experienced by both father and daughter as the ultimate source and reflection of that messy, contradictory, sexual, and sometimes terrifying unconscious world, one they both wish to escape.

Yet the daughter is also tied to, and identified with, the mother. If she takes the male route of escape, it will, literally, kill her mother and that part of her which is like her mother. The mother's identity comes from inside the family. She will cease to exist when her daughter leaves because she cannot be a mother without her reciprocal partner, a child. The daughter is responsible for her mother, in that her leaving destroys the very ground of her mother's being. She must betray her mother if she is to exert her own autonomy. Even paying that terrible price, she will not be really free, since as a female she can never completely enter the world of men.

Thus she must rescue her mother, not only to avoid the guilt of her death but to make possible a total freedom for herself. The mother must become powerful for the daughter to exercise meaningful autonomy. The rage the daughter feels toward the mother is also important. Since dreams are wishes as well as expressions of conflict, the sources of the daughter's anger, so strong as to fantasize her mother's death (although masked by allowing the mother to be the active agent), must be explored. The daughter is angry with the mother for not possessing the sort of power that could free both of them from dependency, on each other and on the father, and which could provide the daughter with a means of entry to the outside world. The daughter sees the mother as both powerful and powerless. If she is so powerful in the emotional sphere, why is she so powerless in the world outside the family and in relation to the father and other men? Is she withholding her power, or has she perhaps given it away to the father? And in exchange for what?

What is the barrier to the mother's possessing the sort of power which could free her daughter (for, surely, the mother is not powerless within the psyche of her daughter)? It is the power of the father, symbolized by the rifle and by his position: the armchair blocking the exit from the room, holding a key to, and a chronicle of, the outside world (the newspaper). The father's source of power is mysterious and impenetrable, like the plastic, expecially since it is exercised silently, with his back to the active participants. Yet his power ultimately determines the character of the drama.

Despite the fact that the rifle (a phallic symbol) is encased in plastic (a symbol of inauthenticity, of inorganic nature), it is still powerful enough to kill the mother. That very wrapping of plastic, making the phallic power invisible to the daughter and incapable of destruction, mirrors the father's apparent lack of involvement in the struggle between mother and daughter and his very real inability to provide emotional support to either mother or daughter. The source of his power is two-fold: the possession of a phallus in a phallocentric world, and his connections to and with the world outside the family, a world which is split between inner and outer, public and private. Only he can connect the daughter to the public world. It is by his grace that she enters there. Yet he can withdraw his permission at any time, especially if she attempts to bring the mother (female identity) into that world. The daughter can neither use nor destroy the phallus, a symbol of both political and sexual privilege (access to the mother).

To whom is the mother singing, and why is all the sound equipment present in the dream? In this particular case, K.'s lover (a male) is a rock musician (reminding us of Freud's remark that what women really look for in their husbands is their mother).[30] That sort of technology is strongly identified with men, since men dominate in rock music, with occasionally a woman vocalist (only apparently) up front. Thus, the symbolism once again points to the mother's powerlessness. She has to use a symbol of male power (the microphone as phallus, the world of rock and roll, a male-written love song to a woman) to appeal—to her daughter certainly, but perhaps also to her husband. The song is partly in French, the language of romance, which also suggests the incomprehensibility of the object of the love. The content of the song is finding "the only words, that I know, that you'll understand; I love you."

The mother is so afraid of not being heard and of the husband's impenetrability that she must amplify her pleas. If her relationship with him were more gratifying, she could ask less of her daughter. Perhaps she is trying to free her daughter in the only ways she knows, either by annihilating herself or (very improbably) by finally getting through to her husband and being able to transfer her needs from her daughter to him. But the second solution would require breaking his phallic power, an outcome which, at least within the dream, seems impossible. Even more repressed and impossible to act on (for both mother and daughter) is the desire to turn the rifle on the father. The mother's shooting herself is a very hostile and angry act, addressed to both father and daughter, and an expression of powerlessness. The act exemplifies one of the main ways women deal with anger, by repressing it and then turning it against themselves and/or by acting out their own conflicts with their daughters, so these become the daughter's conflicts as well.

The Knots of Female Psychological Development under Patriarchy

Let me summarize the typically female psychodynamics the dream encapsulates. (1) Ego boundary confusion between mother and daughter. Women patients often feel as if they must rescue their mother in order to and before they can work on their own problems. Much time at the beginning of therapy may be taken up with a description and analysis of the mother's history and problems, without the recognition of this underlying motive. Women tend to feel guilty that they are somehow betraying their mother in the attempt to resolve and terminate the symbiotic tie. They are much more willing to discuss anger at the father.

(2) Rage at the mother, covered over by a consciously expressed concern for and desire to protect her. Daughters typically feel that they did not "get enough" from their mother. "Getting enough" includes both primary nurturance and encouragement, and strength for autonomy (separation). As I have argued elsewhere,[31] mothers, because of their own ambivalent tie to their mothers, conflicts about being female, and narcissistic relation to their daughters, may be less able to nurture their daughters and provide them with a satisfactory symbiotic experience.

Daughters tend to be terrified of this deep "greedy" need for unconditional love and tend to deny it in the transference relation with a female therapist. With male therapists it may be hidden behind Oedipal material which is safer for the patient to acknowledge and resolve. A therapist not attuned to the special importance of the preoedipal period and the mother-daughter relation for women may never trace the Oedipal material to its earlier roots, leaving patients with a vague sense of dissatisfaction and being "unfinished." Orthodox analysts may incorrectly analyze this feeling as evidence of the "weaker female superego" or unresolved penis envy. Therapy may replicate, not resolve, a woman's deepest psychodynamics by encouraging her to turn to the therapist for protection against the loved and feared infantile mother with the therapist's conscious or unconscious (countertransference) complicity. Patriarchal social relations and male psychological development require that the male therapist, too, deny the power of the mother. This denial may be reinforced by some forms of psychoanalytic theory and training, especially the concentration on Oedipal conflicts and the ego, which often constitute the material of orthodox psychoanalysis. The therapist's own unresolved preoedipal conflicts may continue to affect him and will thus enter the psychodynamics of the analytic situation (and affect the patient) through transference and countertransference. An orthodox female analyst may also have trouble with this material, but it is more likely to emerge in the transference relation with a female patient simply because of their gender identity.

(3) "Penis envy" is largely symbolic and should be traced back to its preoedipal roots. The penis is a means of sexual access to the mother, who is after all the girl's first loved object. This love inevitably has an erotic component that is especially threatening (to both mother and daughter) in an homophobic society. A woman's desire to have a penis is also bound up with a desire to have a baby with the mother, so that symbiotic unity can be maintained. The wish to have a baby is also a wish to *be* a baby, to redo the early developmental process with a "good mother" (the therapist).

Penis envy is also an expression of resentment at the mother. Her power in infancy is contradicted by her powerlessness and compliance with the father. The girl "needs" a penis both to be powerful in the nonfamily world and to rescue the mother from the father (and perhaps to satisfy the mother's erotic and achievement wishes for the child). The girl cannot understand why her mother did not give her a penis. She often feels she is in competition with her father for possession of her mother (feelings that the father often seems to reciprocate). The mother's ambivalent tie to them both permits this situation to remain unresolved.

(4) The separation of nurturance and autonomy within the family is reinforced by patriarchal control of both social relations and economic and political structures. The mother represents, however ambivalently, the only source of nurturance within the family for both father and daughter. Often the daughter, and not the father, is the primary source of nurturance for the mother. Daughters often report confusion from an

early age (three years) as to exactly who was the mother and who the child in the relationship. Daughters serve as confidants, friends, and even lovers in a way that is often confusing and inappropriate to the daughter's developmental process. This behavior often retards a daughter's ability (and mother's as well) to separate. Separation is experienced as abandonment of the mother, and this fear often masks a deeper one—the fear of being abandoned by the mother, or the rage at having been abandoned emotionally by her.

The father represents autonomy, reinforced by patriarchal authority and control outside the family. The daughter sees him as the gatekeeper to both autonomy and the outside, nonfamilial world. Yet the price of identifying with the father is high. It means acknowledging his (at least sexual) control over and privileged access to the mother. The daughter must give up her own preoedipal tie to the mother, and often take on the father's devaluation of and contemptuous attitude for the mother and, by extension, for women as a group. Sometimes, the daughter, especially if there are no sons or she is the oldest sibling, enters not only into a quasi-sexual "little girl" relation to the father, but a protomasculine one as well. This leaves women with what feels like an irresolvable dilemma: to be loved and nurtured, and remain tied to the mother, or to be autonomous and externally successful, to be like a man. The external success is often undercut and limited, not only by patriarchal control outside the home and the alienating quality of work, but by the inner psychic pain caused by this ongoing conflict.

The conflicts outlined above lead me to conclude that differentiation is at the core of women's psychological problems. There seems to be an endless chain of women tied ambivalently to their mothers, who replicate this relation with their daughters. This process occurs because only women take care of infants and do so under certain social conditions, namely, the rule of the father, whose power, while often hidden in the family, is ultimately determinant. He is the possessor of the mother and of rationality. He is representative of society and of culture itself. He generally has far more social wealth than women, whatever his class. His identity is built in part out of denying the mother's (wife's) power and devaluing her, attitudes he conveys to the daughter. She mothers sons who must grow contemptuous of her to be men. Thus patriarchy reproduces itself, reinforced by "the fruits of civilization"—the knowledge and the political and economic systems which reflect and reinforce the splits between nurturance and autonomy, public and private, male and female. As long as patriarchy exists, differences will inevitably be translated into relations of dominance and submission, superiority and inferiority.

Feminists are discovering that these are indeed poisonous, bitter fruits. They nourish only to destroy, first, the potential of half the human race, and now, as Dinnerstein argues, perhaps us all. We cannot re-vision the world with the tools we have been given. The unspoken and the repressed, as Wittig says, must become part of our social discourse and social reality, or there will be no one left to speak at all.

Notes

1. For an introduction to critical theory, see Max Horkheimer, *Critical Theory* (New York: Herder and Herder, 1972), especially the essays "Traditional and Critical Theory" and "Authority and the Family"; Herbert Marcuse, *Negations* (Boston: Beacon Press, 1968); Jürgen Habermas, *Knowledge and Human Interests* (Boston: Beacon Press, 1971), especially the suggestive comments on Freud and the process of psychoanalysis on pp. 214–45. On the possible psychological and social motives for the "domination of nature," see Max Horkheimer and Theodor Adorno, *The Dialectic of Enlightenment* (New York: Herder and Herder, 1972). Their argument cries out for feminist revision along the lines of Dinnerstein's work (see note 3, below). On the family, see the Frankfurt Institute of Social Research, *Aspects of Sociology* (Boston: Beacon Press, 1972), pp. 129–47. For commentaries on critical theory and its problems, see William Leiss, "Critical Theory and Its Future," *Political Theory* 2:3 (1974): esp. 333-35; Jane Flax, "Critical Theory as a Vocation," *Politics and Society* 8:2 (1978): 201–23; Jessica Benjamin, "The End of Internalization: Adorno's Social Psychology," *Telos* 32: (1977): 42–64.
2. See Jane Flax, "The Conflict between Nurturance and Autonomy in Mother-Daughter Relationships and within Feminism," *Feminist Studies* 4:2 (1978): 171–89.
3. Dorothy Dinnerstein, *The Mermaid and the Minotaur: Sexual Arrangements and Human Malaise* (New York: Harper and Row, 1976).
4. Nancy Chodorow, *The Reproduction of Mothering: Psychoanalysis and the Sociology of Gender* (Berkeley: Univ. of California Press, 1978).
5. Especially useful are Harry Guntrip, *Personality Structure and Human Interaction* (New York: International Universities Press, 1961); Margaret S. Mahler, Fred Pine, and Anni Bergman, *The Psychological Birth of the Human Infant* (New York: Basic Books, 1975); and D. W. Winnicott, *The Maturational Processes and the Facilitating Environment* (New York: International Universities Press, 1965).
6. On this point see Guntrip, pp. 55–86.
7. Sigmund Freud, *Three Essays on the Theory of Sexuality* (New York: Basic Books, 1962), pp. 95–96.
8. Ibid., pp. 11–12.
9. On this subject see Gayle Rubin, "The Traffic in Women: Notes on the 'Political Economy' Of Sex," Rayna R(app) Reiter, ed., *Toward an Anthropology of Women* (New York: Monthly Review Press, 1975). On the

differentiation of psychological development by class, see Lillian Breslow Rubin, *Worlds of Pain: Life in the Working Class Family* (New York: Basic Books, 1976).

10. Sigmund Freud, *Civilization and Its Discontents* (New York: Norton, 1961), pp. 60–61.

11. Sigmund Freud, "Femininity," in *New Introductory Lectures on Psychoanalysis* (New York: Norton, 1963), p. 135.

12. Ibid., p. 133.

13. Sigmund Freud, "Female Sexuality," reprinted in Jean Strouse, ed., *Women and Analysis* (New York: Grossman Publishers, 1974), p. 54. This essay has much useful information about the preoedipal period, strikingly misinterpreted by Freud. For example, he notes the "suprising, yet regular fear" in women of being "killed (?devoured) by the mother." He interprets this as a projection of the girl's hostility to the mother "in consequence of the manifold restrictions imposed by [the mother] in the course of training and bodily care" (p. 55). This is basically the same position as that expressed in the much earlier *Three Essays*, despite Freud's acknowledgment in "Female Sexuality" that there is no neat parallelism between the boy's and girl's development. Clearly the fear he refers to has more to do with very early infantile experience (feeding frustration and, more generally, nurturance wishes) and ego boundary confusion between girl and mother. The mother's narcissistic attachment to the child makes the girl feel as if the mother would like to devour her, just as the child would like to devour the mother. This incorporation of the object is part of the internalization process and is felt as greedy in bad object relations.

14. Monique Wittig, "The Straight Mind," *Questions féministes 7 (December 1979); Feminist Issues* 1, 1 (Summer 1980).

15. On this point see Dinnerstein, pp. 91–114, and Adrienne Rich, *Of Woman Born: Motherhood as Experience and Institution* (New York: W. W. Norton, 1976), pp. 73–109.

16. René Descartes, *Discourse on Method* (Baltimore: Penguin Books, 1968).

17. Ibid., p. 54.

18. Ibid., p. 31.

19. Ibid., p. 78.

20. Ibid., p. 79.

21. For an account of early psychological development see Mahler et al., *Psychological Birth*, esp. pp. 41–120.

22. See Winnicott, *Maturational Processes*, pp. 56–63.

23. On narcissism and the reasons for denying the separateness of the object see Otto Kernberg, *Borderline Conditions and Pathological Narcissism* (New York: Jason Aronson, 1975), esp. pp. 3–47 and 213–43.

24. See Melanie Klein, *Envy, Gratitude and Other Works, 1946–1963* (New York: Delta Books, 1977), esp. papers 1–3.

25. Thomas Hobbes, *Leviathan*, ed. C. B. Macpherson (Baltimore: Penguin Books, 1968), pp. 251–57.

26. Ibid., p. 253.

27. See John Locke, *Two Treatises of Government*, ed. Peter Laslett (New York: Mentor, 1960), pp. 344–94. See also Gordon J. Schochet, who discusses *Patriarchalism in Political Thought* (New York: Basic Books, 1975). His perspective differs from mine in that he is interested in the overt content of theories and their history, while I am interested in the latent or repressed content. Consequently our analyses diverge on the relevance of patriarchalism to understanding modern political theory.
28. Aristotle, *The Politics*, tr. Ernest Barker (New York: Oxford Univ. Press, 1962), Book I.
29. Rubin, "Traffic in Women," pp. 198–210.
30. Freud, "Female Sexuality," p. 58.
31. Flax, "Conflict," pp. 171–84.

Jessica Benjamin

The Bonds of Love: Rational Violence and Erotic Domination

Introduction

This essay is concerned with violence—the violence of erotic domination. It is about the strange union of rationality and violence which is made in the secret heart of our culture and only sometimes enacted in the body. This union has inspired some of the holiest imagery of religious transcendence, and now comes to light at the porno newsstands. The imagery of female violation, of erotic domination, is an object of fear and loathing, even when it is not held directly responsible for the degradation of women and attacked accordingly. My concern is not so much with flagrant victimization, with hatred and abuse, as with a fantasy of rational violence. It surfaces as a vital theme of the contemporary pornographic imagination where women are regularly depicted in the bonds of love. But the slave of love is not always a woman or only a heterosexual, for the fantasy of erotic domination permeates sexual imagery in our culture. This fantasy, which mingles love, control, and submission, also flows beneath the surface of "normal love" between adults. But I hope to show how its origins lie in the experience of early infancy, charged with the yearning for and the denial of mutual recognition.

In order to become human beings we have to receive recognition from the first people who care for us. In our society it is usually the mother who is the bestower of recognition. She is the one who responds to our communications, our acts, our gestures, in such a way that we feel that they are meaningful. Her recognition of us makes us feel that vital connection to another being which is as necessary to human survival as food. This psychological or social nourishment, this giving of nurturance, is so evidently essential to mothering that we are tempted to make nurturance and mother synonymous. But feminists have come to be suspicious of the restriction of nurturance to mothering, and the restriction of mothering to women. We have been exploring the psychological repercussions of women's mothering and of the degradation of nurturance in our culture.[1] Why is something so necessary to survival and growth of the individual repudiated and devalued by those who depend upon it? Why does nurturance backfire against those who are appointed to provide it? How does this first experience of the struggle for recognition contribute to the denial of mutuality, the relationship of domination between man and woman?

To answer these questions, feminist writers have begun to examine the complicated process by which human beings are socialized in light of psychological theories of the self. In most Western families the individual acquires a self, or sense of identity, against the background of an individual maternal presence. In psychological terms, the small child begins to *differentiate* its self from the environment, which consists of the mother plus the objects infused by her presence. Most theories based on Freud have stressed that the child grows out of an original sense of oneness with the mother-world into a painful sense of her/his own separateness. The child is torn between the desire to return to that oneness and the desire to become an autonomous person. She or he comes to realize the difference between self and other in two ways: by distinguishing the self from the environment (not-self), and by discovering her/his own identity. Mahler termed these two aspects of differentiation respectively separation and individuation.[2]

The most familiar conflict which arises from differentiation is between the need to establish autonomous identity and the need to be recognized by an other. It is precisely the child's independent acts which require recognition and so reaffirm its dependency. In light of the early relationship between child and mother in which contradiction is first experienced I am going to address three issues. First, how the issues of separation and recognition which arise in the course of differentiation reappear in other relationships of domination, especially erotic domination. Second, how the different ways in which males and females relate to and differentiate from their mother influence the roles they play in such relationships. Finally, the way in which the male experience of differentiation is linked to a form of rationality which pervades our culture and is essential to sadomasochism. This last phenomenon is what I call rational violence.

This analysis is probably not applicable to all forms of violence, or even all male violence against women, even though men's motivations for rape and battery may be similar to those which appear in rational violence. The issues of control and possession, the violent repudiation and derogation of women, must certainly play a role. But I am confining myself to the controlled, ritualized form of violence which is expressed in sexual fantasy life and in some carefully institutionalized sexual practices. There are a great many other forms of violence against women which do not partake of this rational character, in which women are simply assaulted and cannot successfully defend themselves. The danger is that even in such cases women blame themselves and feel guilty for prosecuting the assailant.[3] This makes the topic of rational violence or erotic domination, where participation is voluntary or only a fantasy, seem to some a subtle apology for all male violence. However, understanding the sources of violence should be distinguished from blaming the victim. The relationship between fantasy and real acts, between the pornographic imagination and the perpetuation of violence, must be studied empirically.

My concern here is simply to examine the psychological issues which underlie domination through love, the mutual fantasy of control and submission which we know as sadomasochism. My data are not drawn from studies of sadomasochistic practices but from a single and powerful study of the erotic imagination, the *Story of O.*[4] Therefore these rather schematic speculations ought not to be taken as conclusions. My aim is to suggest an explanation for the assignment and characterization of male and female roles in sadomasochistic fantasy, based on the differences in the way in which boys and girls differentiate. The extent to which real men and women actually identify with such roles is an empirical question. It is apparent that these roles are no longer always played by one sex, that they are no longer assigned necessarily to one gender even though still associated with it. Yet the fantasy of submission and rational control is perpetuated by the splitting of the two basic postures, male and female, in differentiation. One posture, traditionally male, overemphasizes self boundaries, and the other posture, traditionally female, the relinquishing of self. The splitting of these postures is the most important boundary of all.

Differentiation and Male Rationality

In explaining differentiation, most psychoanalytic theories reveal a peculiar bias which empirical observation of infants might rather easily correct. (There are notable exceptions, which we shall come to later.) The infant is conceived as initially uninterested in the world and completely unaware of the existence of the other. This theory, then, places its main emphasis upon the process of breaking the unity, separating from the other. It does not see that discovery of the self and discovery of the other actually go hand in hand, that awareness of self and awareness of the other develop as interdependent processes. Instead this theory places the mutual functions of recognizing the other and establishing one's own autonomous identity in opposition. It sees the child as tied to the mother through physiological dependency, rather than as specifically drawn to her as the other social being he/she comes to know best. The view that the child experiences the mother as an instrument of its own needs corresponds with the devaluation of a child's need to recognize the mother as an independent being or subject with her own needs. Within this theoretical framework it seems natural that the child sees the mother as an object and so attains subjectivity by leaving her, rather than discovering her. The stress is on the establishment of separateness and boundaries, rather than the mutual recognition of subjects.

Chodorow has shown how these problems in psychoanalytic versions of differentiation are connected to an overemphasis on "difference," which reflects male experience. Male children achieve their distinct identity by (more or less violently) repudiating the mother. Initially, all infants not only love their mothers but identify with and wish to emulate them. But boys discover that they cannot be, or become, her; they can only have her. When they grow up, they will be independent and unlike the mother, while girls achieve independence with the expectation that they will continue to be like her.[5] This repudiation of the mother by men has also meant that she is not recognized as an independent person, another subject, but as something Other: as nature, as an instrument or object, as less-than-human.[6] A male child's independence is bought at the price of saying: I am nothing like she who serves and cares for me! I am the recognized and nurtured one, not the recognizer and nurturer. Thus male identity emphasizes difference from the nurturer over sameness, and separation from the mother over individuation. It is based on the one-sided giving or taking instead of reciprocity. For little boys, that aspect of differentiation which involves discovering the other person's self is reduced to establishing dissimilarity and difference from her. No wonder, then, that most theories of psychological development have been largely unable to maintain (even in thought) the tension of simultaneous sameness and difference. They are reflecting the male experience that independent identity can only be gained by unlearning the identification with the mother.

They also reflect the fact that becoming like the mother, as girls do, will probably mean the sacrifice of independent subjectivity or selfhood. It will mean subordination to others and their needs. To the extent that she does individuate, the girl has largely to identify with her father, with the male posture of emphatic differences, for the mother is not an independent figure. Generally, however, the female posture is the opposite of the male—merging at the expense of individuality. The small girl's experience is often that she develops continuity and sameness at the expense of difference and independence.[7] For her the injunction is: I must be like she who serves and cares for me. The temptation to be undifferentiated, to deemphasize boundaries, is reinforced for her as an appropriate form of subjectivity. She becomes all too able to recognize the other's subjectivity, but—like mother—does not expect to be treated as an independent subject herself. Women's own denial of their subjectivity corresponds to the male perception of the mother. She becomes in her own mind object, instrument, earth mother. Thus she serves men as their Other, their counterpart, the side of themselves they repress.

Each gender is able to represent only one aspect of the self-other relationship, either merging or separation. Each gender plays a part in a polarized whole. But neither attains true independence. For even the male posture of attaining independence by denying the mother is a defensive stance: the overemphasis on boundaries between me and not-me means that selfhood is defined negatively as separateness from others.[8]

The question I have considered for some time is how the emphasis on boundaries in male identity is connected to male hegemony in the culture. I have looked for a link between rationality as a "masculine" mental attitude and rationality as a pervasive tendency in the culture as a whole. Evelyn Keller has suggested a link between the way boys differentiate and their development of a scientific or objective approach to the world.[9] The kind of differentiation I have described here as male seems to correspond to the Western rational world view, in "male rationality."* This world view emphasizes difference over sameness, boundaries over fluidity. It conceives of polarity and opposition rather than mutuality and interdependence as the vehicles of growth. That is, it does not tolerate the simultaneous experience of contradictory impulses: ambivalence. Finally, it does not grant the other person the status of another subject, but only that of an object. By extension, this object status is granted to the entire world, which, from early on, was infused with the mother's presence. In these psychic tendencies the basic elements of Western rationality take shape: analysis or differentiation; duality or polarity; and objectivity. Along these lines Keller has argued that the boy's earliest experience of becoming an individual has paved the way for a thought which is "premised on a radical dichotomy between subject and object."[10] This is the dichotomy which, in science and in other rational creations, denies the mutual recognition of subjects.

The rational mind, then, is derived from a one-sided experience of

---

* This is not meant to be a causal model in which psychic dispositions result in social conditions. I am assuming a relationship between the social and cultural conditions of mothering and the way that children differentiate, between the conflicts specific to the experience of differentiation and the mentality or world view of people in a given culture. However, I am not proposing a scheme for these relationships, e.g., that there is a causal line which begins at the relationship of production, moves to the relations of reproduction, on to particular socialization practices, culminating finally in a particular personality type. Rather I want to identify certain themes or conflicts which recur at different levels of social organization, experience, and relationships. In this case I am concerned with the theme of rationality and the conflicts around autonomy and recognition.

differentiation—an experience which closes out the reality of the other. The fact that the subject stands apart from and in opposition to the object means that the giver of nurturance and recognition is radically estranged from the recipient. The recipient cannot, or can no longer, imagine himself in the giver's position. This failure of imagination becomes the great obstacle in emotional reciprocity (e.g., in adult life, where some cannot be given to and others cannot give). Of course, children are capable of giving to and recognizing their mothers, perhaps far more than they are allowed. There is considerable documentation of reciprocal interaction between mothers and infants. At some point, however, this reciprocity is probably interfered with by the vicissitudes of gender identification and differentiation. What we see is the result: the mother is not generally appreciated as a separate person by her child. If the child is able to become independent at all, it is through adopting the male stance of repudiating its identification with its mother—by refusing to be a recognizer, by objectifying her.

Differentiation which occurs without any appreciation of the mother's subjectivity is perfectly consonant with the development of rational faculties. In fact it seems to expedite it. The individual is quite able *cognitively* to distinguish self from other. The person knows that he or she is physically and mentally distinct and able to perform, socially, as if other persons were subjects. But at the deepest level of feeling there is not that sharp and clear sense, that vibrant aliveness, of knowing that I am I and you are you. Rationally or cognitively, the distinction is clear; emotionally and unconsciously the other person is simply experienced as the projection of a mental image. The other person does not exist in his/her own right, and hence the sense of aliveness that could emanate from mutual interaction with him/her is diminished. It is only "as if" he/she were there, while underneath one feels alone. As the male scientist in Christa Wolf's story put it, he always feels "like in the movies."[11] This inability to experience others as real, and concomitantly the self as real, is well known to clinicians today. This feeling of unreality is a result of one-sided or (as I think of it) "false differentiation."[12] Rationality as a substitute for recognition threatens to destroy the sense of reality and selfhood it was supposed to create.

To summarize, both in theory and practice our culture knows only one form of individuality: the male stance of overdifferentiation, of splitting off and denying the tendencies toward sameness, merging, and reciprocal responsiveness. In this "false differentiation" the other subject remains an object, rather than emerging as a person in her/his own right. This way of establishing and protecting individuality dovetails with the dualistic, objective posture of Western rationality. To be a woman is to be excluded from this rational individualism, to be either an object of it or a threat to it. To be a man is not merely to assert one's side of the duality, the supremacy of the rational subject. It is also to insist that the dualism, splitting, and boundaries between the male and female postures are upheld. We shall see how these traditionally gender-specific relationships to boundaries are repeated in the pattern of erotic domination.

Erotic Domination: Master and Slave in Hegel and Bataille

Psychologically, the rational posture can promote an extreme form of individuation, a rigidity of boundaries between self and other, which are unbearably isolating. No subject can really extricate her/himself from dependency on other subjects, from her/his need for recognition. The isolated subject seeks to protect her/himself from this dependency. In order to separate without being alone she/he denies the other's separateness. She/he seeks to resolve the problem of dependency by possessing or controlling the other. Just as she/he seeks to be different and individual by making the other person an object, she/he seeks autonomy by dominating the other person.

Domination contains the threat or the possibility of violence against the other. Violence is predicated upon the denial of the other person's independent subjectivity, and of her/his autonomy. Violence is also a way of expressing or asserting control over another, of establishing one's own self-boundary and negating the other's. Like the other forms of false differentiation, violence is a particularly apt form for the assertion of male identity. It is a way of repudiating sameness, dependency, and closeness with another person, while attempting to avoid the consequent feelings of aloneness. One makes the other an object but retains possession of her/ him. In this sense violence, too, is an attempt to resolve the issues of autonomy and recognition, while denying the other's subjectivity and one's own identification with her/him.

Violence, like rationality, only intensifies the contradictions of dependency. It was Hegel in *The Phenomenology of Spirit* who formulated the classic statement about the dilemma of the subject's unavoidable dependency on another person for recognition. As will become apparent, his formulation reflected an implicit awareness of an idea that psychologists have only recently articulated. Autonomous selfhood develops, and is later confirmed chiefly by the sense of being able to affect others by one's acts. Such confirmation, especially in the first relationship, allows us to develop an appreciation of others' subjectivity. The effect we have on something or someone is a way of confirming our reality. If our acts have no effect on the other, or if he/she refuses to recognize our act, we feel ourselves to be powerless. But if we act in such a way that the other person is completely negated, there is no one there to recognize us. Therefore it is necessary that, when we affect an other, she/he not simply dissolve under the impact of our actions. The other must simultaneously maintain her/his integrity, as well as be affected. So, for example, if the mother sets no limits to the child, if, in effect, she obliterates herself and her own interests and allows herself to be wholly controlled, she ceases to perform the role of an other. It is this self-obliteration on the part of the "permissive" parent which makes the child who "gets everything it wants" so unhappy. She/he ceases to be another subject who can recognize the child's intentions and actions, and the child is abandoned.[13] She/he becomes simply an object, a thing, and no longer exists outside the self. What I am describing here is a dialectic of control: if I completely control the other, she/he ceases to exist, and if she/he completely controls me, I cease to exist. True differentiation means maintaining the essential tension of the contradictory impulses, to negate and to recognize.

Hegel's discussion of the master-slave relationship[14] explains how the need for recognition by another subject becomes a vehicle of domination. The two basic relationships with an other (subject) are recognition and negation. Every action the subject performs on an object negates it. That is, it changes the object so that it is no longer itself, but something other than it was. In acting on things we change them; in transforming them, we are negating their old form. If we try to control them absolutely, we are taking away their form as things existing independently. We are thus completely negating them. If they continue to survive, not impervious to our act, but still recognizably themselves in their altered form, they are not completely negated. In retaining their identity through becoming different, they prove themselves to be self-conscious subjects, "I" 's like myself. For I am I, know that I am I even when I change. In contrast, a thing does not retain its identity through change. It can be completely consumed and destroyed by me, or it can remain unaffected. It is not able, like another subject, both to be negated by me and recognize me.

In sum, Hegel is saying that, in desiring an other, we want to be recognized by her/him. We try to realize this desire in an act, but if this act completely destroys the other, she or he can't recognize us. If it consumes the other, leaving her/him with no consciousness, we become the incorporation, the embodiment of this dead or nonconscious thing. To be alive in relation to an other, two things are necessary: we must act in such a way as not to fully negate the other; and the desire in our act must be recognized by the other. This is why, to return to the idea of true differentiation, it is necessary to have both negation and recognition simultaneously between self and other. To simply separate and assert difference is to negate the other, so that she or he can no longer fully satisfy the self's need for recognition.

Hegel's discussion of domination begins with two subjects pitted against each other in the struggle for recognition. To gain recognition and negate the other, the subject risks his/her own death. But if he/she kills the other he/she is once again alone. Therefore he/she enslaves and subjugates the other instead. Why does the master choose domination over mutuality and reciprocity? This choice is no more problematic for Hegel than for Freud or, following him, Mahler. The nascent self wants to be omnipotent, or rather, has the phantasy that its mental process is identical with the world. Later omnipotence is seen as a regression to this necessary first stage.[15] What Hegel says is that self-consciousness wants to be absolute. It wants to be recognized by the other, in order to place *itself* out in the real world—that is, to prove that it exists objectively. The I wants to prove this at the expense of the other. The I wants to think itself the only one, the whole of the world; it abjures dependency. The I wants to be one and all alone, to negate everything else. It starts out by incorporating everything else, allowing the other to exist only as an object inside itself, in other words, as a mental object. It wants to control everything that matters, as Dinnerstein put it. So for these thinkers, the self only gives up this omnipotence when it realizes its dependency—in Freud, through animal desire or physiological need; in Hegel, through the desire for recognition. The subject discovers that if it completely devours the other (at the animal level) or controls the other (at the human level) it can no longer get what it wanted from the other. So it learns better. But while the subject may relinquish the wish to control or devour the other completely, it does so only out of self-interest. This is a far cry from a real appreciation of the other's right to exist as a person in her or his own right.

Of course Hegel does briefly acknowledge the possibility of mutual recognition between subjects in which both partake of the contradictory elements of negation and recognition. But the polarization of these two moments against each other is a necessary part of the dialectic. Thus, in his scheme, each subject winds up embodying only one moment. Psychoanalytically speaking, this breakdown of wholeness is called splitting. Wholeness for each can only exist if the contradiction or tension is maintained. But it is somehow in the nature of this bond that the tension is broken and the whole is split into opposing halves.

How do we explain this seemingly inevitable splitting? By an essential intolerance of contradiction? By the fact that movement or change can only occur through the dialectic of splitting and reuniting? Although the answer to this question so far eludes us, it is apparent that when the two poles of the unity become split, the relationship of domination emerges. One member of the relationship desires and negates while the other only recognizes. The master-slave relationship can be grasped as a failure of differentiation and of wholeness—the loss of the essential tension.

It was Georges Bataille who first used the Hegelian analysis of the master-slave relationship to understand eroticism, or sexual violation.[16] Bataille centers his treatment of the Hegelian dialectic between self and other around the problem of maintaining the tension between life and death. He quotes Sade to the effect that if one wants to know about death, one ought to look at the erotic, or at sexual excitement. The significance of eroticism, he argues, is that it affords the opportunity of transgression against the most fundamental taboo. This is the taboo separating life from death. Or, it could be called the law of discontinuity, which confines each individual in her/his separate isolated existence, from which she or he can be released by death alone. Death is continuity. It is in death, not life, that each individual is united with the rest, sunk back into the undifferentiated sea. What Bataille is calling death, or continuity, can also be seen as the merging, fusion, or oneness with the mother. This merging or loss of boundaries is experienced as psychic death once we have separated—the proverbial return to the womb. A loss of differentiation is ultimately feared as the threat of death, particularly in the absence of true differentiation which incorporates a sense of oneness. This fear may explain why the individual frantically protects the self's boundary, even at the cost of violating an other's.

The body stands for discontinuity, individuality, and life. Consequently, the violation of the body, erotic violation, breaks the taboo. To break from discontinuity into continuity, in Bataille's terms, constitutes *and* requires a violation. In the act of transgression, the taboo is simultaneously upheld and violated. Violation expresses the fundamental passion; reason, preserving discontinuity and self boundaries, is the law holding it in check. The simultaneously upheld and broken boundary unites these elements in the single act of ritual violation. In this way violence and reason become necessary parts of an act of mastery over death. Whereas violence per se is feared because it represents loss of control, ritual or rational violence upholds control while breaking it. Loss of control is defended against by controlled loss or release.

Bataille discovers the Hegelian dialectic in eroticism by establishing the split between the one who maintains the boundary, or limit, and the one who breaks it. (Or perhaps we should say, the one who allows her boundary to be violated, and the one who does so.) The relationship contains an actor and an acted upon, a negator and a recognizer. Not at all to our surprise, Bataille explains that in the ritualized form of transgression known as sacrifice, the man is the actor and the woman the victim. Still, Bataille argues, the woman performs the function of breaking her discontinuity, of risking death, for both of them. And, I would add, the man upholds the boundaries of reason for her by keeping his violence within ritual limits.

The fact that the woman allows her boundary to be broken and the man breaks it is consonant with the positions each gender traditionally takes in differentiating from the mother. The girl tends to experience her continuity and merging with the mother, and the boy to assert his boundaries. The male position is to make the woman an object, both by his violence toward her and his rational self-control. The female position is to feel herself a passive object and accept her lack of control. Bataille's notion of each partner representing one pole in a split unity, a part of an interdependent whole, suggests that the roles can be reversed. Both partners know and require their opposite half.

Because the transgression Bataille is describing maintains the tension between control and lack of it, it affirms the boundary between life and death. Erotic domination is constructed to avoid the loss of the essential tension. However, this can only work if the master-slave relationship is enacted as fantasy, or at any rate restricted. Otherwise the outcome is the inevitable negation of one subject by another. The problem in the death struggle for prestige is that

> the slave, by accepting defeat . . . has lost the quality without
> which he is unable to *recognize* the conqueror so as to *satisfy*
> him. The slave is unable to give the master the *satisfaction*
> without which the master can no longer rest.[17]

For Bataille, Hegel's idea that each self must be willing to risk death in order to impose itself as an absolute upon the other reveals the impossibility of sovereignty without equality.

The "Story of O"[18]

The total loss of this tension, or of differentiation, is death of the self. Perhaps the most important way in which human beings experiment with the loss of this tension is through sex—death by other means. The imagery and enactment of erotic domination have recently surfaced in ways that make explicit reference to this connection of sex and death. The poster for a movie shows a woman whose exposed throat is circled by a thin red ribbon and bears the caption, "The thin line between love and death is— the Bloodline." It may not be wholly surprising, then, that there is such a strong parallel between Hegel's exploration of the dialectic of control in the master-slave relationship and the description of erotic subjugation in the *Story of O*. Looking for a way to explore some of these problems of false differentiation and male rationality, I was struck by the fact that masochism, or voluntary submission, always requires an other who remains in control. This kind of rational violence, or more precisely violation, seems to reveal a pattern of establishing selfhood by controlling the other, and of losing selfhood by being controlled. The replay of the infant's struggle to differentiate in the adult erotic relationship offers clues about the psychological components of gender domination. Interpreting the *Story of O* in light of Hegel, I am going to try to show how the failure of differentiation culminates in erotic domination.

The *Story of O* is an exceedingly self-conscious attempt to represent the themes of erotic domination—the tension between separation and recognition, rationality and violence, transcendence and negation of self, the active phallus and the passive orifice. Perhaps the greatest objection to this work is its emphasis on O's voluntary submission. But it is only by virtue of O's volition that the allegory of the struggle for recognition can unfold. O must will her lover's desire because in so doing she recognizes his desire. She desires his will, his desire. Thus O is constantly recognizing her lover, and he is constantly negating her. This polarization sets the stage for the end even as the relationship is beginning.

The story is told chiefly from the point of view of O, the woman. The novel makes clear that behind the physical humiliation and abuse which O suffers is a search for an ultimately unattainable spiritual or psychological satisfaction. De Beauvoir pointed out that real masochism consists in wanting the suffering of pain not for its own sake, but as proof of servitude. That is, masochism is essentially a desire for subordination rather than the submission to force or the experience of pain as such. She also states that the masochist desires to be a thing subject to the will of the other in order to *see* herself being an object for the other.[19] Truly, only the ego which has not itself given up the claim to omnipotence wants to submit to the other's omnipotence, thus gaining vicarious satisfaction. She also distinguishes this submissive impulse from the impulse to transcend the self by giving oneself to another person.

This distinction is crucial, as long as we see the relation between the two values. The submissive impulse stands in relation to real transcendence as the part to the whole. The masochist gives up herself while the other remains in control, so she cannot achieve the transcendence of which a whole self is capable. But this is again a case of a unity which has become split. For she exists only in relation to an other who does act, does negate her, is recognized even while she is only the object of his acts. Hence her giving up of self stands for, or signifies, the contradictory unity which she does not achieve. Unfortunately, it is usually only in the knowledge of the parts, in the experience of polarity, that the partners achieve the potential wholeness which unites them.

At the beginning of *Story of O*, our heroine, whose name is evidently given by the letter's designation of the word Open or opening (Ouvert) or of the orifice itself, is brought to Roissy castle, organized by men for the ritual violation and subjugation of women. We know nothing else about it, the men, or her lover, René, and learn little more throughout the book. The first night she is there, the men deliver this speech to O:

> You are here to serve your masters. . . . You will drop whatever you are doing and ready yourself for what is really your one and only duty: to lend yourself. Your hands are not your own, nor are your breasts, nor most especially, any of your orifices, which we may explore or penetrate at will . . . you have lost all right to privacy or concealment . . . you must never look any of us in the face. If the costume we wear . . . leaves our sex exposed, it is not for the sake of convenience . . . but for the sake of insolence, so that your eyes will be directed there upon it and nowhere else so that you may learn that there resides your master . . . it is perfectly all right for you to grow accustomed to being whipped—since you are going to be every day throughout your stay—this is less for our pleasure than for your enlightenment . . . both this flogging and the chain . . . attached to the ring of your collar . . . are intended less to make you suffer, scream, or shed tears than to make you feel, through this suffering, that you are not free but fettered, and to teach you that you are totally dedicated to something outside yourself . . .[20]

A great deal is contained in this short text. First, O is to lose all subjectivity, all possibility of using her body for action; she is to be merely a thing. Second, she is to be continually violated, even when she is not actually being used—the main transgression of her self's boundary occurs through her having to be always available and open. Third, what strikes me as very important, is that her masters are to be recognized by her in a particular indirect form. The penis represents or symbolizes their desire.[21] By interposing it between them they can maintain a self, a subjectivity independent of her recognition. And this subjectivity is expressed through their power over her in a more general way, in their ability totally to organize, calculate, and control the effect they are having upon her. Indeed, what they do is "more for her enlightenment than their pleasure"—even in using her they do not need her. Rather, their acts express a rational control, a rational violation, through which they objectify their rational intentions. Each act has such a goal or purpose which asserts their mastery. They enjoy not so much their pleasure, as the fact that they can take it. They enjoy not so much her pain, as the fact that they have a visible effect upon her: they leave their marks.

Why must they find enjoyment more in their command than in her service, and why must it be mediated through calculation, or symbolized by the penis? Because they must always maintain their separate subjectivity; they must never become dependent. Otherwise, they would suffer the fate of Hegel's master, who in becoming dependent on his slave gradually loses subjectivity to him. A further danger for the master is that the subject always becomes the object which he consumes. ("You are what you eat.") Thus they must be careful never to wholly consume her as *will-less* object, but rather to command and consume her *will*. They always ask her, "O, do you consent?" Of course, in consuming her will, they are negating hers and being recognized in theirs; they are inevitably depreciating her will and turning her into an object. When her objectification is complete, when she has no more will to give, or give up, they cannot engage with her without becoming filled with her thing-like nature. They must perform their violation rationally and ritually both in order to maintain their boundaries and to make her will the object of their will.

Finally, what is significant about the symbolization of male mastery through the penis is that it emphasizes the difference between them and her.[22] It signifies the male pronouncement of difference over sameness. Each act which the master takes against the slave, O, is one which establishes his separateness, his difference from her, his nonidentity with her, through his power to negate her. In the tension between recognition of like humanity and negation of Otherness, he represents the one-sided extreme. What he is doing is continually placing himself outside her by continually saying, "I am not you." He is using her to establish his objective reality by imposing it on her. The rational function, the calculation, objectivity, and control are linked to this one-sided differencing, this "I am not you," in the manner that Bataille saw it as inherently linked with discontinuity. Violence, in the service of reason, has the same intention of asserting the self-boundary of control. The penis symbolizes the fact that, however interdependent the master and slave become, he will always maintain the boundary— the rigidity, antagonism, and polarization of their respective parts.

Through the movement of the dialectic of control, the narrative reveals the consequences of such separation through negating the other. The story is really driven forward by the problematic nature of control as a means of differentiation. Since the slave who is completely dominated loses the quality of being able to recognize, since she who is once possessed no longer exists outside, the struggle must be prolonged. O must be enslaved piece by piece, as it were. New levels of resistance must be found, so that she can be vanquished anew. She must acquiesce in ever deeper humiliation, pain, and bondage, and she must will her submission ever anew. The narrative moves through these ever deeper levels of submission, tracing the impact of each fresh negation of her will, the defeat at her resistance, unto her death.

So far it has appeared that O, by submitting, recognizes her lover's desire, while he only negates her. But this is not entirely true. There is a sense in which, from the very beginning, her enslavement makes her unsuited to recognize him. And he has such control over her that he risks nothing, certainly not (his own) death. She is more the objectification of his desire, not a human subject who recognizes it, and he recognizes in her the object of his desire. Thus while O wants to be recognized by René-the-subject, he uses her as an object in his struggle for recognition.

The narrative problem, the culmination of the dialectic, occurs at the point when O has submitted and can no longer recognize René, and he has exhausted the possibilities of violating her boundaries. The problem is solved by the introduction of Sir Stephen, the older stepbrother to whom René gives O. O herself then realizes that she is an object in René's effort to win prestige from Sir Stephen, who is more important to René than she can ever be. Sir Stephen does not "love" or recognize O (at least, not at first), and so her submission to him is a submission to a pure power who requires no recognition from her in return. She is, he tells her, to be humiliated by one who does not love her in the presence of one who does. Sir Stephen is thoroughly rational, calculating, and self-controlled in his desire.

Equally suggestive is the fact that René looks up to Sir Stephen as to a father. There is more than a hint of the Oedipal relationship here. Sir Stephen is the authority not only for O, but for René. He is the person in whose eyes René wants to be recognized. The entrance of Sir Stephen suggests a reinterpretation of the story up to that point. We now see that René is weak and has always been under the influence of the more powerful, older man. This development in the story reminds us that male domination is rooted in a struggle for recognition between men in which women are mere objects or tokens: the prize. In terms of psychological development the relationship of domination is not only based on the preoedipal drama of mother-child separation, but is perpetuated in the Oedipal triad. In the Oedipal conflict, the father enforces the separation of the boy from his mother, demanding not merely that he relinquish her as a love object, but also as a subject with whom to identify. The father's aggression or interference, which the boy internalizes or identifies with, is reenacted in the repudiation and objectification of the mother. In other words, the boy's posture of repudiating the mother and asserting his own boundaries is inspired by the powerful and different father. Seeking recognition from this father, the boy is aspiring not to be nurtured but to gain prestige. He gains it by repudiating the mother as visibly, as violently, as possible.

The realization that René is willing to relinquish her for Sir Stephen plunges O into despair, for she can only exist if René recognizes her. Without him, without his love which signifies his dependency on her, life is absolutely void. She thinks, paraphrasing a Protestant text she saw as a child, "It is a fearful thing to be cast out of the hands of the living God." We see that her experience has a religious character. This is elaborated not only in the ritual violation of her body as the barrier to continuity, infinity. She herself experiences her lover as a god whom she adores and cannot stand to be parted from. While God represents the ultimate oneness, the ability to stand alone, O represents abject dependency, the inability to tolerate separation and aloneness.

The author tells us that abandonment by God is experienced as punishment and an indication of guilt. Typically, one asks what one has done to deserve this and looks for the cause in oneself. Abandoned by René, punished by Sir Stephen, O finds the guilt in her wantonness, her desire. O is actually willing to risk death in order to continue to be the object of her lover's desire, to be recognized. Her great longing is to be known, and in this respect she is like any lover, for the secret of love is to be known as oneself. But O's desire to be known is rather like the sinner who wants to be known by God. Sir Stephen thrills her, in part, because he knows her to be bad, wanton, "easy," reveling in her abasement, from the moment he meets her.

O's deepest guilt stems not, however, from her desire to be recognized by René or Sir Stephen, but from the possibility that she will be tempted to *act* on her desire. To act is to negate an other, to be a subject. O refuses to masturbate in front of Sir Stephen because her deepest shame is connected to this flagrant act of autonomy, one that says, "I can satisfy myself." We also find out that O has always desired to possess women, to have them give themselves to her, but she has never given herself prior to meeting René. So O is being punished for two aspects of her subjectivity, the desire to be known, and the desire to negate, to act, to be separate. In particular I suspect that the latter, perhaps because it is the prerogative of the male, is her real sin: the assertion of autonomy, of the self as agent.

O is encouraged to whip as well as make love to other women in the course of her enslavement. But her actual independent performance of the active role (before her enslavement) is sinful. In part, the author implies, her refusal to give herself was truly in bad faith, and O's punishment and enslavement is the fate of one who could not truly love. She is not able to give herself as a whole and separate person. Both her inability to tolerate abandonment and separation as well as her guilt-ridden repudiation of all self-assertion inevitably lead O to her death. It is difficult not to see O's continual consent and affirmation in her own enslavement as a flight from the aloneness and separation of the free agent. Yet I do not merely mean to say that O is in flight from freedom. While that may be true, she also seems to be in search of another kind of freedom. It is the freedom of devotion to her god. Although true transcendence and freedom are constituted by the free giving of self in a reciprocal relationship, O finds a kind of substitute transcendence, or loss of self, in her enslavement. This loss of self is the opposite of losing the other, of being alone. We could say that her search for the boundless, for true union, for religious experience, turns into submission and enslavement because she is not separate, cannot bear aloneness. She consents to her enslavement in order to transcend her aloneness (discontinuity) without undergoing separation.

How is pain connected to her transcendence of self? "She liked the idea of torture, but when she was being tortured herself she would have betrayed the whole world to escape it, and yet when it was over she was happy to have gone through it" (p. 152). Most obviously, pain signifies her submission to the other's will. But why does pain have this meaning? What differentiates pleasure from pain, in Freud's terms, is that pain is the point at which stimuli become too intense for the body or ego to bear. Pain is the violent rupture of the self-organization.[23] It is this loss of self-organization which O welcomes, under certain conditions at any rate.* Conversely, pleasure always involves a certain amount of control or mastery of stimuli. Hence it is the master who can know pleasure, the mastery of satisfaction, and the slave who must experience pain. In her violation and loss of self through pain, in the marks of this violation, O's body is "moving" to her masters (as another captive woman is moving to O). This "emotion," however, is always checked and finally diminished as she becomes more a dehumanized object, as it is only the spectacle of her which moves them. O finally attains independence by being willing to go all the way, to risk her life in order to gain recognition. Her experience of psychic death through the self-rupturing pain is her form of transcendence.

Seemingly contradictory, but perhaps complementary, is the use of pain to symbolize birth, selfhood, and separation. The psychic pain of separation is captured in the physical pain inflicted upon the violated. The closeness of birth and death, self-loss and self-awareness in the imagery of pain reminds us that actually the most intense sense of selfhood involves contradictory feelings. True differentiation, I have argued, is a whole, in tension between negation and recognition, affirming singularity and connectedness, continuity and discontinuity at once. O's hope that in complete submission and acceptance of pain she will find her elusive self may be seen as an attempt to experience self by risking death.

If we accept the idea that O's consent to pain and enslavement is a search for transcendence, we still want to know why she chooses this form, rather than the possibility of mutual, reciprocal giving of self. We want to know this in the same way that we want to know why for Hegel the

---

* As de Beauvoir said, the actual violation which the young girl imagines would be terrible if it happened in fact. This is because in imagination the violence is still under control, whereas in reality it is out of one's control.

struggle for recognition ends in the power relationship instead of in reciprocal, equal self-sovereignty. Bataille suggests an answer with his idea of the transgression, or violation, which both breaks and upholds the law. It allows one partner to remain rational and in control, while the other loses her boundaries. In fact, it is the master's rational, calculating, even instrumentalizing attitude which excites submission, the image of his exquisite control which makes for his thrilling machismo. The pleasure, for both partners, is in his mastery. Were both partners to give up self, give up control, the disorganization of self would be total. The masochistic ego would not be able to identify with the part which remained in control. O could not then experience her loss of control as a controlled loss. She could not "safely" give in to her urge to lose control. When the boundary is freely dissolved, rather than broken by one who maintains his boundary, one is left unprotected before the infinite, the terrifying unknown. It may be, then, that the primary motivation for maintaining inequality in the erotic relationship, and ultimately for establishing the master-slave constellation, is the fear of ego loss—the boundless.

And perhaps the boundless infinity of plenitude is as fearful as the infinity of emptiness. The master-slave relationship actually perpetuates the problem it is designed to resolve. The rigid division into master and slave, sadist and masochist ultimately exhausts its potential for transcendence. Neither partner can be both recognized and active-negating. Like the couple in the cuckoo clock, one must always be out when the other is in; they never meet. If the tension dissolves, death or abandonment is the inevitable end of the story, and the *Story of O* is deliberately left open to both conclusions. This ambiguity is appropriate because for the masochist the end or intolerable fate is abandonment, while for the sadist it is the death/murder of the other whom he destroys. The mastery he achieves over the other is unsatisfactory because when the other is drained of resistance she can only be vanquished by death. Metaphorically the sadomasochistic relationship tends toward deadness, numbness, the exhausting of sensation, total immobility. It is caught in the dialectic of objectification, where the subject becomes increasingly like the objectified other he consumes. In one form or another, controlling the other out of existence is the inevitable end. The relation of domination is built upon the fantasy of omnipotence and the denial of the other's separate reality. Consequently it is suffused with the frustration of that feeling of unreality: no one is really there to recognize me.

The assertion of omnipotence and denial of the other is rather a shaky defense against continuity, the boundless. At any moment the perception may dawn on the master that she/he is actually alone because the person she/he is with is no person at all. The slave for her/his part fears that she/he will abandon her/him to aloneness because she/he will get tired of being with someone who is not a person. Only when the slave becomes determined to be a person in her/his own right and assert her/his freedom is the master faced with the fact that she/he, too, is dependent upon her/him for recognition—either directly or indirectly by the master's possession of her/him. This dynamic of dependency is quite familiar in adult erotic relationships. Often, though not always, the male takes the role of asserting difference, the female of dependency. Nonreciprocity is a constant undertow in any dyad. One gives, the other refuses; one pursues, the other loses interest; one plays hard to get, the other pursues; one criticizes, the other feels judged. The aspiration to reciprocity is constantly undermined by deep fear of losing self-boundaries, mental omnipotence. The fear of intrusion, the desire to be self-sufficient, to be unmoved—these are familiar ways of avoiding raw confrontation with the reality that another exists apart from me whom I may yet need.

Some Psychoanalytic Clues to the Origins of Sadomasochism

Two questions remain to be answered. One is whether the assertion of mental omnipotence is, as Hegel depicts it, an original or natural state;[24] or if it is a defensive posture which, in their desire for recognition, people are as loath to maintain as they are to abandon. And second, why does violence play such an important role in erotic domination? To answer these questions we must turn back to the question of differentiation again, and press beyond our earlier explanation that the child repudiates the mother to achieve autonomy. Perhaps the frustration of the sadomasochistic relationship is a clue. Might it signify a repetition of early experience? The nature of aggression or violence and the origin of sadism are such broad topics I cannot do them justice here. But certain psychoanalytical formulations do shed light on the phenomena I am trying to identify as the dialectic of control, on the inevitable and frustrating loss of the partner's reality.

Freud outlined the development of sadism as a complicated process. First, he thought, the infant's relationship to the world is characterized by a primary sadism.[25] By this he meant a desire for mastery in which the infant is quite indifferent to the outcome for the other person. It does not know that its ravenous, sometimes toothy, attack on the breast is hurtful to the mother. Further, its (fantasized) destruction of the object—consuming, devouring, incorporating it in some form—is not experienced with a view to its consequence of affecting the other, let alone hurting her. The infant is not yet aware that it will lose the other by incorporating it. This initial indifference to the fate of the other also allows the possibility that the other will survive any attack. Perhaps the infant even desires and expects the other's survival, as in "eating your cake and having it, too." Real sadism, the desire to inflict pain, only occurs after the child has experienced masochism—only after it has internalized, turned against itself, the original sadism.[26] Through this internalization comes the ability to play both roles in fantasy, to experience vicariously the other's part, which is what gives meaning to the act of violation.

Now, the decisive issue is whether this description of a primary innocent drive for mastery really jibes with the notion that children "naturally" want to maintain omnipotence and impose themselves upon the world. Ultimately what we decide about this may be more a matter of faith than evidence, as was probably true for Freud. But by reasoning from clinical observation we may still find another way to understand violence. This is exactly what the psychoanalyst Winnicott did. Winnicott argued that the destructive act, in its original innocence, might well be understood as an attempt to give up, not maintain, omnipotence.[27] Originally aggression is not an angry reaction to reality, but a primary differentiating drive which helps to establish reality. As stated earlier, the recognition of the subject's acts gives her or him the feeling of meaningful selfhood and relations with others. But it is important that the other is affected, *not* completely negated or destroyed. Winnicott proposes that the baby is always "destroying" the other in fantasy, that it is attacking (negating) it, but is pleased if it finds that the other continues to survive. The baby expects that it has done what it fantasizes, but discovers the ineffectuality of fantasy with relief. The discovery enables it to experience the other as truly having an independent existence, to become aware that the other is truly outside and is not wholly controlled by the self's mental apparatus.[28] This originally innocent attack, or mastery, is not so much an attempt to impose the self on the other, although it may appear to be. Rather, it is an attempt to place the other outside the sphere of mental control or omnipotence. Its aim, or at least its effect, is to collide with the other's resistance and so firmly to establish her/his solid, independent presence. The other's survival spells the death of mental omnipotence, yet this "death" is what really gives the other "life."

Winnicott actually confirms Freud's understanding that initially the aggressive fantasy is not an impulse to dominate or be sadistic. Initially violence is an expression of the impulse to negate, to affect others, to be recognized. But he suggests that there is an interaction between baby and mother which results in what Freud describes as the next steps: first, the internalization of sadism as masochism, then inflicting this hurt upon another person. The failure of the mother to "survive" the attack, that is, to absorb it without reacting, causes the baby to turn its aggression inward and to develop what we know as rage.[29] Rage is a reaction to the other's retreat or retaliation. The original self-assertion is then converted from innocent mastery to mastery over and against the other. Winnicott's account implies that violence begins simply as the differentiating impulse, as a way of placing the other outside the self's boundaries. He (like psychoanalysts generally) does not consider the kind of conditions that would enable a mother, or more generally a first other, to survive as an independent subject for the child. But his analysis does provide a clue to the repetitive and exhausting nature of sadomasochism. When the other does not set a limit, when she does not survive, the child must continue to destroy and attack, continue to seek a boundary for its reactive rage. Now the nature of the attack changes, becomes literally violent, hurtful in intent. The other's failure to survive creates a void for the subject. Even without direct retaliation, if the other caves in and withdraws under my act, my act drops off the edge of that emptiness and I feel that I will soon follow.* In this void, the fear of the boundless begins.

For the masochist as well as the sadist, the search is for the other person's boundary as a protection from emptiness and from rage. The masochist exposes herself to the boundless in herself, while the other continues to survive, to maintain boundaries, to control. But the masochist is also reliving the retaliation for her self-assertion at the hands of the sadist. Neither partner, however, is able to achieve the satisfaction of attacking the other and experiencing the other's survival. There is no relief through finding out that one's aggression is not so destructive after all, through having another presence who can tolerate one's urges and truly stave off the emptiness. In other words, the relationship of erotic domination is a repetition or reliving of an earlier thwarting of the drive for differentiation. It expresses the violence whose original direction was to place the other outside the self. Failing this, it seeks what it could not originally achieve in alienated or symbolic form. But in so doing, it simply repeats the earlier frustration of destroying rather than discovering the other; of submitting to control rather than being recognized.

Extending Winnicott's line of thought, I would suggest that the subject is seeking to express a basic differentiating impulse. This quest persists as violence until it succeeds. The repeated experience of frustration does not so much diminish the differentiating impulse as it converts and distorts its expression by combining it with rage. First, the act of placing the other outside is converted into assertion of control or possession over her/him, in a denial of one's own dependence. Second, the effort to control the violent impulse rationally is substituted for satisfaction of the original need.

---

*I believe a great deal more could be said of the way in which the feeling that one is so ineffectual, one could not possibly harm someone, is responsible for much destructive and violent behavior. It begins with the impervious other.

The effort to control the differentiating impulse instead of acting on it is what makes for the *rational* character of this *violence*. Since the other does not provide a boundary which both contains and permits the differentiating drive one has to provide one's own boundary. One has to play both roles oneself—and, like playing any game by oneself, it is lonely. In adult erotic domination, the sadist has to check and control her/his own impulses; she/he does not have the satisfaction of the other providing a boundary. The masochist does get this satisfaction but not for her/his own differentiating impulse, only vicariously for the sadist's.

Rational violence repeats or reenacts the original process of false differentiation. The containment of violence through adherence to a rational boundary substitutes for the differentiating act of negating the other and enjoying his/her survival. In false differentiation the other may be formally recognized as another subject, but in fact is felt as an object or an instrument. In rational violence the other survives only as an object, not another subject who can recognize and release us. I am arguing that while all violence is a failure of differentiation—an inability to recognize the other's right to exist for herself or himself—rational violence is a special case. It employs the will or volition of the violated and demands the rational control of the violator (in nonrational violence, the victim plays no part at all). The players infuse the relationship with the yearning for recognition and for separateness while protecting themselves from the real experiences of aloneness or reciprocity. Rational violence, as played out in a sadomasochism, is a calculated substitute for real self-transcendence and true differentiation. It is also a substitute for the pain and rage of being unable to successfully destroy and rediscover the other.

In speaking of a substitute—a distorted or alienated expression—for the impulse to differentiate, I am referring to what is often described as a defense.[30] The statement that a particular psychic or interpersonal process serves as a defense is easily misunderstood. It may seem that in terming something a defense, the importance or tenacity or effectiveness of it is being questioned. Quite the contrary. But to term rational violence a defense is to insist that beneath it, however inaccessible, are other yearnings which it both expresses and denies. The essentially defensive aspect of the sadomasochistic relationship lies in the splitting of two impulses which ought to be preserved in tension with one another. The function of the impulses in establishing a sense of reality and independence is impaired. In the process of false differentiation, the one-sided emphasis on separating and drawing boundaries excludes and defends against merging and identifying. In the sadomasochistic relationship, the splitting allows each partner to emphasize and exclude opposing aspects of differentiation—the destructive or negating aspect, and the discovering, recognizing aspect.

The splitting of autonomy from recognition, independence from mutual dependence, is at the root of domination.

Significantly, the tendency of males to emphasize independence and separation in differentiating corresponds to the role of destroying and negating in erotic domination. The male posture, whether assumed by all men or not, prepares for the role of master. He is disposed to objectify the other, to instrumentalize and calculate his relation to her in order to deny his dependency. The female posture disposes the woman to accept objectification and control in order to flee separation both as aloneness and as self-assertion. He asserts individual selfhood, while she relinquishes it.

The Cultural Hegemony of Male Rational Violence

How does this dyadic psychological posture connect to the larger cultural and social forms of male domination? I want to argue that the traditionally male rationality and individuality are culturally hegemonic, while the traditionally female unboundedness and submission are denied and repressed. However morally condemned by society, domination and even violence do not evoke the same fear and loathing as the spectacle of the victim. Further, and crucially, male rationality and violence are linked within institutions that appear to be sexless and genderless, but which exhibit the same tendencies to control and objectify the other out of existence that we find in the erotic form of domination. That is, the male posture in our culture is embodied in exceedingly powerful and dangerous forms of destructiveness and objectification.

While the popular fear of the scientific and technological power to destroy our planet has been abroad since the A-bomb, the idea that in destroying nature man would destroy himself has been abroad far longer. Concern with the tendency of the scientific mind to kill off its object, either literally or in fantasy, is at least as old as romanticism. The romantic critique of male rationality is familiar to us in Frankenstein, or in Hawthorne's Chillingworth, a demon of calculated reason who takes vengeance against the feelings and passions which threaten authority. The sociological critique of rationality found its great articulation in the work of Max Weber at the turn of the century.[31] Weber argued that a certain kind of rational calculation, characteristically Occidental, underlay capitalism. This rationality reduces the process or activity to a mere means, to its product. He called this instrumental reason. Because it permeates our culture, I have suggested the term "instrumental culture."[32] As this form of rationality comes to dominate in our culture, earlier forms of religious and moral authority are replaced. Social interaction becomes depersonalized. The world becomes "disenchanted," devoid of transcendent collective experience. The fact that human needs do not dictate production in capitalism, Weber argued, implies a willingness to subordinate need to profit. For capitalism to develop, this willingness must have been already present in the culture's incorporation of rationality and calculation in the religious and legal forms that preceded industrialization. I think Weber's argument should be extended to mean that male hegemony in the culture is expressed by the generalization of rationality. This would conceptualize one way in which male domination precedes and paves the way for capitalism.

Rationalization and depersonalization in the public spheres of life virtually banish nurturance to the private household, the dwindling maternal world. The repudiation of recognition between persons and its displacement by impersonal objective forms of social intercourse is the social homologue of the male repudiation of the mother. The domestic confinement of nurturance literally sets the stage for the inability to appreciate the mother's subjectivity by depriving her of social recognition. While such connections can only be elaborated in an abstract and schematic way in this essay, it is worth exploring how the differentiation process is affected by culturally embodied forms of male rationality. First of all, I would suggest that privatization of nurturance undoubtedly leads to a weaker position for the mother—and it is her frailty, not her power, which makes her unable to tolerate and encourage her child's differentiation.[33] The more the mother depends upon her child as her task, her meaning, her form of gratification, the less disinterested she is—and the more intense are her feelings around the differentiation process. If she is too permissive and afraid to assert her own needs, she makes the child feel lost. Moreover, if she is socially situated in a way that makes the mothering of only a few children her chief task she is particularly vulnerable to evaluating all her child's acts as touchstones of her own self-esteem, as reflections of her success and failure. This breeds what is essentially an instrumental attitude in the heart of the nurturing relationship. Recognition becomes approval for performance, rather than disinterested appreciation of another person's growth. There are, of course, many varieties of the instrumental attitude which are not informed by overt emotional dependency. For example, constant economic worry and concern or zealous moral standards or fear of community opinion erode maternal disinterestedness. The parents are unable to tolerate a variety of the child's differentiating acts: aggression, exploratory behavior, loud noises, dirt, etc. But today we are probably witnessing a higher degree of social isolation among families and individuals, and consequently a more intensely charged mother-child dyad than in previous eras. The isolation and intensity of the relationship makes the mother both more vulnerable to her child and to the broadcasting of standards of performance and success through impersonal media. There are fewer personal bulwarks against the onslaught of instrumental culture.[34] I would suggest that this tendency toward individual approval and performance in socialization firmly anchors rational or false differentiation today.

The tendency toward rationality in our culture has a number of important consequences. Ironically, domestic privatization seems to encourage strange new collective forms of violation. The secularization of society has eroded many of the previously existing forms of communal life which allowed for ritual transcendence. The experience of losing the self, of continuity, is increasingly difficult to obtain except in the erotic relationship. Consequently sexual eroticism has become the heir to religious eroticism. Erotic masochism or submission expresses the same need for transcendence of self, the same flight from separation and discontinuity, formerly satisfied and expressed by religion. Love is the new religion, and the psychological components of erotic domination are repeated in the eroticized cult politics of our era.

I believe that we are facing unbearably intensified privatization and discontinuity, unrelieved by expressions of continuity. Given that social structure and instrumental culture enforce individual isolation so rigidly, the transgression which attempts to break it may necessarily be more violent. The increase of aestheticized and eroticized violence in our media (return of the repressed) suggests the fallacy in our ordinary understanding of control and self-control. The more rigid and tenacious the boundary between individuals and the more responsible each individual for maintaining it, the greater the danger it will collapse. If the sense of boundary is established by physical, bodily separation, then sexual and physical violence (if not in reality, in fantasy) are experienced as ways of breaking the boundary. The fantasy as well as the playing out of rational violence does offer a controlled form of transcendence, the promise of the real thing. Sadomasochistic imagery may be popular, because it embodies this promise of transcendence without its fearful reality. Similarly, if masochists far outnumber sadists[35] it may be because people are in flight from discontinuity and rationality—especially men who have been charged with upholding them. The rejection of male rationality and control by men because it represents an intolerable strain has become at least thinkable.

Beneath the sensationalism of power and powerlessness the yearning for recognition—to know and be known—lies numbed, not fulfilled. Real transcendence, I have argued, implies that persons are able to achieve a wholeness in which the opposing impulses for recognition and differentiation are combined. The psychological origins of erotic domination can be traced to one-sided differentiation, that is, to the splitting of these impulses and their assignment respectively to women and men. In fact, all forms of gender distinction and domination in our culture bear the mark of this split. I would conclude, not that the issues of differentiation and recognition are the explanation for gender domination, but that they help to reveal some of its inner workings.

While I would like to avoid implying causality and to acknowledge the speculative nature of my analysis, I think the parallels between rational violence and other forms of destructive rationality which have been identified in our culture are too striking to be ignored. The same is true of the parallels between the model of domination which Hegel sketched in his discussion of dependency in the master-slave relationship and the sadomasochism depicted in the *Story of O*. The story illustrates marvelously how the male assumption of mastery is linked to the splitting of differentiation from recognition, to both rationality and violence. It therefore seems safe to say that the same psychological issues run through both political and erotic forms of domination, for they both embody a denial of the other subject. Politically speaking, we are facing the exhaustion of male rationality and the resurgence of erotic fantasy. A politics which denies these issues, which tries to sanitize or rationalize the erotic, fantastic components of human life will not defeat domination but only play into it. The power of a fantasy, the fantasy of rational violence, must be attributed to the interplay of great social forces and deep human needs. Finding the means to dissolve that fantasy, so as to tolerate the tension between true differentiation and mutual recognition, will be no easy achievement.

Notes

1. I refer here to the matrix of thought which has addressed the issue of women's mothering, which includes, above all, the work of Nancy Chodorow, *The Reproduction of Mothering: Psychoanalysis and the Sociology of Gender* (Berkeley: Univ. of California Press, 1978); Dorothy Dinnerstein, *The Mermaid and the Minotaur: Sexual Arrangements and Human Malaise* (New York: Harper and Row, 1976); and Adrienne Rich, *Of Woman Born: Motherhood as Experience and Institution* (New York: W. W. Norton, 1976). See also Jessie Bernard, *The Future of Motherhood* (New York: Dial Press, 1974), for a summary of much relevant literature. Chodorow's thought has been particularly important to me, because she suggested the exploration of object relations theory, a tendency in psychoanalytic thought on which I draw heavily. The larger theoretical framework contributing to my analysis is the critical theory of the Frankfurt School. For a discussion of its import for feminism see my "Authority and the Family Revisited," *New German Critique* 13 (Winter 1978): 35–57. The comments of Evelyn Keller and Jane Lazarre were also particularly helpful in the

formulation of this paper, as were the editorial suggestions of Hester Eisenstein.

2. Margaret Mahler, Fred Pine, and Anni German, *The Psychological Birth of the Human Infant* (New York: Basic Books, 1975). Mahler's work has probably influenced psychoanalytic thinking about infancy more profoundly than any other writer today and has reached widely into popular audiences. Her position is not shared by many other researchers on infancy, however.

3. On rape, see Susan Brownmiller, *Against Our Will: Men, Women and Rape* (New York: Simon and Schuster, 1975).

4. Pauline Réage, *Story of O*, S. d'Estrée, tr. (New York: Grove Press, 1965). As to the broader relevance of this study for the pornographic imagination or sadomasochistic fantasy, the best testimony is probably the power of the text and the exceedingly wide recognition it received. In fact, feminist critics have sometimes mistaken the *Story of O* for an affirmation of female degradation; see, e.g., Andrea Dworkin, "Woman as Victim," *Feminist Studies* 2:1 (1974): 107–11. In addition, the book *Nine and a Half Weeks*, by Elizabeth McNeill (New York: Dutton, 1978), an ostensibly authentic account of a sadomasochistic affair written by the woman participant herself, describes a kind of slavish psychological dependence uncannily similar to that of O. See below, p. 51.

5. Nancy Chodorow, "Gender, Relation, and Difference in Psychoanalytic Perspective," this volume. See also Chodorow, *Reproduction of Mothering*, and Evelyn Fox Keller, "Gender and Science," *Psychoanalysis and Contemporary Thought* 1:3 (1978): 409–43.

6. Simone de Beauvoir's formulation of women as Other, in *The Second Sex* (New York: Vintage, 1974), is obviously the crucial beginning point for the analysis of the subject-other relationship as it applies to men and women. While her work has strongly influenced this essay, I do not necessarily use her concept of Otherness when I use the term "other" here. De Beauvoir uses it to refer to men's exclusion, rejection, and objectification of women, while I use it to refer more generally to the hypothetical confrontation of the self with another subject, which may or may not include these elements.

7. Jane Flax, in "Mother-Daughter Relationships: Psychodynamics, Politics, and Philosophy," this volume, argues that mothers identify more strongly with their daughters and so inhibit their separation.

8. Chodorow, "Gender, Relation and Difference."

9. Keller, "Gender and Science."

10. Ibid., p. 424.

11. Christa Wolf, "Self-Experiment," *New German Critique* 13 (Winter 1978): 109–132. In this story, a woman scientist experiments by undergoing a sex change. When her boss, the head researcher, asks her how she feels now that she is a man, she gives this telling reply. His answer, the punch line, is, "You, too!"

12. This syndrome, in which differentiation is achieved only at the cognitive, conscious level, concealing a despairing sense that no one is really "there,"

has probably been best described and discussed by R. D. Laing in *The Divided Self* (Middlesex: Penguin, 1969). Laing points out that a certain amount of depersonalization, that is, treating the other as an "android robot" rather than another subject, is considered normal and desirable in our culture (p. 47). Severe narcissistic disturbances, which are receiving increasing note among clinicians, also entail an inability to experience others as more than manipulable or resistant objects in the self's world.

13. A variety of psychologists and psychoanalysts embrace this view of how selfhood develops. For example, developmentalists refer to a sense of effectance or of efficacy. See R. Schaffer, *Mothering* (Cambridge: Harvard University Press, 1977) and M. D. S. Ainsworth and S. M. Bell, "Mother-Infant Interaction and the Development of Competence," in K. Connelly and Jerome Bruner, eds., *The Growth of Competence* (London: Hogarth Press, 1973), pp. 97–118. The psychoanalyst D. W. Winnicott writes of parental recognition of the baby's "spontaneous gestures" in "Ego Distortion in Terms of True and False Self," in *Maturational Processes and the Facilitating Environment* (New York: International Universities Press, 1965), pp. 140–52. For a more complete statement on the need for recognition of one's sense of agency and authorship, see Jessica Benjamin, *Internalization and Instrumental Culture: A Reinterpretation of Psychoanalysis and Social Theory,* dissertation, Department of Sociology, New York University, 1978.

14. G. W. F. Hegel, "The Independence and Dependence of Self-consciousness: Master and Slave," ch. IV. A., *The Phenomenology of Spirit* (*Phänomenologie des Geistes*) (Hamburg: Felix Meiner, 1952), pp. 141–50. In using Hegel for such an analysis, I am of course allowing myself the liberty of interpreting him loosely. My usage has been influenced by Alexandre Kojève's *Introduction to the Reading of Hegel* (New York: Basic Books, 1969), especially ch. 1.

15. This idea of a primitive, magical stage, during which people believed in the "omnipotence of thoughts," was developed by Freud as a later elaboration of his concept of narcissism (that is, that the ego is first indifferent, and then hostile to the outside world), as defined in his 1915 essay, "Instincts and Their Vicissitudes," in Sigmund Freud, *General Psychological Theory,* P. Reiff, ed. (New York: Macmillan Collier, 1963), pp. 88–103. This is now generally referred to as primary narcissism. Mahler posits that initially the infant is in a state of absolute primary narcissism or "normal autism" (Mahler et al., *Psychological Birth,* p. 42).

16. Georges Bataille, *Death and Sensuality* (New York: Walker and Company, 1962).

17. Georges Bataille, "Hemingway in the Light of Hegel," *Semiotexte* 2:2 (1976): 1.

18. See note 4, above.

19. See de Beauvoir, *Second Sex,* pp. 444–46. In her discussion of the Woman in Love, de Beauvoir describes the religious enthusiasm of "abolishing the self boundaries which separate her from her lover"—an enthusiasm which

inspires the woman in love with man and the woman in love with God—
but she distinguishes this "ecstatic union" from masochism, even though it
may degenerate into self-debasement and destruction for the woman.

20. Réage, *O,* pp. 15–17.
21. Gayle Rubin provides a more general theory of the phallus as symbol and
mediation of male desire in "The Traffic in Women: Notes on the Political
Economy of Sex," in Rayna R(app) Reiter, ed., *Toward an Anthropology
of Women* (New York: Monthly Review Press, 1975), pp. 157–210.
22. Chodorow, "Gender, Relation, and Difference."
23. See Leo Bersani, *Baudelaire and Freud* (Berkeley: Univ. of California Press,
1977), p. 77; Bersani shows how the poetry of Baudelaire moves increasingly from the fantasy of desire through violence to (murder/) death,
illustrating perfectly the sadist's exhaustion of sensation.
24. Lacan, for example, takes his analysis of the ego from this assumption, and
with it the inescapability of a false differentiation; see Jacques Lacan, "The
Mirror Stage as Formative in the Function of the I," tr. J. Roussel, *New
Left Review* 51 (October 1968): 71–77. The consequences of this analysis
become readily apparent when it is adopted by feminists, as in Juliet
Mitchell's work, *Psychoanalysis and Feminism* (New York: Pantheon,
1974), where the Rule of the Father is seen as an inevitable prerequisite for
development and differentiation.
25. Freud, "Instincts," pp. 91–92.
26. Ibid.
27 D. W. Winnicott, "The Use of an Object and Relation through
Identifications," in *Playing and Reality* (Middlesex: Penguin, 1974), pp.
101–11.
28. Ibid., p. 106. Winnicott also points out that he is really developing an idea of
how the subject relates to reality that is wholly different from that in
classical psychoanalytic thought. "From now on, this stage having been
reached, projective mechanisms assist in the act of noticing what is there,
but they are not the reason why the object is there. . . . [T]his is a
departure from theory which tends to a conception of external reality only
in terms of the individual's projective mechanisms." I would add that in
Freud's theory there is no discovery of reality or of the other as an
emotional issue; there is only a cognitive or functional awareness of
others. That heightened sense of aliveness which accompanies recognition
of another subject enters Freud's theory peripherally, if at all, only in his
comments on love. He does not perceive the problem of intersubjective
reality itself.
29. Ibid., p. 110; "there is no anger in the destruction of the object to which I am
referring, though there could be said to be joy at the object's survival." I
am extending Winnicott's argument by saying that if the object fails to
survive, then anger does become a feature of destruction, and destructiveness becomes actual.
30. A notion crucial to my theoretical perspective here, and which grows out of
the object relations theory of W. R. D. Fairbairn (see his theory of object

relations in *Psychoanalytic Studies of the Personality* [London: Routledge and Kegan Paul, 1952]), is that certain processes which Freud saw as necessarily constitutive of the ego are actually defenses.

31. Weber's most extensive definition of *Zweckrationalitaet,* variously translated as instrumental or goal rationality, appears in *Economy and Society,* G. Roth and C. Wittich, eds., E. Fischoff et al., tr. (New York: Bedminister Press, 1968).

32. See my discussion of instrumental culture in "Authority and the Family."

33. I think that Dinnerstein, who suggests quite rightly the extent to which maternal power of life and death is resented by the child and by all men, neglects the extent to which the mother's own weakness in exercising her own autonomy might underlie the resentment of the use of maternal power.

34. Barbara Ehrenreich and Deirdre English, *For Her Own Good: 150 Years of the Experts' Advice to Women* (Garden City, N.Y.: Doubleday, 1978), is a recent important contribution to the study of how instrumental and universal standards of performance are imposed on women in their capacity as mothers. See also my "Authority and the Family," and Sara Ruddick, "Maternal Thinking," *Feminist Studies* 6, 2 (1980).

35. Gayle Rubin (in conversation) has suggested to me, on the basis of her field research and the discussions in the gay press, that masochists far outnumber sadists.

Part II
Contemporary Feminist Thought in France: Translating Difference

Domna C. Stanton

Language and Revolution: The Franco-American Dis-Connection

> Everything is word, everything is only word . . . we must grab
> culture by the word, as it seizes us in its word, in its language. . . .
> Indeed, as soon as we are, we are born into language and
> language speaks us, language dictates its law, which is a law of
> death . . . you will thus understand why I believe that political
> thought cannot do without thought on language, work on lan-
> guage.[1]

Hélène Cixous's statement contains the premise underlying the work of
many contemporary French women writers: the world is the word; it is
experienced phenomenologically as a vast text which encompasses the
sum total of human symbolic systems. Throughout the history of Western
thought, that text, the Logos, has been founded on the structure of the
binary—the dichotomy between such culturally determined oppositions
as rationality and emotionality, activity and passivity, presence and
absence, in a word, "male" and "female." In Cixous's own terms, ". . . the
complete set of symbolic systems—everything said, everything organized
as discourse—art, religion, family, language—everything that seizes us,
everything that forms us—everything is organized on the basis of hierarchical oppositions which come back to the opposition man/woman."[2]

From this perspective, Hélène Cixous, Julia Kristeva, and Luce Irigaray—three of the strongest female voices in France today—argue that
women's oppression, or more precisely, our *repression,* does not merely
exist in the concrete organization of economic, political, or social structures. It is embedded in the very foundations of the Logos, in the subtle
linguistic and logical processes through which meaning itself is produced.
What we perceive as the *real*, they maintain, is but a manifestation of the
symbolic order as it has been constituted by men. Thus, only by exposing
this phallogocentrism, by deconstructing it—to use the Derridean term,
which has assumed the status of a methodology—can we hope to transform the real in any fundamental way. Cixous asks in *La Jeune née* (1975):[3]

> What would become of logocentrism, of the great philosophical
> systems, of world order, if the rock upon which they founded

their church were to crumble? If it were to come out . . . that the logocentric project had always undeniably existed to found [fund] phallocentrism, to insure for masculine order a rationale equal to history itself? Then all the stories would have to be told differently, the future would be incalculable, the historical forces would, will, change hands, bodies, another thinking as yet unthinkable, will transform the functioning of all society.[4]

In the most systematic feminist deconstruction of the occidental Logos, Luce Irigaray wields the speculum, the instrument of female self-discovery, against Plato and Freud in *Speculum de l'autre femme* (1974) to shatter what she calls "the old dream of symmetry."[5] She examines the strategies of repression which have valorized a single term in the polarity masculine/feminine, reducing woman to man's opposite, *his* other, the negative of the positive, and not as Otherness, as difference in her own right. In the Platonic metaphors which have dominated and determined Western discourse, Irigaray finds a latent scheme/schema to subject woman to the principle of Identity conceived wholly as masculine sameness and male presence. Plato, she argues, precluded a mode of thought that does not originate or terminate in this masculine sameness. If Freud liberated occidental thinking from a certain conception of presence and identity, through the notion of the unconscious, for example, he essentially perpetrated the Logos, when he defined sexual difference only in terms of an a priori sameness—the male phallus—and consigned female sexuality to absence, lack, deficiency. This system of thought and signification must be "radically convulsed"[6] if woman is to exist as Subject, as the speaking subject of her difference.

Following a parallel path, Julia Kristeva strives to deconstruct the Western notion of the subject as an organic and consistent identity. For, as she explains in her essay "La Femme, ce n'est jamais ça," "no sociopolitical transformation is possible which does not constitute a transformation of subjects."[7] From Aristotle on, the subject secures its position through syllogistic logic; it excludes contradiction, and thus never fundamentally doubts or questions itself. Similarly, in Hegel, negativity is a stage affirmed only to be denied; the knowing subject, called "consciousness of self" in *The Phenomenology of Mind*, emerges as unity and passes through one transcendent act of cognition after another. To this "phallic" conception of the subject, Kristeva opposes one always already in process and in question, "no longer simply explaining, understanding, and knowing, but an ungraspable subject because it is *transforming* the real."[8] Kristeva explores the contradictions inherent in dialectical materialism and those implicit in the notion of the unconscious to undermine further the dominant view of "the subject in signifying practice"[9] and to develop a theory of difference. Central to her countertheory of the subject is the postulation of a female principle, which Kristeva calls *the semiotic.* Preceding the imposition of the symbolic—the law and Logos of the Father—it comes before the initiation into the domain of signification, sign, and syntax. This preverbal locus is situated at the moment when the child is bound up with the mother's body, and is conceptualized as a stage of silent production in which the instinctual drives are organized. All subjects articulate themselves through the interaction of the semiotic and the symbolic modalities, Kristeva insists, but the first of these has been consistently repressed by the Logos because it is experienced as a threat. Only the eruption of the semiotic into the symbolic can give reign to heterogeneous meaning, to difference, and thus subvert the existing systems of signification.[10]

The eruption of the semiotic, the female modality, represents an essential *negativity*, a term which also encapsulates Kristeva's definition of the poetic, as her essay "Poetry and Negativity" confirms.[11] Although she claims that this semiotic negativity has been primarily expressed by avant-garde male writers, such as Lautréamont, Artaud, and Bataille, Kristeva emphasizes the need for women to recognize that "modern breaks with tradition and the development of new forms of discourse are harmonious with the women's cause" as "[an] activity of subversion."[12] More precisely, in her preface to the "Recherches féminines" issue of *Tel Quel,* she ascribes to the poetic and the female the identical ideological function of *dissidence,* for both point to what the Logos denies and exiles.[13] "A female praxis," she says in *Polylogue,* "can only be negative, an opposition to what exists, in order to say, 'that is not it,' 'that is still not it.' I mean by 'female' what is not represented, what is not said, what remains outside of nominations and ideologies."[14] In much of women's writing, she discovers that "the notion of the signifier as a network of distinctive marks is insufficient, because each of these marks is charged, over and beyond its discriminatory value as a carrier of signification, by an instinctual or affective force which, strictly speaking, cannot be signified, but remains latent in the phonic invocation or the inscribing gesture . . . [it is] as if . . . this affect did not break through the threshold of signification, and could not find any sign to designate it. . . . Poetic language," she concludes, "has always shared analogous traits."[15]

In the subversion and transformation of the Logos which she envisions, Kristeva does not distinguish the female impulse (*le féminin*) from other polymorphous manifestations of negativity and dissidence. In this respect, she differs notably from Luce Irigaray or Hélène Cixous, whose primary concern is the inscription of the female in language and thought. And yet Cixous herself believes that there are texts marked by *féminité* or femaleness[16] written by men—Jean Genêt, for instance—and thus, that the sex of the author must not be confused with her/his sexuality.[17] Nevertheless, a number of recent texts by French women attest to a prevailing desire to articulate a female language; among them are Irigaray's *Le Langage des démons* (1973) and *Ce Sexe qui n'en est pas un* (1977), Claudine Herrmann's *Les Voleuses de langue* (1976), Annie Leclerc's *Parole de femme* (1974), and Marguerite Duras and Xavière Gauthier's *Les Parleuses* (1974). The content and form of *Les Parleuses*, for example, suggest a concerted effort "to speak the female" through the cracks in the syntax, semantics, and logic of male language. The text consists of five taped conversations between the two women, which have not been edited or, as Gauthier states, "polished and policed . . . to give them a rectitude of thought in compliance with Cartesian logic." That act of censure would have muted "what can be heard in numerous silences, what can be read in what has not been said, what is hatched involuntarily and is enunciated in grammatical mistakes, errors of style, awkwardnesses of expression." Such an enterprise is faithful to the spirit of Duras's body of work, which "allows the cracks, the absences, the blank spaces to inscribe their unconscious effects in the life and acts of her characters." In broader terms, Duras and Gauthier maintain that the subversive function of the female is to reveal the blank in the symbolic chain, to expose its hole: "If full and well-placed words have always been utilised, aligned and accumulated by men," says Gauthier, "it is not impossible that the female might resemble wild, scrawny grass . . . which manages to grow in the chinks of old stones and—why not—finally loosens cement slabs, however heavy they may be, with the power of what has been contained for a long time."[18]

In far more violent images, Hélène Cixous has repeatedly underscored the revolutionary power of *l'écriture féminine*. Whereas speech (*parole*), like our own existence, is inevitably caught up in the dominant system of discourse, writing (*écriture*) "is precisely the very possibility of change, the space that can serve as a springboard for subversive thought, the precursory movement of a transformation of social and cultural structures."[19] Woman must thus write herself: it is the essential act by which she can mark "her shattering entry into history which has always been based on her suppression. To write and thus to forge for herself the antilogos weapon. To become at will the taker and initiator, for her own right, in every symbolic system, in every political process."[20] For Cixous, *écrire* is synonymous with *voler*, "to rob" and "to fly," to reappropriate and to soar. In particular, writing represents the most forceful weapon for reappropriating the female body, which man has confiscated as his property: "It will give her back her goods, her pleasures, her organs, her immense bodily territories which have been kept under seal."[21] Like Madeleine Gagnon, who affirms the need to examine "my body in writing," as she entitles her essay in the collective volume, *La Venue à l'écriture* (1977),[22] Cixous emphasizes the impact of articulating the forbidden aspects of female sexuality: "Let her speak of her sexual pleasure [*sa jouissance*], and God knows that she has enough to say, in such a way that she manages to unblock both female and male sexuality, and to 'dephallocentrize' the body, deliver man from his phallus."[23]

The determined effort to speak female sexuality pervades Cixous's most recent works—*La* (1976), *Angst* (1977), *Le Nom d'Oedipe: Chant du corps interdit* (1978), *Préparatifs de noces au delà de l'abîme* (1978)—and Irigaray's *Ce Sexe qui n'en est pas un* (1977). Using Lewis Carroll's Alice as the symbol of woman's exploration of a new land, the wonderland, Irigaray's text casts a looking glass at prevailing conceptions that presume to define and confine female nature, and emerges slowly, hesitatingly, into the domain of women's speech, free of the fear of not speaking "properly," free of existing, guilt-producing taboos. The closing section, *Quand nos lèvres se parlent*, plays upon the double meaning of *lèvres*—lips and labia— to deny the separation, the dichotomy between self and other. Irigaray explores and expresses love for her own multi-faceted body and the body of another woman:

> Between my/your lips several songs, several ways of saying echo
> each other. Without one ever being separable from the other.
> You/I: they always make several at the same time. How, in fact,
> could one dominate the other? impose its voice, its tone, its
> meaning? They cannot be distinguished. Which does not mean
> that they are blurred. Don't you grasp it at all? No more than
> they grasp you.[24]

Rejecting the notion of knowledge as mastery and the phallic principle of sameness, of identity, Irigaray describes woman's body and being as a rich, unbounded flow:

> You move. You never stay still. You never stay. You never are.
> How shall I say you? Always other. How shall I speak you?
> Staying in flux, without ever coagulating. Solidifying. How can I
> make that current pass into words? Multiple. Without causes,
> meanings, simple qualities. And yet not decomposable. . . .
> These streams without one-way, clearly defined waters. These
> rivers without permanent banks. This body without fixed bor-
> ders. This mobility without end.[25]

According to Irigaray, Cixous, and Kristeva, the articulation of woman's difference must include the domain of the unconscious if we hope to revolutionize the dominant discourse to its very core. For the culture's ideology, observes Cixous, is based on the repression of the unconscious, especially the female unconscious.[26] She maintains, however, that her notion of the female unconscious as the locus where the repressed survives bears little resemblance to the canonical (Freudian) formulation: "When it speaks to you . . . it tells you the old stories which you have always heard, since it has been constituted by the repressed of the culture. But that [level of the unconscious] is always reshaped by the forceful return of a libido, which is not so easily controlled, and by the singular, by the noncultural, by a language which is savage and which can certainly be heard."[27] This unspoken unconscious, free of cultural constraints, must inform the genuinely political, female text. Since such a text has not as yet been written and cannot be predefined, Cixous looks to its future beginning(s) and its volcanic effects: "Let the priests tremble, we're going to show them our sexts!"[28]

For Cixous and many of her contemporaries, the act of speaking and, even more, of writing as a female represents a fundamental birth drive which will destroy the old order of death, not merely its material, economic, social, and political manifestations, but the generative system, which determines the production of meaning. From this perspective, some French women regard the pragmatic empiricism of American feminist criticism as fundamentally doomed. They claim that our critical enterprise aims for equality within the Logos, for an equal share of existing symbolic systems, and thus that it essentially reconfirms the dominant phallogo-centric order. In one of the first attempts to confront this contradiction, the troubling dis-connection between the French and the American theory and practice of feminist criticism, Cixous asked, in her preface to the translation of Phyllis Chesler's *Women and Madness*, whether American women would ever locate repression in the realm of speech acts and in the essence of binary thinking that underlies the very discourse promoting women's liberation.[29] In so doing, Cixous brought into sharp focus the problem explored by Shoshona Felman in the "Textual Politics" issue of *Diacritics* (1975), as she outlined the differences between Chesler's empiricist preoccupation with a clinical history of the institutionalized female on the one hand, and, on the other, Irigaray's investigation of the logic of female repression in *Speculum de l'autre femme*.[30] Although neither critic had concrete proposals for repairing this dis-connection, Cixous urged both French and American women to valorize the female's difference, her otherness as the repressed, the missing signification, in order to undermine the traditional logocentric oppositions between masculine and feminine, intelligence and sensuality, reason and poetry.[31]

Now how have we, American feminist critics, perceived and responded to the theory and practice of *écriture féminine*? Have we made any efforts to mediate between, much less to repair, the Franco-American dis-connection? From all appearances, we have largely ignored this *écriture*; in fact, we are far more ignorant about its presuppositions and its goals than our French counterparts are about American feminist critical praxis. Admittedly, this ignorance may derive from our collective inability to read French with the kind of proficiency that *écriture féminine* requires. And the existing translations are, of course, few and far between: Kristeva's *On Chinese Women*; a couple of articles by or interviews with Cixous and Kristeva in *Substance*, *Diacritics*, or *Signs*—these are, at present, all the available texts in America.[32] Yet the efforts of American feminist specialists in French to introduce the concepts of *écriture féminine* to other Women's Studies scholars, or to apply them to their textual analyses, have also met with indifference, and even with suspicion and hostility.[33]

Such attitudes point up two failings in American feminist criticism. The first is that we have not achieved the inter- or transdisciplinary perspectives which we continue to proclaim essential to Women's Studies. Second, the automatic suspicion of *écriture féminine* suggests that the openness we claim for feminist criticism, in contrast to other modes of analysis, is being undermined by sectarianism and orthodoxy, by what Cheri Register has advocated as *prescriptive criticism*.[34] Every precaution must be taken to guard against the "erection" of a feminist critical imperialism that mouths dogma and prescribes *the* right way to package a feminist product. If we do not preserve openness and diversity through continued, dynamic debate of our differences, if we cease to be receptive to new tools and concepts which may illuminate aspects of female oppression or repression, then American feminist scholarship will fall prey to the sameness and repetition we condemn in masculinist critics, and it will lose its revolutionary impulse.

No less disturbing is the facile rejection of *écriture féminine* as too intellectual and elitist to be feminist. Admittedly, our understanding of Cixous, Kristeva, Irigaray, and others requires knowledge of philosophy, linguistics, and psychoanalytic theory. Even more, one must be willing to decipher dense texts replete with plays on words and devoid of normal syntactical constructions. Through their very mode of writing, however, these texts are striving to practice what they preach by subverting the syntax, the semantics, and even the Cartesian logic of the Logos. As Kristeva has written, ". . . playful language ergo disrupted law, violated, pluralized, maintained solely to allow a poly-valent, poly-logic game which leads to a conflagration of the essence of the Law. . . ."[35] We American feminists tend to consider such wordplay virtuosic and exhibitionistic. We ignore the paradoxical disjunction between *what* we say and *how* we say it, and thus we continue to speak *about* subverting the patriarchal order in pellucid rationalistic discourse. Indeed, the charge of intellectualism and elitism directed at *écriture féminine* is connected to a serious lack of awareness about the nature of our own critical practice that verges on bad faith. Viewed within their specific contexts, Anglo-American feminist empiricism is certainly not any less intellectual than *écriture féminine*. The opposite could in fact be argued: for *écriture féminine* not only combines theory with a subjectivism that confounds the protocols of scholarly discourse, it also strives to break the phallologic boundaries between critical analysis, essay, fiction, and poetry. Moreover, those who maintain that *écriture féminine* is not feminist because it appropriates concepts from such "seminal" thinkers as Saussure, Freud, Lacan, and Derrida choose to forget that it was not feminists but Anglo-American patriarchs who founded, and trained us in, the biographical, thematic, stylistic, sociohistorical, or Marxist literary criticism that we unquestioningly practice. Instead of blinding ourselves to the academic origins and present boundaries of our critical discourse, we should acknowledge that, when compared to the work of other women in our society, feminist scholarship is fundamentally both intellectual and privileged. That admission, however, should not be cause for futile self-flagellation. Nor should it compound the existing, nefarious tendency to assign intellectuality, the capacity for abstraction and speculation, and the use of rigorous modes of analysis to the male, and intuitiveness, sensibility, and emotionality to the female—a type of thinking which validates traditional stereotypes, reinforces the tyranny of the binary, and thus strengthens the phallogocentric order. Rather, we should celebrate our own and all women's heterogeneous contributions to the demolition of the old and the building of a new order of thought and being.

This is not to suggest, however, that the presuppositions and goals of *écriture féminine* should be espoused without serious examination. American and French women should interrogate the premise that the global subversion of the Logos can be achieved through language, and we should question the proposition that there *can* exist a locus outside of the symbolic order from which woman might speak her difference. In *Les Guérillères* (1969), for example, Monique Wittig endorsed the notion that there is no reality outside the symbolic.[36] But whereas in that epic work she argued "that in the first place the vocabulary of every language is to be examined, modified, turned upside down, that every word must be screened,"[37] in her recent paper "The Straight Mind," Wittig insists that emphasis on language has made French women writers lose sight of material reality[38]—a view which many American feminists might echo. We should also point out that French theorizing on the subversion of the Logos has tended to replace, and not merely to supplement, the kind of political activism which Americans consider crucial to their self-definition as feminists. Last, and as some recent French texts seem to confirm, a dis-connection with the *real* can lead to a regressive mystification of the "feminine" and may yield nothing more than a new "lingo," a code doomed to repetition and extinction.[39]

Clearly, then, American feminists can and should alert our French counterparts to the traps and binds into which they may be writing themselves, just as with their help we can comprehend, and hopefully transcend, the limitations of our own feminist critical enterprise. The process and the products of American feminist methodologies will be markedly enriched if we tap the potential of two areas which are central to *écriture féminine*. The first is the considerable work of feminist linguists, which has not received the attention it deserves in American Women's Studies.[40] Feminist linguists can make more meaningful contributions to our future praxis, however, if they systematically question the prevalent empiricist presupposition that linguistic change follows social change rather than determines it,[41] and if they combine pragmatic work in sociolinguistics with more theoretical speculations pertinent to the peculiarities of Anglo-American logocentrism. No less important, American feminist critics, looking to the work of French women, might come to terms with the female unconscious, a problematic which we have ignored or denied because of its predominantly Freudian, phallocratic conception. Going beyond the articulation of feminist protest against the canonical psychoanalytic text, which we found in de Beauvoir, Friedan, Millett, Greer, and Firestone, we can call upon Cixous, Irigaray, and Kristeva to help us investigate and delineate the no-man's-land of a female unconscious.[42] Through these and other interdisciplinary and intercultural exchanges, we may ultimately forge a vital feminist critical power that subverts cultural boundaries and the Logos which promotes dis-connections among women. Transcending our undeniable and important differences, our desire to give voice to woman binds us together in one radical and global project.

In the closing pages of *La Jeune née*, the Marxist-feminist writer Catherine Clément engages in a dialogue with Hélène Cixous in which she voices what might well be Americanist objections to the French connection between language and revolution:

> Clément: Language only replaces one compartment for another, that's all. A true redistribution of elements, a true change cannot take place there, at that level.

> Cixous: Nor do I believe that the revolution is going to be made by language. But there is no revolution without a coming into awareness, without there being people who get up and begin to shout. . . . We can move nothing when we cease to communicate.

> Clément: Unless I interpret what you say in a poetic way, I must

tell you that these phrases have no reality for me. . . . It is a level
of description where I cannot recognize anything that I believe in
political terms. Not that it is "false" of course. But it is described
in terms which seem to me to partake of myth, of poetry.[43]

In trying to articulate her objections, Clément makes the insightful
suggestion that the essential significance of *écriture féminine* may be *poetic*
in the particular and universal sense in which both Kristeva and Cixous
use the term. "Poetry," writes Cixous, "involves gaining strength through
the unconscious . . . , that . . . limitless country . . . where the repressed
manages to survive."[44] It is surely no mere coincidence, then, that two of
our most important feminist poets ascribe to the poetic the same radical
power. "I still believe that the energy of poetry comes from the unconscious and always will," Adrienne Rich has said;[45] in her most recent
work, *On Lies, Secrets and Silences* (1979), she speaks of the crucial,
transformative powers of this energy:

> . . . As long as our language is inadequate, our vision remains
> formless, our thinking and feeling are still running in old cycles,
> our process may be "revolutionary" but not transformative. . . .
> When we speak of *transformation* [instead of revolution] we
> speak more accurately out of the vision of a process which will
> leave neither surfaces nor depths unchanged, which enters soci-
> ety at the most essential level of the subjugation of women and
> nature by men. We begin to conceive a planet on which both
> women and nature might coexist as the She Who we encounter in
> Judy Grahn's poems. Poetry is, among other things, a criticism
> of language. . . . Poetry is above all a concentration of the *power*
> of language, which is the power of our ultimate relationship to
> everything in the universe. It is as if forces we can lay claim to in
> no other way, become present to us in sensuous form.[46]

Audre Lorde's "Poetry Is Not a Luxury" is informed by the very same
vision: "Poetry is the way we help give name to the nameless so it can be
thought. . . . Poetry coins the language to express and charter this revolutionary awareness and demand. . . . In the forefront of our move toward
change, there is only our poetry to hint at possibility made real."[47] In their
own eloquent, forceful voices, Lorde and Rich, Cixous and Kristeva come
together to reinforce the connection between language and revolution (or
transformation), and to proclaim its essential value for the future of
women. If we accept the connection, then these Franco-American expo-
nents of the poetic can surely guide us through the labyrinths of the Logos
to an-other word, and perhaps, an-other world.

Notes

1. Hélène Cixous, "Le Sexe ou la tête?" *Les Cahiers du GRIF* 13 (October 1976), issue entitled, *Elles con-sonnent. Femmes et langages II*, p. 7. ". . . tout est mot, tout n'est que mot. . . . il faut prendre la culture au mot, comme elle nous prend dans son mot, dans sa langue. . . . En fait, dès qu'on est, on naît dans la langue et la langue nous parle, la langue nous dicte sa loi qui est une loi de mort. . . . Vous comprendrez pourquoi je pense qu'une réflexion politique ne peut pas se dispenser d'une réflexion sur le langage, d'un travail sur la langue." The translations in this study are mine, unless otherwise indicated.

2. Ibid. ". . . Tout l'ensemble des systèmes symboliques—c'est-à-dire tout ce qui se dit, tout ce qui s'organise en tant que discours, l'art, la religion, la famille, le langage, tout ce qui nous prend, tout ce qui nous fait—tout est organisé à partir d'oppositions hiérarchiques qui renvoient à l'opposition homme/femme. . . ."

3. Catherine Clément, Hélène Cixous, *La Jeune née* (Paris: Union Générale Editions, 10–18, 1975).

4. Quoted in Elaine Marks, "Women and Literature in France," *Signs: Journal of Women in Culture and Society* 3: 4 (Summer 1978): 841, trans. Anne Liddle.

5. Luce Irigaray, *Speculum de l'autre femme* (Paris: Les Editions de Minuit, 1974). "La tâche aveugle d'un vieux rêve de symmétrie" is the title of the first part of this work.

6. Ibid., p. 176.

7. Julia Kristeva, *Polylogue* (Paris: Editions du Seuil, 1977), p. 523. ". . . Il n'y a pas de transformation socio-politique possible si elle n'est pas une transformation des sujets. . . ."

8. Kristeva, *La Révolution du langage poétique* (Paris: Editions du Seuil, 1974), p. 160. ". . . non plus simplement expliquant, cogitant et sachant, mais un sujet insaisissable parce que *transformant* le réel."

9. Kristeva, "The Subject in Signifying Practice," *Semiotexte* 1:3 (1975): 19–26, followed by a discussion on pp. 27–32.

10. Kristeva's presentation of her theory of the semiotic may be found in *La Révolution du langage poétique* and in *Polylogue*.

11. Kristeva, "Poésie et négativité," *Semiotiké: Recherches pour une sémanalyse* (Paris: Editions du Sueil, 1969), pp. 246–77.

12. Josette Féral, "China, Women and the Symbolic: Interview with Julia Kristeva," *Sub-Stance* 13 (1976): 9–18, trans. Janie Kritzman.

13. Kristeva, "Un Nouveau type d'intellectuel," *Tel Quel* 74 (Winter 1977): 5–6.

14. Kristeva, *Polylogue*, p. 519. "Une pratique de femme ne peut être que négative, à l'encontre de ce qui existe, pour dire que 'ce n'est pas ça' et que 'ce n'est pas encore ça.' J'entends donc par 'femme' ce qui ne se représente pas, ce qui ne se dit pas, ce qui reste en dehors des nominations et des idéologies."

15. Kristeva, "Féminité et écriture. En réponse à deux questions sur *Polylogue*,"

Revue des sciences humaines 168 (177–4), issue entitled, "Ecriture feminité féminisme," p. 497. ". . . La notion de signifiant en tant que réseau de marques distinctives est insuffisante. Parce que chacune de ces marques est chargée, outre sa valeur discriminatoire porteuse de signification, d'une force pulsionnelle ou affective qui ne se signifie pas à proprement parler, mais reste latente dans l'invocation phonique ou dans le geste inscrivant . . . comme si . . . cet affect ne franchissait pas le seuil de la signification et ne trouvait pas de signe pour se désigner. . . . Le langage poétique a, de tout temps, partagé des traits analogues. . . ."

16. Throughout this study I translate *feminité* as "femaleness" and *féminin* as "female" to avoid the pejorative connotations of "femininity" and "feminine" which do not exist in the French terms. I will use the term *écriture féminine* as a generic concept.

17. Cixous, "The Laugh of the Medusa," *Signs* 1:4 (Summer 1976): 885, trans. Keith Cohen and Paula Cohen.

18. Marguerite Duras, Xavière Gauthier, *Les Parleuses* (Paris: Editions de Minuit, 1974), pp. 7–8. ". . . De polir et de policer ces entretiens pour leur donner . . . cette rectitude de pensée qui se plie à la logique cartésienne." ". . . Ce qui s'entend dans les nombreux silences, ce qui se lit dans ce qui n'a pas été dit, ce qui s'est tramé involontairement et qui s'énonce dans les fautes de français, les erreurs de styles, les maladresses d'expression." ". . . Laisse . . . les failles, les manques, les blancs inscrire leurs effets inconscients dans la vie et les actes des 'personnages.'" ". . . Si les mots pleins et bien assis ont de tout temps été utilisés, alignés, entassés par les hommes, le féminin pourrait apparaître comme cette herbe un peu folle, un peu maigrichonne . . . qui parvient à pousser entre les interstices des vieilles pierres et—pourquoi pas?—finit par desceller les plaques de ciment, si lourdes soit-elles, avec la force de ce qui a été longuement contenu."

19. Cixous, "The Laugh of the Medusa," p. 879.

20. Ibid., p. 880.

21. Ibid.

22. Madeleine Gagnon, "Mon Corps dans l'écriture," in Cixous, Gagnon, and Leclerc, *La Venue à l'écriture* (Paris: Union Générale d'Editions, 10/18, 1979), pp. 63–116.

23. Françoise Colin, "Quelques questions posées à Hélène Cixous," *Les Cahiers du GRIF* 13 (October 1976): 12. "Qu'elle dise sur sa jouissance, et Dieu sait qu'elle en a à dire, de telle manière qu'elle arrive à débloquer la sexualité aussi bien féminine que masculine et à 'dé-phallocentraliser' le corps, à délivrer l'homme de son phallus."

24. Irigaray, *Ce Sexe qui n'en est pas un* (Paris: Editions de Minuit, 1977), pp. 208–209. "Entre mes/tes lèvres plusieurs chants, plusieurs dires, toujours se répondent. Sans que l'un, l'une soit jamais séparable de l'autre. Tu/je: font toujours plusieurs à la fois. Et comment l'un, l'une, dominerait-il l'autre? Imposant sa voix, son sens? Elles ne se distinguent pas. Ce qui ne signifie pas qu'elles se confondent. Vous n'y comprenez rien? Pas plus qu'elles ne vous comprennent."

25. Ibid., p. 214. "Tu bouges. Tu ne restes jamais tranquille. Tu ne restes jamais. Tu n'es jamais. Comment te dire? Toujours autre. Comment te parler? Demeurant dans le flux, sans jamais le figer. Le glacer. Comment faire passer dans les mots ce courant? Multiple. Sans causes, sens, qualités simples. Et cependant indécomposable. . . . Ces fleuves, sans mer unique et définitive. Ces rivières, sans rives persistantes. Ce corps sans bords arrêtés. Cette mobilité sans cesse."
26. Cixous, "Entretien avec Françoise van Rossum-Guyon," *Revue des sciences humaines*, p. 490.
27. Cixous, "Le Sexe ou la tête," p. 13. ". . . Quand il vous parle . . . il vous raconte les vieilles histoires que vous avez toujours entendues puisqu'il est constitué par les refoulés de la culture. Mais il est aussi toujours remanié par le retour en force d'une libido qui ne se laisse pas faire si facilement que ça, et par du singulier, par du nonculturel, par une langue qui est une langue sauvage et qui peut très bien se faire entendre."
28. Cixous, "The Laugh of the Medusa," p. 885.
29. Phyllis Chesler, *Women and Madness* (Paris: Payot, "Collection Traces," 1975).
30. Shoshona Felman, "Women and Madness: The Critical Fallacy," *Diacritics*, Winter 1975, pp. 2–10.
31. See Verena Conley's discussion of this problematic in "Missexual Misstery," *Diacritics*, Summer 1977, pp. 70–82.
32. Kristeva, *About Chinese Women* (London: Boyars, 1977), trans. Anita Barros. A chapter from *Des chinoises* was published in *Signs* 1:1 (Fall 1975): 57–82, trans. Ellen Conroy Kennedy. Articles by Cixous have appeared in *Diacritics*, Summer 1977, pp. 64–69, trans. Meg Bortin, and in *Signs* (see above, note 17). Christiane Makward's interview with Cixous and Josette Féral's interview with Kristeva were published in *Sub-Stance* 13 (1976): 9–18, 19–37. The recently published *New French Feminisms*, an anthology edited by Elaine Marks and Isabelle de Courtivran (Amherst: Univ. of Massachusetts Press, 1979), should provide American feminists with a wide sampling of French texts. In addition, a selection from Kristeva's writing is now available in English; see Julia Kristeva, *Desire in Language: A Semiotic Approach to Literature and Art*, ed. Leon Roudiez, tr. Tom Gora, Alice Jardine and Leon Roudiez (New York: Columbia Univ. Press, 1980).
33. Elaine Marks noted this problem in her review essay, "Women and Literature in France," pp. 832–33. Marks's article, along with Carolyn Greenstein Burke's "Report from Paris: Women's Writing and the Women's Movement," which appeared in the same issue of *Signs*, are valuable overviews of the current status of *écriture féminine* and feminist scholarship in France.
34. Cheri Register, "American Feminist Literary Criticism: A Bibliographical Introduction," *Feminist Literary Criticism: Explorations in Theory*, ed. Josephine Donavan (Kentucky: Univ. of Kentucky Press, 1975), pp. 18–24.

35. Kristeva, "Un Nouveau type d'intellectuel: Le Dissident," *Tel Quel* 74 ["Re-cherches féminines"] (Winter 1977): 5. ". . . Langue enjouée donc loi bouleversée, violée, pluralisée, maintenue uniquement pour permettre un jeu polyvalent, polylogique, qui conduit à l'embrasement de l'être de la loi. . . ."

36. Monique Wittig, *Les Guérillères* (New York: Avon Books, 1973), trans. David Le Vay, p. 134.

37. Ibid.

38. See "The Straight Mind," *Questions féministes* 7 (December 1979); and *Feminist Issues* 1, 1 (Summer 1980).

39. In my view, this danger is immanent in the recurring identification of the female in *écriture féminine* with madness, antireason, primitive darkness, mystery, self-diffusion, and self-irridiation, traits which represent a revalorization of traditional "feminine" stereotypes. I discuss this problem briefly in "Parole et écriture: Women's Studies, USA," *Tel Quel* 71–73 (Autumn 1977): 126. Françoise Colin, an editor of *Les Cahiers du GRIF*, has noted the danger signals of a new female "lingo" and stressed the need for multiplicity and heterogeneity in "polyglo(u)ssons," *Les Cahiers du GRIF* 12 ["Parlez-vous française?: femmes et langages I"] (June 1976): 3–9.

40. See, e.g., Mary Ritchie Key, *Male-Female Language* (Metuchen, N.J.: Scarecrow Press, 1975); Casey Miller and Kate Swift, *Words and Women* (Garden City, New York: Anchor Press/Doubleday, 1976); Barrie Thorne and Nancy Henley, eds., *Language and Sex: Difference and Dominance* (Rowley, Mass.: Newbury House, 1975); Alleen Pace Nilsen, Haig Bosmajian, H. Lee Gershuny, and Julia P. Stanley, *Sexism and Language* (Urbana, Ill.: National Council of Teachers of English, 1977); Douglas Butturff and Edmund L. Epstein, eds., *Women's Language and Style* (Akron: Univ. of Akron Press, 1978). See also the various articles written by feminist linguists in *Signs* 3:3 (Spring 1978) and *Women and Language in Literature and Society*, ed. Sally McConnell-Ginet, Nelly Furman, and Ruth Borker (New York: Praeger, 1980).

41. This widespread view is especially notable in Robin Lakoff's *Language and Women's Place* (New York: Harper and Row, 1975).

42. In *Psychoanalysis and Feminism* (New York: Pantheon Books, 1974), Juliet Mitchell tried to counter the prevailing feminist opposition to psychoanalytic categories, but she ignored the crucial issue of language, which informs all contemporary French psychoanalytic thought, and gave an inaccurate and insufficiently critical account of the theories of Jacques Lacan, the current Freudian patriarch.

43. *La Jeune née*, pp. 290–93.

Clément: Le langage ne fait bouger qu'une case à la place d'une autre, c'est tout; la véritable répartition des éléments, le véritable changement ne peut pas se faire là, à ce niveau-là.

Cixous: Je ne pense pas non plus que la révolution va se faire par le langage. Mais il n'y a pas de révolution sans prise de conscience, sans

qu'il y ait des gens qui commencent à se lever et à se mettre à hurler. . . .
On ne bouge plus à partir du moment où on ne communique plus.

Clément: Sauf à entendre ce que tu dis de façon poétique, je t'avoue que
ces phrases sont pour moi dépourvues de réalité. . . . C'est un niveau de
description où je ne reconnais rien de ce que je pense en termes poli-
tiques. Non que ce soit 'faux,' bien sûr. Mais c'est décrit en termes qui
me paraissent de l'ordre du mythe, de la poésie.

44. Cixous, "The Laugh of the Medusa," pp. 879–90.
45. *Adrienne Rich's Poetry*, ed. by Barbara Charlesworth Gelpi and Albert Gelpi
     (New York: W. W. Norton & Co., 1975), p. 113.
46. Rich, *On Lies, Secrets and Silences* (New York: W. W. Norton & Co., 1979),
     p. 248.
47. Audre Lorde, "Poetry Is Not a Luxury," in this volume.

Josette Féral

The Powers of Difference[1]

In a recent discussion of the relationship between history and psychoanalysis, the French historian Michel de Certeau asserted that "theorizing always needs a Savage." The Savage in the West has always been the Woman: simultaneously present and absent, present when absent, and all the more absent when she is there. She is needed so that her difference can act as a confirmation of man's "natural superiority" and of his "birthright" to be the best. Why should he cross the seas in order to find proof of the reality of his strength and violence? His Savage, the Woman, is here, very close, present, and speechless, to take upon herself the full weight of the violence that inhabits such structures as can only exist through her repression. She is a Savage whose existence is denied in its authenticity, in its originality, insofar as it does not support her conquerer's claim. She *is*, but at the same time, she *is not*. She *is* because she *is not*, her only space being the narrow fringe linking her to her oppressor. Only that link makes her live, makes her exist for the other, acknowledges her difference. But this is an illusory recognition, since it depends on a primary, original oppression which recognizes in her difference only that which sets her apart from her oppressor, that which sets as a standard, as a norm—that is, as *value*—the very being of her conqueror. He is the strongest, which means that he holds every right, including that of telling her about herself, that of telling her who *she* is and what *she* wants. This is the right of a usurper, who claims all knowledge for himself and proceeds to set limits for her, to interpret for her her own body and sexuality. Thanks to that vicarious knowledge, his own assertions will become hers. His silences will become hers as well, thus silencing a part of herself for which there is no place in his economy. This is indeed what produces a type of political economy which spares itself the burden of taking difference into consideration. This is a politics of repression, whose scope women have only begun to understand.

What is difference, then, from this perspective, if not a radical disregard of the Other? The Other is One, while I am nothing. In this perspective, difference takes on the status of a necessity, as evidenced in the functioning of capitalist societies, which need their marginals—blacks, Arabs, Jews, hippies, punks—as antidotes, as a reassurance of their own survival. "The *body* of strangeness must not disappear," Hélène Cixous wrote in *La Jeune Neé*, "but its strength must be tamed, it must be returned to the master."[2] Master and slave, conqueror and savage, such are the reductive dichotomies through which the relationships of difference have always been perceived in our Aristotelian West. The Oneness of the master confronts the slave's duplicity, fullness confronts the void, and presence confronts absence. Thus difference has always been construed and perceived through a set of binary oppositions that leaves no room for an authentic difference set outside of the established system. As applied to woman, this means simply that man has cast onto woman, and upon what he calls "femininity,"

> the full weight of the difference of the sexes, the full weight of lack, of death. Man makes her that double of himself which he knows he is, but refuses to acknowledge.[3]

Thus a woman does not become the Other but *his* Other, his Unconscious, his repressed, and she gets caught in the endless and enduring circle of *his* representation. Enmeshed in man's self-representation, woman exists only insofar as she endlessly reflects back to him the image of his manly reality. Inscribed in his identity, designated by a minus sign which emphasizes her deficient being— − phallus, − power, − unity—woman is reduced to being like the plane surface of a plane mirror (as opposed to the concave mirror referred to by Luce Irigaray in *Speculum de l'autre femme*[4]). She has become a mere reproduction, a mere reflection. She exists as a function of what she is not, receiving upon her denied body the etched-out stamp of the Other, as a signature of her void and a mark of his identity. The male Ego cannot dispense with such a reflection, since it receives its existence from it in part, if not in totality. Woman has thus been transformed into the other side of a mirror, present and absent, nowhere to be found but still here, skirting the grasp of the other as well as her own. Male discourse has preyed on this elusive reality for a long time. Man has managed to convert an accident of history into an essence, a fortuitous situation into a natural condition. Colonized and tricked, construed as a robot (as evidenced, for example, by the movie *The Stepford Wives*), woman has always been man's other side, his denied, abused, and hidden side. She has constantly been the embodiment of a nonculture, opposed to structures while remaining nonetheless essentially intent on their preservation.

Society itself is made possible by this repression of woman; it is founded upon the negation of her difference, upon her exclusion from knowledge and from herself. This, no doubt, constitutes an alienating *oppression*. But there exists simultaneously a much deeper and more devious *repression*,

all of which bears upon the female unconscious. For the woman's unconscious is "the noise" in the system, the defect. It is a surplus which
patriarchal society has always wanted to get rid of by denying it any
specificity, thus positing that same society's right to talk about it in terms
of identity with and resemblance to the male model. This unconscious had
to be tamed, silenced out of fear that, were it unexpectedly to return in the
midst of the existing order, it would bring the machine to a deadly halt.
"Does woman possess a soul?" Such was the question addressed by the
Council of Trent in 1545. Four centuries later the very same question is
being raised again, but fraught with four centuries of exploration by an
expanding knowledge. Rephrased, it becomes, "What the hell can we say
about the woman's unconscious?" However, this is an illusory question, a
trumped-up question, a pseudoproblem which is swiftly pushed aside
either by reducing it to already existing models or by translating it into
their mechanistic opposites. What is there to be said about the female
unconscious? Not much, if anything: "that the little girl is a little boy," or
"that the black continent that is woman remains unexplored if at all
explorable." And when it so happens that a woman ventures into this
area, it is with the arrogance of a master, sole possessor of the word, that
the psychoanalyst Jacques Lacan tells her to go back underground. "They
don't know what they are talking about," because they don't know who
they are.

To deny specificity to the female unconscious means nothing else than
to deny her any right to speak up. It means denying that she can hold her
own discourse. French feminists—among whom we can cite Hélène
Cixous, Luce Irigaray, Annie Leclerc,[5] Claudine Herrmann,[6] and the
group "Politics and Psychoanalysis"—have equated the recognition of
the specificity of the female unconscious with the free access to a specific
discourse in the feminine mode (au féminin) and have defined this as a
central focus of their struggle. This does not mean that defining such
discourse would be the *only* way to fight against the existing phallocentrism, but it is certainly one of the *most significant* modalities of the
struggle. This is probably where an American audience—less familiar with
Lacan's rendition of psychoanalysis and more reluctant to accept Freudian views—would be drawn to question their positions. It is probably also
at this point that the two approaches—American and French—exhibit the
most significant differences. This is because the French approach builds
on theoretical foundations of a primarily philosophical and linguistic
nature, whose more prominent initiators include Jacques Derrida, Gilles
Deleuze, and Félix Guattari.[7] This work implies a questioning of knowledge and of the "theo-logocentric" principles that underlie it. It also
demands that established structures founded on the principles of identity
and resemblance be shaken in the name of a revaluation of heterogeneity,

alterity, multiplicity, and difference. Difference, in this context, is not simply defined by reference to a norm—the masculine norm—whose negative side it would be while remaining inscribed within the realm of identity. Rather, difference is to be thought of as other, not bonded by any system or any structure. Difference becomes the negation of phallologo-centrism, but in the name of its own inner diversity.

This is why the established discourse is rejected as essentially male, since it bears the mark of a unifying dominant structure. This is also why the subject of representation is rejected, since it posits as its origin the very notion of resemblance. Therefore, French practice differs from American in that the subversion of the existing language, as it is now being carried out in France, does *not* have as its primary focus an assertion of the similarities between writing in the feminine mode and writing in the masculine mode, with the sole exceptions being themes which everybody acknowledges as different. I refer here, for example, to Mary Hiatt's book on feminine language in literature or that by Casey Miller and Kate Swift entitled *Words and Woman.*[8] It is not surprising that no concerted effort is being made in France to inscribe in language illusory traces whose function would be to designate the locus of woman, as, for example, with what has been achieved in the United States by the use of "Ms." or "Herstory." To do so would be, in effect, to play into the game of power by assuming once more that woman has no place, except in the lacunae of a discourse which allows some minor nibblings, as long as the implicit foundations of phallo-theo-logo-centrism are never questioned.

To put discourse into question is to reject the existing order. It is to renounce, in effect, the identity principle, the principles of unity and resemblance which allow for the constitution of phallocentric society. It means choosing marginality (with an emphasis on the *margins*) in order to designate one's difference, a difference no longer conceived of as an inverted image or as a double, but as alterity, multiplicity, heterogeneity. It means laying claim to an absolute difference, posited not within the norms but against and *outside* the norms. This explains why woman's quest cannot be satisfied by achieving mere socioeconomic equality. That victory implies an insufficient recognition of her specificity as woman and takes the form of momentary concessions, constantly under threat by a patriarchal society which grants them to her in order to control her better. This type of equality is, no doubt, a *necessary* precondition for a profound transformation of structures. But it is in no way *sufficient*, for it ignores in its very principle that this oppression is but one, and only one, of the possible forms of oppression of woman.

To that oppression should be added the more insidious and more destructive repression of her unconscious. In a conversation with Catherine Clément, Hélène Cixous says:

> It is possible to begin transforming a discourse only when the
> existence of the unconscious is taken into account. Where it is
> negated, where psychoanalysis does not exist, nothing changes
> and history goes on.

She also criticizes the present form of literary analyses undertaken by
women because they remain thematic:

> One will work on woman in such and such a period and in such
> and such a text, in exactly the same way as was done with blacks.
> This is a thematic analysis. What is more, it is a kind of work
> which refers us back to the *past*, which in almost all cases does
> not allow a work in the *present*.[9]

If it is true that all problems get into a tangle in the *past*, it is no less true
that they get unraveled in the *present*. This is why it is easy to reply to
those who believe in the primacy of class struggle over woman's struggle
that even in a society as deeply egalitarian as one might wish it to be,
feminine problems would still persist. What is at stake in the woman's
struggle is much more than simply finding a place within the existing
values or discourses. It is the problem of a whole society, questioning its
very foundations and its right to impose its truth as uniquely true. In so
doing, the problem raised by the women's movement is that of a subversion of the "subject" as an entity, as truth, as the subject of knowledge but
also the desiring subject, as a prisoner of micro and macro politics. "They
invented the whole of sexuality while silencing ours," says Annie Leclerc.
"If we invent ours, they will have to rethink their own."[10] We have to
invent or reinvent society, and thus create new values, new discourses, new
words, by refusing to allow woman to accede to the existing values, those
masculine values which have always evaded the problem of difference. We
must substitute for them our own ways of seeing, feeling, and thinking.
Those values should not, of course, become newly imposed norms, thereby
reinstituting an antisystem that would be just as repressive, even though in
reverse; they should not bring about a new dictatorship that does not
modify the deep structures. But they should help, rather, to open up the
system to the prospect of a plurality of possibilities whose recognition, up
to the present time, has been forbidden.

> A woman is a perpetual dissident as regards the social and
> political consensus; she is an exile from power and thus always
> singular, divided, devilish, a witch,

says Julia Kristeva.

> Woman is here to shake up, to disturb, to deflate masculine
> values, and not to espouse them. Her role is to maintain differ-

ences by pointing to them, by giving them life, by putting them
into play against one another[11]

so that the social system will not rigidify and so that the subject will not
die. This *prise de parole* (speaking up), which breaks down the ancient
networks, absolutely cannot find its place in the established discourse,
infused with masculine values. Woman can speak up while borrowing
forms and structures from the established discourse, but only in order to
disrupt them in her attempt to go beyond them toward a different horizon.

For it is true that woman is lost, to quote Julia Kristeva again, on the
narrow fringe that separates, in her words, the *pas encore* (not yet) from
the *pas cela* (not that). Woman's practice is negative with respect to the
dominant structures and this is an opening toward heterogeneity for the
subject. It so happens that woman is very close to such a heterogeneity,
thanks to her way of listening to her body. Hélène Cixous asserts that, "by
writing herself, woman will go back to that body of hers which up to now
has been more than confiscated."[12] And Annie Leclerc replies:

> There is such an overwhelming happiness in pregnancy, such an
> immense happiness in giving birth. I have to talk about it. Not
> about the *jouissance* of my sex, no, not about the *jouissance* of
> my soul, my virtue or my feminine sensitivity, but the *jouissance*
> of my woman's womb, of my woman's vagina, of my woman's
> senses. I have to talk about these, for it is from there only that
> new words will appear, which will belong to the woman and
> originate in her.[13]

New words springing from the very woman who refuses to appropriate
man's words and their implicit founding values, while she chooses to
reinvent her relationships with society. Woman will thus have the arduous
task of reevaluating everything with a fresh look—her own look—stripped
of envy and turned creative. She will attempt to rethink society and its
values, and will thus join forces with the subversive work already being
carried out in a number of avant-garde signifying practices—painting,
music, theater, and literature. The whole social body will thus be put into
question. Such practices take place in France as well as in the United
States, but it seems that France, under the influence of contemporary
philosophical and psychoanalytical trends, puts an excessive emphasis on
theorizing these privileged objects. Less intent on theorizing, American
artists and cultural activists have, however, achieved as much, if not more.

But is such a subversion really possible? It is, perhaps, a model to be
presented, but which may not be realized, for the subject runs the risk of
being lost in the process. The task of woman remains, however, to inscribe
in the social body not so much difference in itself as a multiplicity of

differences. And if it so happens that she has to struggle, to expose and cancel the many oppressions that bear on her—economic, political, and marital; if it so happens that she at times has to make use of masculine discourse to let herself be heard, such steps must be considered only as particular moments in a struggle beyond which a whole different set of possibilities of existence will open. I should add that not all French feminists share this point of view. Some, like Catherine Clément or Monique Wittig, believe that it might end up transforming women into helpless marginals. While working on *past* repressions, a woman should not forget about the present which nurtures her innermost divisions, for it is only in the present that a new politics can be brought about. To her only belongs the difficult task of creating the conditions whereby the future of difference will no longer mean a difference of futures.

Notes

1. In presenting this paper at the Barnard conference, I mentioned that I was not speaking as a representative of the French feminist movement—assuming one exists—and that I was not its official spokesperson, mainly because the French feminist movement and the theory underlying it are very complex. This paper is, instead, an attempt to walk the tightrope referred to by Alice Jardine in her prelude between the American and the French approaches to feminism.
2. Hélène Cixous and Catherine Clément, *La Jeune Née* (Paris: Union Générale d'Editions, 1975), p. 128.
3. Marcelle Marini, *Térritoires du féminin* (Paris: Editions de Minuit, 1977), p. 32.
4. Luce Irigaray, *Speculum de l'autre femme* (Paris: Editions de Minuit, 1974).
5. Annie Leclerc, *Parole de femme* (Paris: Grasset, 1974).
6. Claudine Hermann, *Les Voleuses de langue* (Paris: Editions des Femmes, 1976).
7. See, for example, Jacques Derrida, *Of Grammatology*, trans. Gayatri Chakravorty Spivak (Baltimore: Johns Hopkins Univ. Press, 1974); and Gilles Deleuze and Félix Guattari, *Anti-Oedipus*, trans. Robert Huxley, Mark Seem, and Helen R. Lane (New York: Viking Press, 1977).
8. Mary Hiatt, *The Way Women Write* (New York: Teachers College Press, 1977); Casey Miller and Kate Swift, *Words and Women* (Garden City, New York: Anchor Press/Doubleday, 1976).
9. Cixous, *La Jeune Née*, p. 481.
10. Leclerc, *Parole de femme*, p. 42.
11. Julia Kristeva, *Polylogues* (Paris: Editions du Seuil, 1977), p. 498.
12. Cixous, *La Jeune Née*, p. 179.
13. Leclerc, *Parole de femme*, p. 12.

Christiane Makward

To Be or Not to Be...
A Feminist Speaker

Translated by Marlène Barsoum,
Alice Jardine, and Hester Eisenstein

Introduction

For a feminist critic in contemporary French studies, the status of " *la différence*" is relatively easy to outline in the area concerning us—a different relation to language for women. It is easy to outline simply because French neofeminists have postulated it, at first in fiction works. In the well-known feminist utopia by Monique Wittig, *Les Guérillères*,[1] the women fantasize a language where vowel sounds would have a privileged role, approximating perhaps pure vocal flow. An inarticulated, archaic, intensely pleasurable form of "speech" is dreamed of. The voice as the primary body sound has been subsequently explored by the journal *Sorcières*, in particular. Wittig's book also casts doubt as to the future of the written word and on any and all books, including the "feminaries" which are the texts preserved by the women to help them know themselves and their heritage:

> They say it is possible that feminaries have fulfilled their office.
> . . . All one might do with them in order not to be encumbered
> with useless knowledge is to pile them up in open spaces and set
> fire to them . . . which could be the pretext for celebrations.[2]

In Wittig's footsteps, around 1975, two conceptions of women's relation to language emerged: women's speech (*parole de femmes*) and feminine writing (*écriture-au-féminin*). One can see in Wittig's parable of burning the feminaries a vision of the future of difference. A passionate vindication of difference and a fascinating effort to formulate this difference in theoretical terms undoubtedly constitute the French difference in today's feminist thought. The past ten years have seen the development of what amounts to a neofeminist philosophical movement and the explosion of feminine writing, that is a rapid blooming of first-rate literary works qualifying as "writing-in-the feminine" in that they attempt and succeed in creating new forms to signify or "inscribe" femininity. Such texts want to convey formally, and not just thematically, that they come from women in their positive quest and celebration of a feminine principle not to be defined. The vast majority of texts by women—in the past decade as well as the past eight centuries—do NOT reflect such a purpose, so that it seems appropriate to designate these remarkable recent works as constituting a "new feminine writing."

Some of these writers (Monique Wittig, Marguerite Duras, Chantal Chawaf, Hélène Cixous, Emma Santos, Nicole Brossard, Madeleine Gagnon, etc.) have tried to formulate fragmentary aesthetic principles on feminine writing. Some feminist critics (Luce Irigaray, Michèle Montrelay, Xavière Gauthier, etc.) have worked in the same direction, so that the view of female creativity that emerges can roughly be summarized by the following key words: open, nonlinear, unfinished, fluid, exploded, fragmented, polysemic, attempting to "speak the body," i.e., the unconscious, involving silence, incorporating the simultaneity of life as opposed to or clearly different from logical, nonambiguous, so-called "transparent" or functional language. Different also from preconceived, oriented, masterly constructs and didactic ("male") fiction. The term "fiction" itself is of course inadequate to refer to texts which are altogether nonrealistic and poetical but "bio-graphical," in the sense that they "write" the "body " primarily.

"Writing is to start," writes Chantal Chawaf, "it is always to push the beginning further back, because in language nothing of the body, nothing of the woman has, as yet, been integrated. . . . Everything starts from the body and from the living, from our senses, our desires, our imagination. . . ."[3]

The problem for us, as feminist scholars, is to relate the practice of feminine writing to the theory of femininity. They are in contradiction because, first, feminine writing at its best only differs from other modern poetic texts in the—considerably vast yet clearly distinguishable—area of subject matter, when the female experience and the female body are the very source of creation. And, second, the theory of femininity is dangerously close to repeating in "deconstructive" language the traditional assumptions on femininity and female creativity. This is because the vast majority of those critics and writers—female or male—who have attempted to rationalize their perception of the difference in the relation of women to language have done so on the basis of neo-Freudian postulates. For the main part, the "Symbolic" (the Law, Language, Social Order) is said to function NECESSARILY (or in "essence") on the basis of the repression of women's bodies. Language is said to function through male control of women's bodies at the cost of female silence and submission. The corollary of this conception of language is that the feminine is said to be by definition undefinable, unspeakable and silent, in that "when women think, they think like men" or that thought excludes femininity, or again, that the feminine is unthinkable.

This is roughly where neofeminist thought is currently (in-)stalled on the French scene. Fortunately, women continue to write and speak and agitate even though they cannot theoretically demonstrate that they remain "feminine" in the creative and expressive process.

"Feminist criticism": on the face of it, the two terms are compatible, and clear.[4] But they have developed in such a way that now the problematic of feminist criticism is not methodology, or survival, but its mode of insertion into discourse/discourses, into feminist—or feminine—undertakings (note the fluctuation between the two terms).

Today, the question about feminist criticism is not DOING it, but its very BEING. In literary criticism, we take texts literally: we "take people at their word." We elaborate one discourse upon another: as the scholars say, a "metalanguage." In the case of living writers, this is more of a gamble, in that the classic distinction between written and spoken disappears; *verba manent*, and even *scripta volent*, to evoke Hélène Cixous' fertile metaphor (in the texts of 1975–76).

To speak of feminist criticism is to point to a body of texts that elaborate on other texts . . . but only a partial reading: from the woman's perspective. That is, a reading which seeks out, either the representation of the feminine, or its repression, its mythification, or its modes of expression. It is, thus, not a formal structure, or a new and original methodology, but rather a supple and protean point of view. I would characterize it as an archaeology—criticism of the discourse on "woman" that has been constituted over the centuries, and the texts "she" has produced; or an "archetypology" (a better term might be "stereotypology")—an analysis of the variations on fundamental images or stereotypes of the two sexes; or a feminist stylistics: Suzanne Allen's admirable exploration of the words *outre/autre/utérus* (beyond/other/uterus) in the *Revue des Sciences Humaines*;[5] and Nancy Houston's verbal fireworks in *Les Cahiers du GRIF* (Group de Recherche et d'Information Féministe, Brussels) and in *Sorcières* (Paris).

These readings, or exegeses, or improvisations, as the case may be, have been accumulating for nearly a decade. However, the authors most brilliantly illuminated by the feminist spotlight have been nonmodern novelists and philosophers: Diderot and Voltaire, Sade, Fourier, Balzac, and Freud. Further, there is still a glaring imbalance between the attention given to women's texts, and that to "great writers." Except for George Sand, Colette, Marguerite Duras, and Simone de Beauvoir, few feminist readings of women's texts have reached print. In order to stimulate research in this direction, two publications have been started: the *Bulletin de Recherches et d'Etudes Féministes Francophones* (BREFF) at the University of Wisconsin, founded in May 1976; and *Ecrits de Femmes*,[6] a general reference book of women writers in French. Following the example of their pragmatic American sisters, women in French Studies working in the United States have been carrying on research in the encouraging atmosphere of American universities.

On the French and French-speaking side, the most notable and accessible studies have been a number of special issues in journals such as *Romantisme, Tel Quel, Les Temps Modernes, L'Arc, La Revue des Sciences Humaines, Alternatives, Obliques,* etc., often with major contributions from across the Atlantic. In addition, the feminist journals *Cahiers du GRIF* and *Sorcières* have done much to stimulate a new perspective on texts, language, and cultural discourse in general. And finally, feminist criticism has surfaced within the *Université* itself: in the fall of 1978, a master's thesis by Claire Boniface, "Women and Writing," was defended at *Paris III* (Sorbonne-Nouvelle), under the direction of Simone Fraisse. Recently, also, the first issue has appeared of the *Bulletin d'Information des Etudes Féminines*, a publication of some thirty pages, collaboratively produced by three university groups, PENELOPE (Paris), CLEF (Centre Lyonnais d'Etudes Féministes), and CEFUP (Centre d'Etudes Féminines de l'Université de Provence), on a formula similar to that of BREFF. It contains a great wealth of information, inaccessible up to now, on feminist research in France.

The entry of feminist criticism into the *Université*, the academy, is of crucial importance. This is the place par excellence where, along with the press and the publishing world, ideology is articulated, transformed, or perpetuated. It is where the future "masters" of language, culture, and their transmission are molded. And it is precisely in relation to being academics that feminist critics are encountering a malaise that is fairly specific to the French and francophone community.

Everyone knows that the French have a passion for theory. And in the last few years, the "masters of thought" have been quick to seize upon the "woman question." Jacques Lacan, Jacques Derrida, Jean-François Lyotard, and Vladimir Granoff (to whom we will return shortly) have all conducted seminars and master classes on this theme. In reaction to this discourse about themselves, women have had a variety of responses:

—Some (Julia Kristeva, Michèle Montrelay) have adopted a "politics of the *same*," assimilating, repeating, sometimes even taking the lead in the discussion.

—Some (Luce Irigaray, Hélène Cixous, and the group Politics and Psychoanalysis), by a "politics of the *other*," have denounced this discourse using its own terms, thus making "the other" into "the same" (I will elaborate on this point in greater detail shortly).

—And finally, some women have rejected the discourse, as that of the master, toward whom they are indifferent. This is a politics of the poet, which is no longer a politics of the other, but of the ostrich (*autre/ autruche*)!!

For seven years now, the radical women of the group Politics and Psychoanalysis have sustained a contradiction, barely touched on in their texts (in the dialogue Clément/Cixous, of *La Jeune Née*).[7] The contradiction consists of speaking, either anonymously or through intermediaries, in the language of the masters, petrifying like the gaze of Medusa, all the while using it to denounce, among other things, literature, the publishing business, and the university as "phallic" institutions. For about a year, the *Des femmes en mouvements* group has firmly repudiated the term "feminism," calling it one more "ism," that is, a reformist, opportunistic, capitalist ideology.

Like the *Cahiers du GRIF*, *Des femmes en mouvements* has just published its last issue (January 1979). *GRIF* elaborated at length on the essential reasons for their decision: the drain of energy, exhaustion, the need to go further, and the need to escape institutional routine. These same reasons were expressed by *Des femmes en mouvements* in a few words: "the mortal stability of repetition bores" them (*la stabilité mortelle de la répétition les ennuie*). One can hope (and they have indicated) that the group is looking for a new formula, something less stifling than forever vying with *F* magazine [comparable to our *Ms.* Magazine—Ed.]. On that same page of *au revoir*, the group once again condemns feminists of all persuasions, including academics. It is a critique without explanation—barely more than a declaration: presumably the wickedness of academic feminism is so obvious as to need no proof.

If this kind of radical medicine does not kill, it can cure: we can draw something useful from it, namely a warning. It is difficult to force an established administration, by definition hostile to subversive change, to welcome the very vital forces that threaten its foundations. Academic careers have their competitive and constrictive aspects. They are dehumanizing, from certain points of view, especially that of the body, and this has discouraged or wiped out some of our richest energies. If feminism at its best promotes the libidinal economy—the forces/value of life—AT THE EXPENSE of the political economy—the drive for power—it will have a hard time finding a place in an institution as rigidly structured as the university. Hence the radical critique of academic feminism, which holds that if you use language accessible to the "intellectual community," you cannot possibly speak as a woman (*parler-femme*).

According to this view, every woman who uses academic language, even "feminists," must first put on male garb (although it is amusing to note that academic robes are unisex!). But it would seem that if one has to choose between a feminist academic and an antifeminist academic or defeminized academic—someone not-assumed-in-the-feminine, to speak the language of *Des femmes en mouvements*—then it is best to choose the lesser of two evils, and the shorter expression! Thus, within the university, no woman-speech is possible, for women but only what is characterized, with disapproval, as "feminist discourse," i.e., a phallocratic sham. In this view, linear, directed, logical argument is intrinsically linked to the drive for power, and is not female. By means of an essentialist definition (whose distinguished, if concealed, ancestry we shall trace shortly), woman is incapable of speaking as a woman; therefore, the most female course of action is to observe an hour of silence, or (if you have dramatic talent) to imitate the scream of Artaud at the Théâtre du Vieux Colombier, by way of creating woman-speech. Obviously the problem is that by identifying discourse with power, and then rejecting both, women are resigning themselves to silence, and nonspeech. The speech of the other will then swallow them up, will speak *for* them, and *instead* of them. *Nothing will have taken place but a dis-placement of the feminine.*

Marguerite Duras—a fascinating, true poet, that is, a creatrix—fantasized a world in which men would learn female silence, a world between life and death, between silence and the cry preceding the germination of a genuinely new and unknown life. But she is a poet. Kristeva, on the contrary, thinks that the association of femaleness with silence, "on the fringes of communications decreed as phallic,"[8] is obscurantist and alienating. But two years before, she published an interview with *Les Cahiers du GRIF* in which she herself characterized the marginality of women in culture, what she called the "woman-effect," as essential and defining.[9] Hélène Cixous has also denounced silence, because "it is the traditional confinement, a trap where the future will be lost."[10]

The inscribing of pulsation, the body, the unconscious, the anti-Logos—these are not new; they have in fact constituted the mainstream of poetry for a century. But never before has this been claimed so insistently, so consciously, and never before by women. Rather, these were traditionally the qualities attributed to women as intrinsic defects of their nature, not as a conscious poetics and aesthetic. The "Sottisier," in *Ecrits de femmes*, is pretty amusing on this point.

Women who resist this (entirely theoretical) call to adopt silence as a mark of the feminine (we may recall Valéry's response to the question: why do you write? "Out of weakness!"[11]) begin to speak and write in the feminine (*au féminin*). And here we come to the split between the radicals, who speak, and the women writers, who believe in the work of writing, which inevitably then finds its way to the shelves of bookstores and libraries along with the rest of "literature." Antoinette Fouque, a central figure in the Politics and Psychoanalysis group, an analyst who exercises a strictly oral power, holds that writing is a demand for phallic power, and is thus in agreement with Valéry that it is a narcissistic "weakness." Hence, with a few exceptions, the nonliterary, political orientation of the publications by *Des femmes*. This corresponds to an existentialist concept of the written text.

Beyond either ephemeral political expression or silence, some other characterizations of feminine creativity have emerged: ideas about non-termination, open structures, nonlinearity, movement. Luce Irigaray describes "simultaneity" and "fluidity" as feminine (non-) forms. She writes, in *Ce Sexe qui n'en est pas un:*

> the style of woman rejects fetish-words, correct terms, well-constructed forms.[12]

If movement, plurality, "polylogic"—to paraphrase one of Kristeva's titles—are designed as feminine, it is in reference to a so-called "phallic" or monolithic principle of the ONE, whose nature it is to obscure differences and to bring them back to the same, by functioning with the familiar binary oppositions. Luce Irigaray even pushes the revaluation of difference to the point of finding in the female body both a plurality of differentiating organs and a quality of incompleteness.

Another potentially controversial position is the view that woman does not yet exist; she is not now, but will be born in the future, out of the woman of the past or the present. This is essentially assenting to the decree of Lacan: woman does not exist, because she does not speak herself (*elle ne se dit pas*). However, more down-to-earth voices answer this by saying that "to have an exploited existence, does not mean not to exist!"[13]

This, then, is the impasse: it is impossible to found in theory, to SAY, the feminine without reference to a mythological masculine (the mirror effect), OR without repeating masculine discourse on femininity (the echo effect). It is thus difficult, therefore, to define feminine creativity and writing without opposing them to "the Other," to describe them while dissociating them from the writer's sex. All of these difficulties are beginning to pall. The key words have lost their punch, they are used up, collapsing. We are emerging from a long period of intense ferment in feminist thinking, whose first stage in France was marked by an embracing of DIFFERENCE which unavoidably referred itself to the Other, and therefore to binary opposition. The dogmatism, intolerance of dissent, extreme expressions of uncertainty, even terrorism—all reveal an enormous uncertainty and lack of clarity. The "impasses" of neofeminist thought in France are fruitful, and should certainly not be seen as setbacks, but rather as the period of iconoclastic rejection in the wake of the power vacuum of 1968. Parallel to this, though, the right-wing reaction has been hard at work. Given that the woman's viewpoint has had a certain impact, it has often been exploited, swallowed up, or rendered harmless in women's magazines, the media, and the publishing world. Nevertheless, even in these reactions we can read a profound change.

If neofeminist thought in France seems to have ground to a halt, it is because it has continued to feed on the discourse of the masters. At the root of the problem of the feminine is psychoanalytic theory, which is itself unable to resolve this question. The psychoanalytic impasse—which is the same as the impasse that confronts thinking about the feminine and feminine writing—is a brand-new problem, only eighty years old! An exterior indication of this dilemma is the name-change of the group Psychoanalysis and Politics: they have reversed the name to Politics and Psychoanalysis; their priorities have been reexamined, and praxis is now given preference over the word. Similarly, the name of Antoinette has emerged from the mystery surrounding her since 1972. Could it be that there has been a realization that *in regard to the theory of the feminine*, psychoanalytic discourse is a whirlpool, a fountain of Narcissus, in which the feminine will drown if its passion is to *found itself in theory?*

For the last ten years, Freud has been much disparaged by women: he has been brilliantly attacked, either directly or by implication. This salutary, impressive feminist criticism illustrates one of the great Freudian myths, that of *Totem and Taboo*: the horde of daughters has put the father to death, in order to perpetuate his cult/his word. The Achilles' heel of the Freudian project is his own repression of the woman question. Neofeminists have demonstrated that if he had pushed his analysis further, he would probably have been reduced to silence himself, barring the engendering of the women's revolt then and there (rather than its coming at the end of the sexual revolution, which we owe more to science than to psychoanalysis). He was in some sense reduced to silence by himself, when he came close to the realization that, by his own criteria, the "feminine" position suited him perfectly in his relationships with Fliess, with Martha, and with his own mother. Because of the rupture of an ideal friendship, on the model of the maternal relation to an only son, Freud never wrote his projected essay on human bisexuality.

Vladimir Granoff has followed, step by step, the path of the concept of femininity in the texts and the correspondence of Freud. He underlines the hesitations and reservations surrounding Freud's theory of the feminine, as masterfully dissected by Luce Irigaray in *Speculum de l'autre femme*.[14] Freud postulated "an unconscious whose autonomy has bisexuality as its premise."[15] The fundamental Freudian equation Masculine/active/strong versus Feminine/passive/ weak is termed FUNCTIONAL but insufficient and DESTRUCTIVE to analysis, by his own account.[16] Freud also believed, and said, that the work of civilization goes on AT THE EXPENSE of love in *Civilization and Its Discontents*.[17] Elsewhere, he stressed that his paradigm of Male/Female is the most confused model one could ever encounter in the realm of science.[18] In his theory of the libido, in *Three Essays on Sexuality* (1905), he makes this important reservation:

> IF ONE COULD GIVE A MORE PRECISE CONTENT TO
> THE CONCEPTS OF MASCULINE AND FEMININE...
> one could say the libido is invariably and necessarily masculine
> in men and women, and that the object can be a man or a
> woman.[19]

Eighty years later, psychoanalytic theory has not moved an inch on this point, and neofeminist thought seems to echo the Freudian thesis as restated by Granoff, namely, that THOUGHT IS LINKED TO THE FEMININE BY WAY OF EXCLUSION; that is, WHEN WOMEN THINK, "THEY THINK LIKE MEN,"[20] which also means: the feminine is that which does not think, the UNSAYABLE, or as Marguerite Duras whispers: "that music . . . God . . . nothing." According to this influential mode of thought, the feminine lives at the level of the silent and the unconscious.

At present, the alternative to this impasse of silence is to come back to the initial postulate of bisexuality. That is, to speak as a woman/gynandrous being, and not to allow ourselves to go on demonstrating that discourse is masculine like libido, logic, work . . . all the less, because this is what Freud said a very long time ago. Psychoanalysts of both sexes and theoreticians of femininity, although trying to say something else, have gone on echoing this same discourse. Feminist criticism, which is not an attribute of the "weaker sex," and which remains open to androgynes, is perhaps a feminine undertaking in that it clarifies the contradictions which encumber feminine discourse and the theory of the feminine, not to obliterate or to reduce them, but to go beyond them, to pass through the impasse, to "fly-jump" over them, as Hélène Cixous exhorts us to do in "The Laugh of the Medusa." [21]

The "weakness" of theoretical discourse is intrinsic; it is only theoretical: pure, solipsistic, detached from social, historical, biological reality.

The exploration of the feminine has just made great strides, whose consequences will soon be apparent, with the publication of the proceedings of the Royaumont Colloquium, directed by Evelyne Sullerot, *Le Fait Féminin*.[22] Instead of fighting each other with ultrasymbolic signifiers—whose signifieds are fluctuating and purely conventional—carrying on debates of pure form, people who care about the feminine question, and the pursuit of happiness, justice, and the future of the planet, must educate themselves about the objective, factual differences due to sex. Biological nature continues to be affected by the material and cultural environment, and this phenomenon has been accelerated by the hold of the media over our imaginations. Instead of being entirely absorbed by maternity, women are now in the situation where our "mothering" work is reduced to one-quarter of our lives, and even to zero, in those optimal situations where the milieu and the high standard of living no longer penalize the mother under the pretext of "protecting the best interests of the child" on good Freudian principles.

The other crucial fact brought out by *Le Fait Féminin* is that we are beginning to understand that the "truly human" is a linguistic convention, extrapolated from the most fragmentary observations. Primary thinking functions on the basis of stereotypes, deformed images which are then reflected ad infinitum. After ten years of the woman question, it is time to ask: What do men want? Even if it is established that aggression *is* the fundamental, objective difference between the sexes, the role of the environment, including the nuclear family, is much more determining of psychosexual elements, which spread out into an infinitely shaded spectrum, than any genetic given. *Le Fait Féminin* demonstrates beyond any possible doubt that biological sex is only ONE given, among all those which make of us SO-CALLED "women" and "men," beings that are NAMED and IDENTIFIED much more than born one or the other, and never completely one or the other. In other words, and it is well put, we have to clarify the "HUMAN nature of 'human nature' "[23] before there can be any theoretical progress on sexuality, whether the inquiry is undertaken by the "sons of Freud " or the "daughters of Antoinette."

When Granoff declares that "the feminine is necessarily present in any effort toward the abolition of contradictions," we need to translate this to mean that "feminine" is, among other things, a desire for lasting harmony. It is therefore a *logical* quest, and an effort which doubly contradicts the Freudian association of the feminine, the passive and the nonrational that Granoff holds to elsewhere. But Granoff adds, and this is what we must repudiate, "the abolition of contradictions, that is, of differences."[24] On the contrary: love, which does not exclude civilization by women, consists of not seeing CONTRA/DICTIONS in differences. This is what can be, for women, the founding morality of a research, an analysis, and a feminist criticism whose integration into our "humanities" is long overdue.

Notes

1. Monique Wittig, *Les Guérillières* (Paris: Les Editions de Minuit, 1969).
2. Ibid., pp. 67–68; my translation.

3. Unpublished letter to this writer.

4. This article is a continuation of the following studies: "La critique féministe: éléments d'une problématique," *Revue des Sciences Humaines* 168 (December 1977); "Nouveau regard sur la critique féministe" (forthcoming), in *Revue de l'Université d'Ottawa*; and "La poétique féminine aujourd'hui," in Introduction, *Ecrits de femmes, panorama critique et répertoire des femmes de langue française* by Christiane Makward et al. (Paris: Stock, in press).

5. No. 168 (December 1977).

6. See note 4.

7. Hélène Cixous and Catherine Clément, *La Jeune Née* (Paris: Union Générale d'Editions, 1975). (The Politics and Psychoanalysis group has published a monthly, *Des Femmes en Mouvements*, and runs a publishing house and bookstore, both called *Des Femmes*—Ed. In November 1979 a new periodical, *Des Femmes Hebdo*, appeared.

8. *Revue des Sciences Humaines* 168 (December 1977): 500.

9. No. 7 (June 1975).

10. *Les Cahiers du GRIF*, no. 13.

11. *Le Monde*, December 15, 1978.

12. Paris: Editions de Minuit, 1977, p. 76.

13. *Questions Féministes* 1 (November 1977): 112.

14. Paris: Editions de Minuit, 1974.

15. Vladimir Granoff, *La pensée et le féminin* (Paris: Editions de Minuit, 1977), p. 23.

16. Ibid., p. 42, citing *L'Abrégé* (1938).

17. Ibid., p. 67.

18. Ibid., p. 49.

19. Ibid., p. 48; my emphasis.

20. Ibid., p. 264; my emphasis.

21. In *Signs: Journal of Women in Culture and Society* 1: 4 (Summer 1976): 875–93.

22. Evelyne Sullerot, *Le Fait Féminin* (Paris: Fayard, 1978).

23. Ibid., p. 233, n. 1.

24. Granoff, *Pensée* , pp. 147–48.

Jane Gallop and Carolyn Burke

Psychoanalysis and Feminism in France

Jane Gallop
Introduction

Beginning with Alice Jardine's opening remarks, "The Future of Difference" conference introduced two rather alien components into the American feminist scene: (1) French feminist theory and (2) psychoanalysis. Our workshop, "Psychoanalysis and Feminism in France," seemed a good place to interrogate the two aliens. Two questions seemed central, and if they did not get answered, they did get posed. (1) What is the difference, and is there *a* difference, between French and' American feminism? (2) What use is psychoanalysis to feminism? Why learn another patriarchal discourse?

A tentative answer to the first question: *a* difference, one of many, is that as a feminist goal Americans—like Nancy Chodorow—speak of building a "strong core of self," whereas French—like Josette Féral—talk of the "subversion of the subject." In question is not only a strong core versus a subversion/dispersion of the core, but also a "self" versus a "subject." The "self" implies a center, a potentially autonomous individual; the "subject" is a place in language, a signifier that is already alienated in an intersubjective network.

A tentative answer to the second question: in the place of the Oedipal Father, the primal Father with absolute phallic power, Jacques Lacan has substituted the Name-of-the-Father. Focusing on the patronym, social identity as inscribed in a patriarchal order, inserts the analysis of family structure into a larger social and linguistic order. Whereas Freud's model can lead to an isolation of the family as the seat of psychic dynamics, French psychoanalysis brings a way of seeing the social order, the Law, as it is inscribed in the family. Thus via a French detour, psychoanalysis can provide feminism with a means of understanding the implication of the political in the personal, an important strategic weapon for a practice which must always battle on those two fronts. Rather than being just "another patriarchal discourse," psychoanalysis uncovers the functioning upon and within us of patriarchy as discourse.

Carolyn Burke
Rethinking the Maternal

Incensed by the Freudian equation of anatomy and destiny, American feminists have repeatedly rejected psychoanalysis as an inimical discourse. Because psychoanalysis seemed to perpetuate the idea of woman's different (that is, "inferior") nature, we were resistant to its central concepts. Frequently we sought to demonstrate that significant differences between the sexes simply did not exist, so that these imagined differences could no longer be used against us. Yet, at the same time, there has been a tremendous growth of interest in a separate "women's culture"—new artistic, literary, philosophical, and spiritual forms self-consciously created by women working from a sense of difference. Attempting to see woman not as man's "other," as in the negative sense of "difference," but as a plurality of meanings, we recharge the concept with a new, more positive valence. Now, as theory begins to catch up with artistic experience, we are looking into our reasons for wishing to minimize differences. I would like to suggest that a certain psychoanalysis has its uses in an approach to a feminist theory of difference. Furthermore, it is likely that this approach will lead to a reevaluation of the "female" as understood in relation to the "maternal."[1] Here, as in France, contemporary feminist writing deconstructs and reimagines our ideas of what it means to be mothered and to do mothering, both central experiences in a woman's sense of her difference and her "self." Inevitably, this reevaluation requires a shift in attitudes, a tolerance of uncertainty, and the willingness to accept possible contradictions. The French detour to a different sense of differences does not require our adherence to a body of doctrine per se; rather, it effects a change in the way that we pose our questions. This psychoanalysis allows us to think "difference" differently. And, most important, it does so at a conceptual level that holds the promise of an interdisciplinary feminist theory.

During the last ten years, a discussion of these concepts—difference, identity, the maternal and the female—has been going on within the *Mouvement de libération des femmes* (the Women's Liberation Movement) in France. Although concerns similar to those of American feminists have been voiced by French women writers,[2] the work of Julia Kristeva[3] and Luce Irigaray,[4] to name two prominent theorists, remains largely inaccessible to American readers, in spite of the growing number of translations. Their critical writing, stylistically different and highly theoretical, assumes a reader who possesses a certain intellectual "bagage," as the French call the ideas and codes that one brings to a given subject. In addition to the languages of linguistics, philosophy, literary criticism, and political analysis, both women draw in important ways upon psychoanalysis. They seem to have read a different Freud from ours, and furthermore, they have taken him seriously, whether as teacher, philosopher, poet, or opponent. He is not simply dismissed as the advocate of a reductive female psychology, for both have had to reckon with him as a serious thinker.[5] The American reader of these feminist writers sometimes wonders whether we are talking about the same Freud, and her quandary increases to the point where she wonders whether their analyses are appropriate to our situation.

The missing link between the two Freuds is Jacques Lacan, the eminent and controversial French spokesman for a return to Freudian psychoanalysis (as distinct from psychiatry, psychotherapy, and the whole range of psychologies). Like French intellectuals in general, French feminists inevitably respond to a Freud reinterpreted by Lacan.[6] In his interpretation, psychoanalysis is a far more complex, subtle, and suggestive practice than we, as Americans, have been wont to believe. Indeed, French psychoanalytic theory prompts us to rethink our own relation to Freud's "subversive science": as Laura Mulvey has suggested, "psychoanalytic theory as it now stands can . . . advance our understanding of the status quo, of the patriarchal order in which we are caught."[7] To this end—using psychoanalytic theory rather than being used by it—this essay discusses first aspects of the "French Freud,"[8] then some feminist uses of its perspectives by Julia Kristeva.

To evaluate the differences between American Freudianism and the French Freud, we must undergo an intellectual detoxification. We have to approach Freud without the automatic antagonism aroused by earlier feminist responses. It is likely that our own version of Freud has been colored by those of his followers who stressed the biologistic strands in psychoanalysis, producing the mechanistic model of psychosexuality which we find repugnant. Lacan claims to return psychoanalysis to the more fluid, even contradictory, currents in Freud's thought, in other words, to the realm of the unconscious or that which cannot be fit into any mechanistic schema. At the same time, he dismisses his American counterparts as being reductively mired in our native psychoanalytic school, ego psychology. According to his argument, American psychoanalysis has leaned in the direction of social adjustment and cures, and its practitioners have stressed ego strength at the expense of the unconscious. He claims that Freud's practice has undergone a process of adaptation to American social norms that has altered it almost beyond recognition. In this view, American psychoanalysis (and, by extension, the whole range of psychotherapies here) has adopted a voluntarist position: in placing the emphasis upon the cure as a goal, it has absorbed the pragmatism of our culture.

In our own emphasis upon female ego strength—placing a value upon assertiveness or standing up for one's rights—it is not surprising that feminists have shared in our culture's suspicion of the unconscious.

Although we have by no means rejected the concept, we would prefer to confine its traces to art or literature. We have assumed that just as social ills have their remedies, so personal ills have their cures. Yet many feminists realize that we have analyzed the constraints of the social context more avidly than the contradictions within ourselves. Given the need for political action, it is understandable that we commit ourselves to the ideal of an autonomous and coherent female self. However, the unconscious, the most subversive element in psychic life, seems to be catching up with us. Freud's discovery, that the unconscious is a site of meaning, may provide us with new approaches to our different fields of specialization, and, in the process, change our minds about how we understand the meaning of the self.

A feminist use of psychoanalysis will alter the ways in which the self is conceptualized. At the outset, it sends us back to the very terms of analysis. It is important to realize that Freud's terminology changes slightly, gaining in mystery or concreteness, from one language to another. Comparing the French and English translations of the original German terms, one realizes that they are, in fact, rather different. The Latinate, somewhat reified *ego* sounds far less abstract as *le moi* (and closer to *das ich*). Similarly, the *id* becomes more irrational and unmanageable as *le ça* (*das es*). As for the *superego*, it sits more literally in judgment of us as *le sur-moi* (*das über-ich*). We may have veered away from Freud's use of these terms, all of them rather more lively than in English, in their translation into the more abstract Latinate forms. Stressing *le ça*, Lacan's reading of Freud returns us to the unpredictable, willful, childish, or animalesque in ourselves—that which we have been less than willing to recognize, let alone welcome into our theory. This emphasis in his interpretation inevitably creates a counterweight to the ideal of the strong ego. Similarly, his discussion of selves as "subjects" stresses their decentered quality, man or woman's lack of self-center. It emphasizes Freud's truly subversive view of the unconscious: that which undermines the subject's coherence as a self-determined actor in its own affairs.

From the language of analysis we may turn to Lacan's analysis of language as a model for the structure of the unconscious.[9] In his view, we are constituted by language and by the many cultural "languages" of our particular societies. We learn who we are through the acquisition of language, with its peculiar tendency to posit properties, boundaries, and limits through systems of syntax. Using language, we internalize the laws of the world, especially those that reflect the patriarchal powers. We are, then, divided within ourselves through the use of language, which guarantees the presence of alienating forces within the individual. In this view, "self" becomes "subject" and identity is linguistic, a relational position demarcated by language. This radically different psychoanalysis situates the human subject at the intersection of language and our existence as social beings.

Through language, then, the subject internalizes the values of the patriarchal societies in which we live. These powers are summed up by Lacan as the "Nom-du-Père," a concept with symbolic resonances throughout our social system. What he means by the Name-of-the-Father is social identity given through the patronym, the process of naming under patriarchy. This law stands outside the mother-child dyad until the moment of the Oedipus complex, at which point in the child's psychic development the Name-of-the-Father creates a third term in the family and links it to the social order. The Name-of-the-Father confirms in the child its attempts to situate itself in reality, through the recognition of relational differences. In French, the coincidence in sound between "le non" (no) and "le nom" (name) suggests a relationship: the child learns a place in the system of "nots" (negatives) as it learns a place in the system of names. This law intervenes in the mother-child relationship to establish difference as a concomitant of identity, to initiate the child into the culture of patriarchy. It voices the principle of the Logos as giver of meaning: the one who asserts absolutely, "I am that I am." In Lacan's view, all are marked by the Name-of-the-Father. We have taken it into our psyches with the acquisition of language within the network of familial and social relations.[10]

What can feminists make of such a pessimistic understanding of the human condition? Is this just one more patriarchal discourse which seeks to justify, while describing, the status quo? Can we use it to comprehend our own situation, from within a conceptual framework that undermines our sense of identity? Is it worth considering the idea that the values of patriarchy may be unravelled by means of its own ideological structures? It is possible that acquaintance with the French Freud provides us with a psychoanalysis as a political ally, for Freud's subversive science becomes truly subversive when used in an attempt to counter its own more conservative aspects. Paradoxically, by abandoning the ideals of ego strength and social adaptation, this psychoanalysis returns us to the powers of the unconscious as potential revolutionary.

It is exactly this return to the unconscious that has produced results of great theoretical richness among French women writers. Exploring those issues that Lacanian psychoanalysis does not take up—the "female" in language, her special relation to the maternal, "motherhood" within and beyond the conceptual limits of patriarchal culture—writers like Irigaray and Kristeva have profited from a critical engagement with the French Freud. Kristeva draws on this psychoanalytic tradition in her analysis of the interplay of language, culture, and the female as meaning. Like

Adrienne Rich, she speaks of the knowledge that exists between mother and infant. She investigates the return of that unacknowledged language, in literature as in the psychoanalytic process. Less directly concerned than Rich with "motherhood as experience and institution,"[11] she is, however, much concerned with its implications for the creation of meaning. Herself a psychoanalyst as well as a cultural critic and literary theorist, Kristeva has created an original and syncretic approach that has much in common with the concerns of American feminists.

Kristeva situates the issues of "the female speaker" (or, how does a woman speak) within her general analysis of the process of signification. She is interested in the signifying capacities of language in their interaction with the speaker, for in her view, all social phenomena are symbolic. Most notably since her work on poetic language and the avant-garde (*La Révolution du langage poétique*), she has been concerned with the underside of symbolic language, those aspects in the creation of meaning which she has called the semiotic.[12] The symbolic and the semiotic are two closely related modalities of signification, which, in our cultures, tend to be related as master and slave. That is, the symbolic plays the role of the Logos, or magisterial discourse, and the semiotic speaks through nonsense or "childish" language. This theory has important implications for feminist thought because, in Kristeva's view, the semiotic derives its energy from the realm of the presymbolic, or the preoedipal. It first occurs in the phase of the infant's intense attachment to the mother's body. The semiotic, then, is in close alliance with the unconscious and expresses itself as the organization of instinctual drives through the resources of rhythm, intonation, gesture, and melody.[13]

In the psychic development of the subject, the semiotic stage precedes cognitive knowledge of self as distinct from other. Elaborating upon Lacan, Kristeva asserts that the symbolic is initiated in the "mirror" stage, with the infant's need to deal with absence, representation, and abstraction: that is, with the uses of language.[14] Although the symbolic functions never entirely displace the semiotic, they come to dominate in speech, as in writing. When we learn what we call sentence structure, we absorb a concept of identity as defined by syntax, which posits as a given the subject and its objects. The symbolic is expressed in language that bears the mark of the speaker's conscious control; it depends upon the principle of identity-unto-itself. However, the subject articulates itself through a constant but changing interaction between the two modalities of semiotic and symbolic, and their admixture may be enormously variable. Kristeva's theory of signification as dialectical process allows for the breaks in meaning that we sense in puns, the subversion of the authoritative language of the Logos, and the return of the instinctual drives to pleasure, all of which bring into question the unity of consciousness. In other words, the semiotic voices the return of the unconscious as a different, an *other*, site of meaning which flows counter to the symbolic uses of language.

But what of sexual difference and the implications for feminist theory? Following Freud, Kristeva posits a theoretical bisexuality within the speaking subject, based in the bisexuality of the unconscious. It is important to observe that this bisexuality is "not androgyny but a metaphor designating the possibility of exploring all aspects of signification."[15] In other words, her theory allows for the recognition of sexual difference, of plurality, within the creation of meaning, while the logocentric discourses of our cultures do not. Even more original, and controversial, is her linkage of the semiotic and the maternal. Kristeva associates the semiotic with the stage in psychic development in which the infant perceives the world through the rhythms, melodies, and gestures of the mother's body. If the semiotic is linked with the maternal, the symbolic is associated with the paternal: the realm of Lacan's Name-of-the-Father. But she is not asking whether women speak (or write) differently from men. Instead, she proposes a theoretical model that allows the dialectical functioning of both modalities, "maternal" and "paternal," within texts written by members of either sex. Thus she has long been interested in writers such as Mallarmé, Artaud, Proust, Joyce, and Beckett, in whose work the semiotic constantly threatens to return into the structures of the symbolic. Finally, her concern with writing by women ("écriture féminine") has developed from Kristeva's preoccupation with the revolutionary potential of the avant-garde, those whose creations smuggle the semiotic back into the realm of the symbolic.[16]

In her view, much avant-garde writing in this century has attempted to expand the limits of the signifiable, that is, quite literally, what can be said. She places women's writing within this general development, insofar as it is involved in "a body-to-body discourse with the mother."[17] Such writing creates gaps in meaning, pauses, and silences. It enacts a break from the symbolic within language. The discourse of the Logos is literally ruptured to make room for what it has not allowed to be said. This unsayable, long repressed into the unconscious, includes the language of the maternal, as it does the languages of sexuality, madness, and death. It is in opposition to the consolations of transcendent or theological values. When formulated by those who have the greatest stake in the deconstruction of patriarchal tradition—that is, by women—it is seen as a subversive antagonist to the Logos. In this spirit, Kristeva's "L'Héréthique de l'amour" ("Love's Heretical Ethics") attempts a reconsideration of the problematics of maternal love that allows her to think beyond the conceptual limits of unified discourse.[18]

Her essay begins as an analytic study of the Virgin Mary's symbolic function as archetype of the mother. Unexpectedly, the analysis is interrupted by a lyrical intertext composed of outbursts, cries, and flashes of insight. The intertext ruptures the homogeneity of the main text and forces an opening on the page. The coherence of one discourse, printed across the page, is made to give way to another voice which splits language in two, printed in separate columns carefully juxtaposed in relation to each other. Typographically, the intertext depends upon and echoes the "mother" text; it functions as its child-being-born in a mimesis of the creation of meaning. Commenting upon the more traditional discourse of the parent text, it makes possible an outpouring of the semiotic from within the symbolic. From the constant fluctuation of their dialogue results both an examination of the conceptual and social limits imposed upon "motherhood" in Western culture and a reimagining of that central relationship. Kristeva concludes that the "heretical ethics" of motherhood must be entirely rethought if women are to accede to the language of our differences. In an idiosyncratic and transgeneric manner, her essay demonstrates a use of psychoanalysis that is feminist in its radical rethinking of our cultural paradigms. Exploding their presuppositions about the maternal as a type of the female, it utilizes psychoanalysis toward its own ends.

Such an approach may help to resituate the female in relation to the maternal—that difficult emotional complex of being mothered, mothering, and perhaps being a mother. So far, however, Kristeva has not pursued her analyses into the special relations of mother and daughter. Yet her theory may be useful in our ongoing exploration of what Adrienne Rich has called "the great unwritten story."[19] It may help us to understand the linkage between the female subject and the semiotic, based upon the knowledge of a resemblance to the mother's body. Indeed, the language of mothers and daughters—"subliminal, subversive, preverbal"[20]—bears a revolutionary potential through its different involvement in the modalities of the semiotic. We are only beginning to learn its uses as we unearth in our writing those materials "for the deepest mutuality and the most painful estrangement."[21] The differently psychoanalytic work of Nancy Chodorow and Dorothy Dinnerstein could be fruitfully compared with Kristeva's theories. At this writing, however, neither Chodorow nor Dinnerstein has chosen to investigate the question of the maternal at the level of language. Thus, there has been little dialogue among French and American theorists on this crucial question, even among those writing from feminist interpretations of psychoanalysis in order to examine difference.[22]

For an American, such French uses of psychoanalysis may be more than unfamiliar: they may seem dubiously, or curiously, feminist. Yet Kristeva's recent work takes up the same questions that preoccupy us in this country, and Luce Irigaray's most recent essay, *Et L'une ne bouge sans L'autre*,[23] enacts in poetic prose the explorations of the female as meaning that she presented in earlier, more theoretical writing. On both sides of the Atlantic we are working toward a feminist theory of the maternal, in all its implications. We are engaged, all of us, in "the poetics of discovery and telling, exploring and naming."[24] One might say that much recent feminist writing enacts the eruption of the semiotic into the symbolic, in a rich new language especially suited to the breaking down of boundaries and the deconstruction of patriarchal systems. In her reflections upon the maternal, Adrienne Rich observed that, until very recently, the relationship between mother and daughter "has been minimized and trivialized in the annals of patriarchy."[25] Drawing upon the work of Rich, Kristeva, Irigaray, and others, in their different yet related approaches, we are creating the language with which to reclaim the significance of that relationship. Feminist uses of psychoanalysis that encourage the liberation of the poetic and welcome the traces of the unconscious within their own discourse help us to illuminate "that vast chamber"[26] of unsaid meaning, the language of our difference.

Jane Gallop
Psychoanalysis in France

The science invented by Freud has known very different destinies in France and America.

Briefly (all too briefly in a context where any elision is suspect) American psychoanalysis has become ego psychology, a practice aimed at shoring up that agency in the psyche that Freud said "is not even master in its own house."[27] Ego psychology would help the ego gain domination, although a certain reading of Freud finds that the ego's necessarily fragile, defensive, illusory mastery is the knot of neuroses, the obstacle to happiness.

"A certain reading of Freud": French and American psychoanalysis can be seen as divergent readings of Freud. But to locate the difference, or the cause of that difference, or its center, in a "reading" is already to be on the side of French Freud. Thanks to the work of Jacques Lacan, the development peculiar to French psychoanalysis has been not a growth from Freud but a continual, detailed reading of Freud, reading his most radical moments against his most conservative, in view of a constant vigilance against Freud's and our own tendencies to fall back into psychologism, biologism, or other commonplaces of thought from which his new science was a radical break.

This careful reading, always struggling to hold psychoanalysis' most audacious frontiers, considers the American effort to help the "master of the house" subdue mutinies as ideologically in keeping with the effort to save the threatened nuclear family, based upon traditional sex roles, by strengthening the "master's" domination—that is to say, in keeping with the therapeutic effort to help men and women adjust to their sexually determined social roles. Seen from Paris (even if Paris be in London, New Haven, Baltimore, or Rome), Freud's lot in America has been cooptation: the bold Freud silenced, the timid Freud intoned.

In America, Freud's biologistic side is revised in keeping with the developments of modern biochemistry.[28] In France, Freud's biologism is read as a weak moment, a fearful wish to ground his new science, the science of the Unconscious, in an old science. But the Unconscious is no proper object for biology, and Freud's biological analogies are retreats from the uncharted paths he was exploring back to the relatively safe confines in which he was schooled. The refusal to scurry back to the familiarity of biology opens up a militant psychoanalysis which no longer betrays feminism (by prescribing and abetting adjustment to the roles "destined" by one's anatomical difference), but provides feminist theory with a possibility of understanding "internalized oppression," a concept most efficient when operating within a science of the Unconscious.[29]

The emphasis on the "reading of Freud" differentiates "psychoanalytic literary criticism" in France and in America (although this drawing of lines may be schematic, even paranoid). In France, since the Freudian text is apprehended in its materiality, it cannot be reduced to a univocal system of ideas which would then be applied to other books, literary ones, as a grid for meaning. Rather than a stable image of the psyche which grounds the interpretation of psychic manifestations, including literary language, French Freud simply provides symptoms along with contradictory efforts—either to repress/domesticate/coopt those eloquent productions (the symptoms/texts) or to elucidate/analyze/read them. Freud is not a tool, not even some revelatory Word, but a dynamic of repression, a plural text like any other.

The French reading of Freud has located a particularly troublesome textual knot in psychoanalysis' investigation of sexual difference and female sexuality. Lacan has declared the need for delineation of this problematic in "Propos directifs pour un Congrès sur la sexualité féminine" (*Ecrits*, Paris: Seuil, 1966). Lacan's clearest and most concise articulation of a theory of sexual difference appears in "La Signification du phallus" (also in *Ecrits*).[30] For two longer considerations by Lacan of the "woman question" ("What *does* woman want [anyway]?"—a question Lacan said Freud asked but was afraid to answer), see *Télévision* (Paris: Seuil, 1973) and *Séminaire XX: Encore* (Paris: Seuil, 1975).

In *La Sexualité féminine dans la doctrine freudienne* (Paris: Seuil, 1976), Moustapha Safouan has traced a map for following the vicissitudes of female sexuality in Freud's work. Although a clear and complete inventory, Safouan's book is not a sufficiently critical reading. That "sufficiently critical reading" (necessarily) comes from an overt feminist. Luce Irigaray's *Speculum* (Minuit, 1974) is both a meticulous, psychoanalytic reading of Freud on women and a sharp, mocking critique of the sexist assumptions that constitute a network of timid moments in Freud (biologistic, psychologistic, deterministic, downright protective of the sexual status quo).[31] Both Irigaray and Safouan have learned to read Freud from Lacan, but, whereas the latter systematizes and reduces the audacity out of Lacan/Freud, the former challenges the unavoidable tendency toward conservatism, teasing out what is most insolent in psychoanalysis so as to loosen the hold of Freudian oppression of women.

It is inevitable that Irigaray should turn the critique directly on Lacan, whom she finds sorely guilty of profiting from phallocentrism. This critique, as well as further exposition of her reading of Freud, can be found in *Ce Sexe qui n'en est pas un* (Paris: Minuit, 1977). She condemns Lacan's reactionary positions, yet she does so by using Lacanian strategies and formulations (embracing Lacan at his wildest). But ultimately her entire relation to Freud/Lacan is beyond either embrace or condemnation; it is a reading.

Irigaray is not the only French psychoanalyst both profoundly influenced by Lacan, and yet taking exception to certain conservative moments in his theory. One of the most subtle interrogations of Lacan's authority has been conducted by Jean Laplanche, an ex-student of Lacan's. Laplanche's *Vie et mort en psychanalyse* can be read as a clear and fascinating introduction to Lacanian theory, but it also contains a barely perceptible swerve away from the central thrust of that theory.[32] Such is Laplanche's non-authoritarian strategy that he does not belligerently declare his difference, assert his step beyond. But the difference is signalled in Jeffrey Mehlman's introduction to the English translation of *Vie et mort*: "[*Life and Death*] is deeply in accord with the general orientation of Lacan's reading of Freud, and yet it never invokes—or intimidates its readers with—the magisterial pronouncements of that author. More remarkably still, *Life and Death* ultimately never appeals to the authority of Freud himself" (p. ix). As opposed to Lacan's "magisterial pronouncements," Laplanche refuses intimidation. He refuses the authority of psychoanalysis and in that remains closer, not to Freud or Lacan, but to psychoanalysis at its most radical. Mehlman continues: "For what has authority in this reading is, in the final analysis, the perverse rigor with which a certain bizarre structure of Freud's text persistently plays havoc with the magisterial pronouncements—or authority—of Freud." At its most powerful, psychoanalysis undercuts its own authority.

Laplanche diverges from Lacanian theory in his description of the originary intersubjectivity of sexuality. Whereas Lacan describes that original incursion of others into the infant's psyche as a wound, a lack, a proto-castration, Laplanche adds that it is also a boon; even more, it is absolutely necessary to the child's survival. The "vital order" is not only *"infested,* but also *sustained"* (p. 48) by "that *alien internal entity* which is *sexual excitation"* (p. 24). Lacan does state that the sexual (the intersubjective) is structurally necessary in the constitution of the very ego which seeks to defend itself against that contamination. But by emphasizing the disruptive, violent, infesting side of the sexual rather than the sustaining aspect, and by championing the intrusive sexual over against the conservative, defensive, virginal ego, Lacan maintains a phallic thrust to his science, supported by an investment in the prudishness of the ego and the correlate desire to violate that ego. This turns his battle against ego psychology into an untenable vendetta against the ego. Laplanche, on the other hand, states in the conclusion to *Life and Death* that the ego is necessary so that the unconscious fantasies might "take form" (pp. 125–126).

Life and Death grew out of Laplanche's collaboration with another ex-student of Lacan's, Jean Baptiste Pontalis, to produce the *Vocabulaire de la psychanalyse.*[33] This is the largest of Laplanche's published cooperative efforts. Perhaps the very possibility of a long, devoted collaboration whose goal is to elucidate the vocabulary of other people with more prestige (in particular, Freud and Lacan) is the refusal of authority.

A review of Laplanche and Pontalis' *Vocabulaire,* by the late psychoanalyst Nicolas Abraham, appears in an issue of the journal *Critique* on psychoanalysis (249, 1968). Abraham's brilliant review, "L'Ecorce et le noyau," points to psychoanalysis' potential for the working out of our Oedipal fantasies, its potential for changing our societal sexual structures. He sees the Oedipal/castration complex as part of a dialogue with the mother, which places it not in a separate history of the self's individuation (access to mastery) but in an always intersubjective scenario. Like Laplanche, Abraham also published joint efforts, collaborating with Maria Torok. The work of Abraham and Torok is collected in two volumes recently released by Aubier-Flammarion: *Cryptonymie: Le Verbier de l'Homme aux Loups* and *L'Ecorce et le Noyau.* Part of the eccentric subversion of their work is an uncovering of the distorting effects of the psychoanalyst's ego. *Cryptonymie* is introduced by Abraham's friend Jacques Derrida, a French philosopher who himself wrote a critique of Lacan, "Le Facteur de la vérité" (*Poétique,* 21, 1975), which condemns Lacan's phallocentric system.

Abraham's last text is a sixth act to Shakespeare's *Hamlet* with a theoretical interlude, thus placing psychoanalytic theory in a different, non-masterful relation to literature.[34] This different relationship is precisely the focus of *Yale French Studies* 55–56, *Psychoanalysis and Literature*, edited by Shoshana Felman. In her lucid and concise introduction she suggests that we "reverse the usual perspective in an attempt to disrupt this monologic master-slave structure" (p. 6) where "literature is submitted to the authority, to the prestige of psychoanalysis" (p. 5). Psychoanalysis has usurped for itself a power, an authority which reduces and abuses literature's otherness. Just as psychoanalysis when not coopted as ego psychology calls into question the authority of the ego, so it must question its own equally illusory and defensive prestige. Not that Felman would have the positions reversed, not that literature should have authority over psychoanalysis, but rather that the effect of such a reversal would be a total disruption of "the position of mastery as such" (p. 7).

Felman describes the repressive, traditional American relatonship of psychoanalysis to literature in the same terms that Irigaray describes the relationship of psychoanalysis to women. Felman states that the maintenance of psychoanalysis's authority demands a suppression of literature's plurality and otherness in favor of a unified theoretical discourse. Irigaray, likewise, finds that psychoanalysis's presumption to the truth about women necessitates an exclusion of woman's plural sexuality and all that which is other (and not merely complementary) to phallic sexuality and its unified sexual theory. In both cases, otherness is suppressed to preserve the theory's consistency. Theory's authority is guaranteed by its consistency. Yet French psychoanalysis has been devoted to exposing its own inevitable inconsistencies. Felman's defence of literature's irreducibility and Irigaray's assertion of women's plurality are in keeping with this effort to delineate the contradictions in psychoanalysis's mastery.

If one sees the questioning of authority as an essential feminist effort, then the dialogue between psychoanalysis and literature, as Felman outlines it, may be invaluable for a feminist rethinking of power. According to Felman, "there is one crucial feature which is constitutive of literature but is essentially lacking in psychoanalytic theory, and indeed in theory as such: irony. Since irony precisely consists in dragging authority as such into a scene it cannot master . . . literature, by virtue of its ironic force, fundamentally deconstructs the fantasy of authority" (p. 8). Felman's view of irony subscribes to the theory that irony always exceeds the ironist's control; it necessarily cuts both ways. Once literal meaning is called into question in one instance, it cannot ever be assumed.

If irony undercuts authority, then Lacan's writing, which is full of the most disconcerting irony, is not "magisterial pronouncement."[35] By adding an ironic tone to the discourse of authority, he makes it impossible to take the authority seriously. Thus the question of whether Lacan is authoritarian is a question of how he is read. As Felman suggests, literary perspective is inextricably implicated in psychoanalysis. Freud/Lacan is neither respected nor rejected (that would be falling prey to the transference fantasy where the psychoanalyst is either loved or rejected but never questioned as omniscient), but read.

Notes

1. American theorists who draw upon psychoanalysis to examine sexual difference and differentiation include Nancy Chodorow, *The Reproduction of Mothering: Psychoanalysis and The Sociology of Gender* (Berkeley: Univ. of California Press, 1978); Dorothy Dinnerstein, *The Mermaid and the Minotaur: Sexual Arrangements and Human Malaise* (New York: Harper and Row, 1976); and Jane Flax, "The Conflict between Nurturance and Autonomy in Mother-Daughter Relationships and Within Feminism," *Feminist Studies* 4: 2 (June 1978): 171–91. By the "maternal," I mean that component of relationships between women in which an idealized relation to the mother is reflected. This element in female bonding is present whether or not biological motherhood is involved.

2. See the introductory studies in *Signs: Journal of Women in Culture and Society* 3: 4 (Summer 1978): Elaine Marks, "Women and Literature in France," pp. 832–42; and Carolyn G. Burke, "Report from Paris: Women's Writing and the Women's Movement," pp. 843–55.

3. See Julia Kristeva, *Desire in Language: A Semiotic Approach to Literature and Art*, ed. Leon Roudiez, tr. Tom Gora, Alice Jardine and Leon Roudiez (New York: Columbia Univ. Press, 1980), a collection of her essays. See also Julia Kristeva, "On the Women of China," *Signs* 1: 1 (Autumn 1975): 57–81; Josette Féral, "China, Women and the Symbolic: Interview with Julia Kristeva," *Sub-Stance* 13 (1976): 9–18; and Kristeva, *About Chinese Women* (New York: Urizen Books, 1977).

4. "This Sex Which Is Not One," a translation of the title essay of *Ce sexe qui n'en est pas un* (Paris: Editions de Minuit, 1977), appears in *New French Feminisms*, ed. Elaine Marks and Isabelle de Courtivron (Amherst: Univ. of Massachusetts Press, 1980). "When Our Lips Speak Together," Carolyn Burke's translation of "Quand nos lèvres se parlent," (*Ce Sexe . . .*), is forthcoming in *Signs* 6:1 (Autumn 1980).

5. The only English-speaking feminist theorist to undertake a reconsideration of Freud has been Juliet Mitchell, whose *Psychoanalysis and Feminism* (New York: Pantheon, 1974) appeared when most of her American readers were opposed to the terms of her analysis.

6. For a sociological analysis of Lacan's significance in France, which, however, does not discuss the implications of his work for feminists there, see Sherry Turkle, *Psychoanalytic Politics: Freud's French Revolution* (New York: Basic Books, 1978).

7. "Visual Pleasure and Narrative Cinema," *Screen* 16: 3 (Autumn 1975): 7.

8. The term was proposed by Jeffrey Mehlman, the editor of *Yale French Studies* 48 (1972), to suggest differences between the French and American interpretations.

9. Lacan's dictum, "The unconscious is structured like a language," should perhaps be understood metaphorically. On his use of linguistics, see Anika Lemaire, *Jacques Lacan* (London: Routledge and Kegan Paul, 1977), pp. 38–64.

10. For a fuller account of the Name-of-the-Father in relation to the Oedipus complex, see Lemaire, *Lacan*, pp. 78–92, and Martha Noel Evans, "Introduction to Jacques Lacan's Lecture: 'The Neurotic's Individual Myth,'" *Psychoanalytic Quarterly* 78 (1979): 386–404.

11. The subtitle of Rich's groundbreaking study, *Of Woman Born* (New York: Norton, 1976); although Rich is not centrally concerned with psychoanalysis, her observations have numerous affinities with the French writers discussed in this article.

12. Julia Kristeva. *La Révolution du langage poétique* (Paris: Editions du Seuil, 1974). For a useful account of Kristeva's special use of the term "semiotic" ("*le* sémiotique" rather than "*la* sémiotique"), see Philip E. Lewis, "Revolutionary Semiotics," *Diacritics* 4: 3 (Fall 1974): 28–32. For the following abbreviated account of the semiotic and the symbolic, I am greatly indebted to Alice Jardine, who further clarifies their functioning in her papers, "Theories of the Feminine: Kristeva," delivered at the Modern Languages Association Annual Convention, New York, 1978, and "In Pursuit of the Speaking Subject: Logos and Locus in Woolf and Wittig," delivered at the Northeastern MLA Meeting, Albany, New York, Spring 1978. Any errors in interpretation are, however, entirely my own.

13. If the semiotic expresses itself in the infant's world as babble, rhythm, melody, and gesture, then in the adult's it returns in word play, prosodic effects, nonsense, and laughter—all relatively uncensored traces of the unconscious.

14. On the mirror stage in relation to language, see Lemaire, *Lacan*, pp. 78–81, 176–79.

15. Jardine, "The Speaking Subject," p. 5.

16. Some feminists have criticized Kristeva for her association of the semiotic with the maternal. However, she is not attempting to define an "essence" of the female, but rather to understand the processes of signification and to expand the realm of the signifiable; see Jardine, "Theories of the Feminine," pp. 5–6.

17. Kristeva used this phrase in a discussion of women's writing in relation to the avant-garde, in "Postmodernism?", a lecture delivered at the Modern Language Association Forum on Postmodernism, December 1978.

18. In *Tel quel* 74 (Winter 1977): 39–49.

19. *Of Woman Born*, p. 225.

20. Ibid., p. 226.

21. Ibid., p. 220.

22. One reason for this apparent lack of dialogue may be that American and French theoretical discourses are quite dissimilar in style as well as assumptions. While American scholars are trained to work within the language of their disciplines, Kristeva, like many French intellectuals, draws

ideas from a variety of different fields and interweaves disparate methodological codes.

23. Paris: Editions de Minuit, 1979.

24. Rachel Blau DuPlessis, "Washing Blood," *Feminist Studies* 4:2 (June 1978): 1. This essay introduces the very rich special issue entitled "Toward a Feminist Theory of Motherhood," which does not, however, examine recent French theories on the subject.

25. *Of Woman Born,* p. 226.

26. Virginia Woolf, *A Room of One's Own* (New York: Harcourt, Brace and World, 1929), p. 88; DuPlessis cites this phrase in "Washing Blood," p. 1.

27. "One of the Difficulties of Psychoanalysis," in *Character and Culture* (New York: Collier, 1963), p. 189.

28. See, for example, Karl H. Pribram and Merton McGill, *Freud's 'Project' Reassessed* (New York: Basic Books, 1976).

29. For further explanation of the differences between French and American psychoanalysis, and the greater radical potential of the former, see Juliet Mitchell, *Psychoanalysis and Feminism* (New York: Pantheon, 1974); Louis Althusser, "Freud and Lacan" in *Lenin and Philosophy* (*Monthly Review*, 1971); *French Freud, Yale French Studies* 48, edited by Jeffrey Mehlman; and Jane Gallop, "The Ghost of Lacan, the Trace of Language," *Diacritics* 5:4.

30. This paper appears in the English translation of *Ecrits* (New York: Norton, 1977).

31. For a fine critical reading of the more and the less phallocentric moments in Freud's notion of castration, see Jean Laplanche, "La Castration, ses précurseurs, et son destin" *Bulletin de Psychologie* XXVII:311, 312, 314.

32. Paris: Flammarion, 1970. All quotations are from the translation by Jeffrey Mehlman, *Life and Death in Psychoanalysis* (Baltimore: Johns Hopkins, 1976).

33. Paris: Presses Universitaires de France, 1968. Translated by D. Nicholson-Smith, *The Language of Psychoanalysis* (New York: Norton, 1974).

34. For an excellent discussion of the import of this and Abraham's work in general from an implicitly feminist viewpoint, see Peggy Kamuf, "Abraham's Wake," *Diacritics* 9, 1 (Spring 1979): 32–43. Coincidentally, *Yale French Studies* 55–56 (*Psychoanalysis and Literature*) has an article by Lacan on Hamlet. The two pieces together would provide an interesting contrast on the two psychoanalysts.

35. Felman puts forth a similar argument for Lacan, holding that his language is poetic rather than discursive, in "La méprise et la chance," *Arc* 58 (1974). This issue of l'*Arc*, a special number on Lacan for which all the contributors are women, also includes one of Irigaray's critiques of Lacan. For a further discussion of this *Arc* and Lacan's relation to women, see Jane Gallop, "The Ladies' Man," *Diacritics* 6:4.

Part III
The Language of Difference: Female and Male in Speech and Literary Production

Audre Lorde

Poetry Is Not a Luxury

The quality of light by which we scrutinize our lives has direct bearing upon the product which we live, and upon the changes which we hope to bring about through those lives. It is within this light that we form those ideas by which we pursue our magic and make it realized. This is poetry as illumination, for it is through poetry that we give name to those ideas which are, until the poem, nameless and formless—about to be birthed, but already felt. That distillation of experience from which true poetry springs births thought as dream births concept, as feeling births idea, as knowledge births (precedes) understanding.

As we learn to bear the intimacy of scrutiny, and to flourish within it, as we learn to use the products of that scrutiny for power within our living, those fears which rule our lives and form our silences begin to lose their control over us.

For each of us as women, there is a dark place within where hidden and growing our true spirit rises, "Beautiful and tough as chestnut/stanchions against our nightmare of weakness" and of impotence.

These places of possibility within ourselves are dark because they are ancient and hidden; they have survived and grown strong through darkness. Within these deep places, each one of us holds an incredible reserve of creativity and power, of unexamined and unrecorded emotion and feeling. The woman's place of power within each of us is neither white nor surface; it is dark, it is ancient, and it is deep.

When we view living, in the European mode, only as a problem to be solved, we then rely solely upon our ideas to make us free, for these were what the white fathers told us were precious.

But as we become more in touch with our own ancient, black, non-European view of living as a situation to be experienced and interacted with, we learn more and more to cherish our feelings, and to respect those hidden sources of our power from where true knowledge and therefore lasting action comes.

At this point in time, I believe that women carry within ourselves the possibility for fusion of these two approaches as keystone for survival, and we come closest to this combination in our poetry. I speak here of poetry as the revelation or distillation of experience, not the sterile wordplay that, too often, the white fathers distorted the word poetry to mean—in order to cover their desperate wish for imagination without insight.

For women, then, poetry is not a luxury. It is a vital necessity of our existence. It forms the quality of the light within which we predicate our hopes and dreams toward survival and change, first made into language, then into idea, then into more tangible action. Poetry is the way we help give name to the nameless so it can be thought. The farthest external horizons of our hopes and fears are cobbled by our poems, carved from the rock experiences of our daily lives.

As they become known and accepted to ourselves, our feelings, and the honest exploration of them, become sanctuaries and fortresses and spawning grounds for the most radical and daring of ideas, the house of difference so necessary to change and the conceptualization of any meaningful action. Right now, I could name at least ten ideas I would have once found intolerable or incomprehensible and frightening, except as they came after dreams and poems. This is not idle fantasy, but the true meaning of "it feels right to me." We can train ourselves to respect our feelings, and to discipline (transpose) them into a language that matches those feelings so they can be shared. And where that language does not yet exist, it is our poetry which helps to fashion it. Poetry is not only dream or vision, it is the skeleton architecture of our lives.

Possibility is neither forever nor instant. It is also not easy to sustain belief in its efficacy. We can sometimes work long and hard to establish one beachhead of real resistance to the deaths we are expected to live, only to have that beachhead assaulted or threatened by canards we have been socialized to fear, or by the withdrawal of those approvals that we have been warned to seek for safety. We see ourselves diminished or softened by the falsely benign accusations of childishness, of nonuniversality, of self-centeredness, of sensuality. And who asks the question: am I altering your aura, your ideas, your dreams, or am I merely moving you to temporary and reactive action? (Even the latter is no mean task, but one that must be rather seen within the context of a true alteration of the texture of our lives.)

The white fathers told us, I think therefore I am; and the black mother in each of us—the poet—whispers in our dreams, I feel therefore I can be free. Poetry coins the language to express and charter this revolutionary awareness and demand, the implementation of that freedom. However, experience has taught us that the action in the now is also always necessary. Our children cannot dream unless they live, they cannot live unless they are nourished, and who else will feed them the real food without which their dreams will be no different from ours?

Sometimes we drug ourselves with dreams of new ideas. The head will save us. The brain alone will set us free. But there are no new ideas still waiting in the wings to save us as women, as human. There are only old and forgotten ones, new combinations, extrapolations and recognitions from within ourselves, along with the renewed courage to try them out. And we must constantly encourage ourselves and each other to attempt the heretical actions our dreams imply and some of our old ideas disparage. In the forefront of our move toward change, there is only our poetry to hint at possibility made real. Our poems formulate the implications of ourselves, what we feel within and dare make real (or bring action into accordance with), our fears, our hopes, our most cherished terrors.

For within structures defined by profit, by linear power, by institutional dehumanization, our feelings were not meant to survive. Kept around as unavoidable adjuncts or pleasant pasttimes, feelings were meant to kneel to thought as we were meant to kneel to men. But women have survived. As poets. And there are no new pains. We have felt them all already. We have hidden that fact in the same place where we have hidden our power. They lie in our dreams, and it is our dreams that point the way to freedom. They are made realizable through our poems that give us the strength and courage to see, to feel, to speak, and to dare.

If what we need to dream, to move our spirits most deeply and directly toward and through promise, is a luxury, then we have given up the core— the fountain—of our power, our womanness; we have given up the future of our words.

For there are no new ideas. There are only new ways of making them felt, of examining what our ideas really mean (feel like) on Sunday morning at 7 A.M., after brunch, during wild love, making war, giving birth; while we suffer the old longings, battle the old warnings and fears of being silent and impotent and alone, while tasting our new possibilities and strengths.

Rachel Blau DuPlessis and Members of Workshop 9

For the Etruscans: Sexual Difference and Artistic Production—The Debate over a Female Aesthetic

Thinking smugly, "She shouldn't be working on Woolf." What?

1964. "Doesn't she know that she'd better not work on a woman?" Why was I lucky to know this and what was the threat? Dickinson? Nin? I bought her book, I threw it out. What!

Didn't want it, might confront

> The great difficulties in understanding the language do not
> spring from an inability to read the script, every letter of which is
> now clearly understood. It is as if books were discovered, printed
> in our own Roman letters, so that one could articulate the words
> without trouble, but written in an unknown language with no
> known parallels.
>
> Ellen Macnamara, *Everyday Life of the Etruscans*, p. 181
>
> myself.

Stein says we no longer have the words people used to have so we have to make them new in some way but women haven't had them at all and how can you deconstruct a language you never constructed or it was never constructed by others like you, or with you in mind? How can we have a continuous time a continuous present if we never had a past so what is language to me will it help me discover my life.

Frances Jaffer, poet

1979. The general feeling of the dream was that I was free of the testers; however, I was entirely obligated to take and pass their test.

1965. My big ambition, my hemmed space. Her uncompromising, oracular poems. Her fluid, web-filled writing. Her dream life, surfacing.

Do we have something here? or is the female aesthetic simply an enabling myth? Fish on one foot, hook on the other, angling for ourselves. Woolf: catching "something about the body." Crash.[1] "MOM!" "WHAT!" "You never buy what *I* like! Only what YOU like!" (Fig Newtons) At this rate it will take me ten years, not ten weeks.

A golden bough. The torch is passed on. His son clutches his hand, his crippled father clings to his back, three male generations leave the burning city. The wife, lost. Got lost in burning. No one knows what happened to her, when they became the Romans.

She became the Etruscans?

> Even so, there is nothing to prevent those with a special aptitude
> for cryptography from tackling Etruscan, which is the last of the
> important languages to require translating.

> James Wellard, *The Search for the Etruscans*, p. 192

For some reason I can imitate a sheep rather well, a nasal and effective baaa beeh beeh. When I do this, often the sheep answers. After a round exchange of bleating, sheep becomes suspicious.

My bleats have not the right nuance. Of course. You are not a sheep, you don't sound like a sheep. Sheepish, I am sheepish and embarrassed to mention this

that for me it was always the herding. The herding, the bonding, the way you can speak their language but also have a different language or different needs so hard to say this. Always: I have heard this story from many places—they bond and clump outside your door and never "ask you to lunch" or they talk and be wonderful, lambent, but when you walk up "they turn away" or "they turn on you, teasing, making sexual jokes"

all headed in the same direction, herding and glistening of course some don't. But it has been difficult for these to separate from the rest. Probably the reward system?

Then our disguises. The sexuality, the knife-edge brilliance, the dowdiness, the evasion, the embarrassments, the imprecisions, the deferments; smug primness with which there is no dialogue, combativeness straight into malice. Invisibility, visibility, crossing the legs, uncrossing them. Knights in shining amour. Daddy to the rescue. "Imposing" sex on the situation. "Not imposing" "sex" on the "situation." "Doesn't she know she'd better not work on a woman?" She'd better now work on a woman. "In that grove wander sheep whose fleeces shine with hue of gold. (goad) I bid you take a wisp from the wool of their precious fleece." (*Amor and Psyche*, the second task.)[2] The golden fleece. The golden bough. The female quest?

Frankly, it was *The Golden Notebook* (1966).

Since the sixties I've recognized that my own oppression derived from patterns of social domination internalized so thoroughly that I will never be able to break with them: my competitiveness, my need for the approval of male authority figures, my ability to delay gratification forever in the interest of success—not untypical of women academics, I think.

Sara Lennox,
Department of German,
University of Massachusetts

I remember one preceptor who brought her little white dog to school and trotted it up and down the 4th floor of Hamilton Hall. Mary had a little lamb. What delightful, charming, adorable girls!

Now did I go downstairs, now did I cut up a pear, 8 strawberries, now did I add some cottage cheese thinking to get some more or even some ricotta at the Italian Market so that I could make lasagna so that when B. comes back from NYC he would have something nice and so I wouldn't have to cook again for days; now did I put some sugar on the fruit and then fill the sugar bowl because it was almost empty, now did I go down to the washing machine and did take out two bathroom rugs, clean for the first time in a year, hang on the line, now I did and do wonder that my style repeats key words in a swaying, repetitive motion. Deliberately breaking the flow of thought, which was beginning to come, and with pears, strawberries. The temptation of Eve was fruit, but that's funny, silly. The temptation of Mary, lambs.

Thinking that *they* followed *you* to school.

Throughout the ages the problem of woman has puzzled people of every kind—. . . You too will have pondered over this question in so far as you are men; from the women among you that is not to be expected, for you are the riddle yourselves.[3]

A special aptitude for cryptography.

That dogs and cats acumulated, another dog, another cat. The animal self, the humanoid monkey, there also. All the animals, and I knew they were thirsty. They were mine, and were very thirsty. I had to give them

Put full bowls down, so all the animals can come drink

Something I call an emotional texture, a structural expression of mutuality. Writers know their text as a form of intimacy, of personal contact, whether conversations with the reader or with the self. Letters, journals, voices are sources for this element,

> see "no reason why one should not write as one speaks, familiarly, colloquially."[4]

expressing the porousness and nonhierarchic stances of intimate conversation in both structure and function. Like *Orlando*, like Griffin's *Voices*, like *The Golden Notebook*, these may be antiphonal, many-voiced works, beguilingly, passionately subjective, seeing emotional commitment as an adventure. (as our form of adventure?)[5]

Anaïs Nin and June Miller make contact in a voice, the voice of women exploring, repetitive and supportive. "What a secret language we talk. Undertones, overtones, nuances, abstractions, symbols. Then we return to Henry with an incandescence which frightens him."[6] Holding, honing that voice is Nin's task; the laser of her vocation: "to find a language for intuition, feelings, instincts which are, in themselves, elusive, subtle and wordless."[7]

> "addressing the reader, making herself and her reader part of the narrative . . . an offhand, conversational manner"[8]

I find myself more and more attracted to the porous, the statement that permits interpretation (penetration?) rather than positing an absolute. Not vagueness—I want each component to be clear—but a whole that doesn't pretend to be ultimate, academic.[9]

Meaning, not positing oneself as the only, the sol(e) authority. Sheep of the sun. Meaning, a statement that is open to the reader, not better than the reader, not set apart from; not seeking the authority of the writer. Not even seeking the authority of the writing. (Reader could be writer, writer reader. Listener could be teacher.)

A workshop report which strives to be collective, experimental, different— these model out for us possibilities which we may be able to conceive as revolutionary.

Sara Lennox

Assuming for the moment. That this description—that we can find these traits and name them. One way of proving that the aesthetic can exist would be to find reasons for the existence of this poetics in the gender experiences specific to women, in sexual difference. Deena Metzger speaks of a denial of competition and aggression in women, suggesting that these lead to nonhierarchic forms of mutuality.[10] But this seems incomplete, because female competition of course exists (jealous, "she's said it all" when I heard Christiane Makward; smug, "she should know better than choosing to work on a woman"), wherever there are special rewards for some women at the expense of others. Or just because we are no better than anyone else. Adrienne Rich suggests that motherhood is just such a communal, dialogue-filled experience, and the "shared subjectivity" of that relationship is a gender-based source for structures of mutuality in women's writing.[11] Jean Baker Miller gives a parallel but broader interpretation. Women's lives, she argues, are shaped by nurturance and women take both donor and recipient roles, using tactics of giving and receiving. The dual roles can imply this porous, open structure.[12] (But could as easily suggest dramatic, dialogue form—why does it not?) (because the different roles are not agon-istic?)

The second trait: both/and vision. This is the end of the either-or, dichotomized universe, proposing monism (is that really the name for what we are proposing?) in opposition to dualism, a dualism pernicious because it valorizes one side above another, and makes a hierarchy where there were simply twain.

> a " 'shapeless' shapeliness," said Dorothy Richardson, the
> "unique gift of the feminine psyche." "Its power to do what the
> shapely mentalities of men appear incapable of doing for them-
> selves, to act as a focus for divergent points of view." ". . . The
> characteristic . . . of being all over the place and in all camps at
> once. . . ."[13]

I find a both/and vision moves me most when it is in motion, that is, when dialectic, when born of shifts, contraries, negations, contradictions; when linked to personal vulnerability. When it is essay, and sermon. I want to embrace movement, not fetishize positions. (I don't mean: be opportunistic, and slide.) Structurally, a writing might say different things, not settle on one, which is final. This is not a condition of "not choosing," for choice exists in what to represent, and in the rhythms of presentation. It is nonacademic; for in order to make a formal presentation, one must have chosen among theses: this is the rhetorical demand. One cannot, in formal argument, say both yes and no, if yes and no are given equal value. Either one or the other has got to win. But say, in a family argument? where both, where all, are right? generates another model of discourse.

Rich talks of a new epistemology. "As a woman thinking, I experience no such division in my own being between nature and culture, between my female body and my conscious thought."[14] A reintegration of physical and emotional knowing with rational understanding. Our own "unified field."

The discovery that mind and body are one! (and matter and energy are one)

Frances Jaffer

but also, always in motion. Structure

"must accommodate itself to the shifting perspectives of the writer's observing mind."[15]

Lessing has built a story precisely on this activity, an either-or opposition, which becomes the both/and vision of the female aesthetic. "Dialogue" between one man, one woman who have prototypical traits of masculinity and femininity. He: the tower, is nihilism, the abyss, rigidity, isolation, and control; is courage, reason, and a sickness. The absolutist stubbornness of refusing emotional comfort and security because of the need to impose on his psyche, on his whole being, his unbending intellectual position. Therefore, uncompromising. She: the leaf, a vulval shape in opposition to the phallic tower. She has an irrational happiness, sensuality, pleasure and openness to community. She has common sense, does not drive a philosophical position to the end and bind herself to it.

Having a double self, being able to experience both sides of a dichotomy, is highly valued in Lessing's world. The woman has that skill far more than the man. For while Lessing is at pains to assert "that he had been the other, through her, just as she had, through him," nevertheless the story does not show this. The woman has the power and pain of being neither "one thing [n]or the other"; she says that "what I think contradicts what I feel," but all is pleasure.[16] At the end, experiencing these polarities, she is poised, filled with his deadness, fear, and fragmentation. It is dirt and disgust, yet at the same time, she holds the talismanic leaf of wholeness which incorporates dichotomy. The female mode of seeing holds to one side of a polarity (a "feminine" side) yet is simultaneously that force which includes and transcends male nihilism and rationality. A constellated, integrative form. This vision contains feminine, transcends masculine, asserts female as synthesis. Makes me very nervous. This structure is parallel to the double status of Mrs. Ramsay in Lily's painting (and in

Woolf's *To the Lighthouse*), as one side of the masculine-feminine polarity, fit only to be surpassed; at the same time, as that stroke in the middle, the one unifying lighthouse stroke, which is love and ambition, mother and child, death and pleasure, the female synthesis.

> "A constant alternation between time and its 'truth,' identity and its loss, history and the timeless, signless, extra-phenomenal things that produce it. An impossible dialectic: a permanent alternation: never the one without the other. It is not certain that anyone here and now is capable of it. An analyst conscious of history and politics? A politician tuned into the unconscious? A woman perhaps. . . ."[17]

Or the tones of Woolf's essay *Three Guineas*. One voice is the trial tone and it is rational, legalistic, pursuing points exactly to their logical conclusion. The other tone is discursive, inventing characters, sympathetic, exploring every little nook and cranny. Facts are found through anecdote, not from authority. The first of these voices is masculine, insofar as males have monopolized the terms of law and trial. But when the voice goes beyond laws into the True Law on which to base her life, the voice moves from masculine to female: the Antigone reference ripens, and we talk of women defying the laws of the state. With the feminine, chatty, entertaining voice, the same process occurs. The statements are entirely adversary. This voice moves beyond the feminine into the female: a heroic, intransigent, but unauthoritarian voice which combines reason and emotion, logic and defiance. And the vow, or credo of that work, the formation of the society of outsiders, occurs in the female voice.

> The Etruscan language presents difficulties to the scholar. It can be easily read (the alphabet is of Greek extraction, and the sound value of the signs is known), but, with the exception of only a few words, the vocabulary is not understood.

The Columbia Encyclopedia

Again, the synthetic both/and vision, the contradictory movement between the logically irreconcilable, must have several, multiple causes. Perhaps it is based on the bisexual oscillation between mother and father. For me, one of the climaxes of Nancy Chodorow's analysis is the notion that the Oedipal configuration occurs differently in girls and boys and that because of the way the sexes are reproduced in the family, women have a different object relational experience than men. Women retain men as erotic objects and women as emotional objects; there is an oscillation between mother and father, and a bisexual triangle—mother, father, girl, which differs drastically from the intrapsychic structure of males.

I have felt something of the cheap, Korvette's version of this structure: conflict avoidance. Everybody is right. Can't choose, mother, father. Feel like a chameleon, taking coloration.

Another source is the (relative) freedom women have to draw on both brain hemispheres. Nondominant groups seem to be given a kind of off-hand permission to exercise the socially nondominant hemisphere (in our case, right brain), or more rarely to achieve a balance of the two. Women of achievement may have a parallel, equal development of both hemispheres because they undergo "male" socialization while they also have been marginalized; that would explain the prevalence of both/and vision in Richardson, Woolf, Lessing.

Insider-outsider social status will also help to dissolve an either-or sense of dualism. For the woman finds she is two irreconcilable things: an outsider by her sexual position, by her relation to power; an insider (if middle class) (but how? on her own terms? attached to husband?) by her social position. She is both. Her ontological, her psychic, her class position are double. This is, therefore, the motion of her brain. How then could she neglect to invent a form which produces this incessant, critical, splitting movement. To invent this form. To invent the theory for this form.

From this perspective, our personal, social and historical experience is seen to be shaped by *the simultaneous operation* of relations of work and sex, relations that are systematically bound to each other—and always have been so bound. . . . Feminist thought regards the sexual/familial organization of society as integral to any conception of social structure or social change. And conversely, it sees the relation of the sexes as formed by both socioeconomic and sexual-familial structures *in their systematic connectedness*.[18]

Following this, the female aesthetic will produce art works that incorporate contradiction and nonlinear movement into the heart of a text.

must here snatch time to remark how discomposing it is for her biographer that this culmination and peroration should be dashed from us on a laugh casually like this; but the truth is that when we write of a woman, everything is out of place—culminations and perorations; the accent never falls where it does with a man.[19]

An art object may then be nonhierarchic (an observation which Sheila de Bretteville makes about quilts): showing an "organization of material in fragments," breaking hierarchical structures, making an even display of elements over the surface with no climactic place or moment; having the materials "visually organized into many centers."[20]

Monique Wittig's *Les Guérillères* is thus a form of verbal quilt.[21] We hear her lists, her unstressed series, no punctuation even, no pauses, no setting apart, and so everything joined with no subordination, no ranking. It is radical parataxis. Something droning. Nothing epitomizes another. If fruits are mentioned, many are named, for unlike symbolism, where one stands for the many, here the many stands for the many. Hol-Stein. Mimesis here has a moral point; multiplicity is a form of democracy.

May also be a form of sexuality, that multi-focal female body and its orgasmic capacity, where orgasms vary startlingly, and are multiple. Instead of one (two) pointed climaxes.

"She began to think about 'climax' and 'anticlimax'—what these [formal categories] mean in female and male associations."[22]

April 28

The Body, and its language, which is of course, all language. These notions of writing from the neck up. All that fear, almost terror, of the women at Barnard, of being caught in the old stereotype—woman/body, mother/ nature, an inferior kind of mind, and flee it sisters deny it don't be trapped by our own feminism.

But that male body, how IT dominates the culture, the environment, the language. Since 3,000 B.C. in Sumeria, Tiamat's monsters again and again, and every myth an effort to keep the sun rising. Save the sun, everybody, from the watery deeps, the dark underneath it must go—Into—Every night into such dangers, such soft inchoate darkness, what will become of it, will it rise again will it will it rise again? The language of criticism: "lean, dry, terse, powerful, strong, spare, linear, focused, explosive"—god forbid it should be "limp"!! But—"soft, moist, blurred, padded, irregular, going around in circles," and other descriptions of our bodies—the very abyss of aesthetic judgment, danger, the wasteland for artists! That limp dick—an entire civilization based on it, help the sun rise, watch out for the dark underground, focus focus focus, keep it high, let it soar, let it transcend, let it aspire to Godhead————

Frances Jaffer

Multi-climactic, multiple centers of attention: *Orlando, Between the Acts* where the cows, the rain intervene in art, where the border between life and art is down, is down!

The antiauthoritarian ethics occurs on the level of structure. We call all this "new"; I reuse the word continually;

> sense of a "new form" a "new book" a "new way of writing" layered, "strudled," Metzger says[23]

that use of the word "new" which, in the modern period, has always signaled antithesis to dominant values. These traits, already cited, are one with the almost thrilling ambition to write a great, encyclopedic, holistic work, an ambition to get everything in, inclusive, reflexive, monumental.

The form of the journal. Interesting that for Woolf it was the form of a journal, while for Pound it long ago began as a "rag bag," a market mess of fish but became the form of *Analects*, of codes. *The Cantos.* For Williams, it was the form of antiquarian history—compendia, compilations, local lore, wonders. *Paterson.* For both the male writers, the form is like a city or a world; for the woman it is like her desk. Her desk. Which implies both the hemmed space and the personal scope.

Moreover there looms ahead of me the shadow of some kind of form which a diary might attain to. I might in the course of time learn what it is that one can make of this loose, drifting material of life; finding another use for it than the use I put it to, so much more consciously and scrupulously, in fiction. What sort of diary should I like mine to be? Something loose knit and yet not slovenly, so elastic that it will embrace anything, solemn, slight or beautiful that comes into my mind. I should like it to resemble some deep old desk, or capacious hold-all, in which one flings a mass of odds and ends without looking them through.[24]

Reading my journal later, reading my journal later, it is not random, those connections. It is intentional; I knew more, said more than I knew. The writing is in the interstices, the meaning is between. It is created in the relationship between, between the elements, they are put down at random, and they flare up they are not said by chance; they know better. I allow this to enter, the blankness which I don't control.

We intend to find ourselves. In the burning city.

3/3

She thinks I should try to separate my two types of writing but I told her I'm not editing anything. Not editing. Once in a while if I think something is too private. Take it out before I let anybody see it. But only if really. I told her. The point is no editing. This is a Method. She was surprised. After reading

all the way through to 2/25 and she said Oh it's a process; I thought it was a
production, more of a production.

No production. A discipline, no productions, keep it up, like burning,
hopefully, the protective covering off the mantle on the Aladdin lantern. Blue,
light a match to it, don't touch the mantle with the matchstick, just flame,
burn off the blue. Then it glows white. Itself. Really, more of a yellow. On
Being Blue, all my friends like it, many do, I can't stand it, show-off boys,
Look Ma No Hands.

Burn off, out, the incorporated paralyzing history.[25]

Frances Jaffer

The holistic sense of life without the exclusionary wholeness of art. These
holistic forms: inclusion, nonselection because selection will exclude some
important piece of data, or evidence, or knowledge that the writer is not
yet sure the meaning of. Holistic work: great tonal shifts, from polemic
essay to lyric. A self-questioning, the writer built into the center of the
work, the questions at the center of the writer. And uncensored: love,
politics, children, dreams, close talk. A room where clippings paper the
walls

of course I am redescribing *The Golden Notebook* again. Again.

The artwork produced with this poetics distinguishes itself by the fact that
it claims a social function and puts moral change and emotional vulnerability at the center of the experience for the reader. The artist figures in
Kunstlerromans by women cannot complete or produce their artwork until
processes of growth have been completed, and the growth usually involves
empathy, unguardedness, admission of pain to the self.[26]

Rich makes this kind of argument about feminist criticism: that the critic
is not, and should not show herself to be, untouched. Rather, if the critic
needs the work, the terms of her need and of her passion for an author's
writing should be inscribed in the work, for the authenticity of need
creates response.[27]

The fact that there is an imbedded, fictional artwork with a process of
creation visible in Gilman, in Lessing, in Woolf, in Olsen, in Stead—along
with the interruptions, hiatuses, emotional weight and tender risk, the
difficulty of voicing, and the achieved statement—this tends to demystify
the activity of an artist. Not a godlike creator, conjuring the work *ex nihilo*

from an inexplicable crucible, instead portraits of the female artist show the artist as a producer, a maker of a social product.

Sometimes the distinction between high art and artisanal products is blurred. The female artist (in the fictional realm. And in real life?) takes the fruitful from artisan—the idea of art as a gift to another, art for personal use, art personally intervening, a message

> Shaker Spirit Drawings, mainly by women, are inspired messages and guides to the recipient, as illustrated visionary poems

> Mrs. Ramsay, in *To the Lighthouse*, that *boeuf en daube* an old recipe from her grandmother

> Margaret Laurence, author of *The Diviners*, speaks of folk seers divining for water, of folk singers whose words unite Canada's disparate ethnic strains

> Zora Neale Hurston's *Their Eyes Were Watching God*, in which black folk life is the metaphor for community participation and psychic wholeness

> Woolf, using anonymous ballads, nonsense, nursery rhymes, ancient counting-out songs as the climax—the climax!—of book after book

> Alice Walker's mother's garden

all ways of talking about the missing makers of high art. And about actual art. A manifestation of "social creativity."[28]

> Although the language seems to contain both Indo-European and non-Indo-European elements as well as traces of ancient Mediterranean tongues, it cannot be classified into any known group of languages.
>
> *The Columbia Encyclopedia*

The female artist depicted in works by women writers is a site for the reconciliation of domestic sphere and vocation. A "daughter" artist draws her inspiration from an ambivalently regarded maternal muse who has such female skills as healing, bricolage, nurturing, empathetic care. The daughter transposes that artistry to a relatively permanent form.

When should I offer a possible definition? The female aesthetic: the production of formal, epistemological, and thematic strategies by members of the group Woman, strategies possibly born in contradiction, overdetermined by two elements of sexual difference—by women's psychosocial experiences of gender asymmetry and by women's historical status in an (ambiguously) nonhegemonic group.[29]

The term "artistic production"? it emphasizes that any text *is* made, tries to show those forces that went into its making, the materials the artist faced, collected, resolved. The word production points to the fact that an artist works with cultural and social materials that s/he did not invent.[30]

Radical teacher's technique: bring an object to class and have students describe it. After "it is red," and so forth, one can discover that describing the qualities of an isolated thing-in-itself severs the object from its relations; that every thing can be seen better as a culmination of processes. A process of makings, human choice and necessity. Any work is made to meet itself at the crossroads. Any work is a strategy to resolve, transpose, reweight, dilute, arrange, substitute contradictory material from culture, from society, from personal life. And the female aesthetic? Various strategies of response and invention shared by the group Woman at distinct moments.

To epitomize some of this: Nin's diary. Her diary as form and process is a stratagem to solve a contradiction often present in acute form for women: a contradiction between the desire to please, making woman an object, and the desire to reveal, making her a subject. The culturally sanctioned relationship to art and artists which Nin imagines (ornament, inspiration, sexual and psychic reward) is in conflict with the direct relationship she seeks as artist, colleague, fellow worker.

And Nin's diary as fact and artifact transposes these conflicting forces. It reveals and protects simultaneously, allowing her to please others while also attempting honesty to herself. The diary is a work which Nin deploys in a unique fashion which indicates its strategic function. Whenever the diary is attacked, whenever Otto Rank or Henry Miller deny that writing it is the proper or fruitful use of Nin's energies, whenever she is criticized for her compulsion in continuing it, she immediately seduces that critic by means of the diary, showing *to* him some specially prepared section written *about* him. Thus the diary can be either public or private; Nin will choose to reveal or to conceal what it says based on the balancing of double (sometimes duplicitous) needs to please herself and placate another.

Kill the diary, they say; write novels; but when they look at their portrait, they say: "That is wonderful."[31]

She can therefore organize the satisfaction of creating in a private way, without competing with men, but when she needs to win their approval for her pursuits, she is able to convince them how necessary and important is her work.

The diary is also a synthesis between permanent and impermanent achievements. All of Nin's traditionally feminine creations are ephemeral: a generous and subtle atmosphere, artful and astonishing clothes, arresting, courtesan manners. Woman's body, woman's face, the prime aesthetic objects which we create, are ultimate symbols of transience, as countless *carpe diem* conceits testify. Nin notes a wonderful moment when even she is overwhelmed by her own decor.

to walk into my house is to walk into down, into color, into music, into perfume, into magic, into harmony. I stood on the threshold and reexperienced the miracle, forgetting I had made it all, painted the walls Chinese red, turquoise. . . .[32]

Culturally valued male creation, on the other hand, has most often taken shape in permanent forms: books, statues, paintings, architecture. The diary is then a solution to another aspect of the conflict between the feminine, nurturing woman and the self-actualizing artist: it is permanence in impermanence. A diary was a mode of expression in which she did not at first seek permanence (i.e. publication); therefore, it did not violate the unwritten rules about feminine achievement whose limitations Nin simultaneously endured and transformed.

The "psychosocial experiences of gender asymmetry" in my definition have barely to be glossed in the context of these assembled papers. But existing, these differing experiences produce different consciousness, different cultural expression, different relation to realms of symbols and to symbol users.

And therefore, and therefore, there is a female aesthetic

> "from this [difference in priorities between men and women]
> spring not only marked differences of plot and incident, but
> infinite differences in selection, method and style"[33]

as there is a male:

> "It is a commonplace of criticism that only the male myths are
> valid or interesting; a book as fine (and well-structured) as *Jane
> Eyre* fails *even to be seen* by many critics because it grows out of

experiences—events, fantasies, wishes, fears, daydreams, images of self—entirely foreign to their own."[34]

Female aesthetic begins when women take, investigate, the structures of feeling that are ours. And trying to take them, find also the conflict between these often inchoate feelings, coded as resistances, coded as the little animals, and patriarchal structures of feeling—romantic thralldom, female fear of male anger, debility.

This question about the female aesthetic leads to another: is it necessary for a writer consciously to see herself as producing formal, epistemological, and thematic strategies? Or, is it necessary for a writer to see herself and her work in terms of the "two elements of difference . . . psychosocial experiences of gender asymmetry and . . . historical status in an (ambiguously) non-hegemonic group"? (Women authors who say they are anti-feminist are surely responding to their "difference," so the "possible definition" here offers some grounds for discussion. But what about writers who don't seem to take up these questions at all? Are there such?)

And then another question: in what sense is all this (the "strategies") produced by membership in (rather than members of) the Group Woman? Here, I think of Macherey: "In what relation to that which is other than itself is the work produced?"[35]

Louise Yelin, critic

I am watering cattle who are thirsty. There is a frisky white one, looks Indian, with a friendly pointed face and horns with pink tips. She pokes me, playful, calling attention to herself. I know she is mine. But one thing I must immediately establish. That she is not male. I pick up her little curtain. There. Fleshy pink udders. She is pink and white. I have watered the cattle and they have given me a guide.

Yet it is also clear that there would be reasons not to see the female aesthetic. Why might someone object?

First, a desire to say that great art is not made by the factoring out of the sexes, is "androgynous" as Woolf uses the term in *A Room of One's Own*. The desire, simultaneously, to state that greatness is (must be?) universal, and that anything else is special pleading.

> "Women, said Rank, when cured of neurosis, enter life. Man enters art. Woman is too close to life, too human. The feminine quality is necessary to the male artist, but Rank questioned whether masculinity is equally necessary to the woman artist."[36]

This seems to have been the neo-Freudian formula of (at least) *les années vingt, trente*. D. H. Lawrence said the same kind of thing to H. D. You should be woman; you must not take the male point of view.[37] Women may then respond with a strategy of self-chosen, proud ghettoization (Richardson's "feminine psyche") or may respond as Woolf did. For in 1929, in that neo-Freudian context, Woolf's androgyny position is a triumph, rejecting the ghettos, stating that woman's art contains the man, contains the woman. And in all this, where is the female aesthetic? It is both strategies of response and invention; either the "feminine psyche" (our version of *négritude*) or "great art is androgynous"—a sexual fusion transcending sex.

Then, there is the desire at all costs to avoid special pleading, anything that looks like women have gotten by because of our sex; this is an earlier generation's rejection of the courtesan for the firm-chinned professional, who does not call attention to her sex. "Doesn't she know she'd better not work on a woman" speaks to this fear of being ghettoized. Of being patronized. But it happened, anyway. Any way. Probably the reward system?

Also, the desire not to seem inferior, insofar as "female=inferior" is a familiar equation. This is a highly understandable fear, since the differentials between men and women traditionally have been structured to valorize one side at the expense of the other. Differentials (which are potentially neutral, even pleasant, sources of joy) are made to be "preferentials": yet another way of marginalizing women.

Another fear: that any aesthetic is bound to be misused, misappropriated, and this one is surely extremely vulnerable, with its blurring of all the elements we have firmly regarded as setting art apart: blurring between art and life, blurring between social creativity and "high" art, blurring between one's journal and one's poem, blurring between the artifact (aesthetic distance) and the experience (personal and social distance or sheer immersion), a blurring between composition which has been chosen, and the speaking voice, which can gabble, garble, say anything: all meaning a possibility that some artists will write badly.

"looseness quickly becomes slovenly. A little effort is needed. . . ."

I see that the next day I wrote in my journal,
   "The trouble with trying to create art from up close is that one has to know exactly what one is doing: both the psychological truth and the form used to convey it. Most women's fiction these days fails because a simple truth

    is rushed toward with a sloppy example, generic language. Accuracy and
    patience are the keys."
So this is from the inside, that is, from my point of view as someone reading
a bit of women's writing and trying to do it myself. (What I don't quite
understand is that your aesthetic seems to apply wonderfully to the spate of
women's novels that have come out of the women's movement, while most of
the books you speak about are pre-movement works, which really only have
these characteristics to a lesser degree.)

I have to tell you that I don't love one single novel that has come out of the
1960–70s women's movement. I don't think there is anyone concerned enough
about either language or the real details of daily life. My sense is that
everyone has been in a rush. (I feel in this rush too sometimes. Who wants to
be a poor nobody at 40?) Sure there are wonderful moments here and there in
different pieces of fiction. But no one has been concerned enough about
FORM for me.

I would love someone (me?) to write a wonderful novel using the aesthetics
you speak of—that are in my little list—mutuality, porousness, intimacy,
recontacting a both/and, using both sides of the brain, non-hierarchic, anti-
or multi-climactic, wholistic, lacking distance . . . perhaps didactic—but I
think this person would have to be a particularly strong and careful artist.
Just as a ballet dancer who does parodies or looks clumsy on stage must have
already passed through every capacity to be graceful and on target. I think
that feminists, feeling rightly oppressed by the existing forms—and the way
they were rammed down their throats—often want to overthrow form
altogether. They don't read the classics, don't study how a novel or poem is
made. They think something will come out naturally, and it does. But it's not
beautiful, much of the time. Another analogy: the yogi works for years and
years to be able to relax, let go. When a writer jumps in and lets go, she or he
is simply sloppy.

None of this conflicts with what you said in our workshop. It's just another
vantage point. Or perhaps also a corrective, in the sense that I fear too many
women can take your aesthetic and churn out crap in three easy lessons.
While to do the things you speak of, one has to be so fine, so self-knowing, so
precise, so careful. It's really like petit-point to get so close to one's subject,
keep it porous, open, multi-climactic, and still keep it art.

Carol Ascher, writer

The art of artlessness is so much harder than the art of artfulness. To be
able to keep many strands in the hand—and all being the strand of art! If

a writer takes literally the notion—the myth—of including everything just exactly as it happened, then is produced an account book, a record of unexamined principles of selection, the illusion that natural rhythms transfer themselves into art. We have had innocence already: some of Pound's *Cantos*, Richardson's *Pilgrimage*; structurally innocent in hopeless ways. Woolf spoke of an art form *based on* the journal, not the journal itself.

But why think of this? every literary movement has its terrible writing, which does not invalidate the movement? Yes, of course, but a literary movement that calls the institution, the axioms of art into question, seems more slidy, more dangerous than a movement that does not challenge the boundaries of Art. Thinking back over the 1950s, the Hall, Pack, Simpson anthology and other manifestations of that aesthetic, I guess there were as many inauthentic poems written then, but they did not sprawl in the way that some of ours do. Were just mold at the core.

Perhaps this aesthetic comes at the end of a struggle, not at the beginning. Is an arrival, not a point of departure. That may be why I cite Woolf, Lessing—not our contemporaries. That may be why the *Kunstlerromans* that present this aesthetic often do so in an imbedded, fictional artwork, held by a formally exacting, structurally nuanced frame.

As for further disincentives to seeing a female aesthetic: the imperative not to focus on the sexual, since sexual categories have always been used so destructively; our use of them, is it not "playing into their hands"?

> "Another reason women don't like their art to be seen through their bodies is that women have been sex objects all along and to let your art be seen that way is just falling right back into the same old rut."[38]

Objections to seeing a female aesthetic might then be based on the fear of being trapped (retrapped), held, colonized, but now by women, obliged to write "this way," not another. When we have just begun to get free.[39]

The possible characteristics of a female aesthetic that you suggested seemed familiar and true certainly of my own work. Therefore I wanted to find out something else and maybe offer something else (if only doubts or impatience with the deterministic limitation of non-hierarchic, layered, "porously intimate," subjective, etc. work) but felt disappointed and thwarted.

Mira Schor, painter

Because locating just one set of strategies, my description is (description, not prescription) necessarily incomplete. It does not move toward, does not deal with an absolutely parallel, but aesthetically opposing use of oracular, gnarled, compressed tactics, suggesting "the difficulty of articulating the experience at all."

> "There emerges a complex psychology of linguistic parsimony related to a professional identity. Haunted by the specter of the sweet-singing 'poetess,' the woman poet may have come to the 'modern' style of the early decades of the twentieth century by a very different route than her male counterparts."[40]

So this essay points to one set of responses. One among several differing possibilities. The actual traits matter on one level, but the function performed is crucial in this analysis. I propose no absolute. Although the essays I write lie precisely within this range

> incorporating metonymy and metaphor into one structure. Roman Jakobson associated the metonymic pole of language (juxtaposition) with prose, with fiction, and the metaphoric pole (resemblance) with lyric poetry. In this essay, juxtaposition, resemblance both occur; linear and constellated forms co-exist; the work is analytic and associative at once.

my poetry differs greatly, suggesting "the difficulty of articulating the experience at all."

But to test whether this is true, whether what you are calling women's themes do appear in women's writing, would you not have to use objective methods, devise objective tests of this knowledge?

Mirra Komarovsky, sociologist, in the workshop

We have covered the whole range of the anxiety inherent in scientific methodology—from Mirra [Komarovsky]'s comment that the individual scholar must prove her thesis to have validation for more than herself (by the "objective," "scientific" method), to my concern that to define a female aesthetic is to establish a rigid norm of female creativity, which repeats the patriarchal tyranny of an "objective" absolute way of doing things.

Lou Roberts, coordinator, Women's Studies,
Sarah Lawrence College

Can I prove it? I can prove that different social groups produce differences in cultural expression. I can prove that women are a social group. I can point to examples of differences in our relation to the symbolic order and in our cultural expression.

But I cannot prove that only women, that women only, use this aesthetic.[41] And this failure is actually the strongest proof of all.

Women are "(ambiguously) non-hegemonic" because as a group, generally we are outside the dominant systems of meaning, value, and power "which are not merely abstract, but which are organized and lived."[42] To talk of society and culture as involving "hegemonic" practices does not mean that a hegemony is a ten-ton stone that comes out of the sky and crushes you into shape.

Hegemony is not to be understood at the level of mere opinion or mere manipulation. It is a whole body of practices and expectations; our assignments of energy, our ordinary understanding of the nature of man [*sic*] and of his world. It is a set of meanings and values which as they are experienced as practices appear as reciprocally confirming. It thus constitutes a sense of reality for most people in the society ... but ... is not, except in the operation of a moment of abstract analysis, in any sense a static system.[43]

A hegemony is a social and psychic "process" whose "internal structures are highly complex," which does not simply exist, or exist to crush all comers, but rather has "continually to be renewed, recreated, defended and modified" as well as "continually resisted, limited, altered, challenged."[44]

Women, in a nonhegemonic position, barred from the cultural institutions of renewal, defense, and modification:

In Europe, with the development of the university system from the twelfth century on, the "mainstream" of European intellectual history was carried on without us. The clerical status of scholars in the middle ages automatically excluded women from the formal training which would fit them for the learned world and, as you know, this situation was not rectified in modern times until very recently. Moreover, self-study was for most women virtually impossible because the formal training was carried on in a highly technical Latin (and Greek after the humanist movement), unintelligible even to the ordinary literate lay person. There is, I think, a reasonable argument to be made that this resulted in the creation of an aesthetic which was in many respects feminine. All over Europe, vernacular literature, particularly French literature, began its development at about the same time that the universities began theirs. Students of that large grab-bag grouped together as "courtly love" literature are well aware that its development depended heavily on the patronage of women and that some of its enduring output was even written by women—Marie de France, the Comtesse de Die and some others. Similarly there is a rather large body of mystical literature composed by women barred from the study of theology or philosophy which was either dictated in vernacular to be translated by a clerk (the corpus of Hildegarde of Bingen) or written directly in vernacular. By the 14th and 15th century, the work of Margery of Kemp, Christine de Pisane and others was widely disseminated and deeply influential in the development of the vernacular corpus.

This work tends to be "popular" and often highly personalized. Margery Kemp's book is the first autobiography in the English language. No doubt students of the history of literature could carry this argument much further along into modern times. The modest point I wished to make myself is that it is possible to suggest that at least once before in Western history, women did make a substantial contribution to the formation of what might—in the context of our workshop—be called a non-patriarchal language, the "mother-tongue" which they spoke in contrast to the formal language of scholars.

Jo Ann McNamara, Department of History, Hunter College

proceed to alter and challenge.

Along with what Raymond Williams calls hegemony, there are other, parallel, but not dominant, forms of social practice. Residual social practice is often conservative, or, better, traditional; for women, this would be an ethnic, kinship-based, female-centered community, male-centered family. Emergent forms are "new meanings and values, new practices, new significances, and experiences" which "are continually being created." Williams's analysis extends emergent social practices (which in classical Marxist theory had been reserved exclusively for new classes—a relatively rare historical event) to "sources of real human practice which [the dominant mode] neglects or excludes." I would like to suggest that while hegemonic values assert and assume that women belong to the majority, to the hegemony, in fact women are virtually always (ambiguously) nonhegemonic. A great number are residual, drawing on the practices of "some previous social formation" like religion, the male-centered family, and stereotypical femininity, however newly packaged.[45] Whoever "we" are—you reading this, thinking it—we are emergent— "alternative or oppositional to the dominant elements."[46]

Why are women as a group "(ambiguously) non-hegemonic"? A woman may be joined to a dominant system of meanings and practices by her race (say, she is white), but not by her sex; she may be joined via her class (upper middle), but not her sex. She may be joined through her sexual preference (say she is heterosexual), but not her race or sex. She may be working class, black, and a woman—then unambiguously nonhegemonic in ascribed status. But that person might be internally oriented toward hegemonic norms (June Jordan's poem "If you saw a Negro lady" speaks to this possibility).

"(Ambiguously) non-hegemonic." For women, then, existing in the dominant system of meanings and values that structure culture and society may be a painful double dance, clicking in, clicking out—the divided consciousness. For this, the locus classicus is Woolf.

Again if one is a woman one is often surprised by a sudden splitting off of consciousness, say in walking down Whitehall, when from being the natural inheritor of that civilisation, she becomes, on the contrary, outside of it, alien and critical.[47]

That shifting focus, bringing the world into different perspectives, is the ontological situation of woman because it is our social situation, our relationship to power, our relationship to language.

Why have I based this essay on a Marxist theory of culture? It is the best way to explain—and not to explain away—the idea that the "female aesthetic" is not exclusively female. For the "female aesthetic" is simply a version of that aesthetic position that can be articulated by any nonhegemonic group.

And neatly enough, other nonhegemonic groups are used as analogies for women's writing. Russ talks about nineteenth-century Russian fiction (in comparison with Western European writing) as showing traits parallel to writing by women:

"pointless" or "plotless" narratives stuffed with strange minutiae, and not obeying the accepted laws of dramatic development, lyrical in the wrong places, condensed in the wrong places, overly emotional, obsessed with things we do not understand, perhaps even grotesque.[48]

So what we here have been calling the female aesthetic turns out to be a specialized name for those practices available to those groups—nations, sexes, subcultures, races, emergent social practices (gays?)—which wish to criticize, to differentiate from, to overturn the dominant forms of knowing and understanding with which they are saturated.

As this manifesto about *négritude*:

Consider then the white European standing before an object, before the exterior world, before Nature, before the *Other*. A man of will, a warrior, a bird of prey, a pure act of watching, the white European distinguishes himself from the object. He holds the object at a distance, he immobilizes it, he fixes it. Equipped with his instruments of precision, he dissects it in a cold analysis. Moved by the will to power, he kills the Other and, in a centripetal movement, he makes it a means to use for his own practical ends. He *assimilates* it. . . . The black African is first of all in his colour as if standing in the primordial night. He does not see the object, he *feels* it. He is like one of those worms of the Third Day, a pure sensing field. Subjectively, at the end of his sensing organs, he discovers the Other. . . . So the black African sympathizes with, and identifies with the Other.[49]

For blacks excluded from a Western world of whiteness will affirm a connection to rhythms of earth, sensuality, intuition, subjectivity and this will sound precisely as some women writers do.

High modernists are the most problematic nonhegemonic group, because they make a conservative, sometimes *fascisante* criticism of bourgeois culture, with "positive" values ascribed to hierarchical social order, sometimes buttressed by religion, but also, astonishingly, linked to peasant-based agriculture (as opposed, of course, to our urban, industrial morass). These writers constitute themselves as a group-against, whose common bond is opposition to the social basis on which their world in fact rested. Modernists show the strength of a politicized culture based on a shared revulsion to World War I, on one hand, and to the Russian Revolution on the other. This set of individuals with residual values (Eliot, Pound, Yeats, Lewis, Lawrence) depends on responses to a once-existing, and somewhat mythologized social basis in peasantry and patriarch. Aristocrat, head, *il capo*. A revolution from the right.

Literature by women, in its ethical and moral position, resembles the equally nonhegemonic modernism in its subversive critique of culture. (Not from a residual, conservative position, no need to admire that.) In women's writing, as in modernist, there is a didactic element, related to the project of cultural transformation, of establishing values. In women's writing, as in modernist, there is an encyclopedic impulse, in which the writer invents a new and total culture, symbolized by and announced in a long work, like the modern long poem.

And women are beginning to produce just such works, often in the encyclopedic form of essay, compendia, polemic, collage (*Woman and Nature, Silences, Gyn/Ecology*).[50]

> I imagine Hélène Cixous fits here, too, and her dissertation was even on Joyce! Perfect.

Then, literature by women, in its phenomenological position, is associated with postmodernism, and with the democratic tolerance and realism of a Williams or the generative blankness and fecundity of Stevens. Any list of the characteristics of postmodernism would at the same time be a list of the traits of women's writing: inwardness, illumination in the here and now (Levertov); use of the continuous present (Stein); the foregrounding of material (Woolf); the muted, multiple, or absent telos; a fascination with process; a horizontal world; a decentered universe where "man" (indeed) is no longer privileged. But women reject this position as soon as it becomes politically quietistic, as it can and does. For when the phenomenological exploration of self-in-world turns up a world that devalues the female self, when that exploration moves along the tacit boundaries of a social status quo, she cannot just "let it be," but must transform values, rewrite culture, subvert structures.

As my political analysis became more sophisticated, as I became a Marxist shaped by the Frankfurt School and then a feminist, I was able to present a theoretical explanation for my intuitions: (**they were mine, and were thirsty**) *I understood that, at least for middle-class Americans under late capitalism, the form* (structure, "language") *of the culture is the sustaining force of social domination. But, though I was implicated in those forms, I also knew— perhaps because of my somewhat marginal position as a woman, a petite bourgeoise?* (**She became the Etruscans?**)—*that I recognized these forms to be not self-evident and natural, but intolerable and changeable, and that occasionally I discovered, and tried to transmit through my teaching and writing,* (**printed in our Roman letters**) *examples and visions of how things could be other and better.*

It's been clearer and clearer to me, since I've been a feminist, (**some ricotta at the Italian Market**) *that we women were never completely integrated into the structures of capitalism ("ambiguously non-hegemonic") and that our difference,* (**a vulval shape**) *whether only psycho-social or somehow biological as well, has given us a privileged position* (**horns with pink tips**) *from which to rebel and to envision alternatives. What's difficult, though, is to believe in those glimmers,* (**entirely obligated to take and pass their test**) *to hold fast to them, even more, to model them out and explore them—and this is the importance to me of women's writing.* (**like her desk. Her desk**) *If it's* *really the forms, the language, which dominate us, then disrupting them as radically as possible can give us hope and possibilities. What I'd like to try to understand and explain to other people* (**you yourselves are the riddle**) *is how the* form *of women's writing is, if ambiguously,* (**of double [sometimes duplicitous] needs**) *nonetheless profoundly revolutionary (as are, in their confusing ways, modernism and post-modernism, also written from positions of marginality to the dominant culture).*

But I've also been thinking recently that we need a writer who would be for feminism what Brecht was for modernism—who understands, to put it a little crudely, that literature doesn't change things, people *do.* (**a process of makings, human choice and necessity**) *Our literature and thinking still seem quietistic to me, in that they require us to understand and respond, but not to act on our understanding, certainly not to act collectively.* (**a room where clippings paper the walls**) *Moreover, I think we haven't even grasped the most radical implications of feminism for a theory which mediates back to practice: that we have a vision which men have barely glimpsed of what dialectical thought is really about—about a total, specific, feeling and thinking subject, present in her interaction with "objective" materials, overcoming the division between thought and action.* (**The golden bough. The golden fleece. The female quest?**)

I've been angry recently that, while theory proliferates, we have given up on what was compelling about the late sixties and early seventies—that feeling of infinite possibility which challenged us to think and live differently. So many of those experiments have fallen by the wayside, victim to the economic situation and our own discouragement and exhaustion.

Sara Lennox

Exploration not in service of reconciling self to world, but creating a new world for the new self:

> "If I take over the world, let it be to disposses myself of it immediately, let it be to forge new links between myself and the world."[51]

given the revolutionary desire (that feeling of infinite possibility) for a nonpatriarchical order, in the symbolic realm and in the realms of productive, personal, and political relations.

May-June 1979
for the Etruscans

Notes

With special thanks to Carol Ascher, Frances Jaffer, Sara Lennox, Jo Ann McNamara, Lou Roberts, Mira Schor, and Louise Yelin for their responses. The Jaffer material is excerpted from the as yet unpublished manuscript *Procedures for Having Lunch.* Citations about the Etruscans come from Ellen Macnamara, *Everyday Life of the Etruscans* (London: Batsford, 1973), from James Howard Wellard, *The Search for the Etruscans* (New York: Saturday Review Press, 1973), and from *The New Columbia Encyclopedia*, ed. William H. Harris and Judith S. Levey (New York: Columbia Univ. Press, 1975).

1. Virginia Woolf, "Professions for Women," *The Death of the Moth and Other Essays* (New York: Harcourt Brace Jovanovich, 1942), p. 240.
2. Erich Neumann, *Amor and Psyche: The Psychic Development of the Feminine. A Commentary on the Tale by Apuleius* (Princeton: Princeton Univ. Press, 1971; first published 1952). This work contains a root metaphor for me, worked out in more detail in "Psyche, or Wholeness," *Massachusetts Review* 20: 1 (Spring 1979): 77–96.
3. Sigmund Freud, *New Introductory Lectures on Psycho-Analysis*, tr. W. J. H. Sprott (New York: W. W. Norton & Company, Inc., 1933), pp. 154–55.
4. Virginia Woolf, "Mrs. Thrale," *The Moment and Other Essays* (New York: Harcourt Brace Jovanovich, 1948), p. 52.
5. B. Ruby Rich, "The Films of Yvonne Ranier," *Chrysalis: A Magazine of Women's Culture* 2 (1977): 115–127. "Melodrama, and by extension even soap opera, deal in the drama of emotional involvement, substituting the risks of emotional commitment for the risks of physical danger" (p. 119).
6. Anaïs Nin, *The Diary of Anaïs Nin, Volume I (1931–1934)*, ed. Gunther Stuhlmann (New York: The Swallow Press and Harcourt, Brace and World, Inc., 1966), p. 34.
7. Ibid., p. 276.
8. Julia Penelope Stanley and Susan J. Wolfe (Robbins), "Toward a Feminist Aesthetic," *Chrysalis* 6 (1978): 68.
9. Anita Barrows, "Form and Fragment," typescript, pp. 7–8, for the projected Lydia Koolish anthology concerning women writers on women's writing (Ph.D. thesis, Stanford University).
10. Deena Metzger, "In Her Image," *Heresies: a feminist publication on art & politics*, May 1977, p. 2.
11. I cannot now trace this reference.
12. Jean Baker Miller, *Toward a New Psychology of Women* (Boston: Beacon Press, 1976), p. 51.
13. Dorothy Richardson, "Leadership in Marriage," *New Adelphi* 2nd series, 2: 4 (June-August 1929): 247.
14. Adrienne Rich, *Of Woman Born: Motherhood as Experience and Institution* (New York: W. W. Norton and Company, Inc., 1976), p. 95.
15. Stanley and Wolfe, "Feminist Aesthetic," p. 67.
16. Doris Lessing, "Dialogue," *A Man and Two Women* (New York: Popular Library, 1958), pp. 239, 241.

17. Julia Kristeva, *About Chinese Women*, tr. Anita Barrows (New York: Urizen Books, 1977; published as *Des Chinoises* in 1974), p. 38.
18. Joan Kelly, "The Doubled Vision of Feminist Theory: A Postscript to the 'Women and Power' Conference," *Feminist Studies* 5:1 (Spring 1979): 222, 223.
19. Virginia Woolf, *Orlando* (New York: New American Library, 1960; originally published 1928), p. 204.
20. Sheila de Bretteville, cited in Metzger, "Image," p. 5.
21. Tr. Peter Owen (New York: Avon Books, 1973; first published in French, 1969).
22. Frances Jaffer, "Review of Ellen Moers' *Literary Women*," *Chrysalis* 1 (1977): 136.
23. Metzger, "Image," p. 7.
24. Virginia Woolf, *A Writer's Diary*, ed. Leonard Woolf (New York: Harcourt, Brace and Company, 1953), p. 13 (1919).
25. Compare this passage from *A Writer's Diary*, 1919: "Not to play the part of censor, but to write as the mood comes or of anything whatever, since [on rereading] I was curious to find how I went for things put in haphazard, and found the significance to lie where I never saw it at the time. But looseness quickly becomes slovenly. A little effort is needed . . ." (p. 13).
26. Rachel Blau DuPlessis, "Female Artist and Fictional Artwork in Twentieth Century Women's Writing," unpublished typescript.
27. Elly Bulkin, "An Interview with Adrienne Rich: Part II," *Conditions: Two* (1977): 61. Compare the following from Lucy Lippard, *From the Center: Feminist Essays on Women's Art* (New York: E. P. Dutton & Co., Inc., 1976), p. 2: "From inside, from where I live, there is a new freedom to say how I feel, and to respond to all art on a far more personal level. I'm more willing to be confessional, vulnerable, autobiographical, even embarrassing, if that seems called for."
28. Silvia Bovenschen, "Is There a Feminine Aesthetic?" *New German Critique* 10 (Winter 1977): 111–137, partially reprinted in *Heresies* 4 (Winter 1978). In a peroration, Bovenschen asks, "What if we alternated painting our faces with painting on canvas? What if we turned recipes into poetry?" The figure of the female artist creates a mechanism for the fusion Bovenschen speaks of.
29. This was the definition I offered at the Barnard Conference to Workshop 9.
30. Terry Eagleton, *Marxism and Literary Criticism* (London: Methuen & Co., Ltd., 1976), pp. 68–69.
31. Nin, *Diary I*, p. 301.
32. Ibid., p. 241.
33. Virginia Woolf, "Women Novelists," *Contemporary Writers* (New York: Harcourt Brace Jovanovich, 1965), p. 27. Review dates from 1918.
34. Joanna Russ, "What Can a Heroine Do? Or Why Women Can't Write," in *Images of Women in Fiction*, ed. Susan Koppelman Cornillon (Bowling Green, Ohio: Bowling Green University Popular Press, 1972), p. 14.
35. Pierre Macherey, *A Theory of Literary Production* (Boston: Routledge and Kegan Paul, 1978), p. 154.

36. Nin, *Diary I*, p. 309.
37. H. D., *Bid Me to Live (A Madrigal)* (New York: Grove Press, Inc., 1960).
38. Lippard, *From the Center*, p. 92.
39. I have attempted to give a historical approach to strategies women might choose, and to suggest that all the strategies, even those that contradict each other, may be grouped under the term "female aesthetic." However, it is also clear that, at this moment, certain strategies prevail. Confirmation of the concentration of contemporary and modern women on the strategies I have enumerated can be found in Barbara Currier Bell and Carol Ohmann, "Virginia Woolf's Criticism: A Polemical Preface," in Josephine Donovan, ed, *Feminist Literary Criticism: Explorations in Theory* (Lexington: The Univ. Press of Kentucky, 1975), pp. 48–60, and in Melissa Meyer and Miriam Schapiro, "Waste Not/Want Not: Femmage," *Heresies* 4 (1978): 66–69.
40. Jeanne Kammer, "The Art of Silence and the Forms of Women's Poetry," in *Shakespeare's Sisters: Feminist Essays on Women Poets,* eds. Sandra M. Gilbert and Susan Gubar (Bloomington: Indiana University Press, 1979), p. 156.
41. Others who have attempted to account for the lack of sexual specificity of the female aesthetic offer several explanations. Josephine Donovan, "Feminist Style Criticism," in Cornillon, ed., *Images*, argues that there is a difference between male and female sentences; in one word: authority. Authority of tone. Since tone comes from social authority, a male writer projects firmness, directness, confidence. This is tempting (despite such exceptions as Lessing), but seems circular. Knowing that thus and such an author is male, one can respond to general authority, not to the specific stylistic traits of the passage. Donovan also argues that a major property of female writing is an interest in psychological realism, a concern for inner, almost subterranean events. However, Henry James, James Joyce, and D. H. Lawrence betray the same interest. Woolf is indeed analytic and selective in her *tropismes*. Stanley and Woolf (in the "Feminist Aesthetic" article) argue that men who use this mode are well out of the mainstream, are in the minority. Because the feminine mode is illegitimate, those men who use this mode are relatively few compared to the far greater number of male writers who do not. However, if few, the male writers implicated in this aesthetic are among the most influential, like William Carlos Williams or Robert Duncan. Finally, Woolf offers a clue, which has been very difficult for me to penetrate. In her essay "Romance and the Heart," on Dorothy Richardson, we begin well: "She has invented, or, if she has not invented, developed and applies to her own uses, a sentence which we might call the psychological sentence of the feminine gender. It is of a more elastic fibre than the old, capable of stretching to the extreme, of suspending the frailest particles, of enveloping the vaguest shapes" (*Contemporary Writers,* p. 124). But we learn immediately that "other writers of the opposite sex have used sentences of this description and stretched them to the extreme": and it is (I think) impossible to tell if she means the conventional "opposite sex" (women) or the sex opposite from the one she

is talking about (men). But this is a small problem to what follows: what distinguishes this woman's sentence. For "it is a woman's sentence, but only in the sense that it is used to describe a woman's mind by a writer who is neither proud nor afraid of anything that she may discover in the psychology of her sex" (pp. 124–25). Does this say that one can call this a woman's sentence only because it is producing a contents that deals with women? So a sentence or any formal and stylistic feature belongs to one sex or another by virtue of its social function.

42. Raymond Williams, "Base and Superstructure in Marxist Cultural Theory," *New Left Review* 82 (Nov.–Dec. 1973): 9. Williams acknowledges his debt to Gramsci.

43. Williams, "Base and Superstructure," p. 9.

44. Raymond Williams, *Marxism and Literature* (Oxford: Oxford Univ. Press, 1977), p. 112.

45. Williams, "Base and Superstructure," pp. 11, 13, 10.

46. Williams, *Marxism and Literature*, p. 124.

47. Virginia Woolf, *A Room of One's Own* (New York: Harcourt, Brace & World, Inc., 1929), p. 101. Compare Richard Wright's observation in 1956: "First of all, my position is a split one. I'm black. I'm a man of the West. These hard facts condition, to some degree, my outlook. I see and understand the West; but I also see and understand the non- or anti-Western point of view. . . . This contradiction of being both Western and a man of color creates a distance, so to speak, between me and my environment. . . . Me and my environment are one, but that oneness has in it, at its very heart, a schism." In *Présence Africaine* 8–9–10 (November 1956), the proceedings of the First International Conference of Negro Writers and Artists, cited in *The Black Writer in Africa and the Americas*, ed. Lloyd W. Brown (Los Angeles: Hennessey & Ingalls, Inc., 1973), p. 27.

48. Russ, "Heroine," pp. 14–15.

49. Léopold Sédar Senghor, *Liberté* I, cited in *Selected Poems/Poésies Choisies*, translation and introduction by Craig Williamson (London: Rex Collings, 1976), pp. 12–13. *Négritude* (a black aesthetic) is a highly controversial concept. Distinguished black writers and critics (Wole Soyinka, Ralph Ellison) oppose it; equally distinguished black writers and critics (James Baldwin, Senghor) embrace it.

50. Susan Griffin, *Woman and Nature: The Roaring Inside Her* (New York: Harper & Row, Publishers, 1978); Tillie Olsen, *Silences* (New York: Delta, 1978); Mary Daly, *Gyn/Ecology: The Metaethics of Radical Feminism* (Boston: Beacon Press, 1978).

51. Wittig, *Guérillères*, p. 107.

Sally McConnell-Ginet

Difference and Language:
A Linguist's Perspective

Rather than a single, unified topic, the title "Difference and Language" points to a cluster of related issues and questions. Let me begin by quickly "placing" both myself and my approach. My own scholarly perspective on language has been shaped by early training in mathematical logic and the philosophy of language and, more recently and more significantly, by my training and research in theoretical linguistics. My feminism grows out of a variety of personal and political factors, ranging from relatively early marriage and motherhood to fairly active participation in New Left political organizations during the 1960s. My feminist investigation of language has developed through teaching and research in an interdisciplinary Women's Studies Program. It has drawn as well from a growing network of friendships and contacts with other women (and some men) who are also approaching questions about the interaction of language and sex from a feminist starting point, though often from theoretical and methodological assumptions quite different from my own.[1] Not only has this interaction across traditional disciplinary boundaries led to new ways of looking at and finding out about women's experience, it has also been an important stimulus in leading me to somewhat different views of language and linguistics than I once had. I don't pretend to represent linguistics as a profession but only my particular subjective self, whose perspective on language owes much to the mutual influence of feminist concerns and formal linguistic training.

Linguistics is often defined as the science of language. As a "scientist" I ask different questions and have different aims and methods than those whose concern with language springs from more artistic or literary concerns. For example, I am interested in describing in precise detail the linguistic structures that people put to use in a wide variety of situations. Science is, of course, not only descriptive but also seeks to articulate explicitly and to test general principles that help explain the phenomena of ordinary (and extraordinary) life. We all know at some intuitive level that the socially dominant leave a more lasting imprint on the linguistic resources of their community than do subordinates. We also know that there are often "different" patterns of language use in the community that survive in spite of not being "approved" by those in control. *How* does this happen? What are the mechanisms through which language interacts with society and culture on the one hand, and with our inner mental and emotional life on the other? *Why,* for example, might women's relation to language be different from men's? What are the linguistic consequences of familiar and traditional arrangements between the sexes? What are the social and cultural consequences for women of familiar linguistic practices? Neither linguistics nor any other discipline can answer such questions, but it is now possible to begin to formulate them more carefully, as a first step in the systematic investigation of the connections between language and the political and psychological conditions of women's lives.

To be a scientist is not, in my view, to be "neutral," "objective," "value-free." All serious intellectual inquiry springs from human minds and feelings, develops in socially and culturally situated contexts of human activity. The questions we ask (or don't ask) reflect what we care about. Science, however, does not assume that the answers to those questions will be what we want them to be, that our feelings alone shape the world we share with other selves; or that our intuitions are always a reliable guide to understanding empirical phenomena. "Hunches" play a crucial role in the formulation of hypotheses. But these are seldom taken as adequate evidence in themselves because of their essentially "private" character. We must, of course, take our experience and our convictions seriously and not be led, for example, to distort or deny women's perceptions because they don't fit what is allowed by some orthodox "scientific" theory. Feminist scholars have suggested that many accepted theories and explanatory models are based on a male-centered view of human behavior and social life.[2] Bringing women into the picture gives a richer view of human experience, and women's own analyses of their experience offer critically important evidence which the male-dominated scientific community has too often ignored. Scientific methods and theories that cannot handle the phenomena that we recognize from our personal experiences are clearly inadequate. Feminist scholarship is beginning to reshape some of our conceptual frameworks and to develop new approaches to empirical investigation.

Science is "objective" in the sense that it strives to adduce publicly accessible evidence in support of an intersubjective, shared understanding of our world. Scientists do not conduct their inquiries in isolation. The world is extraordinarily complex, and scientific thought develops through a cooperative exploration of various kinds of phenomena. This necessary division of intellectual labor can lead to a sterile compartmentalization of human thought, with increasingly narrow and specialized fields accessible only to a few initiates. Specialized vocabulary can be very helpful but can also hinder communication with "noninitiates." There is also an unfortunate tendency for a kind of intellectual "imperialism" to take hold, for specialists to forget that their own work provides only a partial perspective on the world. In spite of these limitations, however, specialization does make possible a much deeper level of understanding of certain kinds of phenomena. Generally available linguistic categories and informal observations provide only a relatively superficial view of many aspects of experience. Collaboration can help keep boundaries open between different approaches. Specialists can distill some of their results for generalist audiences.

As a linguist interested in women's concerns, I have found it essential to draw on ideas originating in other disciplines as well as outside of academia. Yet I retain a basically linguistic approach: a view of language as a complex structured system that is somehow represented in each language-user's mind. The form will be slightly different for each user, though basically very similar; the major differences are likely to be in the vocabulary, the stock of words we have available. The basic system can be put to use in a variety of different ways: writing a poem, asking a riddle, giving a lecture on mathematics. Such uses don't comprise different languages in a linguist's sense of "language," although at least some of the differences among them may be characterized in linguistic terms. However, the whole spectrum of language *uses* provides evidence of the language *system* that underlies them, and also helps shape the system itself.

Thus, my first reading of "Language and Difference" suggests that the very concept of language, and what it means to explore it, will be different for a linguist, a poet, and a literary scholar. Our panel discussion at the conference—including all three—was self-reflexive: we exhibited differences not only in our personal starting points for thinking about language and its implications for feminist theory and practice, but also in our uses of language itself. Our vocabularies, our styles of discourse, differed. Such a panel does not—and should not—erase those differences, for it offers new potential for enriching our individual perspectives.

My second reading of "Language and Difference" is a sketch of one way in which the existence of difference, of opposition or contrast, has been taken as fundamental in the analysis of language. The address title *Ms.*, for example, is not just distinguished from *Mr.* by its gender-marking; *Ms.* enters into a more elaborate network of differences than *Mr.*, implying (at this particular stage in our history) a choice from the three-term set that also includes *Miss* and *Mrs.* This difference, however, is viewed against a backdrop of sameness or similarity: these forms can all serve as titles preceding a surname. Opposition, difference that "counts" linguistically, is understood relative to what are sometimes called paradigmatic connections. Linguistic analysis proceeds by opposing or contrasting elements that share a substantial portion of their linguistic properties, that are in important ways *not* different, the same. Linguistic meaning implies choices or alternatives: differences against a background of partial sameness. In my view, language is not a fixed structure but a constant interplay of actions and reactions that are interpreted relative to multiple and changing structural possibilities. Use of a title, for instance, can also be looked at in the light of a larger system of address options—last name only, first name only, nickname, epithet, or endearment.[3] In general, linguistic choices are only partially fixed: they are continually being created and transformed in dynamic processes of speaking and hearing, writing and reading.

I want to expand on the general methodological point that difference is interpreted relative to partial sameness in discussing my third reading of the title "Language and Difference": what is the relation between sexual difference and language and its use? This question generates two distinct though related questions. Do the sexes use language in systematically different ways? Is the language used about women and to women significantly different from that used about and to men? We also need to consider what is believed about such differences, what their psychological and social impact might be, how they are interpreted and evaluated within the linguistic community, and how and why they might be developed and maintained. We are just beginning to acquire some insight into such issues, but it is already clear that sexual difference and language interact in countless complex and subtle ways. Unless sexual difference is considered in the light of similarities that cut across sexual divisions, in a context of partial sameness, its interactions with language will either seem uninteresting or incomprehensible.

From one viewpoint, differences in the relation of the sexes to their language are relatively trivial. Both girls and boys acquire the language spoken around them in roughly the same way and, except in those few communities in which the sexes are rarely in contact, they come to recognize a basically common system. Still, the structural system— including the stock of vocabulary, grammatical constructions, and sound patterns—can be put to many different uses, and we can understand ways of speaking that we would never use. Thus, even within a basically common system, different people adopt characteristically different approaches to expressing themselves. In addition, and perhaps more importantly, the vocabulary we choose, the style of pronunciation, the sentence structures—all these formal details of "how" we say it—are potentially a part of "what" we say and are affected by such factors as the relative privacy of the occasion, the topic, how speakers assess the social relationships between themselves and their hearer, and so on. Factors of this kind operate for both sexes, and studies that look at sexual difference and language use must take into account the enormous variety of uses of language, the diverse contexts in which language users find themselves, and the vast array of aims they pursue through linguistic means. Even if the sexes had identical resources available—unlikely in most communities because of differences in social mobility, educational and occupational opportunities, networks of friends, and prescriptions on "proper" language use—the fact that our situations and aims are so often different might lead to certain kinds of difference in how women and men tend to use language.

For the developing child, language acquisition and linguistic experience may well play a major role in establishing notions of sexual difference. They may also help create and maintain ways of behaving and thinking that keep sexual differences so important in social arrangements and cultural ideologies. We don't know much about how language and its use frame the child's beliefs and expectations, but we do know that patterns of language use provide the basis for a rich and often very disturbing set of inferences about both differences between the sexes in society and culture and the values attached to such differences. It seems likely that covert messages about sexual differences could be at least as powerful as the overt messages, especially for the child whose experience is limited.

First the child observes how people (especially adults) speak to and of women and men, girls and boys. Girls with brothers, boys with sisters may tend to receive more frequent examples of this differentiation in speech directed toward them by adults, but most children in our culture spend a considerable portion of their adult-supervised time in contact with children of the other sex. In one household I know, the male child is frequently addressed by both parents as "son," the female as "honey" or "dear"—a small but potentially powerful message.

In general, girls and boys acquire not only very different conceptions of their roles (compare the partially similar verbs "to mother" and "to father," for example—and the absence, in most children's experience, of "to parent") but also different evaluations of themselves and their activities. Not only are many of the terms referring to women both specifically sexual and also negative, but, perhaps even more importantly, they tend to be *homogenized:* that is, differences among women tend to be obscured for the child by our linguistic practices. The originally elevated "lady" might seem to the child at first to be the mate of the grand "gentleman" and indeed is in some contexts. Yet, as Robin Lakoff has pointed out, mother may be a "cleaning lady" whereas father cannot be a "garbage gentleman."[4] Not only children but mature women are referred to and addressed as "girls;" "boys," on the other hand, learn that they will one day grow into manhood. Terms referring to men, in contrast, *do* retain their power to mark difference and individuality within the sex, but they tend to lose their sex-specificity, a linguistic reflex of the false *universalization* of masculinity and male experience. For example, when they go to school, girls have to learn that words like "man" and "he," which they first acquired in contexts of male reference, are sometimes to be interpreted as applying to human beings generally. Girls seem to believe this more than boys in interpreting others' uses but are more sensitive than their brothers to the potential exclusion and likely to eschew such forms in favor of options like "person," "she or he," singular "they," and the like.[5] Females may arrive at a more complex appreciation of sexual differences than males—and possibly also of the connection between forms and their meanings. Males may be led to view their own sex as a relatively unimportant feature of their identity, important only in differentiating themselves from females, whose sex is seen as a personal characteristic that overrides all other qualities.

The impact on the child of acquiring ways of speaking about the sexes will undoubtedly depend on many factors. At what age, in what situation, and from whom does one first acquire "motherfucker?" Which forms become part of one's actively used vocabulary and which remain passive? In what ways does the rest of one's experience support or contradict the "homogenization" of women, the "universalization" of men's experience?

Children of both sexes almost always have their first, primary linguistic interactions with an adult female, usually the mother. We don't know precisely what difference this makes, although it may help shape notions of appropriate speech *to* women and to men. The very young child typically encounters father as a relative stranger and may speak to him more "deferentially" and less "intimately" than to mother. Distance may lend a measure of authority and status to father. We have no idea how extensive such phenomena are, or, more importantly, what role they might play in shaping our later modes of speaking to women and to men. Yet the different roles of the father and the mother in the child's world provide one of the earliest sociolinguistic lessons in the modification of speech as a function of social relationships with those to whom one is speaking. A fruitful line of investigation might be to compare the development of skills in language used in those children reared by both parents with those reared mainly by the mother. To the extent that mother and father provide different models of language use, the child may take these as typical or expected of women and men, respectively.[6]

It is important, however, not to exaggerate the influence of parents on children's acquisition of particular ways of speaking. We know that once the child moves beyond the very early stages of confinement in the home, peer influence is generally the most important determinant of speech. For most children, the natural play groups that form are single-sex (although there are various interactions between the girls' and boys' groups and occasional cross-overs). The child may acquire ways of talking that are distinctive to its sex mainly through contact—just as I learned English rather than French because of my social environment. Yet the different ways are not, in these cases, sex-exclusive, and each sex interprets the other's styles, strategies, and favored patterns against its own assumptions. Some evidence suggests more collaborative strategies in girls' play groups ("Let's go") as opposed to more competitive in boys' ("Get outa here").[7] It is possible that in later interaction the competitor may try to interpret the collaborator as just an unsuccessful competitor. Again, seeing masculine experience as universal promotes the assumption that the expectations developed in male contexts cover the entire linguistic community. One can succeed in defining a situation as competitive without assent from coparticipants, whereas collaboration is not possible without agreement. Many studies of adults show that men tend in a variety of ways to "control" conversational interactions with women.[8] Of course, this is linked to other nonlinguistic mechanisms that support male dominance, but some women may be easily dominated by men in part because their view of conversation and their strategies for approaching it have been shaped in situations where resisting dominance was not a major concern. More studies of girls and women talking in peer-groups will help to clarify these issues.

Thus differences—and similarities—in the relation of the sexes to their language have important implications for understanding not only our participation in intellectual, artistic, and political activity but also our ordinary social lives. The mechanisms through which individuals come to use language as they do are remarkably similar. What varies are the social situations and the cultural values that frame our lives, as well as, of course, those distinctive individual capacities and those particular experiences that our accidental histories (including those dictated by our biology) provide. To understand sexual differences in relationship to language, it is essential to look at other kinds of sociocultural and psychological differences that cut across sexual boundaries and are connected to the uses of language, by identifying factors (relative power of speaker and hearer, for instance) that work in essentially the same ways no matter which sex they happen to characterize. These need not work in precisely the same way: gender meanings draw on and interact with other dimensions of significance. Linguistic indicators of hesitation, for example, may be heard as characteristic of "women's language" because women have learned this self-protective strategy as a defense against attack. The indicators may survive, however, in contexts where the strategy is not needed or is ineffective, because they now also play a role in symbolizing identity "as a woman." To understand how and why language is significant in our experience as women, we cannot focus on sex in isolation from the other factors that shape our lives.

The assumption that sexual difference outweighs all other factors ignores and devalues the differences among women and perpetuates the male-centered view of women as homogeneous. Some women create beautiful metaphors and poetic images, others are skilled at establishing and maintaining conversational ties, and others develop new vocabulary and theoretical discourse for describing and analyzing women's experience. For an individual woman, only some of these uses are genuine options: our abilities, concerns, and tastes will lead us to try to become skilled at only a fraction of the possible uses of language. But all our lives are enriched if we are fully integrated into a community that offers a wide range of kinds and styles of discourse. As Audre Lorde made so clear to us, "poems are not a luxury," nor, I would add, are the personal observations we share with intimates, or the theoretical frameworks we build to interpret scientific research. Social life depends on our going beyond the resources available to single individuals. To create a society and culture that takes women's interests and concerns seriously, we cannot afford to cede to men exclusive responsibility for any of the diverse functions language serves. The challenge, of course, is to put all those functions to work *for* women rather than against us—to move from static dichotomies and rigid hierarchizing differences to ongoing interactive and dynamic processes of fruitful differentiation in a context of feminist community. Language is the major means of linking individual selves and creating a culture that transcends our personal limitations by making use of all kinds of differences among users and uses of language.

Notes

1. I cannot list everyone but I must particularly mention Ruth Borker and Nelly Furman (in anthropology and literature, respectively), with whom I co-edited *Women and Language in Literature and Society* (New York: Praeger, 1980) and with each of whom I have had the great pleasure of team-teaching. Editing this book and reading many other papers, published and unpublished, greatly enriched my own thinking about language and the sexes. Correspondence and conferences have brought me into contact with many of the people involved in related work. I have had particularly fruitful exchanges with Barrie Thorne and Nancy Henley, coeditors of *Language and Sex: Difference and Dominance* (Rowley, Mass.: Newbury House, 1975) and with Cheris Kramarae, who is coediting a revised edition with them and who coauthored with them a review article, "Perspectives on Language and Communication," *Signs: Journal of Women in Culture and Society* 3:3 (Spring 1978): 638–51. Francine Frank, whose

"Women's Language in America: Myth and Reality" appears in *Women's Language and Style*, ed. Douglas Butturff and Edmund L. Epstein (Akron, Ohio: Univ. of Akron Press, 1978), pp. 47–61, has been a close colleague from linguistics, as has Patricia C. Nichols, whom I first met as a coparticipant in the *Conference on the Sociology of Languages of American Women,* proceedings edited by Betty Lou Dubois and Isabel Crouch (San Antonio, Texas: Trinity Univ. Press, 1976). Anthropologist Ann Bodine's work (see, for example, "Androcentrism in Prescriptive Grammar," *Language in Society* 4:2 [1975]: 129–46) helped arouse my interest, and she organized the symposium on Language and Sex Roles at the 1974 American Anthropological Association Meetings, at which I presented the initial version of what eventually became "Intonation in a Man's World," *Signs* 3:3 (Spring 1978): 540–59. For me, as for many others, Robin Lakoff's *Language and Women's Place* (New York: Harper Torchbooks, 1975) provided considerable stimulus when parts of it first appeared in 1972 in mimeographed form. Other books that incorporate influence from linguistics include Mary Ritchie Key, *Male/Female Language* (Metuchen, N.J.: Scarecrow Press, 1975), and A. P. Nilsen, H. Bosmajian, H. L. Gershuny, and J. Stanley, eds., *Sexism and Language* (Urbana, Ill.: National Council of Teachers of English, 1977). Selected papers from a section on Language and Sex, 9th International Congress of Sociology, August 1978, are being compiled by Cheris Kramarae and M. Schulz; J. Penelope (Stanley) and G. Valdés-Fallis are assembling papers presented at the December 1978 Modern Language Association; a generally perceptive nonacademic discussion of several issues is Casey Miller and Kate Swift, *Words and Women* (Garden City, New York: Anchor Press/Doubleday, 1976).
2. See Mary Brown Parlee's analysis of work in the psychology of women in the inaugural issue of *Signs* (1975), pp. 119–38, for examples. My "Intonation in a Man's World" and "Address Forms in Sexual Politics," in Butturff, ed., *Women's Language,* pp. 23–35, develop this general point with respect to analysis of the use of particular linguistic forms.
3. See my "Address Forms in Sexual Politics"; Cheris Kramarae's "Sex-Related Differences in Address Systems," *Anthropological Linguistics* 17:5 (1975): 198–210; Nessa Wolfson and Joan Manes, " 'Don't "Dear" Me!' ", in *Women and Language.* See also Una Stannard, *Mrs. Man* (San Francisco: Germainbooks, 1977), for an interesting discussion of the significance of women's names and titles.
4. See Lakoff, *Language and Women's Place.*
5. Wendy Martyna has done excellent research in this area, much of which is summarized in her "The Psychology of the Generic Masculine," in Mc-Connell-Ginet et al., *Women and Language.* Bodine's work is mentioned in note 1.
6. See Carole Edelsky, "Acquisition of an Aspect of Communicative Competence: Learning What It Means to Talk Like a Lady," in *Child Discourse,* eds. S. Ervin-Tripp and C. Mitchell-Kernan (New York: Academic Press, 1977), for a discussion of children's developing sense of stereotypic women's and men's speech.

7. Marjorie Goodwin, "Directive-Response Speech Sequences in Girls' and Boys' Task Activities," in McConnell-Ginet et al., *Women and Language*, reports such results. This paper is part of the much larger study of natural speech used by groups of working-class black girls and boys in Philadelphia that comprised her recent Ph.D. dissertation in anthropology at the University of Pennsylvania.

8. See, for example, Pamela Fishman, "Interactional Shitwork," *Heresies* 1:2 (May 1977): 99–101; and "What Do Couples Talk About When They're Alone," in Butturff, ed., *Women's Language*, pp. 11–22; Don H. Zimmerman and Candace West, "Sex Roles, Interruptions, and Silences in Conversation," in Thorne and Henley, eds., *Language and Sex*, pp. 105–29; and West and Zimmerman, "Women's Place in Everyday Talk: Reflections on Parent-Child Interaction," *Social Problems* 24 (1977): 521–29.

Naomi Schor

For a Restricted Thematics: Writing, Speech, and Difference in *Madame Bovary*

Translated by Harriet Stone

It is time to say out loud what has been whispered for some time: thematic criticism, which was given a first-class funeral a few years ago, is not dead. Like a repressed desire that insists on returning to consciousness, like a guilty pleasure that resists all threat of castration, thematic criticism is coming out from the shadows. This new thematic criticism is not, however, a nostalgic textual practice, a "retro" criticism, a regression to the styles (of reading) of the 1950s. Just as hyperrealism in painting is a return to the figurative passed through a minimalist grid, neothematism is a thematism passed through the filter of structuralist criticism. One could even argue that a certain structuralism, namely structural semantics, was in fact never anything but recuperation of thematism, a structuralist neothematism.

But it is not our purpose to study the persistence of thematics; the point is not, within the narrow framework of our study, to anticipate a history of contemporary criticism which is yet to be written. Rather it is a question of opening an inquiry into the continuity that links thematics, structural semantics, and even "poststructuralism." This very undertaking, this implicit valorization of continuity, is precisely what to our eyes constitutes thematics' characteristic, distinctive feature: I shall term thematic all textual practices that suffer from what might be called, in the manner of Bachelard, an Ariadne complex, all readings that cling to the Ariadne's thread ("fil conducteur"), whether it be the "synonymic chains"[1] of Barthes, the "chain of supplements"[2] of Derrida, or the "series"[3] of Deleuze. Be it vertical, horizontal, or transversal, the Ariadne's thread haunts the texts of Barthes, Derrida, and Deleuze, not in the typically structuralist form—that is, metalinguistic—of the Greimasian isotope, but in a poetic form: the thread ("fil") has become an extended metaphor. As Deleuze's "spider web,"[4] Barthes's "braid,"[5] and Derrida's "texture"[6] indicate, the relationship between the "textual" and the "textile"[7] is on its way to becoming one of the obsessive metaphors of current criticism. How are we to explain this obsession common to thinkers otherwise so different? One seductive hypothesis is that they all draw from the same source, namely Proust's metaphoric repertory. The following quotations from

Richard (on Proust), Derrida (on Plato), and Barthes (on the pleasure of the text) substantiate this notion:

> Thematization thus clearly resembles weaving. The interweaving of all thematic series assumes in the Proustian daydream the form of a net in which the matter of the work is caught, or that of a network, both innervational and cybernetic, that enables us to circulate in it from link to link, knot to knot, "star" to "star" with the utmost freedom; because "between the least significant point in our past and all the others there exists a rich network of memories offering a plethora of communications."[8]

> The dissimulation of the woven texture can in any case take centuries to undo its web: a web that envelops a web, undoing the web for centuries; reconstituting it too as an organism, indefinitely regenerating its own tissue behind the cutting trace, the decision of each reading. There is always a surprise in store for the anatomy or physiology of a critique that might think it had mastered the game, surveyed all the threads at once, a critique that deludes itself too, in wanting to look at the text without touching it, without laying a hand on the "object," without risking—which is the sole chance of entering into the game by getting a few fingers caught—the addition of some new thread. Adding, here, is nothing other than giving to read. One must manage to think this out: that it is not a question of embroidering upon a text, unless one considers that to know how to embroider is still to take heed to follow the given thread. That is, if you follow me, the hidden thread.[9]

While taking the opposite view from Derrida insofar as hidden meaning is concerned, Barthes adopts his textile metaphor; Derrida's *istos* becomes Barthes's *hyphos:*

> *Text* means *Tissue;* but whereas hitherto we have always taken this tissue as a product, a ready-made veil, behind which lies, more or less hidden, meaning (truth), we are now emphasizing, in the tissue, the generative idea that the text is made, is worked out in a perpetual interweaving; lost in this tissue—this texture— the subject makes himself, like a spider dissolving in the constructive secretions of its web. Were we fond of neologism, we might define the theory of the text as an *hyphology* (*hyphos* is the tissue and the spider's web).[10]

The metaphors that these authors weave again and again are extremely significant, since according to Freud the only contribution of women "to the discoveries and inventions in the history of civilization" is a "technique," "that of plaiting and weaving."[11] The thread unraveled by Ariadne, cut by the Fates, woven by Penelope, is a peculiarly feminine attribute, a metonym for femininity. There is thus cause to speculate about the relations (necessarily hypothetical at the current stage of our knowledge) between a thematic reading and a feminine reading, by which I certainly do not mean that reading practiced uniquely by women. If my hypothesis concerning the femininity of thematism were justified, this would explain its culpabilization on the one hand and, paradoxically, its masculine recuperation on the other. This hypothesis presupposes a question: does reading have a sex? And this question in turn brings up another: does writing have a sex? It is, as we will attempt to demonstrate, precisely this question of the sex of writing that underlies *Madame Bovary*. We can no longer read *Madame Bovary* outside of the "sexual problematic"[12] that Sartre analyzed in its author, but we must no longer separate the sexual problematic from the scriptural problematic, as did Baudelaire, who was the first to qualify Emma Bovary as a "strange androgynous creature."[13]

Let us note at the close, in order to weave the many threads of our introduction, that there exists in *Madame Bovary* the description of an object which can be readily inscribed in the line of thought that we have just evoked. I am referring to the green silk cigar-case that Charles picks up when leaving la Vaubyessard and that Emma so preciously keeps. Read, or reread, in light of the preceding remarks, this passage seems to assume a new meaning: the green silk cigar-case becomes the emblem of the imbrication of weaving, the text, and femininity. *Madame Bovary* thus contains not only an objective correlative of its production, but a protocol for its interpretation as well:

> It had been embroidered on some rosewood frame, a pretty piece
> of furniture, hidden from all eyes, that had occupied many
> hours, and over which had fallen the soft curls of the pensive
> worker. A breath of love had passed over the stitches on the
> canvas; each prick of the needle had fixed there a hope or a
> memory, and all those interwoven threads of silk were but the
> continued extension of the same silent passion.[14]

To conclude these prolegomena, I would like to put to the test a new thematics that I propose to call a "restricted thematics" because, if the definition of the field of possible themes must henceforth answer to the call for literary specificity, the reciprocal play of speech and writing will replace the time/space paradigm privileged since Proust, with speech occupying the field of time, and writing inscribed in that of space. Unlike the "general" thematic reading which always tends toward "an infinite reading" (Richard, op. cit., p. 8), which exists, that is, in an anamorphous relationship with the text, restricted thematics would be the equivalent of an anastomosis, sectioning the text in order to bring together binary opposites (on the semantic plane), doubles (on the actantial plane), and repeated sequences (on the evenemential plane).

> *En somme, cette femme est vraiment grande, elle est surtout pitoy-*
> *able, et malgré la durete systématique de l'auteur, qui a fait tous*
> *ses efforts pour être absent de son oeuvre et pour jouer la fonction*
> *d'un monteur de marionnettes, toutes les femmes* intellectuelles *lui*
> *sauront gré d'avoir élevé la femelle à une si haute puissance, si loin*
> *de l'animal pur et si près de l'homme idéal. . . .*

Baudelaire

As a starting-point for our reflection, let us recall René Girard's statement concerning Flaubert's "grotesque antithesis":

> As Flaubert's novelistic genius ripens his oppositions become
> more futile; the identity of the contraries is drawn more clearly.[15]

If—as we are firmly convinced—this breakdown of opposites is manifest at all levels of the Flaubertian text and along its entire diachronic course, how does it apply to the writing/speech opposition, explicitly thematized by Flaubert in *Sentimental Education*, during a conversation between Frédéric and Madame Arnoux: "She admired orators; he preferred a writer's fame."[16]. Does this orators/writers opposition also participate in the obsessional tyranny of the identity of the contraries, in this system of growing in-differentiation?

The speech axis permits a first division of the characters in *Madame Bovary* into two large categories: those who are adept at speaking, such as Rodolphe and Homais, and those who are not, such as Charles and Emma. But the insufficiency of this first distribution is instantly apparent since certain characters adept at speaking are not good listeners. The speech axis must be subordinated to the communication axis, a bipolar axis with at one end an encoder/emitter, at the other a decoder/receiver. Depending on whether or not a character exhibits the aptitudes for encoding and decoding, we can forsee four combinations:

(1) encoding +   (2) encoding −   (3) encoding +   (4) encoding −
     decoding +   decoding −   decoding −   decoding +

If we examine the characters named above[17] in light of these *roles*, certain aspects of the speech problematic in *Madame Bovary* emerge.

From his first appearance, Charles reveals himself to be an impotent speaker:

> The new boy then took a supreme resolution, opened an
> inordinately large mouth, and shouted at the top of his voice as if
> calling someone, the word "Charbovari." (p. 3)

Incapable of articulating the syllables of his name, Charles can but repeat
the words of others:

> Charles's conversation was commonplace as a street pave-
> ment, and every one's ideas trooped through it in their everyday
> garb, without exciting emotion, laughter, or thought. (p. 29)

What distinguishes Charles's conversation from that of the glib speaker is
not so much its painful banality, but its neutrality. His is an inefficient
speech, lacking resonance, a speech in which nothing is transmitted from
the enunciator to his interlocutor. Nevertheless, it must be noted that this
"zero" on the encoding plane will have a great word, his last:

> He even made a phrase ("un grand mot"), the only one he'd
> ever made:
> "Fate willed it this way." (pp. 254–55)

The effect of this grandiloquent sentence is, however, doubly subverted by
its receptor, Rodolphe:

> Rodolphe, who had been the agent of this fate, thought him
> very meek for a man in his situation, comic even and slightly
> despicable. (loc. cit.)

First irony: the receptor is, in fact, the encoder. It is Rodolphe who was
the first to put the word "fate" into circulation in the novel when he
composed his letter breaking with Emma:

> Why were you so beautiful? Is it my fault? God, no! only fate is
> to blame!
> "That's a word that always helps, " he said to himself. (p. 146)

And Charles reads this letter (pp. 249–50). As we will see below, once
launched, this word will continually reappear. In using it in talking to
Rodolphe, Charles only completes the series, closes the circuit: Rodolphe
→ Emma → Charles → Rodolphe. Second irony: the original encoder (the
"voluntary deceiver"[18], presents himself as judge and condemns his imi-
tator (his involuntary dupe). Flaubert thus puts the parrot and the
hypocrite back to back.

With Charles the inability to encode goes along with an inability to
decode which makes him unable to understand Emma. For Emma,
speaking to Charles is a last resort:

> At other times, she told him what she had been reading, some
> passage in a novel, a new play, or an anecdote from high society
> found in a newspaper story; for, after all, Charles was someone
> to talk to, an ever-open ear, an ever-ready approbation. She even
> confided many a thing to her greyhound! She would have done
> so to the logs in the fireplace or to the pendulum of the clock.
> (p. 44)

Charles's qualifications as a listener are minimal; they can be reduced to
the possession of an ear and the promise of his ever-identical reaction. The
equivalence established among Charles, the greyhound, the logs, and the
pendulum says a great deal about his inability to decode, for the progression from the animate to the inanimate, the choice of the logs and the
pendulum in the domestic code, with their semes of hardness (hence the
figurative meaning of "bûche" [log]: "stupid person") and mechanicity,
confirms Charles's nullity: he actualizes combination #2, which is doubly
negative.

Initially, Rodolphe seems gifted with all the faculties that Charles lacks.
This is not to say that his discourse is more "original" then Charles's, but
that he draws from the same dictionary of received ideas as Emma: he
speaks her language. The juxtaposition in the oft-commented-upon chapter of the agricultural fair of Rodolphe's conventional seduction of Emma
and the functionaries' set speech serves only to underscore the parallelism
of the two discourses: opposed on the spatial (vertical) axis, Rodolphe and
the two orators echo each other on the speech axis, as the intersection of
the two discourses indicates. The only difference between Rodolphe's
speech and that of Charles is that Rodolphe's acts upon Emma; it evokes
dreams, it becomes action, love.

A clever encoder, Rodolphe is also a cunning decoder of corporeal
semiology; he is a diagnostician of great talent:

> Monsieur Rodolphe Boulanger was thirty-four; he combined
> brutality of temperament with a shrewd judgment, having had
> much experience with women and being something of a connois-
> seur. This one had seemed pretty to him; so he kept dreaming
> about her and her husband.
> "I think he is very stupid. She must be tired of him, no doubt.
> *He has dirty nails, and hasn't shaved for three days.*" (p. 93,
> emphasis mine)

But it is precisely that which enables him to decode this *clue*, namely his
experience, that prevents him from decoding Emma's oral messages.
Having spent his life repeating, indeed perfecting, an invariable scenario
whose only variant is the partner, Rodolphe cannot go beyond clichés,
ready-made formulas. Everything happens as if Rodolphe's decoding

mechanism were programmed to function only with information that has already been received. We find in Rodolphe the same "linguistic deafness"[19] that Genette analyzes in certain Proustian characters who, he remarks, only hear what they can or want to hear, that is, in the extreme, what they can or want to say. Rodolphe's decoding of Charles's speech (see above) exemplifies this form of listening by projection. Emma's case is, however, far more complex:

> He had so often heard these things said that they did not strike *him* as original. Emma was like all his mistresses; and the charm of novelty, gradually falling away like a garment, laid bare the eternal monotony of passion, that has always the same shape and the same language. He was unable to see, this man so full of experience, the variety of feelings hidden within the same expressions. Since libertine or venal lips had murmured similar phrases, he only faintly believed in the candor of Emma's; he thought one should be aware of exaggerated declarations which only serve to cloak a tepid love; *as though* the abundance of one's soul did not sometimes overflow with empty metaphors, since no one ever has been able to give the exact measure of his needs, his concepts, or his sorrows. The human tongue is like a cracked cauldron on which we beat out the tunes to set a bear dancing when we would make the stars weep with our melodies. (p. 138, emphasis mine)

The increased intervention of the narrator from the "him" of disassociation (indirect intervention) to the "as though" of judgment (direct intervention) translates the importance that Flaubert attaches to this passage, in which he puts forth his speech problematic. In effect, this passage does no more than reiterate an invariant opposition: unique feelings versus common speech. In other words: how does one communicate difference by means of sameness, how does one give an individual charge to words used by all? With Flaubert the renewal of the cliché is not so much a matter of style as metaphysics, for, on a purely linguistic plane, there is in his work as a constant inspiration by the cliché, an aspiration by the received idea. Thus in *Sentimental Education* the cliché favors more than it prevents the communication of passionate feelings: "He . . . poured out his love more freely through the medium of commonplaces" (p. 197). But what the cliché cannot communicate is unicity. Two presuppositions underlie this passage: first, there is a "dissimilarity of feelings," original feelings, unique essence; second, in an ideal system of speech there is a total adequation of the word and the psychic signified. Flaubert's oral ideal is, to use Genette's expression, nothing but a new "avatar of cratylism,"[20] which is hardly surprising in this avowed Platonist.

Madame Bovary tests the romantic notions of exceptionality and ineffability, for the destiny of the romantic hero is bound up with a theory of speech.[21] The "double intervention"[22] noted above translates the doubling of the narrative sequence; we could adopt here the writer/novelist distinction proposed by Marcel Muller to account for two of the seven voices in *Remembrance of Things Past*,[23] attributing to the "writer" Rodolphe's point of view, and to the "novelist" Emma's. To assign Rodolphe's decoding a minus sign—Rodolphe would actualize combination #3— amounts to espousing the cause of the novelist, who supports Emma's essential superiority/difference, betrayed not only by the inferiority of those who surround her, but also by speech, which is not up to her level. René Girard, it should be noted here, adopts the point of view of the writer, indirectly justifying Rodolphe: "the opposition between Emma and Charles, and between Emma and the citizens of Yonville is essential only in Emma's mind."[24]

If, however, we follow the thread of the thematic paradigm speech/ writing, we find that the structuring opposition of the novel is neither Emma versus Rodolphe nor Emma versus Charles (nor is it the commonplace of traditional criticism, Homais versus Bournisien); the privileged doublet is none other than Emma versus Homais, a fundamental opposition half-expressed, half-concealed by their names, which should be read "Femm(a) versus Hom(ais)"—*Femme* (Woman) versus *Homme* (Man). This reading consists of remedying Emma's lack by restoring her truncated "F" to her, and of cutting off Homais's supplement by putting his adjunctive suffix in parentheses. How can one fail to see in the operations to which Flaubert subjected the terms of sexual opposition to generate the characters' names, the equivalent of castration on the plane of the signifier? We could thus term the castration axis the arch-axis, the principal axis that subordinates all the other semantic axes of the novel.

Opposed to Emma's inability to find the words necessary to express her thoughts (one of the corollaries of the cratylian theory being that thoughts/feelings *precede* speech), is the always reiterated adequation of the pharmacist's thoughts and words:

> Perhaps she would have liked to confide all these things to some one. But how tell an undefinable uneasiness, changing as the clouds, unstable as the winds? Words failed her and, by the same token, the opportunity, the courage. (p. 29).

> "What a dreadful catastrophe!" exclaimed the pharmacist, who always found expressions that filled all imaginable circumstances. (p. 96)

Emma's incapacity, let us note, is intermittent; her cyclothymia is also a pathology of speech:

> On certain days she chattered with feverish profusion, and this
> overexcitement was suddenly followed by a state of torpor, in
> which she remained without speaking, without moving. (p. 48)

This alternate encoding can be represented as follows:

Emma: encoding $+/-$

Nevertheless, on the speech-encoding plane, Homais is the undisputed
winner. Of all the characters in the novel, he is the only one to work
tirelessly at his expression. For him talking is both a delight (*jouissance*)
(". . . for the pharmacist much enjoyed pronouncing the word 'doctor,' as
if addressing another by it reflected on himself some of the grandeur of the
title" [p. 120]), and an art ("Homais had meditated at length over his
speech; he had rounded, polished it, given it the proper cadence; it was a
masterpiece of prudence and transitions, of subtle turns and delicacy
. . ." [p. 181]). Unlike Rodolphe, Homais does not speak a stilted language, but takes pleasure in hearing and reproducing new thoughts, stylish
expressions. Thus we see him, in the course of a conversation with Léon,
reveal his extraordinary mimetic gifts, speaking "Parislang":

> . . . he even used slang to impress [. . .] the "bourgeois," saying
> "flip," "cool," "sweet," "neat-o," and "I must break it up," for
> "I must leave." (p. 202)

If Rodolphe is a smooth talker, if he dexterously manages the code of the
vile seducer, Homais has a gift for *languages* (Latin, English, slang) that
he handles with the love of a savant, an expert in transcoding.

But if on the communication axis Homais wins out over Emma, who, it
must be remembered, does not shine as a decoder, allowing herself to be
easily duped by the clichés that Rodolphe reels off to her both before and
after their affair ("It was the first time that Emma had heard such words
addressed to her, and her pride unfolded languidly in the warmth of this
language, like someone stretching in a hot bath" [p. 112]; "She yielded to
his words . . ." [p. 226]), when one turns to that delayed communication,
writing, the balance of forces is equalized. Certain readers, unaware of
Emma's scriptural activities, will perhaps be surprised at this affirmation.
It is, however, in the area of writing that the Emma/Homais rivalry turns
out to be the most violent; it is to the extent that they practice two different
forms of writing that their sexual opposition becomes significant. The
medal that motivates Homais and whose reception closes the novel—"He
has just been given the cross of the Legion of Honor" (p. 255)—is destined
to crown his writings, which are numerous. He is the classic pedant
scribbler, having published " 'at my expense, numerous works of public
usefulness, such as' (and he recalled his pamphlet entitled, *On Cider, Its*

Manufacture and Effects, besides observations on the wooly aphis that he had sent to the Academy; his volume of statistics, and down to his pharmaceutical thesis)" (p. 253). Compared to this journalistic logorrhea, what has Emma published? Nothing, but she does write. What, to my knowledge, has escaped critical notice is the thematic and structural relationship between *Madame Bovary* and the first *Education*: the Emma/ Homais couple is a new avatar of the Jules/Henry couple. Even those who have taken literally the famous exclamation *"Madame Bovary, c'est moi"* have bypassed the essential, the too-evident, in their concern for the anecdotal similarities between Emma and Gustave. Emma is also the portrait of an artist, but of the artist as a young woman, and it is this difference, this bold representation of the writer as a woman which disconcerts, which misleads, and which, for these reasons, must be examined.

Emma's search for love's passion is doubly motivated by literature. First there is "external mediation,"[25] the desire to transform the (dead) letters that she has read into lived experience, to coincide with literary models:

> And Emma tried to find out what one meant exactly in life by the words *bliss, passion, ecstasy,* that had seemed to her so beautiful in books. (p. 24)

When she becomes Rodolphe's mistress, this much longed-for identification seems to be realized; Emma progresses from the passive status of a reader to the active status of a heroine:

> Then she recalled the heroines of the books that she had read.
> . . . She became herself, as it were, an actual part of these lyrical imaginings; at long last, as she saw herself among those lovers she had so envied, she fulfilled the love-dream of her youth.
> (p. 117)

Finally, with Léon she attains her goal: from a heroine-for-herself she is transformed into a heroine-for-others: "She was the mistress of all the novels, the heroine of all the dramas, the vague 'she' of all the volumes of verse" (p. 192).

But this first love-letters link conceals another of prime importance to our study: Emma seeks a lover not only to become a novelistic character, but especially to become an author. When, in the early stage of her marriage, Emma settles in to wait for "something to happen," she outfits herself in advance with a writer's tools:

> She had bought herself a blotter, writing-case, pen-holder, and envelopes although *she had no one to write to*. . . . (p. 43, emphasis mine)

What Emma lacks is not a lover, but a receiver ("destinaire"), and what she desires through this receiver-pretext for writing is literary fame. To convince oneself of this, one need only compare the above quotation with another seemingly innocent remark which follows one page later. Emma wants Charles to become a great doctor because:

> She would have wished this name of Bovary, which was hers, to be illustrious, to see it displayed at the booksellers', repeated in the newspapers, known to all France. (p. 44)

By bringing together these two segments of the same sentence, of the same phantasm, we witness the emergence of Emma's profound ambition: to be a famous novelist. Why then is this wish expressed on the one hand by an intermediary, projected onto Charles, and on the other hand occulted by the separation of the means (writing instruments) from the end (to be famous)? This repression, this censure, results from Emma's sex. What she envies in a man is not so much the possibility of traveling, but the possibility of writing; what she lacks in order to write are neither words nor pen, but a phallus.

Imbued with eighteenth-century literature, Emma cannot conceive of a literary production other than a novel by letters, and the taking of a lover is the necessary condition for this form of writing. Once she becomes Rodolphe's mistress, Emma begins her epistolary novel. Rodolphe serves as both her initiator and her receiver:

> From that day on they wrote to one another regularly every evening. Emma placed her letter at the end of the garden, by the river, in a crack of the wall. Rodolphe came to fetch it, and put another in its place that she always accused of being too short. (p. 117)

This little game of hide-and-seek inaugurates Emma's apprenticeship, which will go through three stages, the first of which is marked by the persistence of the illusion of communication. Rather than renounce this illusion, Emma brings to correspondence all those desires unsatisfied by conversation, continuing to valorize *exchange*, clinging to the double role of sender/receiver that defines the interlocutor. Thus Emma complains of the brevity of Rodolphe's letters; thus she demands verses from Léon:

> She asked him for some verses—some verses "for herself," a "love poem" in honor of her. (p. 201)

If initially Emma writes to receive letters, to take pleasure in the communication forbidden, impossible on the speech plane, writing subsequently becomes the adjuvant of a "waning passion" in the manner of an aphrodisiac:

> . . . in the letters that Emma wrote him she spoke of flowers,
> poetry, the moon and the stars, naive resources of a waning
> passion striving to keep itself alive by all external aids. (p. 205)

It is only during the third stage when the receiver-lover has been demysti-
fied, unmasked as the double of her husband—"Emma found again in
adultery all the platitudes of marriage" (p. 211; an excellent example of
the identity of opposites!)—that Emma must yield to the evidence: she no
longer loves Léon, but she continues more and more to love to write. It is
only at this stage that Emma fully assumes her role as writer:

> She blamed Léon for her disappointed hopes, as if he had
> betrayed her. . . .
>   She none the less went on writing him love letters in keeping
> with the notion that a woman must write to her lover.
>   But while writing to him, it was another man she saw, a
> phantom fashioned out of her most ardent memories, of her
> favorite books, her strongest desires, and at last he became so
> real, so tangible, that her heart beat wildly in awe and admira-
> tion, though unable to see him distinctly, for, like a god, he was
> hidden beneath the abundance of his attributes. . . . She felt him
> near her; he was coming and would ravish her entire being in a
> kiss. Then she would fall back to earth again shattered; for these
> vague ecstasies of imaginary love would exhaust her more than
> the wildest orgies. (pp. 211–12)

The "but" signals the passage from one stage to another, the final
subordination of love to writing, the metamorphosis of writing dictated
by conventions into writing that flows from the heart. The latter writing is
diametrically opposed to conversation-communication in that it presupposes the absence of a receiver, compensates for a lack, thereby embracing
emptiness. As Freud demonstrates in *The Poet and Daydreaming*, the
fictive character, like this composite being who is sketched by Emma's
pen, is the product of all the unsatisfied desires of its creator. Transcoded
into psychoanalytic terminology, the "phantom" that Emma perceives is
a phantasm. Moreover, writing, such as Emma practices it (such as
Flaubert practiced it), is a solitary pleasure: the phantasmic scene is
seduction. The pleasure that Emma experiences in rewriting Léon, in
giving herself a lover three times hyperbolic, is intensely erotic.

To write is to leave the prey for the shadow, and, in the end, writing is to
become the shadow itself: the author-phantom must succeed the charac-
ter-phantom. Thus, just before swallowing the arsenic, Emma appears to
Justin "majestic as a phantom" (p. 229). The apprenticeship of the
heroine-artist can lead only to death, but to an exemplary death, because
suicide generates language. In the novel to die a natural death (*belle mort*)

is to commit suicide, because suicide is the very act that links the coming
to writing with the renunciation of life. Like Madame de Tourvel, like
Julie, Emma does not die without having written a last letter: "She sat
down at her writing-table and wrote a letter, which she sealed slowly,
adding the date and the hour" (p. 230). Of this letter we know only the
first words: " 'Let no one be blamed . . .' " (p. 231). The fragmentary state
of this letter is highly significant, because the gap created by the ellipsis
leaves forever unanswered the essential question: in this ultimate letter,
ultima verba, does Emma complete the final stages of her apprenticeship,
does she succeed in inventing for herself a writing that goes beyond clichés,
beyond the romantic lies that they carry with them? The first words are
only a (negative) repetition of Rodolphe's words, tending to invalidate
any hypothesis of last-minute literary conversion. This letter immediately
evokes the imitative circuit. If, in the letter that Charles composes right
after Emma's death, we find both thematic (novelistic ideas) and stylistic
(use of the imperative: " 'Let no one try to overrule me' ") echoes of
Emma's previous letters, we are struck, too, by the firmness of expression
resulting from a very bold use of asyndeton. In fact, one could cite this
passage as an example of the Flaubertian enunciation which, according to
Barthes's formula, is seized by "a generalized asyndeton"[26]:

> I wish her to be buried in her wedding dress, with white shoes,
> and a wreath. Her hair is to be spread out over her shoulders.
> Three coffins, one oak, one mahogany, one of lead. Let no one
> try to overrule me; I shall have the strength to resist him. She is
> to be covered with a large piece of green velvet. This is my wish;
> see that it is done. (p. 239)

Is this writing a personal find of Charles's, whose writing up to this point
vied in ineptitude with his speech (note the fifteen drafts that he writes to
have Dr. Larivière come *before* Emma's death), or can one see in it the
pale reflection, traces of Emma's last letter?

In the Flaubertian novelistic universe, in which substitution chains
organize the narrative, nothing is less evident than the principles of closure
that govern this neurotic serialization. Since in Emma's mind the Viscount
= Léon = Rodolphe (p. 106), what prevents her from continuing indefi-
nitely this substitution of one lover for another? In theory the series is
open-ended; the resources of a substantial rhetoric and logic are inexhaus-
tible.[27] In effect, Emma's death is not synchronic with the exhaustion of
the narrative because, after her death, she is replaced by other characters:
formerly the *subject* of substitution, she becomes its *object*. Thus Félicité,
her maid, wears her dresses: "[she] was about her former mistress's height
and often, on seeing her from behind, Charles thought she had come back
. . ." (p. 249); and Charles begins to imitate her:

> To please her, as if she were still living, he adopted her taste,
> her ideas; he bought patent leather boots and took to wearing
> white cravats. He waxed his moustache and, just like her, signed
> promissory notes. (p. 250)

But, on the actantial plane, on the plane of the novel's structuring
opposition, Emma/Homais, Emma is succeeded by the blind man, a
Beckettian character whose *symbolic* value has for a long time preoccupied
the critics[28] and whose function still remains to be pinpointed. According
to our reading, his function is above all heuristic: whereas the opposition
between Emma and Homais is implicit, concealed by anagrams, that
between the blind man and Homais is explicit, manifest on the evenemential plane.

The blind man's doubling of Emma is prepared a long time in advance:
from his first appearance the blind man finds in Emma a listener; his
melancholic song evokes an echo in Emma's mind (p. 193); later she gives
him her last five-franc coin (see in this scene the opposition: Emma's
excessive generosity versus Homais's excessive greed; by her *gift*, Emma is
united with the blind man against Homais [p. 219]). Finally, on her
deathbed, Emma hears the blind man, believes she sees him, and pro-
nounces her last words: " 'The blind man!' " (p. 238). The seme common
to Emma and the blind man is monstrosity, physical in the one, moral in
the other. It is precisely the blind man's monstrosity that brings upon him
Homais's hostility: Homais would like to cure the blind man, that is,
reduce his difference, "normalize" him. The blind man/Homais sequence
only repeats the clubfoot/Homais sequence; in both cases the science
preached by the pharmacist is never anything but the means of replacing
heterogeneity with homogeneity, thereby earning the gratitude and esteem
of his clients. Nevertheless, unlike the crippled clubfoot, the blind-man-
ever-blind flouts Homais, publicly exhibiting the wounds that the pharmacist's recommendations and pomades could not cure. Homais, unable
to silence this embarrassing witness to the inefficacy of his speech, begins
to pursue him through writing; a fierce fight ensues between the garrulous
blind man and the prolix pharmacist:

> He managed so well that the fellow was locked up. But he was
> released. He began again, and so did Homais. It was a struggle.
> Homais won out, for his foe was condemned to lifelong confine-
> ment in an asylum. (p. 251)

The superimposition of the Emma/Homais // blind man/Homais rival-
ries reveal within writing the same opposition that we detected above at
the center of speech: efficacy versus inefficacy. We can thus posit the
following equivalence:

$$\frac{\text{Efficacy}}{\text{Inefficacy}} \simeq \frac{\text{Rodolphe's speech}}{\text{Charles's speech}} \simeq \frac{\text{Homais's writing}}{\text{Emma's writing}}$$

While Emma's writing remains, so to speak, a dead letter, transforming nothing, producing no impact on the external world, Homais's writing is able to exile if not kill, and becomes a means of social advancement.

Moreover, this superimposition permits the disengagement of an attribute, an invariant qualification of the *victim*: the victim, woman or blind man, is a being who lacks an essential organ, in fact, as Freud repeats at several points, the same organ, since according to his theory blindness = castration. The victim's final failure is inscribed in his/her body; Emma's monstrosity is physical as much as it is moral. The blind man's doubling of Emma punctuates the text, assures it readability: woman, this "defective" monster ("*monstre à la manque*"), is the privileged figure of the writer, and especially of the writer Flaubert, a "failed girl" ("*fille manquée*") according to Sartre's thesis. It would, moreover, be easy to demonstrate that Emma's writing apprenticeship is consistent with an attempt to change sex, to reverse castration. The refusal of femininity, the temptation of virility, are not given once and for all from the beginning; before going that route, Emma will try to follow the path of integration, to accept the feminine destiny that Freud charts for the "normal" woman: marriage and maternity. But, just as marriage ends in failure, Charles being unable to succeed *in Emma's place*, motherhood ends in disappointment: George, the phantasmic phallic-son, turns out to be only Berthe, a child worthy of Charles. Thus, much before Freud, Flaubert well understood that in order for maternity to fully satisfy penis-envy, the child must be male (which would condemn over half of all women to inevitable neurosis):

> She hopes for a son; he would be strong and dark; she would call him George; and this idea of having a male child was like an expected revenge for all her impotence of the past. A man, at least, is free; he can explore all passions and all countries, overcome obstacles, taste of the most distant pleasures. But a woman is always hampered. Being inert as well as pliable, she has against her the weakness of the flesh and the inequity of the law. . . .
> She gave birth on a Sunday at about six o'clock, as the sun was rising.
> "It's a girl!" said Charles.
> She turned her head away and fainted. (p. 63)

Unable to obtain a phallus by "phallic proxy,"[29] Emma seeks to satisfy her desire to change sex through transvestism. Partial at the beginning of the novel, the disguise is completed just before Emma's death:

> Like a man, she wore a tortoise-shell eyeglass thrust between two buttons of her blouse. (pp. 11 12)

> . . . she parted [her hair] on one side and rolled it under, like a man's. (p. 89)

> "[How could] I go riding without proper clothes?"
> "You must order a riding outfit," he answered.
> The riding habit ["amazone"] decided her. (p. 113)

> On that day of Mid-Lent she did not return to Yonville; that evening she went to a masked ball. She wore velvet breeches, red stockings, a peruke, and a three-cornered hat cocked over one ear. (p. 212)

But, as Sartre demonstrates, for Flaubert sexuality belongs to the realm of the imagination; disguise is, then, only an *analogon* of Emma's imaginary sex. In the last analysis, it is only on the imaginary plane, i.e., on the plane of the role *played* in the couple, that Emma's growing virility asserts itself. The order of her affairs, Rodolphe before Léon, thus assumes its meaning: whereas in her relationship with Rodolphe Emma plays the female role, traditionally passive, in her relationship with Léon the roles are reversed: ". . . he was becoming her mistress rather than she his" (p. 201).

It is not by chance that the writing apprenticeship and the "virility apprenticeship," if I may call it that, follow paths which ultimately converge at the time of Emma's affair with Léon, for their affair marks the triumph of the imaginary over the real, this being the precondition of all writing. If, insofar as the effect *on* the real is concerned, Homais's writing surpasses Emma's, considered in terms of the "reality effect," it is without any doubt Emma's (Flaubert's) writing that surpasses Homais's, for the "reality effect" can only be achieved through a total renunciation of any real satisfaction, can only be the just reward of sublimation, i.e., castration. For Flaubert writing thus has a sex, the sex of an assumed lack, the feminine sex.

It would seem, however, that all these oppositions are outweighed by Flaubert's radical distrust of language in general, a distrust evident in Emma's most bitter discovery, namely that ". . . everything was a lie" (p. 206). For the Flaubert of *Madame Bovary* language is constantly undermined by its potential for lying, lying in the largest sense of the term, including hyperbole as well as the willful distortion of facts, and mystified idealization as well as cynical reductionism. The generalization of lying erases both the differences between forms of writing and the differences between writing and speech. Emma's letters and Homais's published pieces thus participate in the same "a-mimesis": both he and she depart from reality, embellishing facts, adjusting them to their needs. They "invent"—"Then Homais invented incidents" (p. 251). On the other hand, Emma's idealization—"irrealization," Sartre would say—of Léon on paper is only the resumption, the materialization of the oral self-idealization of the two lovers that occurs on the occasion of their reunion in Rouen:

> . . . this was how they would have wished it to be, *each setting up an ideal* to which they were now trying to adapt their past life. Besides, *speech is like a rolling machine that always stretches the sentiment it expresses.* (p. 169, emphasis mine)

Things would be too simple if there were not at least one exception to the rule; hence old Rouault appears to escape the treason of language. His annual letter enjoys a harmony both metaphoric (letter = writer) and metonymic (letter = reality contiguous to the writer). The hiatus between writer, words, and things is here reduced to a minimum. In fact, in the Flaubertian system the opposite of lying is not telling the truth, but immediacy, because the least distance between the sender and the receiver, the writing subject and the Other, as well as that between man and Things, opens a gap through which lies penetrate:

> She held the coarse paper in her fingers for some minutes. A continuous stream of spelling mistakes ran through the letter, and Emma followed the kindly thought that cackled right through it like a hen half hidden in a hedge of thorns. The writing had been dried with ashes from the earth, for a little grey powder slipped from the letter on her dress, and she almost thought she saw her father bending over the hearth to take up the tongs. (p. 124)

Examined more closely, this model of paternal writing is in fact threatened from all sides. In spite of the spelling mistakes and the "intradiagetic"[30] metaphor which guarantee the writer's adherence to words and things, the gap is there, manifest in the form of a lack: thought is compared to a "half hidden" hen. Adherence is thus only partial, and if this letter conveys writing-matter (letter + ashes), it is the matter itself that represents "the price to be paid": the symbolic Father is the dead Father.

Two consequences follow from this. First, for the characters who, unlike old Rouault, maintain relations with the world that are strongly mediated by written as well as spoken language, such as Emma, there is only one way in which to enjoy immediacy, and that is to step outside language. The two great erotic scenes of the novel link bliss (*jouissance*), plenitude, with the suspension of all linguistic communication. The initiation by Rodolphe culminates in one of the great Flaubertian silences, to borrow another expression from Genette[31]:

> Silence was everywhere. . . . Then far away, beyond the wood, on the other hills, she heard a vague, prolonged cry, a voice which lingered, and in silence she heard it mingling like music with the last pulsations of her throbbing nerves. (p. 116)

If in this scene the spoken word is supplanted by a non-articulated, a-semantic cry, in the coach scene the written word is torn to shreds, reduced to insignificance:

> One time, around noon, in the open country, . . . a bare hand appeared under the yellow canvas curtain, and threw out *some scraps of paper that scattered* in the wind, alighting further off like white butterflies on a field of red clover all in bloom. (p. 177, emphasis mine)

The euphoric form of the letter is thus the sperm-letter: in *Madame Bovary*, as in *The Temptation of Saint Anthony*, happiness is "being matter."

But if fictional characters, these "paper beings," find their happiness beyond or without language, what of the writer who is condemned to work in an articulate and signifying language? The writer cannot be for Flaubert but a pursuer of lies, making do for want of something better, with available means, i.e., language, language which is always both judge and plaintiff, source of lies and condemner of lies, poison and antidote, *pharmakon*. There is in *Madame Bovary* a character who appears to fulfill this prophylactic function. It is, as if by chance, a doctor, Doctor Larivière, a character with quasi-divine attributes: "The apparition of a god would not have caused more commotion" (p. 233).[32] Note in what terms Flaubert describes his diagnostic gifts:

> His glance, more penetrating than his scalpels, looked straight into your soul, and would *detect any lie*, regardless how well hidden. (p. 234, emphasis mine)

These are exactly the same terms that Flaubert uses to define his stylistic ideal when, in a letter to Louise Colet contemporary with the writing of *Madame Bovary*, he criticizes Lamartine for not having "this medical view of life, this view of Truth."[33] Truth, it must be remembered, is for Flaubert a matter of style. To be true, the writer need only substitute for the doctor's look the equivalent instrument in his art, i.e., his style:

> a style . . . precise like scientific language . . . a style that would
> penetrate into ideas like the probe of a stylet. (loc. cit.)

The structural homology of the two sentences in question, with, on the one hand, the scalpel-glance which "looked straight into your soul," and on the other the "stylet-style" which "penetrates into ideas," underscores the identity of scriptural approach and surgical procedure. There is nothing less passive, less feminine, than the relationship with language known as "les affres du style" (pains of style): the reader of the correspondence concerning *Madame Bovary* cannot but be impressed with the aggressive and even sadistic relationship of Flaubert with the sentences and paragraphs of his novel that he sets about dissecting, unscrewing, undoing, unwriting, to use expressions found throughout his letters.[34] To convey the inarticulate, one must disarticulate. As Sartre observes, "style is the silence of discourse, the silence in discourse, the imaginary and secret end of the written word."[35]

Flaubert's stylistic ideal completes his writing ideal; if Flaubert's writing refers to what one might call, playing a bit on Kristeva's terms, a "gyno-text," then his style aspires to a "phallo-text," a masculine "pheno-text":

> I love above all else nervous, substantial, clear sentences with
> flexed muscles and a rugged complexion: I like male, not female,
> sentences. . . .[36]

In the last analysis the "bizarre androgyn" is neither Flaubert (Sartre) nor Emma (Baudelaire), but the book, locus of the confrontation, as well as the interpenetration of *animus* and *anima*, of the masculine and the feminine.

By definition a *restricted* thematic study cannot claim to be all-encompassing. We are thus able to take note of a final demarcation separating the new thematic criticism from the old: concerned with thematic structure or, better still, structuring themes, new criticism must not go beyond the framework of the individual novel (poem, drama). (This does not, of course, exclude intertextual allusions and references.) Defining the corpus in this manner, restricted thematics reintroduces a diachronic dimension into the always synchronic or a-chronic apprehension of traditional thematic criticism, thereby substituting "a new hermeneutic, one that is syntagmatic, or metonymic" for "the classical hermeneutic that was paradigmatic (or metaphoric)."[37] As we have observed, the writer/speech paradigm overdetermines not only the actantial distribution of characters but also the consecutive progression of the narrative sequences. I mean *overdetermine* because a thematic approach cannot by itself account for the multiple functioning of a text, but, given its "intent," one cannot really do without it.

Postscript

To publish a (brand-new) translation of a not so recent (1976) article as a record of my workshop is to perpetrate a sort of hoax, though perhaps a necessary one: short of a verbatim transcription, there exists no acceptable and, above all, accurate mimesis of such an eminently oral event. I did not read this article at the workshop (though I did draw very heavily on it); indeed, I did not read from any prepared text; rather I spoke (or as one malcontent would have it, "lectured"!) from a couple of pages of notes. Were I to publish these notes, they would surely be even less intelligible than an unedited transcript of the proceedings, so in order to enter into the record a halfway faithful account of what actually happened, I have in effect prepared a third text, based on my notes, a tape of the session (graciously provided by the Barnard Women's Center), and my own recollections. Adherence to some unwritten code of academic ethics is not, however, my prime reason for adding this postscript; I simply wish to indicate how in the context of the conference—its agenda and its proceedings—points merely alluded to in the article were amplified, and how in the course of the workshop other points were raised.

As announced in the short description of the workshop I had prepared for prospective participants, my intention was "to explore the complex ramifications of Flaubert's well-known but little understood exclamation: 'Madame Bovary is me.' " The question I wanted to raise was: what happens when a male author identifies with his female protagonist to the point of fusion or *con*fusion? I call this mysterious creative process *female im-personation*. Obviously this process is at work in all male-authored gyneco-centric literature, but there is some justification for granting *Madame Bovary* paradigmatic status, for, as Mary McCarthy notes in her "foreword" to the Signet edition, "there is hardly a page in the novel that he [Flaubert] had not 'lived,' and he constantly drew on his own feelings to render Emma's. All novelists do this, but Flaubert went beyond the call of duty. Madame Bovary was not Flaubert, certainly; yet he became Madame Bovary. . . ."[38]

Now what further makes *Madame Bovary* a privileged example of female im-personation is the fact that this paper sex-change operation is singularly complicated, a great deal more so than I had suggested in my article, where I make some glancing allusions to Baudelaire and Sartre before going on to discuss how the anxiety of sexual difference informs the structure of the novel, pitting as it does a male and a female writing principle against each other. In the context of this conference, the sources of this anxiety in Flaubert's autobiography seemed to me to require a great deal more attention. Two critical texts would provide a common ground for discussion: Baudelaire's still pertinent essay on *Madame Bovary*, wherein the question of Emma's sex is raised for the first time, and Sartre's monumental biography of Flaubert, wherein for the first time the question of Flaubert's sexuality is raised. The anxiety of difference which pervades *Madame Bovary* draws its affective resonance from Flaubert's own complex sexual organization.

Using xeroxed handouts of pages drawn from Baudelaire's essay, we focused on the following passage in which the poet-critic is explaining how Flaubert succeeded against all odds in transforming a trivial subject (provincial adultery) into a great work of art: the process described amounts to a form of symbolic castration.

> To accomplish the tour de force in its entirety the author had only to divest himself (as much as possible) of his sex and to become a woman. The result is a marvel; in spite of all his zeal as an actor, he could not keep from infusing virile blood into the veins of his creation, and Madame Bovary, in what is the most forceful, most ambitious, and also most contemplative in her nature, has remained a man. Just as Pallas Athena sprang full armed from the head of Zeus, so this strange androgynous creature has kept all the attraction of a virile soul in a charming feminine body.[39]

Reduced somewhat schematically, for Baudelaire: male author + female protagonist = androgyn. Now two interdependent and obviously questionable assumptions ground this formulation: one, "man" is a monolithic being; two, man is superior to woman. Thus, both here and in a subsequent passage, where Baudelaire goes on to detail Emma's masculine traits, all her positively valorized attributes are ascribed to her vestigial virility. Perhaps Baudelaire's most telling gesture is his inclusion of hysteria among Emma's "masculine" virtues; indeed—and this reveals the locus of Baudelaire's own identification with Flaubert's heroine—he sees in her an image of "the hysterical poet" (146).

Baudelaire's text elicited several comments from the participants, relating to the etymology and symptomatology of hysteria, and its possible motivation of the name of Bovary, which, as one astute participant pointed out, contained the word ovary. It was only later, after the workshop was over, that I realized that the (B)ovary hypothesis did not work quite as well in the original French, for Bovary does not rhyme with *ovaire*, though they do, of course, share the same stem. In retrospect, I'm glad I didn't think of this objection on the spot. The intervention was important not for its ultimate validity or contribution to Flaubert studies—which, by the way, do feature far wilder onomastic fantasies—but for its contribution to the *working* of the workshop. It was a welcome sign of the participants' willingness to join in some of the wordplay I had put on the board. (It also provided comic relief!)

From Baudelaire we shifted to Sartre. Here I restricted myself to the not so modest task of presenting in hopelessly simplified form Sartre's remarkable analysis of Flaubert's "*sexual problematic.*"[40] (I was fortunate enough to have among the participants a woman who was writing her thesis on *L'Idiot de la famille* and was thus able to help me in my presentation.) According to Sartre, when Flaubert looks at himself in the mirror, "his initial impulse is to see himself as a woman" (693). This observation should not, however, be taken to mean that Flaubert is a homosexual, or at any rate a male homosexual; rather, Sartre argues, Flaubert's sexuality is passive, and because he (Flaubert) associates passivity with femininity, he wishes to play the feminine role in his sexual fantasies and encounters. In other words—Flaubert's own—he is a "lesbian." Here Sartre makes a useful and important distinction between the homosexual and the *perverse*: "by this word I mean to designate any erotic attitude in which there is derealization *in the second power*" (694). This is precisely what occurs during Emma's love affair with Léon. But before we get to Sartre's reading of those scenes, we must consider another useful distinction he introduces, the one between adrogyny and hermaphroditism. For him, as for Baudelaire, Emma is an androgyn, but his constituent equation is radically different: "Emma is androgynous: in the arms of Rodolphe—a real man . . .—she swoons. . . . When she goes to make love with Léon, it is she who is the hunter" (710).

This alternatively active and passive sexual behavior does not, in Sartre's vocabulary, qualify as perverse; what is perverse and, by the same token, anxiety-producing are the erotic games Emma and Léon play, enacting their fantasies in fear and trembling. Perversion, Sartre insists, is not linked to specific sexual practices—one can be perverse while making love in the orthodox missionary position. Perversion is a pathology of the imaginary. When Emma and Léon make love, they form a doubly hermaphroditic couple, for each partner is endowed with a real (biological) sex and an "unreal" (imaginary)) one: "What Léon is after in Emma is the satisfaction of what has become *his vice*, the desire to imagine that he is a woman being caressed by a woman. Emma too is worried: through the role she is playing, that she cannot help but play, it would seem that she perceives the unreal threat of a permanent sex change" (711). What is of particular interest to us in Sartre's analysis is the connection he makes between perversion and anxiety, which is, in this instance, an anxiety of difference. To follow his immensely subtle and persuasive reading is to see how the novel moves ineluctably toward the collapse of sexual differences. The event that comes closest to this final catastrophe is the masked ball, which is presented as the ultimate degradation, for on that occasion masquerade is inseparably linked to slumming, which is to say, a breakdown of class difference.

The question of the breakdown of difference elicited a fair amount of discussion. One participant felt very strongly that Emma had been "sold the American dream," and suffered the fate of a *déclassée*, excluded from the predominant discourse. Others pointed out other instances of collapsing differences in the novel: see, for example, the celebrated Chapter VIII, with its description of the Agricultural Show. Viewed in my perspective, this strictly local event can be seen as a reenactment of the Carnaval, with its ritual suspension of all structuring differences, as well, of course, as their ultimate restoration. The masked ball appears then to be a degraded repetition—a pleonasm, for in Flaubert, as Sartre points out, repetition always implies degradation—of the central, euphoric version of the festival. Similarly, Flaubert's disquieting use of syllepsis—as in, "At one and the same time she wanted to die and to live in Paris" (77)—could be taken to figure that breakdown of difference.

In lieu of a conclusion, I shared with the participants in the workshop an inchoate insight that had come to me as I listened to Audre Lorde make prose sing. I began to rethink Emma's deathbed scene, and her famous, enigmatic last cry: " 'The blind man!' " (302). In my article I stress the negative attributes common to both Emma and the beggar, in particular their "castration." Now I wonder if I had not overlooked, in an act of critical deafness, their obvious *positive* link: a certain relationship to music. The blind beggar is after all also a singer, and throughout the novel Emma's quest is set to music: in the convent, at her wedding, at home (her piano), in Tostes (the organ-grinder), at la Vaubyessard, at the opera in Rouen, throughout the novel there is an insistent musical accompaniment to the heroine's life, a melodic subtext, as it were. What is significant, then, in the beggar's song are not the words, but the music. If, as had been suggested, Emma is denied access to the predominant discourse, she enjoys privileged access to that preverbal, preoedipal register that Julia Kristeva has retrieved from beneath the symbolic: the pulsating, rhythmic semiotic.[41] Somehow, in the course of the conference, my topic had changed from the anxiety to the joy of difference.

Notes

1. Roland Barthes, *S/Z*, tr. Richard Miller (New York: Hill and Wang, 1974), p. 93.

2. Jacques Derrida, *Of Grammatology*, trans. Gayatri Chakravorty Spivak (Baltimore: The John Hopkins University Press, 1976), p. 152.

3. Gilles Deleuze, *Proust et les signes* (Paris: P.U.F., 1971); *Logiques du sens* (Paris: 10/18, 1973). (All translations unless otherwise indicated are those of the translator of this article—trans.)

4. Deleuze, "Table ronde," in *Cahiers Marcel Proust* 7 (1975): 91.

5. Barthes, op. cit., p. 160.

6. Derrida, *La dissémination* (Paris: Seuil, 1972), p. 71 (translation mine—N.S.).

7. Derrida, *La dissémination*, p. 73.

8. Jean-Pierre Richard, *Proust et le monde sensible* (Paris: Seuil, 1974), p. 221.

9. Derrida, *La dissémination*, pp. 71–72; my thanks to Barbara Johnson for allowing me the use of this paragraph from her translation (Jacques Derrida, *Dissemination* [Chicago: Univ. of Chicago Press, forthcoming in 1981]).

10. Barthes, *The Pleasure of the Text*, tr. Richard Miller (New York: Hill and Wang, 1975), p. 64.

11. Sigmund Freud, "Femininity," *New Introductory Lectures on Psychoanalysis*, tr. James Strachey (New York: Norton, 1961), p. 132.

12. Jean-Paul Sartre, *L'Idiot de la famille*, I (Paris: Gallimard, 1971), p. 703.

13. Charles Baudelaire, *Ouevres complètes* (Paris: Pléiade, 1961), p. 652.

14. Gustave Flaubert, *Madame Bovary*, tr. Paul de Man (New York: Norton, 1965), pp. 40–41. (All page numbers refer to this edition.) Cf. Claude Duchet, "Romans et Objets: L'Exemple de *Madame Bovary*," *Europe* 485–87 (Sept.-Nov. 1969): 172–201. To Duchet's remarks about the cigar-case I would add only the following: if in the last chapter of the first part of the novel the cigar-case is opposed to the wedding bouquet, in the novel in general it is opposed not to a manifest, but to a virtual object. In effect, the textile activity of the aristocratic Penelope who wove the luxury object is opposed to that of the proletarianized Penelope, Berthe, who, it must be remembered, ends up in a "cotton-mill" (p. 255). Thus Flaubert privileges weaving both as a model of textual production and as a means of closure; the Bovarys' decline and Emma's failure translate into the transformation of the silk thread into the cotton thread, i.e., into the degradation—the "Manchesterization," as Duchet would say—of the Ariadne's thread.

15. Rene Girard, *Deceit, Desire & the Novel*, tr. Yvonne Freccero (Baltimore: Johns Hopkins Univ. Press, 1965), p. 152.

16. Flaubert, *Sentimental Education*, tr. Robert Baldick (London: Penguin, 1978), pp. 92–93. Cf. in *Madame Bovary* this bit of dialogue between Emma and Léon: " 'That is why,' he said, 'I especially love the poets. I think verse is more tender than prose, and that it makes one weep more easily.' 'Still in the long-run it is tiring,' continued Emma, 'and now, on the contrary, I have come to love stories that rush breathlessly along, that frighten one' " (p. 59). This superimposition valorizes the invariant relationship which in Flaubert subordinates the speech/writing, poetry/prose paradigms to the man/woman paradigm, enabling us to establish the following equivalency:

$$\frac{\text{woman}}{\text{man}} \simeq \frac{\text{orators}}{\text{writers}} \simeq \frac{\text{prose}}{\text{poetry}}$$

Moreover, this first conversation retroactively announces their sexual relationships: Emma's masculinity versus Léon's femininity. The genres have a sex and each sex selects, prefers the complementary or supplementary genre-sex. We will return to this notion below.

17. This "survey"—partial but motivated—obviously cannot account for all the oral manifestations in the text. Among the main characters, Léon's omission is particularly conspicuous. Let us state briefly that the relations of Léon and Emma are marked by the seal of silence; either they do not talk to each other, or their words are not recounted: "Had they nothing else to say to one another? Yet their eyes were full of more serious speech, and while they forced themselves to find trivial phrases, they felt the same languor stealing over them both; it was like the deep, continuous murmur of the soul dominating that of their voices" (p. 68). "She did not speak; he was silent, captivated by her silence, as he would have been by her speech" (p. 75). ". . . Then they talked in low tones, and their conversation seemed the sweeter to them because it was unheard" (p. 71). All this will culminate in the coach scene. Léon is shy, and shyness is the degree-zero of speaking.

18. Claude Bremond, *Logique du récit* (Paris: Seuil, 1973), p. 263.

19. Gerard Genette, "Proust et le langage indirect," *Figures II* (Paris: Seuil, 1969), p. 228.

20. Genette, *Poétique* 11 (1972): 367–94; 15 (1973): 113–33; 15 (1973): pp. 265–91.

21. Hence the numerous similarities between the speech problematic in Flaubert and Constant, cf. Tzvetan Todorov, "La Parole selon Constant," *Poétique de la prose* (Paris: Seuil, 1971), pp. 100–17.

22. Victor Brombert, *Flaubert par lui-meme* (Paris: Seuil, 1971), p. 59.

23. Marcel Muller, *Les Voix narratives dans la Recherche du temps perdu* (Geneve: Droz, 1965), pp. 8, 91–175. The question of Flaubertian *irony* (or in other words, of point of view) must be raised here, a question which creates what Barthes terms "a salutary discomfort of writing . . . for the very being of writing . . . is to keep the question *Who is speaking?* from ever being answered" (Barthes, *S/Z*, p. 140).

24. Girard, p. 149. Does the problematic case of Rodolphe require the insertion of a new combination, a combination between types 1 and 3: encoding +, decoding +/−?

25. Girard, p. 9 and passim.

26. Barthes, *The Pleasure of the Text*, p. 9.

27. See Raymond Debray-Genette, "Les Figures du récit dans *Un coeur simple*," *Poétique* 3 (1970).

28. For a discussion of the diverse symbolic readings of the blind man see P. M. Wetherill, "*Madam Bovary*'s Blind Man: Symbolism in Flaubert," *Romantic Review* 61:1 (1970).

29. Luce Irigaray, *Speculum de l'autre femme* (Paris: Editions de Minuit, 1974), p. 106.

30. See Genette, *Figures III* (Paris: Seuil, 1972), pp. 236–41, and Jacques Neefs, "La figuration réaliste," *Poétique* 16 (1973): 472.

31. See Genette, "Silences de Flaubert," *Figures* (Paris: Seuil, 1966), pp. 223–43.

32. For a magnificent demystification of this entire passage the reader should consult Sartre, op. cit., pp. 454–61.

33. Flaubert, *Extraits de la correspondance*, ed. Geneviève Bollème (Paris: Seuil, 1963), p. 71.

34. See Barthes, "Flaubert et la phrase," *Nouveaux essais critiques* (Paris: Seuil, 1972), p. 141.

35. Sartre, *L'Idiot de la famille*, II, p. 1618.

36. Flaubert, *Extrait de la correspondance*, p. 30.

37. Genette, "Table ronde," in *Cahiers Marcel Proust*, pp. 91–92.

38. Mary McCarthy, "Foreword," in Gustave Flaubert, *Madame Bovary*, tr. Mildred Marmur (New York: New American Library, 1964), p. x. Any subsequent references to the novel will be to this edition.

39. Charles Baudelaire, *Baudelaire as a Literary Critic*, tr. Lois B. Hyslop and Francis E. Hyslop, Jr. (University Park: Pennsylvania State Univ. Press, 1964), pp. 143–44.

40. Sartre, *L'Idiot de la famille*, I, p. 703. All translations are mine; the emphases are Sartre's. All subsequent page references will be included in the text.

41. Julia Kristeva, *La révolution du langage poétique* (Paris: Seuil, 1974), pp. 17–100 and passim.

Clare Coss, Sondra Segal, and Roberta Sklar

Separation and Survival: Mothers, Daughters, Sisters—The Women's Experimental Theater

The Women's Experimental Theater

The Women's Experimental Theater creates and performs theater by and for women. We are concerned with the evolution of a feminist theater aesthetic and the establishment of women's theater as a form of expression within the arts. The program for W.E.T. includes the creation and performance of collaborative works; the development of experimental methods of acting through workshops; the nurturance of writers, directors, and performers; and public research with women on themes relevant to our experience. Based in New York City, the Women's Experimental Theater performs and offers workshops throughout the country.

Our current work, *The Daughters Cycle*, by Clare Coss, Sondra Segal, and Roberta Sklar, is a trilogy exploring the roles, relationships, and possibilities for women in the family. *The Daughters Cycle* is directed by Sondra Segal and Roberta Sklar. The excerpts presented at the Barnard conference were performed by Mary Lum, Mary Lyon, Debbie Nitzberg, and Sondra Segal.

The Daughters Cycle (a dramatic trilogy: *Daughters, Sister/Sister, Electra Speaks*) is a testimony to the uniqueness and stature of the female experience. Conceived, created, and performed by women, it represents a new approach to the discovery and expression of a female aesthetic for the theater.

Daughters is a ritual that moves through themes of birth, the ambivalent and interchangeable nature of mother/daughter roles, the underlying contracts negotiated between mothers and daughters, the commonality of all women as daughters, and a naming and reclaiming of our matrilineage. *Daughters* is the founding play of the trilogy.

Sister/Sister reveals the mercurial relationship between sisters within the context of the family and reflects realities common to all sibling relations. The play presents struggles, defeats, and triumphs sisters experience over issues of loyalty and betrayal, competition and support, closeness and distance, sameness and difference. Act I is an amusing and painful search into childhood and its impact on sisters as adults. Act II focuses on relations and responsibilities between adult sisters. It is a mourning for the death of the family romance and a celebration of choice.

Electra Speaks, the culminating play in this trilogy on women in the family, is a study of the women in the *Oresteia*—Clytemnestra, Electra, and Iphigenia—as mothers, daughters, and sisters. It is a probing and disturbing retelling of one of the major myths of our culture and an analysis of the ways in which the lines of demarcation are drawn between women in the patriarchal family.

In *Electra Speaks* we pose the question, whose interests are served by the institutionalized division between women in the family? We seek to project previously ignored experiences of women in the archetypal family. If something goes unspoken, it becomes unspeakable. In Part III of *The Daughters Cycle*, Electra sees what happens to her sister, her mother, herself—sees what happens to women in the House of Agamemnon—and chooses to speak. Her speaking takes her toward separation and action.

In our firm belief that women have a separate experience, we have been engaged in developing research forms and presentational forms as well as content that articulate the female experience. We use experimental theater techniques and structures developed specifically for this research. The research stage for each of these plays has included workshops which call upon large numbers of women to explore and share their experience within their family roles; dialogue with feminist scholars; workshops with skilled performers; and a collaborative dialogue among the three authors. Prescriptions from history and demands of the popular culture are identified and challenged by women in a theater environment that compels a focus on the woman's experience, distinct from a male measure or point of reference.

The theory and practice of feminist issues can be seen as organically intertwined and continually generative in the theatrical medium. It has been our experience with workshops and presentations of the plays that the action of the audience as witness to the act of the women on stage is a spontaneous redefining of the self as separate and of the self as survivor. Each of the plays begins and ends with a naming ritual, an ongoing research form that provides an opportunity for the audience member to join with the performers after the play in searching for and naming the women in her own matrilineal heritage. In this way the trilogy continues. The naming never ends.

The question, how is a woman to know herself and take claim to herself, is a thematic thread that weaves through The Daughters Cycle. The family, a major formative institution; the mother, a person who is supposed to embody the laws of that institution; a daughter, a person who is supposed to fulfill the institution's demands; a sister, a person whose value is supposed to be ignored or denied by the institution; all are revealed through testimony, physical and vocal imagery, poetry, and dialogue that range in mood from humor to dread. The feminist theory underlying our choice of work in the theatrical medium assumes that when women become available to themselves they can have an impact on and change the very institutions that seek to deny and crush that expression.

Excerpts from *Daughters* and *Sister/Sister*

Note: Four actors perform *Daughters* and *Sister/Sister*. The voices in these excerpts are indicated with character names, with performers' names, and occasionally as Voice I, II, III, and IV.

1. *Why Do I Weep*, a letter to my sister (from *Sister/Sister*).
2. *The Matrilineage* (from *Daughters*).
3. *The Homecoming:* The daughter speaks for the mother (from *Daughters*).
   Rosie (a monologue for two voices).
   Chew and Lille.
   The Questioner.
4. *The Quadrologue* (from *Sister/Sister*).
5. *The Contracts* (from *Sister/Sister* and *Daughters*).
   The Sister Unit on Family Position.
   The Sisters Review the Family Rules.
   The Pledge.
   The Daughters' Contract.
6. *The Matrilineage* (from *Daughters*).
7. *The Matrilineage* with the audience.

1. Why Do I Weep, a letter to my sister (from *Sister/Sister,* specifically on the theme of separation and survival)

Why do I weep before I see you?
And after I see you?

Who am I weeping for?

Do I weep for what we've lost

or for what we still bring with us into the present?
Am I saying farewell to something each time I see you?
Is that why I weep?
saying goodbye
to what?
to my child self?
you in childhood?
dead expectations of Mother and Dad?
what I felt you took from me that I can never regain?

Who do I weep for?
Daddy's girl?
Mother's
what was?
or what never was?
the family romance
the loss of the family romance

How far have I come away from all of this?
from all of you?
Is it all
are you all
lost to me?

Or do I weep at how close it all still is
that every visit with you
my sister
is a visit to the past
to those original family scenes, to powerlessness,
competition, unmet need

Is it that?

Is it that we talk
here in the present
trying to keep our safe, good place with each other
surrounded by shapes of ourselves
and of them
shapes that live in us still
when we are apart
and more so
when we are together.
The past is like the sun in our eyes
it is light
but light that keeps us from seeing

and oh how hard we work to see, sister
to see each other.

I'm weeping
I'm weeping for all of us
who yearn for sight
as much as we yearn for the family romance.

Don't give up
don't leave me now
now that there are tools for seeing.

When I say I love you
what does that mean?

I love you.

What do I want from you?
closeness without sameness
support without competition
loyalty without betrayal
an ending to those ancient dualities
an ending to living in comparison

separation without loss

I want to separate from you without losing you

You've been there all along
we've seen the same things
there's no way to say farewell to you
and I've never really wanted to.

and yet
I weep for fear of losing you
the you with whom I seek
a sisterhood of consciousness and friendship

Our relationship is so complex
so laden with the past, with the intensity
    of each of our connections to each of our parents,
    with the intensity of family life
So laden with the dependency of early childhood,
    the desperation of sibling rivalry,
    the threat of separation.
So full of being torn apart and of being alone.

How can we

see one another through all that
see ourselves and one another with consciousness
and with compassion

I want you to see me
separate
see my shape
because I am in space
see my form
because there is light around me
see me changing
because there is room for movement
see me as figure
not on the field of family
not on the field of the past
or at least
not only those ways
but also separate
from you
separate
from them
close
but with space and light between us so that you can see me
and I can see you.

BLACK OUT

2. *The Matrilineage* (from *Daughters*, the prologue or setting for the play)

I am Sondra

I am Clare

I am Mary

I am Debbie

I am Mary

I am Roberta

I am Sondra
daughter of Lille
daughter of Sarah Rebecca

daughter of Tzivia
daughter of a woman from Austria

I am Clare
daughter of Alistine
daughter of Marie Josephine
daughter of Marie Josephine
daughter of a woman from southern France

I am Mary
daughter of Chew Kwong Ping
daughter of Nok Yip Lee
daughter of a peasant woman from my ancestral village of
Son Woy in Canton, China whose name I don't know

I am Debbie
daughter of Arlene
daughter of Frances
daughter of Celia

I am Mary
mother of Jennifer
daughter of Agnes
daughter of Mary Regina
daughter of Eva

I am Roberta
daughter of Rose
daughter of Golda
daughter of Ruchel
daughter of a woman from Odessa
whose name I don't know

I am Sondra
daughter of Lille
daughter of Sarah Rebecca
daughter of Tzivia
for whom I was named
Tzivia had five daughters
Chaicha, Roncha, Bette, Esther, and Sarah
each of these women came to this country in her teens
Tzivia never saw any of her daughters again
she was the daughter of a woman from Austria

I am Clare
daughter of four women who brought me up

daughter of Alistine
who gave birth to me
daughter of grandmother Josie
who took care of me my first four months of life
daughter of Dolores Dobrosky
who came to work for my mother when she was sixteen
and I was seven months old
my earliest memory is Dolores leaning over my crib
smiling
daughter of Aunt Clare
who taught me artifice and survival

I am Mary
daughter of Chew Kwong Ping
when I was growing up I was fortunate enough
to have my own room
My bed was right under a large picture window
Whenever my mother heard me coughing in the night
she would come into my room right away
lean across my bed and close the window
because she didn't want me to catch a cold
she was the daughter of Nok Yip Lee

I am Debbie
daughter of Arlene
daughter of Frances
when I was very young I used to sleep
in the same room as my grandmother Frances
before I went to sleep she'd always say
pleasant dreams
I remember never knowing what she meant by saying that
until I was much older

I am Mary
mother of Jennifer
daughter of Agnes
on June 26th my daughter Jennifer graduated from high school

I am Roberta
daughter of Rose
when my mother died five years ago
as the rabbi spoke a eulogy for her
he named her repeatedly as Rose
daughter of Aden, her father
he never mentioned her mother

since that time I have had the opportunity
to name my mother publicly
Rose
the daughter of Golda, her mother
the daughter of Ruchel, her grandmother
the daughter of a woman from Odessa
whose name I don't know

I am Sondra
daughter of Lille
daughter of Sarah Rebecca
daughter of Tzivia
daughter of a woman from Austria
whose name I don't know

I am Clare
daughter of Alistine
daughter of Josie
daughter of Josephine
daughter of a woman from Gascony in southern France

I am Mary
daughter of Chew Kwong Ping
daughter of Nok Yip Lee
daughter of a peasant woman from my ancestral village
of Son Woy in Canton, China whose name I don't know

I am Debbie
daughter of Arlene
daughter of Frances
daughter of Celia

I am Mary
mother of Jennifer
daughter of Agnes
daughter of Mary Regina
daughter of Eva

I am Roberta
daughter of Rose
daughter of Golda
daughter of Ruchel
daughter of a woman from Odessa
whose name I don't know

3. The Homecoming: The Daughter Speaks for the Mother (from *Daughters*)

Rosie (a monologue for two voices)

Chorus: The Homecoming
             The daughter speaks for the mother.
             (The two women who portray the mother/daughter totem in
             the Primary Connection step downstage center with two
             crates. They sit mid-stage next to one another and speak both
             simultaneously and separately as Rosie.)

Chorus: What's your name?

Rosie I &
Rosie II: Rosemary.

Rosie II: Rosie.

Chorus: What's your husband's name?

R. I & II: John.

R. I: John Ryan.

R. II: John Harper Ryan.

R. I: That's my husband's name.

Chorus: What does he give you?

R.I: A kitchen full of stale cookies.

R. II: He's got steady work nowadays—union—a truck driver for
             Nabisco.

R.I: Can never throw away one damaged package.

R. II: All I ever see are cookies—malomars, oreos, lemon wafers,
             but where does his paycheck go? Talk about damage—that
             never gets near the house, much less the kitchen.

R. I: He drives, then he drinks. Thank God in that order. "When the sun reaches below the rear-view mirror, I get a powerful thirst on me." And then he's off with his poker-playing buddies, talkin' up the open road.

R. II: Whenever I complain that the kids need new shoes or clothes—he says . . .

R I & II: "You're a lucky girl, Rosie, and you don't even know it."

Chorus: Do you like Johnny?

R. II: He's still pretty good lookin'.

R. I: Yeah, he can be a lot of fun sometimes.

Chorus: Tell us about your children.

R. I & II: They make up for him.

R. II: They really do. The youngest is an angel. She's my blessing. In her last year of high school. That girl is going to college, I swear she is.

R. I: Going to major in chemistry, can you beat that?

R. II: She's smart.

R. I: She takes after my side of the family.

R. II: She's going to make something of herself, that's for sure.

R. I: My oldest boy, Billy, he left home at sixteen—joined the Navy—but he still writes home twice a month—and he sends me a little silver spoon from every country he's been to. He even had a special cabinet made for me to hang them all up.

R. II: Now I have a kitchen full of stale cookies and little silver spoons.

R. I: I don't really know Billy any more—see him every few years for a few days at a time. He always took off out of the house as a kid—a real loner, Billy.

R. II: Getting away from the fights. Johnny and I were always
           fighting before he got steady work.

R. I: He was always under my feet, Johnny. I'd come home from
           work, I worked as a bank teller while I put myself through
           college at night, and there he'd be moping around the house,

R. I & II: guzzling beer,

R. I: just waiting to pick a fight.

R. II: Then I'd come home and he'd go out, leaving me with all the
           kids.

R. I: Out with his beer drinking buddies.

R. II: He never helped with groceries or the kids or cooking or
           nothing.

R. I: Billy being the oldest had it harder than any of the other kids.

R. II: And there's Maureen—

R.I & II: Mo's a fool—

R. II: married to get out of the house. I told her she could go to
           college on a scholarship.

R. I: Get yourself an education.

R. II: But you can't tell Mo word one. Mo knows everything. She's
           stubborn and beautiful. Just like her father.

R. I: She goes around with her nose up in the air. But she was such
           an easy baby. One time her highchair fell over on the heat
           register on the floor, and she never cried.

R. II: That girl never cried.

R. I: There she was, lying on the hot register, thank God I walked
           by and found her. She has a little scar right here on her nose
           and the back of her right hand from that hot register. I nursed
           Maureen for the longest time. She was such an easy baby.

R. II: She's having a hard time with that husband of hers—he's a real loser . . . lets her wait on him hand and foot.

R. I & II: Always out of work.

R. II: My Maureen works so hard,

R. I & II: I get a pain right here in my heart.

R. II: I tell her, Maureen, before you get kids hanging around your neck, get rid of him, Maureen.

R. I & II: "I love him, ma."

R. I: Mike—

R. II: my youngest boy—

R. I: is shy and clumsy. I think I got the wrong baby in the hospital when I look at Mike.

R. II: Always had to go in and have those heavy looks from his teachers and counselors.

R. I: What are we going to do with Mike?

R. II: Never studies.

R. I: Never does his homework.

R. II: Plays hookey all the time.

R. I: Doesn't like sports. He lives in a dream world.

R. II: Johnny and I tried to talk to Mike. But he explodes. He goes around quiet and shy and then say word one and he explodes.

R. I: Johnny can't stand Mike now. He yells and screams at him all the time. He beat him up once for nothing.

R. II: 'Cuz he wouldn't give him the answer he wanted about girls.

R. I: I said to Johnny,

R. I & II: hitting me is one thing. You start beating up on my children and that's it. You've seen the last of me.

R. I: He never tried that again.

Chorus: Who's your best friend?

R. II: Connie.

R. I: It's hard for me to be with women, they put me off—

R. I & II: but not Connie.

R. II: We met at college at night—

R. I: sat next to each other in math class, can you beat that?

R. II: She dropped out after her first year to marry Red. His name is John too, but everyone calls him Red 'cuz of his hair. Not that he has that much left of it.

R. I: She married Red to get out of that apartment with her father.

R. II: Connie got herself tied down to a no good bartender. She'd do everything but genuflect for that man.

R. I: For awhile there Connie and I would meet on Sundays with the kids—go on picnics—to the beach—

R. II: they never cared.

R. I: Johnny and Red never cared.

R. I & II: Never missed us.

R. I: Sundays were

R. I & II: ballgames and beer and poker to them.

R. II: Connie was so popular. Guys would line up to date her. She kept a list inside her closet door—had dates three months in advance when I first knew her.

R. I: Then she fell for a good-looking face and

R. I & II: a gift for gab.

R. I: Connie always says to me: Rosie, what happened? Rosie—
           there was Frank—

R. I & II: there was Joe Spinozi—

R. I: Rosie, there was Milo.

R. I & II: What happened, Rosie?

R. II: I'll tell you what happened.

R. I: What happened? She could have married the cream right off
           the top,

R. II: or finished college,

R. I: but she fell for looks and a

R. I & II: gift for gab.

Chorus: How do you like to spend your time?

R. II: What time?

R. I: Who has time? When I'm not working, cleaning up after
           everybody or,

R I & II: or trying to keep track of Johnny, what time is left?

R. II: The last time I saw a movie, Maureen dragged me to a rerun of
           An American in Paris.

R. I: That Maureen, she thinks I looked like Leslie Caron when I
           was younger—in my snapshots.

R. II: None of the kids, except Angie, keep their clothes, their rooms
           in any kind of condition. They're all pigs.

R. I: They're just like their father.

R. II: Except for Angie.

R. I & II: I never have any time—

R. II: Angie says, ma—let me take you to Puerto Rico for a week's
            vacation—and I say yes—that's what I'll do. I'll just up and
            walk out of here for a week. Let Johnny see what this house
            would look like without me around picking up after every-
            body.

R. I: That'd be a real eye-opener for all of them.

Chorus: Where's your mother?

R. II: Momma's been gone now for several years.

R. I: God rest her soul. Everyone called her Grandlady from the
            time Billy was born . . . her first grandchild.

R. II: Except for me, I always called her Mama. When people used to
            say, what was it like in your day? She'd rise up as tall as she
            could get and say—My day! My day! This is my day! I'm alive,
            aren't I. This is my day.

R. I: She came over when she was sixteen—worked as a maid—then
            one summer she and her sister took a trip upstate—she met a
            farming man, married him and had six big boys

R. I & II: and me.

R. I: Only two of them, Pat and Robbie, stayed on after Pop died.
            Momma had crystal blue eyes and black black hair—and the
            whitest skin.

R. II: She had always planned to live with me when I got married,
            but she couldn't stand the sight of Johnny.

R. I: She wanted something better for me. She told me to concen-
            trate on college and forget Johnny or I'd be wasting my life
            with all charm and no sense and she was right too.

R. II: I went up to be with her when she was dying—

R. I: pregnant with Michael . . .

R. II: shouldn't have been traveling. Momma had written me a long
            goodbye letter in case I didn't make it in time.

R. I: "Sweeter through adversity. Don't you believe it for one min-
            ute."

R. II: She used to say that all the time. Momma and I were best
            friends until I married Johnny. Then it was always harder for
            us to talk. She always thought Johnny was a mistake for me.

R. I: When she was dying she took my hand and kept asking me to
            get the little red velvet pin cushion shaped like a heart—I
            didn't know what she was talking about—her hair never
            turned grey—it was black black

R. I & II: till the day she died.

R.I: To this day, I can never see a full black head of hair without
            seeing Momma.

Chorus: What did you want for yourself?

R. I: Ooo, what did I want for myself?

R. II: I wanted to go back upstate and open a clinic out in the
            country. I went to nursing school—at night, you know.

R. I: I always thought that Johnny and I would leave the city and
            I'd run a clinic—like where I grew up in farm country. We
            never had a doctor anywhere near when I was growing up.

R. II: And I wanted to go to Rome and maybe Paris. But Rome first
            and see all that old beauty over there.

R. I: I married Johnny to get out of the house, just like my Maureen
            did.

R. II: Pop wanted me to stay at home and work on the farm and
            take care of him and Momma. I eloped with Johnny and came
            back to tell Pop. We had a big fight in the barn. He almost
            killed me. He just went berserk. Said I couldn't leave. Momma
            was scared. That was the first time I ever saw her scared.

R. I: She sneaked me money for us to go to New York City, as far away as we could get.

R. II: But Pop got over it and dropped the whole thing after a few months. It was Momma who didn't like Johnny.

R. I: What did I want for myself? I got my B.A. degree at night—it took years to get my nursing degree—I'm a school nurse now.

R. I & II: I do a good job.

R. II: They didn't want to hire me because I was so old by the time I got my degree. But I kept at it and threatened to make a human rights case out of it if I didn't get hired at my age.

R.I: I work hard as a school nurse in this city—

R. I & II: believe me.

Chorus: Do you have a word of advice?

R. I & II: Nobody ever listens to my advice.

R. I: Do what you want to do—and if you can't do that, do what you have to do; find a way.

R. II: And if marriage is the only way—

R. I & II: then do that.

R. II: But be careful who you marry. Somedays you can end up more lonely than if you lived alone.

R. I: And your kids won't make any difference when it comes to being lonely.

R. I & II: Don't think they will.

Chorus: Who takes care of you now?

R. I & II: What do you mean?

Chorus: Who takes care of you?

R. I: I take care of myself, who do you think?

R. II: I don't need to trap one of my kids for my old age.

R. I: Once Johnny died, I moved into this little apartment. I can take care of it myself. No steps to climb and a grocery right next door.

R. II: Connie's still on the other end of the phone when I need her.

R. I: And I don't expect to hear from my kids. Billy still comes through once in a blue moon.

R. II: Mo is swamped with three kids and her husband still laying around like a helpless baby.

R. I: Angie's got a good career for herself now.

R. I & II: God bless her.

R. II: I've lost track of Mike. He'll turn up, like a bad penny.

R. I: I take care of myself.

R. II: Angie's promising a trip to Rome—I'm not holding my breath. I'm learning Italian from the records—maybe I'll go on a tour someday. Maybe I'll go with Connie. You can't lean on your kids.

R. I: The only one I've ever been able to count on is myself and that's never going to change.

R. II: I take care of myself.

Chorus: What's your name?

R. I & II: Rosemary.

R. II: Rosemary Kenyon.

R. I: My married name is Ryan. Mrs. John Ryan.

R. II: But my friends call me Rosie.

Chew and Lille

MARY: My mother, Chew Kwong Ping Lum, was born in the village of
        Son Woy in Canton, southern China. She married my father
        when she was 19 through an arranged marriage. She came from
        a very poor family—she was a peasant's daughter. She worked
        very hard. Her life was very hard. When she married my father
        she went to live with his family and kept house for them while
        he came to the States to look for work, and didn't see him again
        for twenty years. She was his family's insurance that their son
        would return. He fought in World War II and in '47 brought my
        mother back to the States as a war bride. She said something
        about growing up in China when the bombs fell—I think she
        meant Japanese bombs. Her father, my grandfather, had died
        very young fighting in one of the civil wars. She was the oldest
        daughter and had to take care of her younger sister. She
        remembered carrying her sister, running for cover a lot.

DEBBIE: My mother's name is Lille. She was the second daughter in a
        family of six children. She grew up in a very very very small
        town called Point Merion, Pennsylvania. They were poor and
        the only Jews in town. Several times crosses were burned on
        their front lawn.

        Out of all the children my mother sees herself as the good one.
        Sylvie was the little one, Pearl was the funny one. Rose was the
        pretty one, and my mother was the good one. She took respon-
        sibility in the family. She got a job at the age of 15. She said
        there was a roomful of 200 girls being interviewed at the same
        time. When they asked what office skills they had, she raised her
        hand for everything, whether she knew how to do it or not. She
        got the job and was paid fifteen dollars a week which supported
        the family.

MARY: I'd like to tell you what I mean by a war bride. My mother
        wasn't allowed to come over with my father in 1928. The
        government here had issued a law called the Chinese Exclusion
        Act of 1924, which specifically forbid Chinese women to come
        over with their husbands. It made it very difficult even for
        Chinese men to get to this country unless they knew someone
        who could get them in—so my mother couldn't come, otherwise
        she might have been here in 1928. My father came over, found
        work, and sent money back to his family. In '41 when the war

broke out, he enlisted. The government said that if you enlist and fight in the war and come out alive, you can bring your wife over as a war bride. He had to go through some sort of procedure where it looked like he met her during the war, something like that. A lot of Chinese men did that. They fought in the war, and then they brought their wives over as war brides. That's how my mother got here.

DEBBIE: My mother's mother, my grandmother, came from Galicia, Austria. I picture her living on a farm, doing farm work. She came here when she was 16 and never saw her mother again. Her sisters had already come over and were living in Pittsburgh. When she first arrived they more or less used her as a maid. I know that my grandmother was beautiful, she had rosy cheeks, she was a very healthy women—a big woman. She used to tell me that. She had come to this country on a boat. She spoke no English.

I have a feeling when she met my grandfather, it was arranged. I'm not sure. She got married when she was 18. He was a tinker, a traveling salesman with a wagon full of household goods. Her greatest shame was that he was much shorter than she was, and in pictures of them he is always sitting on a high stool. She raised six children, farm animals, had a garden, did all the heavy work because he traveled. They didn't see him much, except when he came home for shabbos. She did all the work of running the place. It was primitive. She did the laundry, farming, they grew vegetables that they lived on, had chickens, a cow. They kept kosher. They had beans for protein. She spoke English, but she never learned to read or write.

MARY: My mother never learned to speak English. I always thought she knew more than she said she did, because she had been here for thirty years. Since then I have realized that she said she didn't understand English in order to maintain her dependency on me and my sister, and on my father.

I think she did that to keep us all together. We tried to teach her English and she was too embarrassed to speak it. When they first came over in '47 my father had a laundry and my mother went to work in one of the garment factories in Chinatown. After a while she said she didn't like it. Then she got fired because the boss said she was too slow. After that my father said she could stay at home and work with him. They were together twenty-four hours a day for thirty years.

DEBBIE: There are only a few stories I know about my grandmother. One of them is about her ladies—Bubbie's ladies. They'd play canasta at different women's homes. She'd say, "Tonight I'm going to my ladies." I went with her once. They spoke mostly yiddish and played canasta and had a good time. My grandmother loved it when I played canasta with her. She would always tell me the same stories about herself—and how she had once been beautiful and healthy and young with rosy cheeks and black hair.

MARY: My mother had a good sense of humor. Although I found it irritating at times. My sister and our friends thought it was cute. I can't think of anything specific right now. I know she laughed a lot. I guess I never fully appreciated her sense of humor or who she was as a person.

My mother's definition of a daughter is one who is dutiful and obedient. A good daughter would find herself a nice husband, get married, and have grandchildren, of course, and either live at home or marry a man who can afford to buy a house so the family can all live together.

I think she considered herself a good daughter in the traditional sense. Very much so.

DEBBIE: My mother loved school. She was crazy about school, and would have liked to continue. She wanted to go to college and study drama. She graduated from high school when she was fifteen. She hadn't started school until she was fairly old because of taking care of her younger brothers and sisters. So I guess she could only have gone to school for seven or eight years. I never realized that. She reads constantly. She always did. Instead of children's books, she used to read to us whatever she was reading—the *Scarlet Letter, Jane Eyre, Crime and Punishment*.

My mother also worked with my father in his store—a kosher meat market—for about thirty years. I always thought the work was like slave labor. They worked six days a week, fourteen hours a day, and only took one week off during the year. In recent years when I helped them out at busy holiday times, I saw that she loved it. I was shocked. She was very very busy and it was a completely social setting. She worked very fast, lots of demands, activity, phones ringing, a lot of pressure. She turned to me at one point and said, "Isn't this fun!" I didn't think it could be after more than thirty years.

MARY: My mother lived half her life in China, came over here and still maintained the old customs. I think that's another reason why she never bothered to learn English. She preferred to use Chinese because she wanted to maintain her culture. And she was also the last to yield. My father was the first to compromise. He'd say, well, we moved our daughters into a white neighborhood and they have been exposed to a different culture all their lives. He was more able to compromise and to accept our different ideas and our differences.

My mother administered the punishment. She was the one who disciplined. She hit. She used a broomstick. That's how bad I got. She used a hanger. I got pretty bad. Although at the time I didn't think I was bad, I thought I was just exercising my independence. But she thought differently.

DEBBIE: My mother has a mind of her own. Her friends have always been important to her. In her adult life her best friend is Ida—someone she's been close to for thirty-five years. Ida's a lot of fun. Now she lives in Florida. When my parents moved to Florida my mother said she didn't move too close to Ida because she didn't want to live in anyone's pocket. She likes independence. She never was a good neighbor. Doesn't want people dropping in. She likes to have her own house. Actually, I think she feels the same way about her kids. Each of us sees my parents about three times a year. We're a very close family. We all see ourselves as a very close family.

But we don't live in each other's pockets.

MARY: There's something else I'd like to say about my mother. In spite of her supposed lack of English and knowledge of this culture—see, I never saw this in my mother until late. My father saw it and my sister saw it before I did. She was able to get around. She was able to function and survive and do what she had to do, in spite of the fact that she never spoke English. She wasn't helpless. She was a very strong woman.

The Questioner

The *Daughters* form a straight line facing the audience and speak the following questions by sections as indicated.

Does your mother feel loved?
Is she terrified of aging?
Does she have a best friend?
What do they talk about?

Can you talk about your mother without crying?
Do you hate yourself when you're with her?
Do you have to forgive her?
What do you want from her now?

Is your mother healthy?
Is she alone?

Is your mother still alive?

Did your mother work it out with her mother?
Was she ashamed of her mother?
Are you?

Does your mother have a mother?
Do you have a daughter?
Are you alone?

Does your mother feel loved?
Can you talk about her without crying?
Is there still time to work it out?

Are you terrified of aging?
Are you healthy?
Do you look like your mother?

Did your mother work it out with her mother?
Did she hate herself when she was with her?
Does your mother hate herself when she is with you?
Is she ashamed of your life?

Do you have to forgive her?
Are you her disappointment?
Was she her mother's disappointment?
Can you forgive her?

Do you feel loved by your mother?
Do you have a daughter?
Can she forgive you?

Can you talk about your mother without crying?
What do you want from her now?

Can you talk about your mother without crying?

4. *The Quadrologue* (from *Sister/Sister;* four sisters' voices on the theme of shared responsibility in adulthood)

SONDRA:

Who actually comes when somebody calls from the hospital
and needs help?
Who talks to the surgeon?
Is the one who talks to the surgeon the one everyone expected
to or was it a surprise?
Who sees to it that everyone knows?
Who is responsible for making the funeral arrangements for a parent?
Who talks to the rabbi?
Is he going to give the same old eulogy and everyone stand
around crying?
Who goes through all the old family photos and divides up the furniture
and stands there and sells things?

DEBBIE:

Can sisters know each other after the death of a parent?

SONDRA:

Can we sort out the past from the present so that we can
know each other?

BLACK OUT

SONDRA:

When Mother knew she was dying, who helped her?
Who held her?
Who was it?
Was it the oldest sister?
Was it the responsible sister who held her?
Who held her?

Who?
Was it the baby girl holding her mother?
Was it the baby girl changing into her mother?
Which sister held her mother?

I held my mother.
I grew into the one who mothers the mother.
I held my dying mother while we were each changing.
I cared for my mother until there was no mothering left
only my mother dying
leaving life
leaving me
leaving us
leaving her daughters
wanting to be mothered.

I'm the sister who grew into my mother's mother.
I grew through my mother's death into myself
my mother's mother
my own mother
myself.

And where were my sisters then?
Were they changing into themselves, too?
Were they separating out into themselves?

I grew up and I changed.
I'm not sure what happened to my sisters.
But I changed.

MEG:

For a couple of years they used to come over on Saturday night.
Mom and dad.
We all ate together and watched TV
and they'd sleep over.
It was too much for them to go home
especially since they were coming back the next day.
Anyway we'd watch TV and mom would doze a little
and in the morning dad and Al and the boys would go out
and play ball.
Mom would sit out on the porch and turn the pages
of the Sunday papers and sleep a little in the sun.
And no one really noticed that way, not really.

So I never mentioned anything

to my sisters I mean.
We all had breakfast and lunch together
and mom would help a little and talk with the kids
and none of us really noticed that she was in pain
and couldn't do very much.
Well she didn't really want us to notice.
That's how she wanted it.
She wanted it to slip by
and I helped her do that.

It went on for a couple of years.

Each week she was up to less and less.
She was still working part-time, sewing every morning.
But she told me more and more
she had to sleep away the afternoons.
Don't get me wrong
she wasn't old.

She was only sixty, that's not old.
I didn't mention it to my sisters.
What good would it do?

My mother turned to my younger sister when
things got really bad.
The youngest one was mad that I hadn't told her.
We had a big fight on the phone.
She kept going on about why had I let it go on so long.
But there was nothing anyone could do.
It was better not to mention it.
There was no reason to tell.
There was nothing anyone could do.
I know my mother wouldn't have wanted
any of us to see her that way.
There was no reason to tell.
I did what I could
after that I couldn't do any more.

SONDRA:

Three of us carried my mother's dying
in turns and in unequal shares.
My oldest sister's part ended when mine began.
She carried it and she dropped it
and I took it with my middle sister
and for awhile we carried it together.

And then I carried my mother
and her dying
without my sisters
to the end.

My friends helped me.
My friends
my chosen sisters were there the whole time
and through to the end.

I grew up and I changed.
I'm not sure what happened to my sisters
but I changed.

MARY:

I didn't know

nobody told me
none of my sisters told me
it's not my fault that I didn't know
nobody told me
maybe I didn't want to know
anyway nobody told me
nobody told me anything.

(She holds image with her elbows bent, her hands opened out flat on each
    side.)

DEBBIE:

I was pulled apart in the middle of all this.
pleasing and caring
I was pulled all over the place
my mother
my father
my husband
my kids
I was pulled all over the place

I tried
I tried to keep my promise to my mother
after all a promise is a promise
I promised to take care of my father when she couldn't
well not in so many words
but everyone expected me to take care of him

to feed him
to give him meals
to take care of him
to do everything for him

I promise
I promise to take care of him, ma, I promise
I tried
I tried
to take care of him
I tried to take care of him, ma

I went to the cemetery with my sister
to visit my mother's grave
I had asked her to take me there
I didn't tell my older sister or my father
It's not that it was a secret
I just wanted to go with her

We went together
the two of us
me and the youngest one
I told her
I know it's a terrible thing to say
but when dad dies
I won't even go to his funeral.

SONDRA:

She said to me
I won't even go to his funeral
it was almost two years since mother had died
we went to the cemetery together
she hadn't been there in two years

we went up on the hill
together

she had wanted me to take her there
I didn't really want to
I didn't really want to be there with her because
I didn't want to have to take care of her but
I couldn't say no to her either.

I had missed her after my mother's death
I had been angry
and I had missed her

we had a falling out
and we hadn't spoken

we went up on the hill together
we paced around
a stranger had been buried next to my mother
there were little stones on her tombstone
little pebbles
signifying visitors
who had been there?
my father?
my oldest sister?
she couldn't have been there

we walked back and forth
little steps
the sun in our eyes
finally
she put her arm around the tombstone
goodbye ma
she kissed the tombstone
she kissed the tombstone!
I saw my sister saying goodbye to my mother
she kissed the tombstone
not knowing any other way

later
we sat in a diner
over coffee
exhausted
we talked about our father
our bitterness
each of us bitter against him
ashamed of it
she was ashamed of it
and I was raging
there was some comfort for us in that
finally
we left the diner

a few days later
we went to the wedding of our nephew
the son of our eldest sister
that was why we were all together that week
to celebrate a wedding

the three sisters
the three of us
sisters
were together
for the first time
since our mother had died
to celebrate a wedding

she sat us at separate tables at the wedding
I left before it was over.

MARY:

I didn't know
did she know she was dying
I didn't know
nobody told me
none of my sisters told me
it's not my fault that I didn't know

my oldest sister didn't tell me
I only saw my mother once that year
on a stopover flight
I couldn't believe it
did she know she was dying
if she didn't know it's not my fault
it's not my fault if I didn't know

nobody told me
Okay. Maybe I didn't want to know
and anyway
nobody told me
nobody ever told me anything.

DEBBIE:

Can sisters know each other after the death of a parent?

SONDRA:

Can we sort out the past from the present so that we can know each
    other?
(SONDRA rests her hand on DEBBIE's shoulder.)
                    BLACK OUT

5. *The Contracts* (from *Sister/Sister* and *Daughters*)

The last series of excerpts from both *Daughters* and *Sister/Sister*: the contracts negotiated between women in the family. From *Sister/Sister*: a series of transformations through feeling states and dynamics between sisters. Changes come rapidly and with the inflections of childhood.

The Sister Unit on Family Position

One by one the performers form a family portrait at the left platform. They take a pose after each performer's first line:

SONDRA: No one loves anyone more than I love my mother.
MEG: I preserve the picture of my family.
DEBBIE: I agree to share with my mother the picture of my sister no matter what my sister does.
MARY: I hide the closeness with one sister from another sister.
SONDRA: I agree to see my sisters the way my parents see them.
MEG: I agree with my mother to respect one sister more than the other sister.

(The following lines are said continuously as one statement, as the performers speak from the family portrait.)
DEBBIE: I agree not to be closer to any one of my sisters than I am to my mother.
SONDRA: and to be closer to one of my sisters than I am to my mother from time to time but when my mother is available to leave that sister for my mother
DEBBIE: and I agree to never be open with my sister
MARY: and I agree to be open with my sister
MEG: and not let my mother know.

LIGHTS UP

(THE PERFORMERS meet on Platform Left to form THE SISTERS. They begin a series of transformations.)
MARY: I'm the oldest. The spoiled one.
SONDRA: I'm the middle. The guilty one.
DEBBIE: I'm the youngest. I'm the special one.
MEG: I'm the oldest. The responsible one.

I'm the good one.
I'm the interesting one.
I'm the guilty one.

I'm the forgotten one.
I'm the sexual one.
I'm the spoiled one.
I'm the special one.

SONDRA: (addressing an audience member)
    I love you the best.
(THE SISTERS join her)
    I love you the most
    I love you better.
    I love you the most.
(Their focus turns to the other side of the theater, and back again to the other side.)

The Sisters Review the Family Rules

MEG/MOTHER
(Pointing and shaking her finger in a wide arc at the audience)

Don't—
Don't—
Don't—
Don't start a fight.
Don't eat, you'll spoil your dinner

DEBBIE/FATHER

Don't leave anything on your plate.
Don't sit too close to the TV.
Don't touch your sister's things.
Don't be selfish.
Don't trust anyone outside the family.

MOTHER

Don't come crying to me.
(She grabs her right hand with her left hand to stop it from pointing and shaking, and sits down. FATHER stands at her side.)
I don't know how you all turned out so different.
I raised you all the same.
I love you all the same.

FATHER

She loves you all the same.

MOTHER
Love your sisters all the same.

FATHER
Be like your sister.

MOTHER
If you want to be beautiful, you have to suffer.

FATHER
If you can't say something nice, don't say anything at all, young lady.

MOTHER (prompting FATHER)
The more you know—

FATHER
The more you know—

MOTHER (prompting)
The more you'll have—

FATHER (quickly)
The more you know, the more you'll have to do.

MOTHER (Rising, eyes closed, hands in prayer)
Walk with God and you'll never walk alone.

FATHER
You can't have what you want just because you want it.
You should be ashamed of yourself.
You're so cute, I'm going to eat you up.

MOTHER
You're so cute, I'm going to eat you up.

FATHER
It will all work out for the best.
Don't come crying to me.
We just want you to be happy.

MOTHER
Don't tell your father, I'll tell him.

FATHER
Don't tell your mother, I'll tell her.
If you really loved me. (spoken to MOTHER)

MOTHER
You'll find out when you grow up.
When you have your own house you'll do it your way.

FATHER
She didn't really mean it.

MOTHER
Put yourself in her place.

FATHER
Remember the family.

MOTHER
Come home for the holidays.

FATHER
Get married in chronological order.

MOTHER
Share and share alike.

FATHER
Give us a sign that you'll take care of us forever.

MOTHER
Don't leave.

FATHER
No matter what.

The Pledge

DEBBIE: (Kneeling, she pledges)

> I promise not to have more than my sister.
> I promise I won't give more to myself than to my sister.
> I won't love myself more than I love my sister.
> I promise I won't take care of myself more than I take care of
> my sister.

BLACK OUT

The Daughters' Contract

The Oath

Performers are evenly dispersed throughout the playing space.

CALLER

(Calls out each agreement. DAUGHTERS swear to each agreement by
repeating it after it is called.)

I agree to make the same agreement over and over with everyone always.

I agree to make my body forget its primary connection.

I agree to be happy.

I agree to stand up straight.

I agree to be like you.

I agree to be quiet.

I agree never to know what I want.

I agree not to kill myself.
     (one voice trailing)
     Not me, Mommy

I agree to always need you.

I agree to want and not get.

DAUGHTER
(Each DAUGHTER calls out her own agreements)

Voice I

I agree that my body belongs to you.

I agree to do what I want and pay and pay and pay.

I agree that you and I are special.

I agree never to have an independent moment.

I agree to eat for you.

I agree to be in a fog.

I agree to love you no matter what.

I agree to want too much.

I agree not to earn more money than my father.

I agree to survive no matter what.

I agree never to put you in a nursing home.

I agree not to be sexual.

I agree to be sexual.

I agree that the word home will always mean where you are.

I agree to leave you and come back to you in the end.

Voice II

I agree not to fight.

I agree to drink milk for lunch.

I agree to go to bed early.

I agree to eat well.

I agree to work.

I agree not to take anything for free.

I agree to obey.

I agree not to ask for too many things.

I agree to see both sides.

I agree to worry about money.

I agree to grow up.

I agree to love you, no matter what.

Voice III (CALLER)

I agree to live for you.

I agree to be humble.

I agree to sacrifice.

I agree to get married just so you can have grandchildren.

I agree to call home every day.

I agree to give up my dreams for you.

I agree to live in the family tradition.

I agree not to be conspicuous.

I agree never to leave you alone.

I agree not to be myself.

I agree to be nice to relatives I don't like.

I agree not to be sexual.

I agree to be sexual.

I agree not to question you.

I agree to remember your sacrifice.

I agree to take care of you, no matter what.

Voice IV

I agree not to think for myself.

I agree to be sweet and quiet.

I agree not to say I'm afraid.

I agree not to be conspicuous.

I agree to button my coat and keep it buttoned.

I agree not to play rough.

I agree that it's greedy to want too much.

I agree that I'm a lucky girl and to realize how fortunate I am.

I agree not to slam the door.

I agree to be sorry.

I agree not to be wild.

I agree to get married and have children.

I agree that Daddy didn't really mean it.

I agree to survive, no matter what.

CALLER
(DAUGHTERS repeat after each call)

I agree to be the victim.

I agree not to notice the depth of my deprivation.

I agree to want what you can't give.

I agree not to look for it anywhere else.

I agree to leave you and to come back to you in the end.

The Round: Caller and Daughters

Spoken together once, then a round. Each DAUGHTER becomes possessed physically and vocally by the oaths she is speaking. The intensity

and volume of voices and movements increase to a din of oath taking—a freeze.

ALL DAUGHTERS

YOU WON'T BE YOU.
I WON'T BE ME.

YOU WON'T BE YOU.
I WON'T BE ME.

I AGREE
I AGREE
I AGREE
I AGREE

I AGREE NOT TO SEE
   NOT TO BE
   NOT TO KNOW
   NOT TO TELL
   NOT TO FEEL
   NOT TO THINK
   NOT TO LOOK
   NOT TO WANT
   NOT TO NEED
   NOT TO SAY

I AGREE
I AGREE
I AGREE
I AGREE

I WON'T BE YOU.
YOU WON'T BE ME.

I WON'T BE YOU.
YOU WON'T BE ME.

I AGREE TO MAKE THE SAME AGREEMENT OVER AND OVER AGAIN WITH EVERYONE ALWAYS.

(THEY freeze)

BLACK OUT

6. *The Matrilineage* (from *Daughters*)

I am Sondra
sister of Audrey and Ronna

we are the daughters of Lille
who is the daughter of Sarah Rebecca
daughter of Tzivia
daughter of a woman from Austria

I am Mary
mother of Jennifer
daughter of Agnes
daughter of Mary Regina
daughter of Eva

I am Debbie
daughter of Arlene
daughter of Frances
daughter of Celia

I am Mary
sister of Doris
we are the daughters of Chew Kwong Ping
daughter of Nok Yip Lee
daughter of a peasant woman from my ancestral village
of Son Woy in Canton, China

7. The Matrilineage with the audience

We now invite you to join us in reclaiming the women in our matriline and
participate in the collecting of matrilineal oral history for all of the women
present.

The women form a circle and begin the naming ritual.
    I am Betsy
    daughter of Martha
    daughter of Elizabeth
    who crossed the country in a covered wagon
    and is one of the women who settled the state of Wyoming.
    She is the daughter of a woman
    whose name I don't know.

    I am Marie
    daughter of Rose Margaret
    who was born in Port-au-Prince
    who was the daughter of Granmere

    I am Carol
    daughter of Rachel

daughter of Augusta
Rachel worked in a defense plant during World War II.
She wanted to be a riveter but had to work
on the assembly line instead. . . .

Sixty women named their matrilineages at the culmination of the workshop.

SUMMARY of the postperformance discussion with the audience

The discussion that followed the performed excerpts from *Daughters* and *Sister/Sister* centered on four questions: Why a feminist theater? What is feminist acting? How is the collaboration carried out? Why is the focus of *The Daughters Cycle* on the family?

The work of the Women's Experimental Theater is predicated on the belief that women have a separate and distinct experience. Feminist theater calls upon the woman in the audience to be woman-identified, to experience herself as the center of her own life. Being woman-identified is synonymous with being self-identified. The audience member is witness to this expression in our work.

The feminist actor gives testimony to the ability of women to change. We witness the woman performer as she applies consciousness and choice in her presentation of self and character at the same time, and as she demonstrates the capacity to shape and choose her own emotional experience. We see a woman in the playing space who is just herself. Then we see her enact another and also herself at the same time. We also see her comment on it. All of these levels are a testimony to our own capacity to do the same in our own lives. The woman in the audience also recognizes publicly the validation of her own experience, the commonality of her experience with other women. There is something in this process that enables all of us, the performers and the audience, to risk looking into our separateness and our differences.

What happens in the theater is an ongoing transformation. The immediacy of the theatrical act is what draws us to it. Theater is an inherently collaborative art form. Our collaboration as artists comes from our interest in working together with other women and the enormous stimulation and growth that this process generates. In addition to our own dialogue and work with the actors, we develop research forms for use in workshops with women outside of the acting company and outside of the theater context. *The Daughters Cycle* trilogy has been developed with the research participation of over two hundred women. The matrilineage, the questioner, and the testimony forms which appear in the excerpts were developed specifically as the themes of these plays were investigated.

The focus in *The Daughters Cycle* is on women in the family. Every political movement has a major institution to focus on and be critical of, in a way that either dismantles it or significantly changes it. The patriarchal family is a powerful institution that depends upon and perpetuates the subjugation of women. Through our explorations we take claim to the women who have existed in the roles of mother, daughter, and sister. Our work is not about the study of our oppression or the oppressor. It is an articulation of our experience, a reclamation of our survivals, and a search for the possibilities between women in the family.

The work of the Women's Experimental Theater derives from the deepest regard for women. It is a continuously deepening regard for every aspect of who women are, who women have to be, and who we will become.

The following is a guide for the structure of the matrilineal research.

The Matrilineage[1]

A standing circle is formed for the naming/reclaiming. One by one each woman enters the ritual by speaking her own name. There are four rounds.

 I. *Her own name*
    I am Sondra
 II. *Her biological matrilineage searching back as far as she can*
    I am Sondra (mother of [her daughter] if applicable)
    daughter of Lille
    daughter of Sarah Rebecca
    daughter of Tzivia
III. *Her matrilineage plus any new names she recalls or wants to add and a short piece of information about any one of the women named*
    I am Sondra
    daughter of Lille
    daughter of Sarah Rebecca
    who came to this country when she was sixteen
    and never saw her mother again
    daughter of Tzivia
    daughter of a woman from Austria
IV. *Her matrilineage as in Round II*
    She may choose to say only a part of it, or her own name.

Note

1. The matrilineage is part of the play *Daughters*. If you wish to use it, please acknowledge in the following way:

> The Matrilineage, from *Daughters*,
>   by Clare Coss, Sondra Segal, Roberta Sklar
> The Women's Experimental Theater
> 98 East Seventh Street
> New York, New York 10009   (212) 866-7785

Part IV
The Naming of Difference: Morality, Power, and Social Change

Quandra Prettyman

Visibility and Difference: Black Women in History and Literature—Pieces of a Paper and Some Ruminations

The paper I read as a workshop warm-up, although elegantly titled "Visibility and Difference," seemed to me even as I read it somewhat graceless. With each draft, its center had seemed to shift. Shades of an academic beginning remained in the biographical sketches of four black women whose careers and lives had spoken to me of mutual concerns.

There were two nineteenth-century figures: Sojourner Truth—familiar to most of the participants; and Frances Ellen Watkins Harper—a significant but nearly forgotten figure, abolitionist, feminist, temperance worker, independent working woman, prolific writer. The early twentieth-century figures were two novelists, Nella Larsen and Zora Neale Hurston, whose works raise questions which we perceive today as particularly feminist concerns.

My loose thesis was that a connection between black women and feminist concerns is a natural one and one with a long history. I considered renaming the workshop "The Tradition of Black Feminism," for I saw that by whatever route women travel toward feminism (the quest for economic security, the quest for personal fulfillment, the quest for self-defined sexuality), black women have traveled, usually before, certainly not behind.

There are no new questions. I am a woman. How will I tend my children? How will I tend my house? How will I tend my brain? Linda Brent, in 1861, hoped her readers would "excuse deficiencies," for, she explained:

> I was born and reared in Slavery. . . . Since I have been at the
> North, it has been necessary for me to work diligently for my
> own support, and the education of my children. This has not left
> me much leisure to make up for the loss of early opportunities to
> improve myself; and it has compelled me to write these pages at
> irregular intervals, whenever I could snatch an hour from house-
> hold duties.[1]

The early antagonism of many black women to the women's movement took me by surprise, although I well understood its basis in our history. Movements for black civil rights had been deserted before as white women shifted their political energies away from the cause of black freedom to feminist causes. Some black women spurned the women's movement because it seemed to offer nothing new. For some of us, "rights" were already "burdens."

What perplexes some black women about the feminist movement is that it appears that a large number of white women wish to look at us without observing that we are black. What perplexes us is that we know we are black and female. What remains perplexing to me are those black women who wish to look at me without observing that I am female. I intend no participation in my abasement as either a female person or a black person.

One of Sojourner Truth's contemporaries described her as "one who is nobody but a woman, an unlettered woman, a black woman, and an old woman, a woman born and bred a slave."[2] More than a hundred years later, Shirley Chisholm said of herself and her experience as that self:

> I am both black and a woman. That is a good vantage point
> from which to view at least two elements of what is becoming a
> social revolution: the American Black Revolution and the
> Women's Liberation Movement. But it is also a horrible disad-
> vantage. It is a disadvantage because America, as a nation, is
> both racist and anti-feminist. Racism and anti-feminism are two
> of the prime traditions of this country.[3]

Our times and our children's lives demand that black women live with a double consciousness and sing a dual song—of gender and of race.

"You call yourself a self-made man," Sojourner Truth once remarked. "Well, I am a self-made woman." Self-made. Simone de Beauvoir has commented somewhere that Americans have difficulty understanding existentialism because we are natural existentialists, creating our history daily. Similarly, black women are natural feminists. By this I do not mean natural matriarchs. I mean that black women have been working women since we first were disembarked here. By working women, I mean women who hold full-time jobs outside their homes.

These earliest American working women found themselves victimized by two double standards which have become familiar to greater numbers of American women as they have entered the work force. At work, these women were frequently expected to perform the same jobs as men; at work, they were required additionally to function peculiarly as women— that is, as a sexual object in the most concrete meaning of that term, and as a sexual product in an equally concrete sense. These first American working women, according to another double standard, were expected to do something called women's work as well. Black female slaves left their homes at sunup to work all day and returned at sundown to tend insofar as possible to the needs and demands of their own families.

It was somewhere between here and the latter half of my paper that I saw my axis had truly altered. I could not fit Frances Ellen Watkins Harper in between Sojourner Truth and Nella Larsen. The connecting link was buried in my earliest jottings:

> Note that with freedom Sojourner Truth chose her name.
> Frances Ellen Watkins Harper kept all her names. Unlike S.T., she was born free. Unlike S.T., she was born into comparatively comfortable circumstances. Unlike Sojourner, she was married legally, etc.

"She was married legally" was the burden of the paper. This was the spot on which white women were parked, and the spot where we had found potholes. This was the question raised by Marcia Ann Gillespie in a February 1972 *Essence* editorial with which I prefaced my workshop:

> The oppression that some of them seek escape from, home-making, raising their children, doing what they choose in any given day, is what Black women, tired from that neverending job, tired of leaving their children with aunts and neighbors, would run to. . . . They sit and talk about "meaningful jobs," "getting more meaning into their lives," "discovering their po-tential," with all the sincerity this leisurely and comfortable white middle class can muster, and I remember that we are still struggling to survive with any kind of work, trying to stay alive and then some.[4]

Zora Neale Hurston's Janie answered that. Home from her third marriage, she talks with her friend Phoeby:

> "Ah done lived Grandma's way, now Ah means to live mine."

> "What do you mean by dat, Janie?"

> "She was born in slavery time when folks, dat is black folks, didn't sit down anytime dey felt lak it. So sittin' on porches lak de white madam looked lak uh mighty fine thing tuh her. Dat's what she wanted for me—don't keer whut it cost. Git up on uh high chair and sit dere. She didn't have time tuh think whut tuh do after you got up on de stool uh do nothin'. De object wuz tuh git dere. So Ah got up on de high stool lak she told me, but

Phoeby, Ah done nearly languished tuh death up dere. Ah felt like de world wuz cryin' extry and Ah ain't read the common news yet."

"Maybe so, Janie. Still and all Ah'd love tuh experience it just for one year. It looks lak heben tuh me from where Ah'm at."

"Ah reckon so."[5]

Hurston's Janie answered in 1937. Further back, there was the legally married (and legally widowed) Frances Ellen Watkins Harper, who wrote of the particular anguish of the slave mother. But her concern for the quality of women's lives also produced "Vashti," of woman's pride and refusal to be treated as a possession, and "A Double Standard," with its concluding couplet, "And what is wrong in woman's life / In man's cannot be right."[6] Her deep involvement in the Temperance Movement sprang from this concern with the quality of women's lives. The physical abuse of women was a special concern:

Men talk about missionary work among the heathen, but if any lover of Christ wants a field for civilizing work, here is a field. Part of the time I am preaching against men ill-treating their wives.

The education of women was another:

Part of my lectures are given privately to women, and for them I never make any charge, or take up any collection. . . . I am going to talk with them about their daughters, and about things concerned with the welfare of the race.[7]

Daughters. The welfare of the race. Marriage. William Wells Brown included these advisory quatrains in his 1863 sketch of Frances Ellen Watkins Harper:

Nay, do not blush! I only heard
    You had a mind to marry;
I thought I'd speak a friendly word;
    So just a moment tarry.

Wed not a man whose merit lies
    In things of outward show,
In raven hair or flashing eyes,
    That please your fancy so.

But marry one who's good and kind,
    And free from all pretense;

> Who, if without a gifted mind,
> At least has common sense.[8]

I teach in a women's college where the students in my black literature class are, for the most part, black and female. I have been perplexed by their inability to cope effectively with the predicament of the central character of Nella Larsen's *Quicksand*.[9] Daughter of a white woman and a black man, Helga Crane moves from color culture to color culture without finding fulfillment in either. There is, among my students, an ideological rejection where the theme offends their racial identity: why doesn't Helga find fulfillment in being black? There is also a rejection in the question, posed with hostility, that recurs: "What I want to know is, what does she do for a living?"

A *New Yorker* cartoon shows two men neck-deep in quicksand. "Quicksand or not, Barclay," one says to the other, "I've half a mind to struggle." What does Helga *do*? She struggles in racial and sexual quicksand; and it is the sexual quicksand which suffocates her—and this makes her particularly appropriate to a contemporary discussion. Helga is a middle-class woman, a middle-class black woman. Her frustrations resemble those of the majority of early white feminists. That one can describe her as frustrated is what is most pertinent here. Sojourner Truth had agony, anguish, anger; "frustrated" does not apply to her. Helga "could neither conform nor be happy in nonconformity" (33); self-made Sojourner Truth could not experience that dilemma. Helga laments her "lack of acquiescence" (33); for Sojourner Truth, social acquiescence could only be a posture.

Helga doesn't know what is the matter with her. She knows only that she has an impulse to flee. And she creates the necessity to flee, usually through precipitous speech. She is frustrated in her life as a woman. The frustration is sexual. On one hand, there is her inability to find satisfying work. (The men in the novel find contentment in their work or, when discontent comes, move to other work which brings contentment.) On the other hand, there are Helga's attempts to repress her own sexuality. She is a prisoner of the notion that she should find satisfaction in things which bring her no satisfaction, such as teaching school, or being thought beautiful. With only "half a mind" to struggle, Helga commits suicide—she marries.

Quicksand is not about marrying. Not marrying is what Helga *does*. She does not marry James Vayle, the black teacher with whom she works in Naxos; "she had wanted social background, but—she had not imagined that it could be so stuffy" (35). She does not marry Dr. Anderson, although "he had been too liberal, too lenient, for education as it was inflicted in Naxos" (98). She does not marry the Danish artist Axel Olsen, pleading race this time: "You see I couldn't marry a white man. I simply couldn't . It isn't just you, not just personal, you understand. It's deeper, broader than that. It's racial" (151).

Then Helga does marry—disastrously. The end of *Quicksand* finds Helga Crane Green mired in a life she loathes, pregnant with her fifth child.

"Our dreams," Audre Lorde said in her presentation, "point the way to freedom." Zora Neale Hurston's heroine Janie does discover, and make real, her dream. Born Janie (of no last name), she is by the end of the novel the three-times wed, triple-named Janie Killicks Starks Woods. *Their Eyes Were Watching God* is a remarkable novel about marrying and marriage.

Janie's first marriage, to Logan Killicks, is arranged by her grandmother. She wants to protect her from hard labor: "Ah didn't want to be used for a work-ox and a brood-sow and Ah didn't want my daughter used dat way neither" (31). She wants to protect her from the sexual abuse she has known—herself by her white master, her daughter by her black teacher: "And Ah can't die easy thinkin maybe de menfolks white or black is makin' a spit cup outa you" (37). She seeks for Janie the sanctuary of marriage.

But Killicks soon violates the promise of the marriage. He buys a mule for Janie to use in plowing. She seeks refuge in traditional roles. "You didn't need mah help out dere, Logan. Youse in yo' place and Ah'm in mine." His reply comes from an equally venerable tradition. "You ain't got no particular place. It's wherever Ah need yuh. Git uh move on you and dat quick" (52).

Joe Starks, an ambitious man headed for the top, appears. He tells Janie that she has no business with a plow. "A pretty doll-baby lak you," he tells her, "is made to sit on de front porch" (49). Soon Janie is married to the man who becomes the town's most successful merchant, its chief property-owner, and its mayor.

When Starks is elected mayor, the townspeople ask Janie to speak. Starks replies for her, "Thank you fuh yo' compliments, but mah wife don't know nuthin' 'bout no speech-makin'. Ah never married her for nothin' lak dat. She uh woman and her place is in the home" (69). To Janie's plaint, "Ah feels lak Ah'm jus' markin' time," he offers that his being "a big voice" will make her "a big woman" (74).

Starks's efforts to oppress and repress Janie rest on traditions as venerable as those used by Killicks. "Somebody," he informs her, "got to think for women and children and chickens and cows" (110). And when dinner is not up to par, in the traditional manner by which husbands express dissatisfaction, "somebody" slaps her "until she had a ringing sound in her ears." The slap sends to the surface Janie's wifely way of handling dissatisfactions; "she found she had a host of thoughts she had never expressed to him, and numerous emotions she had never let [him] know about" (112).

Then Janie Killicks Starks meets Vergily Woods, known as Tea Cake. Tea Cake is out of tradition. He is younger than Janie; he is poorer than Joe; he is without the community roots Logan had. The first thing he does is teach Janie to play checkers.

Janie will learn that she can share her host of thoughts and numerous emotions with him. Shortly after they meet, Janie begins teasing him when he buys her a Coke from her store, "We got a rich man around here," she teases, "buyin' passenger trains uh battleships this week?" He turns the question back, "Which one do *you* want?" And Janie makes a safe flirtatious answer: "Oh, if you'se treatin' me tuh it, Ah b'lieve Ah'll take de passenger train. If it blow up, Ah'll still be on land." Tea Cake replies, "Choose de battleship if dat's whut you really want" (153).

"Have de nerve tuh say what you mean," he tells her when she adopts traditional feminine obliqueness. They share the world together, hunt and fish together, go to movies and dance together. Wanting to be together, Tea Cake comes home from the fields to see her. Wanting to be together, Janie joins him working in the fields. "So you aims tuh partake wid everything?" Tea Cake once asked her (186); and they shared it all.

"Tea Cake ain't draggin' me off nowhere Ah don't want tuh go," Janie tells her friend Phoeby. "Ah wants to utilize mahself all over."

In rescuing Janie from a rabid dog, Tea Cake is bitten. He refuses medical attention, and Janie keeps him at home until he madly attacks her. Then with a skill he had shared with her, she shoots him.

In Janie's second appearance as a widow, there are none of the "expensive veils and robes" which covered her first. She is, instead, "in her overalls," for this is not an appearance, this is reality; a dream transformed into a real thing and now dead. "She was too busy feeling her grief to dress like grief" (281).

At the beginning of *Their Eyes Were Watching God*, Janie has just walked back into town. The townspeople gossip with explicit questions which mask from them the real questions implied:

> What she doin' coming back here in dem overalls? Can't she find
> no dress to put on?—Where's dat blue satin dress she left here
> in?—Where all dat money her husband took and died and left
> her? What dat ole forty year ole 'oman doin' wid her hair
> swingin' down her back lak some young gal?—Where she left dat
> young lad of a boy she went off her wid?—Thought she was
> going to marry?—Betcha he off wid some gal so young she ain't
> even got no hairs—why don't she stay in her class? (10)

The questions boil down to three:

> Can a black woman live her own way?
> Can a black woman partake of everything?
> Can a black woman utilize herself all the way?
> There is a fourth. Can any woman?

Notes

1. Linda Brent, *Incidents in the Life of a Slave Girl* (Boston, 1861; reprint ed. New York: Harcourt Brace Jovanovich, 1973), p. xiii.
2. *Narrative of Sojourner Truth; A Bondswoman of Olden Time, Emancipated by the New York Legislature in the Early Part of the Present Century; With a History of Her Labors and Correspondence Drawn from Her "Book of Life"* (Battle Creek, Mich., 1878; reprint ed. New York: Arno Press, 1968), p. 181.
3. "Racism and Anti-Feminism," *Black Scholar*, January-February 1970, p. 40.
4. "Getting Down," p. 27.
5. *Their Eyes Were Watching God* (Philadelphia, 1937; reprint ed. Urbana: Univ. of Illinois Press, 1978), pp. 171–72. All further references to this work appear in the text.
6. In my presentation I read a group of Harper's poems. A representative sample can be found in William Robinson, ed., *Early Black American Poets* (Dubuque, Iowa: William C. Brown, 1970).
7. William Still, *The Underground Rail Road* (Philadelphia, 1872; reprint ed. New York: Arno Press, 1968), p. 773.
8. William Wells Brown, *The Black Man, His Antecedents, His Genius, and His Achievements* (Boston: Thomas Hamilton, 1863), p. 162.
9. Nella Larsen, *Quicksand* (1928; reprint ed. New York: Collier Books, 1971). All further references to this work appear in the text.

Barbara Omolade

Black Women and Feminism

The question of black women's relationship to feminism has been raised primarily to discover why black women have not joined the women's movement in large numbers and have been generally hostile to feminism. In other words, it has been raised as a strategic and organizational issue by white feminists in order to develop better ways to recruit black women into their movement. The question rarely gets raised as a political or theoretical issue seeking greater clarity and understanding of black women and white women: their differences and similarities, their separate histories and possible common interests. In discussing this issue, there is a need to put aside the narrow and limited confines of feminism as defined and dominated by mainly middle- and upper-class white women to reach a broader analysis that could include the experiences of all women under white male domination. By confining their theories to their own particular history and culture, white feminists have denied the history and culture of women of color and have objectively excluded them from equal participation in the women's movement.

White feminists claim that sexism and women's oppression cut beyond all racial and cultural boundaries and reach back to the fundamental purpose and function of the patriarchal family, which limited women to being childbearers and homemakers. But this view cannot be merely rhetorically spouted to get black women to march for the Equal Rights Amendment. For black women to begin to consider political alliances with white women, the rhetoric has to be either documented and proven or abandoned.

Even the most cursory examination of the cultures and history of black women, for example, would force feminists to raise questions about the universal oppression of women under patriarchy. The experiences of black women in West Africa before the colonial period, prior to 1490, and the experiences of white women in Western Europe during the same period (the Middle Ages) were quite different. Women in Western Europe were nonpeople, citizens without basic civil rights,[1] while black women enjoyed high status, and the civil and human rights accorded all tribal members.[2]

A thorough study of the role of women in traditional cultures has to be undertaken by African feminists; here we merely pose the theoretical framework and directions of that research. We assert simply that black women are not white women with color but are women whose color has obscured their historical and cultural experiences as Africans, as chattel slaves and as more than half the population of the black community. Their color has also obscured *their* assessment and understanding of their own experiences. Therefore, any attempt at dialogue between black women and white feminists must begin with a knowledge of the history of black women as *they* understand it, and the limitation of feminist theory as developed thus far.

Black women came to this country as captured chattel slaves from tribal communities that dotted the West African coast. Like their male counterparts they came against their will and under the force of European men possessing superior military technology. The 500 years of domination by white Europeans over the world's peoples of color wreaked havoc with the underpinnings and interworkings of the societies it exploited. Propped up by racism and male chauvinism, European cultural imperialism distorted, dismissed, and mocked the thoughts and actions of black women in traditional African societies. Black women and men in traditional African societies were conscious human beings who designed and constructed their own societies to meet their defined human needs. This seemingly self-evident statement is often overlooked by historical studies that depict black people beginning as slaves with no thoughts and ideas about the world.

African women in traditional culture were human, were citizens, and were valuable members of society. There is no concept in Africa that designates people as sub- or nonhuman, existing apart from the range of tribal law or human consideration. In contrast to European society, which continued the Greek tradition of granting the father the absolute right to sell, kill, or abandon his children,[3] African societies never condoned the mistreatment and abandonment of children regardless of their sex. There was sex-role differentiation; men and women had clearly designated roles and tasks. But this did not undermine the rights of women to participate in the tribal decision-making process, i.e., tribal and family councils; to have redress against mistreatment even by their husbands; and to have the right to own property and accumulate personal wealth and goods from their labor. As Chancellor Williams points out in *Destruction of African Civilization*, Africans were operating under a continent-wide constitution which outlined the rights of each member of the community, including women.[4]

African women were valued as childbearers, a sign to many feminists of oppression and restriction. But Africans viewed motherhood as an honor necessary for the tribe's continuance. Motherhood had a more critical place in the society than fatherhood; "the mother is sacred, her authority is so to speak unlimited."[5] In addition, African women did not belong to the husband's family, but continued to belong to their own family after marriage and were only temporarily separated from it.[6] Feminists might legitimately raise the question of paternal rule over the women's family, since the African woman was still not free from patriarchal domination and protection. The crucial aspect here is not an assertion that African women were liberated in the context of industrialized twentieth-century societies, but whether they were citizens with political rights and economic freedoms that differed from European women living at the same time.

Preindustrialized traditional societies were characteristically overwhelmed by the struggle for physical survival. "In those primitive ages," Diop asserts, "when the security of the group was the primary concern, the respect enjoyed by either of the sexes was connected with its contribution to this collective security."[7] It is in this context that African tribal unity and egalitarianism must be understood.

When comparing black women in traditional African society and women in Europe, a qualitative difference in world view emerges. In Europe between 1500 and 1700 millions of women were burned at the stake as witches, ostensibly for communicating with God or practicing medicine outside the male-dominated church. But the witch hunts were a systematic attempt to eradicate any "heretical" thinking as well as independent activity of women.[8] In contrast, female organizations in Western African tribes flourished and were responsible for educating women about sexuality, obstetrics, and gynecology. Men were forbidden by tribal law to interfere;[9] even clitoridectomy was originally part of the practices of these female societies. There was no religiously reinforced system justifying male domination or a male priesthood controlling knowledge and excluding women in Africa. African men never pondered, as medieval church fathers did, whether women "had immortal souls" or were bestial in nature.[10] The religious systems in Africa included powerful female gods that often designated men and women as their god-children, requiring both to emulate and be obedient to her.

There was no economic system in Africa where women were either appendages, household ornaments, or worthless drudges. African women were workers encouraged to work and participate in the survival of the tribe and clan. Wealthy men were proud of their wives for working and managing market stalls which traded goods and crafts. Their activities enhanced the family's status and wealth.

Thus African women captured as slaves were brutally wrested from a society where they participated as human beings with firmly entrenched rights and status. It is not surprising, therefore, that from the beginning African women as well as men independently and collectively resisted enslavement. They did not want to leave Africa and clearly understood that their human rights were left on its shore.

There was no chattel slavery in Africa. The slaves of traditional African society were captured in wars, and had rights to manumission, to a family, and even entry into certain tribes as equal members. The trickling African slave trade began with the trade of African slaves to the Europeans. As more and more wealth began to accumulate in the hands of unscrupulous kings and tribal chieftains vying for power, unrestrained by more egalitarian tribal law, tribal members were taken and sold as slaves for minor offenses or without cause. This process was accelerated by Europeans attempting to foster the tribal divisions in Africa so they could reap profit and power for themselves.[11]

African women captives were given no special privileges because of their sex. Men and women were force-marched, carrying heavy loads, to the coast to meet the Europeans and their ships. In addition, African women were systematically raped by slave catchers and slave holders. (This slavery-initiated practice has continued until fairly recently; because of their racial and class status, black women have been the source of available sex for white men.)

Irrespective of whether the father was rapist, slave-holder, or lover, slave women were expected to reproduce slaves, to assure even greater profits for the slaveholder. However, the prime reason black women and men were brought here as slaves was to work, to develop and extend the plantation system. The skills and strength of African women and men in large-tract agriculture, practiced communally in Western Africa, made them the most profitable source of labor for the white ruling class. Tremendous profits were realized in spite of the two-month slaveship journey, the loss of life due to disease and torture, and the "seasoning" process which turned captive Africans into productive slaves.

As workers, as mothers, and as forced sex partners, slave women were basic to the success of the slave system. On their sheer physical strength to work twelve hours in the field, bear and raise babies, and have sex on demand rested the fortunes of the slave owners.[12] The brutal oppression suffered by black women gave rise to their militant resistance to the slave system. In this resistance the black woman was not alone, but was supported by the equally brutalized black man. For he, too, had been stripped of his birthright of liberty and the cultural right to define his own manhood. In fact, the use of men and women as chattel slaves gave rise to a unity and equality in resistance probably unknown before in the history of male/female relationships. Patriarchal protection of women ended when black women were enslaved, irrespective of their sex-defined roles in tribal law. They were on their own in facing the oppression, and thus worked hard with the black man in developing strategies and tactics for resisting slavery. Petitioning, escape, noncooperation, and armed struggle were the means they used.

This resistance took place within the context of a developing black society. The forging of a black society with cultural integrity and independence as its binding force and human and civil rights as its goal has long been neglected in studying the history of black people in this country. The black society has been able to build religious and educational institutions and develop social and community programs. The most important function of the black society, with black communities as its geographic base, has been the protection and sustenance of black people against the ravages of a racist and often fascist system.

In ignoring the existence and importance of a black society, historians have emphasized the roles of so-called exceptional and exemplary black people in Afro-American and American history. The individual contributions of Frederick Douglass, Harriet Tubman, and Sojourner Truth, though they were great, are discussed as if their achievements were miracles for black people to attain. Given the theoretical basis of unity in the black community and the practical need for a collective response to oppression, Harriet Tubman could not have emerged by herself. She was not merely affected by the brutality of her individual slave experiences, but represented the collective aspirations of all slaves for freedoms. Her revolutionary consciousness was shaped by those collective aspirations, which enabled her to "see" herself as an instrument to free her people. More concretely, Harriet Tubman could not have helped free slaves without the support of the slave community which lied and covered for runaway slaves, giving them an edge on pursuing masters, which stole food and protected runaways and isolated spies and betrayers.[13] She could not have helped free slaves without the "free" black community being there to receive slaves when they escaped and to defend them against slave catchers.

By denying our collective aspirations for freedom and emphasizing certain individuals, feminists and feminist historians dismiss the question of political ideology and the conscious organizational response of black women and men to slavery. For example, they begin accounts of the abolitionist movement in the white community with William Lloyd Garrison, the Grimke sisters, and others.[14] Their mention of blacks is cursory and matter-of-fact. They ignore the fact that it was black people who first called in an organized way for the abolition of slavery.

The call emerged as part of a growing movement by black people from pre-Revolutionary days which linked the struggle for an end to racism in the North with the struggle to resist slavery in the South.

> Under the impact of this revolutionary spirit, Negroes them-selves, led by Absalom Jones, Prince Hall, and William Cuffee, became involved in the struggles; they protested the payment of taxes to a government denying them the rights of citizens; and they demanded freedom as a reward for fighting in defense of their country. Negroes also organized resistance to the slave trade and, in New England, even petitioned state legislatures for emancipation. . . . These early protests against American slavery yielded rich rewards. By 1808 the African slave trade was abol-ished, slaves were freed in Vermont, New Hampshire, Massachu-setts, and Ohio, and gradual emancipation was provided for in Rhode Island, Pennsylvania, New Jersey, New York, and Con-necticut. Although slave labor in these states had already de-creased in importance as an economic factor and was being replaced by free labor, these early anti-slavery activities hastened the day of freedom.[15]

Thus, at least fifty years before 1832, when local and national abolition societies met in Philadelphia to form the American Anti-Slavery Society, black people had begun to organize resistance to slavery. The American Anti-Slavery Society apparently grew from the second annual meeting of the Convention of Colored Men, who had organized the year before to oppose emigration of black people to Africa as a solution to slavery and to press the demand for "life, liberty, and the pursuit of happiness" for black people. In 1831 the Convention invited Garrison, Lundy, the Tappan brothers, and other white abolitionist leaders to attend also. The next year the American Anti-Slavery society launched its work with black people to end slavery.[16]

The abolition movement brought together white women and the black community in a united front organized against white male power around the question of the abolition of slavery. White women correctly linked the oppression of slaves with their own oppression as women while the black community understood that alliances with white women would benefit their struggle against chattel slavery. However, the united front did not assure the equal inclusion of black women into feminist circles. There was outright racist exclusion such as the dissolution of the Massachusetts Female Anti-Slave Society at Fall River in 1838 when black women began attending meetings. And there was subtle racist exclusion such as failing to link their early concerns about women's rights with black women organized in antislave societies and the underground railroad.[17] Both kinds weakened the unity between black and white women in fighting both racism and male chauvinism. It was not surprising therefore that white women viewed black abolitionist support, including that of early black feminist/abolitionist Frances Harper, for the Fifteenth Amendment, giving former slaves (male) citizenship and voting rights, as a betrayal of their own struggle for suffrage. Though Frederick Douglass and Frances Harper attempted to explain the difference between white women getting the vote and black people, former chattel slaves, getting the vote as legal recognition of their citizenship, white women nonetheless went ahead and formed the National Women's Suffrage Association.[18] Thus white women formally broke the organized united front between those opposing racism and slavery and those opposing male chauvinism.

White women continued to organize as women, excluding black women, either explicitly or de facto. White women organized for entry as equals in the white-male-dominated economic and political system, while black women and the black community continued their struggles against racist and economic exploitation. This division continues to exist today, with white women organizing in opposition to white men, while black women have united with black men to struggle for national liberation from white male rule. These separate paths, though shaped by racist and class exploitation, come directly from the histories of black and white women before they came to this country.[19] White women have had to fight for identity within a culture which has denied them a place as human or equal, while black women have had to fight for the survival of a culture which had defined them as equal and human but whose values and practices were undermined by European imperialism.

Furthermore, black women have joined white women's organizations and helped to develop feminist ideas and strategies, especially around suffrage, and have helped to lobby for white women to support black community struggles against racism. White women, on the other hand, have largely ignored the work of black women within their own community. Thus the tradition of black women organizers for social change has been neglected, especially by many feminist organizers.[20]

One of these black women organizers, Ella Baker, bears closer examination because of her impact on the recent civil rights movement and her influence in shaping and defining the role of black women political activists in the last thirty years. She began organizing consumer cooperatives in New York City during the Depression but by the end of the 1930s was a field organizer for the National Association for the Advancement of Colored People, recruiting members primarily in the South. She traveled, often alone, throughout the South organizing people to join the NAACP as a way of fighting the racism in the rural South. She tried to awaken the black people in their communities to a feeling of common need and that in numbers there is strength. She started with where people were at, helping them to identify the organization with the people they knew and who had helped them.[21] She believed "very firmly in the right of people who are under the heel to be the ones to decide the action they are going to take."[22]

These views, enabling people in the community to decide the direction and form of political action, were critical to building the mass movement in the black South against segregation and racism. The Montgomery Bus Boycott was initiated by Rosa Park, a black woman whose personal refusal to accept segregated seating on a bus precipitated the boycott and the later Freedom Rides. One year after four students sat in in protest against not being served food at a lunch counter, 70,000 students sat in throughout the South. Both these mass movements demonstrated the influence and soundness of Ms. Baker's theory of organizing community people. Ms. Baker worked for the Southern Christian Leadership Conference, which grew out of the Montgomery Bus Boycott at the time of the sit-ins.

> She called a conference of the students who were from the sit-ins to better coordinate their activities. The SCLC felt that they could influence how things went. They were interested in having the students become an arm of SCLC. "They were confident that this would be their baby because I was their functionary and had called the meeting." She refused to participate in persuading the students to join SCLC and subsequently resigned.[23]

She went to work for the Student Non-violent Coordinating Committee, the independent student group that became one of the most powerful black grass-roots organizations during the 1960s.

Though essential to the administrative development of three major civil rights organizations and critical to their reaching black community people throughout the South, Ms. Baker has insisted upon a supportive and back-seat role. She states,

> I knew from the beginning that as a woman, an older woman in a group of ministers who are accustomed to having women largely as supporters, there was no place for me to have come into a leadership role. The competition wasn't worth it.[24]

Neither was the feminist theory and practice available which could have supported Ms. Baker in taking that leadership. There was no organized women's movement. The revolutionary examples of women in Vietnam, China, Cuba, and Angola were either not known or were yet to happen. There was no theory of revolutionary feminism to help her "come into a leadership role." She did not have a feminist perspective, though she acknowledges the significant role of black church women in the civil rights movement. Nor does she advocate anyone following her pattern, though most black women who participated in the civil rights movement did.

Following the legacy of Ella Baker, activist black women organizers have defined their role as supporting black male leadership, rather than "splitting" the unity of the movement for black liberation. Many have chosen to ignore or condemn the call of feminists to join them in fighting sexist oppression, as a ploy to sidetrack them from the larger issue of racism. Unfortunately, black men and their black women supporters lacked the understanding, though they experienced it, of the link between racism and sexism. The very biology of black women embodies that link. The separation and prioritizing has prevented the black community from correctly understanding the insidious and vicious nature of capitalism, which is propped up by racism and male chauvinism simultaneously. In fact, many black male leaders have restricted, rather than developed, the political participation of black women in the liberation struggle.

White feminists who could have educated and helped black women understand the nature of male chauvinism were blinded and confused by their own racism. They failed to develop a feminist view of racism which sees the interrelationship between racism and sexism, expressing itself in a militant and activist stand against racism. Instead, white feminists have frequently defined women's liberation in terms of employment opportunities and changing sex roles. They successfully ignore the history of black women as workers in Africa and this country, which have proven that economic independence from men is not liberation. Even more striking, most of black women's work has been under the direct supervision of white women as domestics or office workers. Even in hospitals, where many black women are employed, they are frequently supervised by white females. These women have been as domineering, arbitrary, and racist as white men. How can they ask black women to join them if they haven't even acknowledged white skin privilege?

The racism of white feminists has prevented unified and effective actions around issues that concern all women, such as rape. The definition of the issue of rape as posed by white women has excluded black women. White women speak out only about brutal rape and sneak attacks in the night, and rarely mention the business rape that women of color face from white men who own the factories and head the households where they work as servants. White women have also turned to the criminal justice system to prosecute rapists as a solution. But many black women are raped by black men, and reporting them to white cops, aside from raising questions about loyalty to black people in the face of common enemies, places them in positions of being ignored, mocked, or even threatened with rape by the policemen themselves.

In conclusion, to enable black women to pursue a dialogue with white feminists, a feminist theory needs to be developed and expanded to include our priorities and experiences. We have to begin to speak of a feminism that is black in its essence and historical roots and that is not isolated from the black community. We must speak of a feminism that seeks the root cause of our oppression under capitalism and links our struggles with the liberation struggles of other peoples of color in the world. Our feminism must expand the theories of revolutionary nationalism. It must aim at destroying male chauvinism in our brothers, while understanding that they have been the staunchest ally of black women in our fight for freedom. But this feminism cannot be defined or demanded on our behalf by white women or black men. No other group can demand liberation for us, because in doing so they take away our own capacity to organize and speak for ourselves.

The racism of white women will not allow them to give us the right to speak on our own behalf, and the male chauvinism of black men will not allow them to give us the right to speak on our own behalf. *We must take the right to speak from them.* The feminism of white women does not define us, nor can it lead us. When black women begin to organize in large numbers and become a political force, white women will have to say either that they only speak for themselves or that they stand with us against racist and sexist oppression.

Notes

1. Eleanor Flexner, *Century of Struggle* (Cambridge: Belknap Press, 1959, rev. 1979), p. 7.
2. Chancellor Williams, *Destruction of Black Civilization* (Chicago: Third World Press, 1974), pp. 180–85.
3. Robert Flacelliere, "Daily Life in Greece at the Time of Pericles," in Michael Cherniavsky and Arthur Slavin, *Social Textures of Western Civilization: The Lower Depths* (Lexington, Mass.: Xerox College Publication, 1972), p. 129.
4. Williams, *Black Civilization*, pp. 180–85.
5. Cheikh Anta Diop, *Cultural Unity of Black Africa* (Chicago: Third World Press, 1959), p. 37.
6. Ibid., p. 36.
7. Ibid., p. 34.
8. Barbara Ehrenreich and Deirdre English, *Witches, Midwives and Nurses: A History of Women Healers* (Old Westbury, N.Y.: The Feminist Press, 1973), pp. 4–6.
9. Williams, *Black Civilization*, p. 177.
10. Sheila Rowbotham, *Women, Resistance and Revolution* (New York: Vintage Books, 1974), p. 20.

11. David Brion Davis, *The Problem of Slavery in Western Civilization* (Ithaca, N.Y.: Cornell Univ. Press, 1967), pp. 469–70.
12. Barbara Omolade, "Black Motherhood" (unpublished master's thesis), pp. 63–73.
13. Angela Davis, "Reflections on the Black Slave Woman's Role in the Community of Slaves," *Black Scholar*, December 1971, pp. 2–15.
14. Flexner, *Struggle*, p. 8; Gerda Lerner, *The Grimke Sisters from South Carolina: Rebels Against Slavery* (Boston: Houghton Miflin Co., 1967).
15. Philip Foner, ed., *Life and Writings of Frederick Douglass* (New York: International Publishers, 1975), Vol. I, p. 29.
16. Victor Ullman, *Martin R. Delaney: Beginnings of Black Nationalism* (Boston: Beacon Press, 1971), pp. 9–14.
17. Sharon Harley and Rosalyn Terborg-Penn, eds., *Afro-American Women: Struggles and Images* (New York: Kennikat Press, 1978), pp. 18–20.
18. S. Jay Walker, "Frederick Douglass and Women's Suffrage," *Black Scholar*, March-April 1973, p. 24.
19. Elizabeth Hood, "Black Women, White Women: Separate Paths to Liberation," *Black Scholar*, April 1978, pp. 45–55.
20. Ibid.
21. Ellen Canterow and Susan O'Malley, "Ella Baker: Organizing for Civil Rights," in *Moving the Mountain: Women Working for Social Change* (New York: Feminist Press, 1980), pp. 9–13.
22. Ibid., p. 18.
23. Ibid.
24. Gerda Lerner, *Black Women in White America: A Documentary History* (New York: Vintage Books, 1973), p. 351.

Carolyn G. Heilbrun

Androgyny and the Psychology of Sex Differences

As my title indicates, I want to begin by offering some background on the relation of two concepts—androgyny and sex differences—to each other. In the period since *Toward a Recognition of Androgyny* was published, seven years ago,[1] the concept of androgyny has enabled many people, in many disciplines and ways of life, to question the veracity of sex differences, their immutability and their ultimate power to affect our lives. These changes, on which I will elaborate more fully in a moment, are certainly profound and of utmost importance to feminism.

Yet the word "androgyny" itself has fallen upon hard times. Ironically enough, when my book first appeared, I feared that I would offend unbearably those who had their being in the macho–sex-kitten dichotomy, the inevitable quarterback-cheerleader assignment of life's roles. Certainly the reviews reflected the fact that this group in our society was momentarily upset, but oddly enough they soon quieted down, and soon, indeed, began swaying in the winds of changing trends. So Anatole Broyard, who in 1973 had sneered at the idea of androgyny as useless, preposterous, and disgusting, provided this for my unbelieving eyes in a 1976 review:

> While friendship in one's own sex may be deeply assuring, it is
> also conceivable that, in overstressing this kind of contact, we
> may be begging the question of our deep-seated androgyny.
> What men are accustomed to call the "otherness" of women may
> correspond to the unexplored parts of themselves for which
> many of them feel such a profound yearning.[2]

The fun continued when I learned that a section from *Toward a Recognition of Androgyny* had become part of a recent LSAT exam. One can see why: it tested the candidate's ability to distinguish what was said from his or her assumptions about what was said. Let me add, however, that I was neither paid nor officially informed of the use of the passages. Still, the word and the concept of androgyny were catching on and freeing many from the prison of gender and the bonds of appropriate behavior.

Something even more pleasing to those who hate the idea of stereotypical sex roles was that androgynous comments from the past began to surface. Here is a single example: in her excellent introduction to *Aurora Leigh* in 1978, Cora Kaplan quoted Elizabeth Barrett Browning's comment, in a letter to Miss Mitford, about Charles Kingsley:

> I like him and admire him. Few people have struck me as much
> as he did last year in England. "Manly," do you say? But I am
> not very fond of praising men by calling them *manly*. I hate and
> detest a masculine mind.[3]

Yet to many feminists, and to those whose intelligence and commitment I most respect, the word "androgyny" became a dirty word, fought against with a determination I don't altogether understand. Let us take, for example, the works of a woman for whom I have the most profound admiration and respect: Adrienne Rich. In 1973, simultaneously with my own book, she published a poem which I did not then know, entitled "The Stranger."

> Looking as I've looked before, straight down the heart
> of the street to the river
> walking the rivers of the avenues
> feeling the shudder of the caves beneath the asphalt
> watching the lights turn on in the towers
> walking as I've walked before
> like a man, like a woman, in the city
> my visionary anger cleansing my sight
> and the detailed perceptions of mercy
> flowering from that anger
>
> if I come into a room out of the sharp misty light
> and hear them talking a dead language
> if they ask me my identity
> what can I say but
> I am the androgyne
> I am the living mind you fail to describe
> in your dead language
> the lost noun, the verb surviving
> only in the infinitive
> the letters of my name are written under the lids
> of the newborn child[4]

In her new book of poems, *The Dream of a Common Language*, this verse appears:

There are words I cannot choose again:
humanism   *androgyny*
Such words have no shame in them, no diffidence
before the raging stoic grandmothers:

their glint is too shallow, like a dye
that does not permeate

the fibres of actual life
as we live it, now[.][5]

In Rich's great book, *Of Woman Born*, she complained that

androgyny has recently become a "good" word (like "motherhood" itself!) implying many things to many people, from bisexuality to a vague freedom from imposed sexual roles. Rarely has
the term been accompanied by any political critique.[6]

And, to my great sorrow, Rich expunged her poem "The Stranger" from
her collected poems, so in retracing her career through that edition, one
would never have known it had been there.[7]

I have only one more example. In a recent issue of *Heresies*, "On
Women and Violence," the editorial states:

At birth, infants are assigned a gender. This division of all people
into *mutually exclusive* and *non-overlapping* sex roles is assumed
to be natural. But this development is not the unfolding of some
genetic blueprint: it requires learning a complex set of rules and
rituals which create rather than reveal what it means to be a man
or a woman in a society.

Exactly. But further down the page, we read:

Androgyny is not the answer. Men expressing their "male side"
leaves unchallenged sexist definitions of what is masculine and
feminine.[8]

The reader will, I hope, have noticed that the first quotation expressed
androgyny as I understand it, but not the second. My confusion is
increased when I read again and again that the French feminists all
support "bisexuality" for everyone, but not androgyny. But of course,
bisexuality, which was Freud's word, not only retains the definitions of
masculinity and femininity, but reinforces them as binomial, emphasizing
rather than diminishing the sacred "dichotomy."

Meanwhile, where it matters, the concept of androgyny, bisexuality, or
whatever we choose to call it, has done and is doing its work. The progress
in this area—the psychology of sex differences—is what I want to talk

about next. Why then do I pause so long over the political fate of the term "androgyny"? It is not because I do not understand the objections to it. In addition to those I have mentioned, they are, first, that in the history of the androgyne, it has been the male who assumes female aspects, leaving the female to keep all the inconvenient female duties, like typing and laundry. And second, as Adrienne Rich has pointed out to me, the media have taken up androgyny in a way which she, and certainly I, find profoundly offensive. But I, and perhaps she, find everything the media do profoundly offensive.

What troubles me, I think, is the tendency of the women's movement, like all other political movements, to break into factions which use energy attacking each other rather than the problem. In the *Heresies* editorial, for example, why not simply make a statement to the effect that gender need not determine sex roles? Why do the editors also find it necessary to take a swing at androgyny, which is certainly not the philosophy of those who perpetrate violence upon women, or who resist the Equal Rights Amendment? If we are to undermine the slavery for women inherent in old ideas of sex difference, why should we begin by quarreling publicly about the term?

Here then is how a psychologist puts it: Sandra Bem's "pioneer work on androgyny has stimulated alternative theories and new methodology in the area of sex roles."[9] In Bem's view,

> even if people were all to become psychologically androgynous,
> the world would continue to consist of two sexes. . . . Thus,
> being female typically means that you have a female body build;
> that you have female genitalia; that you have breasts; that you
> menstruate; that you can become pregnant and give birth; and
> that you can nurse a child. Similarly, being a male typically
> means that you have a male body build; that you have male
> genitalia; that you have beard growth; that you have erections;
> that you ejaculate; and that you can impregnate a woman and
> thereby father a child. . . . Precisely because these are biological
> givens which cannot be avoided or escaped, except perhaps by
> means of very radical and mutilating surgery, it seems to me that
> psychological health must necessarily include having a healthy
> sense of one's maleness or femaleness. But I would argue that a
> healthy sense of maleness or femaleness involves little more than
> being able to look into the mirror and to be perfectly comforta-
> ble with the body that one sees there. . . . But beyond being
> comfortable with one's body, one's gender need have no other
> influence on one's behavior or life style. Thus, although I would
> suggest that a woman ought to feel comfortable about the fact

that she can bear children if she wants to, this does not imply that she ought to want to bear children, nor that she ought to stay home with any children that she does bear. Similarly, although I would suggest that a man ought to feel perfectly comfortable about the fact that he has a penis which can become erect, this in no way implies that a man ought to take the more active role during sexual intercourse, nor even that his sexual partners ought all to be female.[10]

Those wise words were written in 1975. I will return shortly to the minor phrase from the passage just quoted, "except perhaps by means of very radical and mutilating surgery," because, in my view, the tremendous attention given these days to transsexuals like Jan Morris and Renée Richards has brought the whole discussion of sex differences to a new sharpness of definition. But let me review, first, what has been accomplished in the area which we may, for now, call androgyny. Psychological tests for masculinity and femininity, once almost universally employed, have now been largely abandoned. In their place has been substituted an "androgynous" test which attempts to measure the integration of the entire personality. It will come as no surprise to anyone who has thought of these matters that those who measure as the most androgynous are the most intelligent, the most mature, and the most integrated within themselves. Those at the extreme ends are, if men, strongly inhibited from tender or emotional behavior. Those women at the extreme end of femininity on the scale are inhibited not only from "masculine" behavior as such, but from any behavior where what is "appropriate" is left unspecified.[11]

Likewise, it has been demonstrated that the psychological tests for moral maturity, once widely used, conflate human behavior with male behavior, while they define a woman with male behavior as unfeminine, and a woman with female behavior as nonhuman. These tests have been recognized for what they are and abandoned; other tests are being developed.[12]

Most important, and here of course the work of Nancy Chodorow must be particularly mentioned,[13] there have evolved indications that the sexes are not ideally defined (supposing that they must be "defined" at all) *against* each other. Until very recently, men assumed they could define masculine behavior primarily as *not* feminine, *not* what girls do, thus leaving girls passively to accept what was left, which wasn't much.

Yet, most recently, the phenomenon of transsexualism has given us the sharpest insights into the psychology of sex differences. What is obvious, of course, is that those who need to transform themselves from one sex to the other are the most committed to the stereotypical sex roles. Those doctors who perform these mutilating operations never question whether it is necessary to change one's body in order to find where one "belongs." Psychoanalysts like Robert Stoller find that the source of transsexualism lies in the mother's use of the newborn boy as a penis: she, unhappy as a woman, uses her son, who in turn conceives of himself as part of her, feminine. This entire concept, of course, is based on the inevitability of sex difference.[14]

I particularly recommend two articles on this subject. The first is by Janice G. Raymond, on "Transsexualism: The Ultimate Homage to Sex-Role Power,"[15] and the second is by Marcia Yudkin, on "Transsexualism and Women: A Critical Perspective."[16] Both authors, and the second refers to the first, demonstrate how the entire phenomenon of transsexualism, from the individual's needs to the treatment now meted out, is the result of defining sex roles as absolutely distinct, as at opposite ends of the old masculinity-femininity scale. The fact that most transsexuals are male-to-reconstructed-female helps to underline this phenomenon. They rejoice, after their dominant roles as males, in the passivity of their female life.

The best possible demonstration of this is in *Conundrum* by Jan Morris. The reader is urged to look up this book, particularly pages 149, 150, 153, and 157, where the story told in the transsexual's own words conveys more sharply than can any paraphrase the connection between being perceived as "female" and being therefore "female" in the stereotypic way. Unfortunately, since I was denied permission to quote from *Conundrum*, I must paraphrase Jan Morris's language.

She tells us that she became more of a woman as she was treated as a woman. If she was perceived to be incompetent at any task (and we must remember that she had been an extremely competent male), she became incompetent at it—even if the task was only reversing cars or opening bottles. When her lawyer one morning addressed her with the words "my child," treating her as an inferior, she found that she accepted the state of inferiority. Since, as she learned, men preferred women to be less competent in every way than themselves, she obliged them by being so. The annoyance at being thought inadequate was compensated for by the pleasure of having tasks done for her.

She began to feel small and neat, though she was the same size as in her male form. Her "feminine" clothes, with bangles and matching accessories, made her feel vulnerable, a feeling she enjoyed. She liked to make up her face to be ready to be looked at by the world. When a passing workman smiled at her, she felt as pleased as she used to feel at the good reception of one of her/his books.[17]

Yet here is what a "real woman" feels like:

> I have to confess that, in the sense in which transsexuals use the
> phrase, I do not feel myself to be "really a woman"; I feel myself
> to be "really" just a person, sex unspecified. Of course, I know
> that I am female, just as I know that I am 5'6", have brown hair
> and blue eyes, and am 25 years old; but I do not let any of those
> facts define me and I prefer to be in circumstances where others
> do not define me by those time-honored physical facts. If I
> juxtapose this intuition with time-honored philosophical anal-
> yses of what it is to be a person, an interesting irony emerges.
> Not only is the declaration that a woman is "just a person"
> distinctly an oddity in the history of philosophy, but "person"
> turns out in most of the philosophical systems of the past to
> mean implicitly "male person," with women ignored, regarded
> as nonpersons, or regarded as just marginally persons. The irony
> deepens when I report my further sense that I do not consider
> myself a "woman in a woman's body," as I should if the trans-
> sexuals' versions of womanhood as an inner reality which can
> match or fail to match biological facts were correct for everyone.
> This intuition too contradicts some philosophers' insistence that
> women are essentially women rather than human beings who
> happen to be of the female sex.[18]

Marcia Yudkin concludes her critical perspective on transsexualism
thus:

> But where does this leave me with reference to the concept of
> "woman"? Perplexed. I seem to have perpetrated a dizzying
> reconstruction of the concept of "woman," shown how in com-
> mon usage—and common experience, for a language often pene-
> trates and structures experience—it is a confused amalgam of
> biological and social levels. If one legislates some clarity into the
> concept, as I have done by separating the biological and social
> levels and calling them by separate terms, "female" and
> "woman," one gets an astonishing answer to the question with
> which I began: are transsexuals who have undergone surgery and
> are able to "pass" successfully as women *women*? Yes, and in a
> sense they are more genuinely women than I am, for they typi-
> cally have a strong identification with the female sex role: they
> like having doors opened for them, prefer to be in subordinate
> positions, want to marry a man and mother children, all of
> which I do not.[19]

"Androgyny," then (or whatever term we prefer), is not, as Rich says, "vague." Precisely, it seeks to suggest that sex roles are societal constructs which ought to be abandoned. I am willing enough to let the word androgyny go since I seek the ends, not the word. But I think we might as well recognize that it began what is a wonderfully liberating process, and that if it inspired Rich, for example, to that beautiful poem she has now disclaimed, can we not at least recognize "androgyny" as a step along a path that may be the most important, and is certainly the most revolutionary, traveled by humanity?

One final point needs to be addressed, and that is the question of why some lesbians object so to androgyny. To this I would respond that, in my own experience, a lesbian's response to androgyny depends on how separatist she is. Lesbian separatists certainly hate and attack the word. But those, like Carter Heyward, who believe that the Christian Church must recognize homosexuality, themselves use the word to suggest the opposite of homophobia.[20]

What I want to end by suggesting is that transsexuals may stand for those of us caught in stereotypical roles, caught, yet wishing to escape. For such people, at such a moment, the concept of androgyny is liberating. It is only a transitional stage. I do not believe it can long satisfy anyone who, like Adrienne Rich, has become her own person and found her own voice, her own self. Androgyny is a necessary stopping place on the road to feminism. We must not claim more for it, but it must be allowed to be what it is.

Notes

1. Carolyn G. Heilbrun, *Toward a Recognition of Androgyny* (New York: Alfred A. Knopf, 1973).
2. *New York Times*, October 5, 1976, p. 43.
3. "Introduction," In Elizabeth Barrett Browning, *Aurora Leigh and Other Poems*, ed. Cora Kaplan (London: The Women's Press, 1978), p. 30.
4. In *Diving into the Wreck* (New York: Norton, 1973), p. 19.
5. In "Natural Resources," *The Dream of a Common Language* (New York: Norton, 1978), p. 66.
6. *Of Woman Born: Motherhood as Experience and Institution* (New York: Norton, 1976), p. 76.
7. Adrienne Rich, *Poems: Selected and New, 1950–1974* (New York: Norton, 1974).
8. "Editorial," *Heresies* 6 (Summer 1978): 24.
9. Alexandra G. Kaplan and Joan P. Bean, eds., *Beyond Sex-Role Stereotypes: Readings toward a Psychology of Androgyny* (Boston: Little, Brown, 1976), p. 47.
10. Sandra L. Bem, "From Traditional to Alternative Conceptions of Sex Roles," in Kaplan and Bean, *Beyond Sex-Role Stereotypes*, p. 60.

11. Ibid., p. 59.
12. See Inge K. Broverman et al., "Sex-Role Stereotypes: A Current Appraisal," in *Women and Achievement*, ed. Martha Mednick, Sandra Tangi, Lois Hoffman (New York; Halsted/Wiley, 1975), pp. 32–45. See also Carol Gilligan, "In a Different Voice: Women's Conceptions of Self and Morality," this volume.
13. See "Gender, Relation, and Difference in Psychoanalytic Perspective," this volume, and *The Reproduction of Mothering: Psychoanalysis and the Sociology of Gender* (Berkeley: Univ. of California Press, 1978).
14. Robert J. Stoller, *Perversion: The Erotic Form of Hatred* (New York: Pantheon, 1975), pp. 141–42.
15. In *Crysalis* 3 (1977): 11–24; see also her book, *The Transsexual Empire: The Making of the She-Male* (Boston: Beacon Press, 1979).
16. Marcia Yudkin, "Transsexualism and Women: A Critical Perspective," *Feminist Studies* 4:3 (October 1978): 97–106.
17. Jan Morris, *Conundrum* (New York: Harcourt, Brace, 1974), pp. 149, 150, 153, 157.
18. Yudkin, "Transsexualism and Women," p. 103.
19. Ibid.
20. Carter Heyward, "Ruether and Daly, Theologians: Speaking and Sparking, Building and Burning," *Christianity and Crisis* 39:5 (April 12, 1979): 66–72. See also Heyward, "Coming Out: Journey without Maps," *Christianity and Crisis* 39:10 (June 11, 1979): 153–56. This point was raised in the discussion during my workshop at the Barnard conference; unfortunately, the tape was too poor to permit further transcription.

Tucker Pamella Farley

Lesbianism and the Social Function of Taboo

Because the conference was originally designed to discuss difference primarily as a male-female problematic, I wanted to choose a title that would perform several functions. The first would be to create a safe space for lesbians to talk, without at the same time creating a token enclave that others, whose defensiveness and tension about sexual difference are as yet submerged and unresolved, could use unconsciously as a dumping ground. The analysis of male-female difference, utilized oppressively as the basis for male supremacy and glorified as natural, is at least respectable. But other differences, like those of color and sexual identity, which are also used oppressively, are simultaneously glaring and invisible. We are always caught up in the dual necessity of surviving the oppression that makes those embodying difference into scapegoats and tokens,[1] and transforming it: moving beyond victimization to creative activity.

So this was to be the second use of my title: to move both ways, engage both perspectives, acknowledge oppression, and build a way out. To tap the hidden sources of our power. Like compressed energy anywhere, what has been hidden, kept down, generates power, force, strength. An oppressed group performs the negative function of supporting the oppressive; but it also acts, in its liberatory movement, to transform those relations. Everybody knows this on some level, or nobody would need either to deny it or to participate in it: nobody would need to struggle around it. Difference would have no function in oppression; oppression would have to be different. For oppression uses difference—especially differences that can be made to seem natural, according to whatever social (that is, scientific or religious) constructs we use to delineate a "law." Yet transforming those very characteristics which we in this society today feel to be at the *base* of "human identity" can be threatening as well as liberating. Both dynamics function together; for all of us—lesbian, black, white, heterosexual—they call each other into being.

Finally, I wanted to indicate that this process of transformation, of a dynamic, of change, takes place in a historical context, in which we are all implicated. None of us wants to participate in "the social function" of oppression. To speak of a social function is to speak of a systemic process which, as is true of any system, has structures and procedures that, by certain criteria, benefit some at the expense of others, and an ideology that obscures this dynamic. Heterosexuality, built on the gynophobic laws of male supremacy, is such a system—and we have been raised by it, in an age of racism and imperialism. Because of this, our survival has required—even as we rebel—participation in our own oppression. It is our task to locate and refuse the means by which we participate, to render them socially dysfunctional—to recognize, in the dialectic of oppression, that subversive transformation in which we each play a different and crucial part.

So: "Lesbianism and the Social Function of Taboo." In the workshop we went around the room and introduced ourselves; I spoke, and then we had a discussion, with about forty women participating. I began with several premises. The first is that in fact as lesbians, we know several things not "generally known"—not, that is, well accommodated in heterosexist knowledge.

We know women can act in nonfeminine ways, can act as males do, can behave in combinations of ways both baffling and enticing, but not gender-determined. Murray Hall, a woman who twice married women and was a Tammany Hall politician for thirty years, successfully passed as a man and evaded public detection of her gender until she died in 1901.

> "I wouldn't believe it if Dr. Gallagher, whom I know to be a man of undoubted veracity hadn't said so," said Senator Bernard F. Martin. "Well, truly, it's most wonderful. Why, I knew him well. . . . Suspect he was a woman? Never."[2]

If behavior is not gender-determined, then all the systems of knowledge and all the social systems built on the assumption of heterosexuality and inherent male-female differences are inaccurate. There are psychological and social systems to enforce the coincidence of gender and role, and they may appear inherent. But they can and do change, as an adequate history of sexuality and of women will show. In this period, where the supposed universality of male supremacy is threatened, its ideal opposite, the essential feminine, rises to challenge it. *Yet both are constructs used by people as labels for forces in conflict,[3] whose outcome will transform them both, and whose process already does.* In the modern period new combinations emerge as visible from these changing relations, manifest themselves in individuals, in groups, and by affecting all relations in the system.

We also know that woman is central. Not only in our own lives, though certainly in our own lives, women are definitive, valuable, influential. Yet also in the way we see the world and its relations are women central. This vision is outside of History (an intellectual construct built by "men"), and contradicts it. While the class war has been recognized—and distorted—in History, having become a form of "male-dominated" struggle, "the battle of the sexes" has been distorted—and unrecognized—in the culture. During the early industrial period, free women's wages for cotton, tobacco, laundry, and other domestic work challenged the slave system and provided an alternative to the feudal structure, both on the farms and plantations and in marriages and homes. Unpaid labor was being displaced by paid labor in both places. The process has engendered bloody wars, which continue to this day. *Yet the evidence of a woman-centered view of relations is kept confined, to the realms of "folk," or joke, to the insane—to "the unconscious," which contains it.*

Furthermore, not only is woman central to the maintenance of human life, and life-sustaining systems. In particular, lesbians know a nonpatriarchal secret: the primary significance of the mother. It is she—not Freud's patriarchal father—in a system, who is the central figure in shaping our identity and culture, a fact which History determinedly and systematically denies.

Thus History, Culture, and Science lie. Lesbians know this; however much we might have swallowed the myth that *we* were wrong for seeing the lie, we refuse to live wholly by it. We defy the patriarchal, heterosexual constraints against woman-love and so somewhere in our experience exists the dangerous evidence that recorded knowledge is inaccurate.

A second premise follows: that identity is created in social systems, in which all participate. There is something about "heterosexual society" which produces so-called homosexuals. The pertinacity with which we have survived despite massive and nearly universal repression is testimony not only to the amazing strength and power of the individuals who have lived but also to the questions we must inevitably raise about the historical development of ideas, posited as "universal," that classify "human nature" outside of this social interaction. We are familiar with the contamination theory used to bar us from parenting, from teaching jobs, and from other "sensitive" areas where ideology is transmitted, for fear we will teach "heterosexuals" to be "homosexuals." The obvious reply that we came from heterosexual families, schools, and cultures is ignored over and over again. The very persistence of the denial and fear indicates that on some level people do understand both that heterosexual identity is created socially—at the expense of nonconformers who must be kept down to maintain heterosexuality as a system—and that the entire society takes part in this process.

Take the identity, "slave." A slave is created by force and the maintenance of several fictions as "reality" on the part of a society. There can be no slave without a master, certainly, but no master without a complex social system lending him the power to appropriate the life of the slave for her labor power and ability to reproduce. The identities of both master and slave are sustained by everybody else—in the master's family, in town among shopkeepers, tradespeople, and artisans, in the courthouse, the homes, and churches, on the streets, and, to some extent, dialectically by the dynamics of resistance to slavery, by those still needing to mask their resistance in order to survive. The point is that *social identity is created by and maintained coercively in the social system.* As lesbians we are learning this about sexuality as well, learning to reject individual guilt for not behaving as heterosexual females are supposed to behave, learning "even" to be proud of that.

A third premise is that any system pretending to exclusiveness, like heterosexuality, uses scapegoats. *By definition heterosexuality denies homosexuality; but it both requires and suppresses the scapegoat. Her function is to be the unthinkable alternative,* the nonchoice of heterosexuality; to validate it by being a mistake; to preserve the system, the ideological construct and its material, institutionalized forms. To be wrong, so the other can be right; to be bad, so the other can be good; to be unnatural, so the other can be natural: to be Different. The need for such reassurance is very great. So many of the pressures of the patriarchal system push toward consciousness the sense of something wrong, bad, not natural about its arrangements, that the need to demonstrate the opposite, and divide women, is constant—and growing, as the feminist movement which gives voices to those suspicions and becomes itself a force, grows.

If the function of what is denied is to shore up something trying to be different and better (whatever is doing the denying and benefits most from it), then the processes of denial have to be overt, while the processes of shoring up have to be covert. This dual reality is further complicated by a factor we are all familiar with from other contexts: *the denial, the oppression of any category of people—whose difference is exploitable according to the logos/force employed by any other—takes overt and covert forms as well. Not only are the oppressed made to disappear, rendered invisible and even obliterated. So too are the means of oppression made to disappear, rendered invisible, obliterated.* Nobody sees them. Even the victims are made to feel—often too successfully—we are responsible, guilty, for our difference-as-badness. (Whether the "badness" is called evil, sick or criminal depends on the model of law.) And too often the guilt runs us; we escape self-destructively into elaborate systems whose mutually reinforcing and interdependent (and exchangeable) roles that defy "reality" simultaneously appear to resemble the heterosexual dependency system. We are unacceptable, and that which makes us so is acceptable. That we retreat, deny, rebel against this process is only evidence, even sometimes to ourselves, of our insanity. We may be told that we have "a personality problem" if we see things differently, or that we're "sick"; if we point out trouble we are "troublemakers"—or "criminals." Not only behavior but people become taboo. This doubleness, which includes keeping the lid on while apparently taking it off in a token instance, is a social function that maintains the taboo even more effectively than the force and violence which lie beneath it and, by being so much more reprehensible at performing the same function, dignify it. Liberalism is the direct result of the doubleness of a reality that maintains itself by denying another.

The social system includes this conventional, institutionalized, ideologically invisible violence as heterosexual sanction; it is the underside of the social institutions, conventions, and ideology of heterosexual/patriarchal society. Because each aspect of the system, as well as the system itself, maintains male supremacy, each victimizes women and each is embattled. We see these contradictions within and outside of the family, that legal unit that serves to contain and control the kin systems which formerly determined social relations, particularly as given shape by the movements against legal wife battery and child abuse, incest, rape, enforced sterilization, and other abuses of reproduction and abortion, and for child care and women's liberation in every sphere. *What most divides women in this historical stuggle for self-determination is the taboo against women loving women, the taboo that forbids women to step out of the socially defined behavior for females, that maintenance of a "natural" difference by which some are served and others serve.*

This taboo has been so widespread, and the repression of lesbianism so successful, that while male homosexuality, also a severe challenge to heterosexuality and patriarchy, has covertly been both incorporated and punished, lesbianism has been almost invisible. The massive oppression and repression of nonmale, and nonheterosexual, behaviors is built upon a gynophobia strong enough to challenge matriarchal society if it ever existed, and prevent it if it didn't. *Our civilization is built on systemic woman-hating, and is maintained by systemic denial of the fact. Like the parasitic dependency of the ruling class upon those it exploits, the dependency of "men" upon "women" is a great secret of History. To keep it, same-sex social/sexual relations—which provide the evidence to disprove the "necessity" of exploiting dependency relations of gender difference—are made taboo.* Social identity is shaped by the intimate experience of patriarchal dependency relations, enticing us to participate in them as adults as we were forced to as infants. These relations pervade class society, whose functioning depends upon them, at all levels. The taboo is a crucial, invisible support.

Thus the social function of the lesbian taboo is to support "civilization." Difference is used as a tool for maintaining divisions in the hierarchies of power. It follows that "History"—the male record of civilization—has been a socially masculine construct, by definition hiding, containing, and refuting female power function. History silences and requires silence. It is not amendable; it is a weapon. By definition, "civilization" has been a coercive system to reproduce dominance relations—all of which have benefited social "men"—and maintain them throughout several modes of economic and social production. Civilization requires and is founded upon compliance.

What is repressed materially is appropriated: the labor and resources of women, poor people, blacks, the earth, the universe. Their energies appear either to disappear (become used) or become mysterious, wild, untamed, chaotic, and destructive until understood, mastered, tamed, categorized, and controlled by men.

This repression, hidden by history, is recorded in the "unconscious."

So, "reality" is a political construct, denying and run by its denial of what it taboos. As marriage is supported by prostitution, so the family is by incest, and heterosexuality by homosexuality. The key is that "women" must "love" "men." What is hidden is woman at the center of these relations. From her vantage point, they would all look different.[4]

Finally, we spoke of how lesbian culture is calling for a radical transformation of vision, the empowering of women, and the building of a new culture sustaining, not destroying, the different lives and energies of our universe.

Notes

1. Olga Broumas captures the complexity of this process in her poem "Cinderella" (in *Beginning with O* [New Haven and London: Yale Univ. Press, 1977], p. 57), which transforms the traditional tale by assuming a feminist stance. "Cinderella" evokes the pain of a woman, successful at using the master's tools, who finally refuses to buy into patriarchal success, putting her, as it does, in the position of participating in the oppression of her sisters, dividing her against herself.
2. Jonathan Katz, *Gay American History* (New York: Thomas Y. Crowell Co., 1976), p. 234.
3. Political economists and historians have devised a model to describe the conflict of social groups as the moving force in history, and psychoanalysts have devised a model of the psyche which mirrors it. But both are finding that those forces posited as different—dark, not white; irrational, not rational; untamed, not civilized (according to the patriarchal logos)—are, as they come to power, challenging the systems that contained them. Psychology and History are constructs different from, and laid down upon, reality. For a fuller discussion of these models and how they

function in daily life, see my paper "Taking Medicine," for the New York Women's Studies Association Colloquium "Frontier or Backwater: Can Feminism Survive in the University?", Brooklyn College, 1977.

4. These ideas were first developed in my paper "Beyond Marx and Freud: Some Theoretical Considerations," at the session "Power, Oppression and the Politics of Culture: A Lesbian Feminist Perspective," at the Fourth Berkshire Conference on Women's History, Mount Holyoke College, 1978.

Carol Gilligan

In a Different Voice: Women's Conceptions of Self and of Morality

The arc of developmental theory leads from infantile dependence to adult autonomy, tracing a path characterized by an increasing differentiation of self from other and a progressive freeing of thought from contextual constraints. The vision of Luther, journeying from the rejection of a self defined by others to the assertive boldness of "Here I stand" and the image of Plato's allegorical man in the cave, separating at last the shadows from the sun, have taken powerful hold on the psychological understanding of what constitutes development. Thus, the individual, meeting fully the developmental challenges of adolescence as set for him by Piaget, Erikson, and Kohlberg, thinks formally, proceeding from theory to fact, and defines both the self and the moral autonomously, that is, apart from the identification and conventions that had comprised the particulars of his childhood world. So equipped, he is presumed ready to live as an adult, to love and work in a way that is both intimate and generative, to develop an ethical sense of caring and a genital mode of relating in which giving and taking fuse in the ultimate reconciliation of the tension between self and other.

Yet the men whose theories have largely informed this understanding of development have all been plagued by the same problem, the problem of women, whose sexuality remains more diffuse, whose perception of self is so much more tenaciously embedded in relationships with others and whose moral dilemmas hold them in a mode of judgment that is insistently contextual. The solution has been to consider women as either deviant or deficient in their development.

That there is a discrepancy between concepts of womanhood and adulthood is nowhere more clearly evident than in the series of studies on sex-role stereotypes reported by Broverman, Vogel, Broverman, Clarkson, and Rosenkrantz (1972). The repeated finding of these studies is that

The research reported here was partially supported by a grant from the Spencer Foundation. I wish to thank Mary Belenky for her collaboration and colleagueship in the abortion decision study and Michael Murphy for his comments and help in preparing this manuscript.

the qualities deemed necessary for adulthood—the capacity for autonomous thinking, clear decision making, and responsible action—are those associated with masculinity but considered undesirable as attributes of the feminine self. The stereotypes suggest a splitting of love and work that relegates the expressive capacities requisite for the former to women while the instrumental abilities necessary for the latter reside in the masculine domain. Yet, looked at from a different perspective, these stereotypes reflect a conception of adulthood that is itself out of balance, favoring the separateness of the individual self over its connection to others and leaning more toward an autonomous life of work than toward the interdependence of love and care.

This difference in point of view is the subject of this essay, which seeks to identify in the feminine experience and construction of social reality a distinctive voice, recognizable in the different perspective it brings to bear on the construction and resolution of moral problems. The first section begins with the repeated observation of difference in women's concepts of self and of morality. This difference is identified in previous psychological descriptions of women's moral judgments and described as it again appears in current research data. Examples drawn from interviews with women in and around a university community are used to illustrate the characteristics of the feminine voice. The relational bias in women's thnking that has, in the past, been seen to compromise their moral judgment and impede their development now begins to emerge in a new developmental light. Instead of being seen as a developmental deficiency, this bias appears to reflect a different social and moral understanding.

This alternative conception is enlarged in the second section through consideration of research interviews with women facing the moral dilemma of whether to continue or abort a pregnancy. Since the research design allowed women to define as well as resolve the moral problem, developmental distinctions could be derived directly from the categories of women's thought. The responses of women to structured interview questions regarding the pregnancy decision formed the basis for describing a developmental sequence that traces progressive differentiations in their understanding and judgment of conflicts between self and other. While the sequence of women's moral development follows the three-level progression of all social developmental theory, from an egocentric through a societal to a universal perspective, this progression takes place within a distinct moral conception. This conception differs from that derived by Kohlberg from his all-male longitudinal research data.

This difference then becomes the basis in the third section for challenging the current assessment of women's moral judgment at the same time that it brings to bear a new perspective on developmental assessment in general. The inclusion in the overall conception of development of those categories derived from the study of women's moral judgment enlarges developmental understanding, enabling it to encompass better the thinking of both sexes. This is particularly true with respect to the construction and resolution of the dilemmas of adult life. Since the conception of adulthood retrospectively shapes the theoretical understanding of the development that precedes it, the changes in that conception that follow from the more central inclusion of women's judgments recast developmental understanding and lead to a reconsideration of the substance of social and moral development.

Characteristics of the Feminine Voice

The revolutionary contribution of Piaget's work is the experimental confirmation and refinement of Kant's assertion that knowledge is actively constructed rather than passively received. Time, space, self, and other, as well as the categories of developmental theory, all arise out of the active interchange between the individual and the physical and social world in which he lives and of which he strives to make sense. The development of cognition is the process of reappropriating reality at progressively more complex levels of apprehension, as the structures of thinking expand to encompass the increasing richness and intricacy of experience.

Moral development, in the work of Piaget and Kohlberg, refers specifically to the expanding conception of the social world as it is reflected in the understanding and resolution of the inevitable conflicts that arise in the relations between self and others. The moral judgment is a statement of priority, an attempt at rational resolution in a situation where, from a different point of view, the choice itself seems to do violence to justice.

Kohlberg (1969), in his extension of the early work of Piaget, discovered six stages of moral judgment, which he claimed formed an invariant sequence, each successive stage representing a more adequate construction of the moral problem, which in turn provides the basis for its more just resolution. The stages divide into three levels, each of which denotes a significant expansion of the moral point of view from an egocentric through a societal to a universal ethical conception. With this expansion in perspective comes the capacity to free moral judgment from the individual needs and social conventions with which it had earlier been confused and anchor it instead in principles of justice that are universal in application. These principles provide criteria upon which both individual and societal claims can be impartially assessed. In Kohlberg's view, at the highest stages of development morality is freed from both psychological and historical constraints, and the individual can judge independently of his own particular needs and of the values of those around him.

That the moral sensibility of women differs from that of men was noted by Freud (1925/1961) in the following by now well-quoted statement:

> I cannot evade the notion (though I hesitate to give it expression) that for women the level of what is ethically normal is different from what it is in man. Their superego is never so inexorable, so impersonal, so independent of its emotional origins as we require it to be in men. Character-traits which critics of every epoch have brought up against women—that they show less sense of justice than men, that they are less ready to submit to the great exigencies of life, that they are more often influenced in their judgments by feelings of affection or hostility—all these would be amply accounted for by the modification in the formation of their super-ego which we have inferred above. (pp. 257–58)

While Freud's explanation lies in the deviation of female from male development around the construction and resolution of the Oedipal problem, the same observations about the nature of morality in women emerge from the work of Piaget and Kohlberg. Piaget (1932/1965), in his study of the rules of children's games, observed that, in the games they played, girls were "less explicit about agreement [than boys] and less concerned with legal elaboration" (p. 93). In contrast to the boys' interest in the codification of rules, the girls adopted a more pragmatic attitude, regarding "a rule as good so long as the game repays it" (p. 83). As a result, in comparison to boys, girls were found to be "more tolerant and more easily reconciled to innovations" (p. 52).

Kohlberg (1971) also identifies a strong interpersonal bias in the moral judgments of women, which leads them to be considered as typically at the third of his six-stage developmental sequence. At that stage, the good is identified with "what pleases or helps others and is approved of by them" (p. 164). This mode of judgment is conventional in its conformity to generally held notions of the good but also psychological in its concern with intention and consequence as the basis for judging the morality of action.

That women fall largely into this level of moral judgment is hardly surprising when we read from the Broverman et al. (1972) list that prominent among the twelve attributes considered to be desirable for women are tact, gentleness, awareness of the feelings of others, strong need for security, and easy expression of tender feelings. And yet, herein lies the paradox, for the very traits that have traditionally defined the "goodness" of women, their care for and sensitivity to the needs of others, are those that mark them as deficient in moral development. The infusion of feeling into their judgments keeps them from developing a more independent and abstract ethical conception in which concern for others derives from principles of justice rather than from compassion and care. Kohlberg, however, is less pessimistic than Freud in his assessment, for he sees the development of women as extending beyond the interpersonal level, following the same path toward independent, principled judgment that he discovered in the research on men from which his stages were derived. In Kohlberg's view, women's development will proceed beyond Stage Three when they are challenged to solve moral problems that require them to see beyond the relationships that have in the past generally bound their moral experience.

What then do women say when asked to construct the moral domain; how do we identify the characteristically "feminine" voice? A Radcliffe undergraduate, responding to the question, "If you had to say what morality meant to you, how would you sum it up?," replies:

> When I think of the word morality, I think of obligations. I
> usually think of it as conflicts between personal desires and
> social things, social considerations, or personal desires of your-
> self versus personal desires of another person or people or what-
> ever. Morality is that whole realm of how you decide these
> conflicts. A moral person is one who would decide, like by
> placing themselves more often than not as equals, a truly moral
> person would always consider another person as their equal . . .
> in a situation of social interaction, something is morally wrong
> where the individual ends up screwing a lot of people. And it is
> morally right when everyone comes out better off.*

Yet when asked if she can think of someone whom she would consider a genuinely moral person, she replies, "Well, immediately I think of Albert Schweitzer because he has obviously given his life to help others." Obligation and sacrifice override the ideal of equality, setting up a basic contradiction in her thinking.

Another undergraduate responds to the question, "What does it mean to say something is morally right or wrong?," by also speaking first of responsibilities and obligations:

> Just that it has to do with responsibilities and obligations and
> values, mainly values. . . . In my life situation I relate morality
> with interpersonal relationships that have to do with respect for
> the other person and myself. [Why respect other people?] Be-
> cause they have a consciousness or feelings that can be hurt, an
> awareness that can be hurt.

*The Radcliffe woman whose responses are cited were interviewed as part of a pilot study on undergraduate moral development conducted by the author in 1970.

The concern about hurting others persists as a major theme in the responses of two other Radcliffe students:

> [Why be moral?] Millions of people have to live together peacefully. I personally don't want to hurt other people. That's a real criterion, a main criterion for me. It underlies my sense of justice. It isn't nice to inflict pain. I empathize with anyone in pain. Not hurting others is important in my own private morals. Years ago, I would have jumped out of a window not to hurt my boyfriend. That was pathological. Even today though, I want approval and love and I don't want enemies. Maybe that's why there is morality—so people can win approval, love and friendship.

> My main moral principle is not hurting other people as long as you aren't going against your own conscience and as long as you remain true to yourself. . . . There are many moral issues such as abortion, the draft, killing, stealing, monogamy, etc. If something is a controversial issue like these, then I always say it is up to the individual. The individual has to decide and then follow his own conscience. There are no moral absolutes. . . . Laws are pragmatic instruments, but they are not absolutes. A viable society can't make exceptions all the time, but I would personally. . . . I'm afraid I'm heading for some big crisis with my boyfriend someday, and someone will get hurt, and he'll get more hurt than I will. I feel an obligation not to hurt him, but also an obligation to not lie. I don't know if it is possible to not lie and not hurt.

The common thread that runs through these statements, the wish not to hurt others and the hope that in morality lies a way of solving conflicts so that no one will get hurt, is striking in that it is independently introduced by each of the four women as the most specific item in their response to a most general question. The moral person is one who helps others; goodness is service, meeting one's obligations and responsibilities to others, if possible, without sacrificing oneself. While the first of the four women ends by denying the conflict she initially introduced, the last woman anticipates a conflict between remaining true to herself and adhering to her principle of not hurting others. The dilemma that would test the limits of this judgment would be one where helping others is seen to be at the price of hurting the self.

The reticence about taking stands on "controversial issues," the willingness to "make exceptions all the time" expressed in the final example above, is echoed repeatedly by other Radcliffe students, as in the following two examples:

> I never feel that I can condemn anyone else. I have a very relativistic position. The basic idea that I cling to is the sanctity of human life. I am inhibited about impressing my beliefs on others.

> I could never argue that my belief on a moral question is anything that another person should accept. I don't believe in absolutes. . . . If there is an absolute for moral decisions, it is human life.

Or as a thirty-one-year-old Wellesley graduate says, in explaining why she would find it difficult to steal a drug to save her own life despite her belief that it would be right to steal for another: "It's just very hard to defend yourself against the rules. I mean, we live by consensus, and you take an action simply for yourself, by yourself, there's no consensus there, and that is relatively indefensible in this society now."

What begins to emerge is a sense of vulnerability that impedes these women from taking a stand, what George Eliot (1860/1965) regards as the girl's "susceptibility" to adverse judgments of others, which stems from her lack of power and consequent inability to do something in the world. While relativism in men, the unwillingness to make moral judgments that Kohlberg and Kramer (1969) and Kohlberg and Gilligan (1971) have associated with the adolescent crisis of identity and belief, takes the form of calling into question the concept of morality itself, the women's reluctance to judge stems rather from their uncertainty about their right to make moral statements or, perhaps, the price for them that such judgment seems to entail. This contrast echoes that made by Matina Horner (1972), who differentiated the ideological fear of success expressed by men from the personal conflicts about succeeding that riddled the women's responses to stories of competitive achievement.

> Most of the men who responded with the expectation of negative consequences because of success were not concerned about their masculinity but were instead likely to have expressed existential concerns about finding a "non-materialistic happiness and satisfaction in life." These concerns, which reflect changing attitudes toward traditional kinds of success or achievement in our society, played little, if any, part in the female stories. Most of the women who were high in fear of success imagery continued to be concerned about the discrepancy between success in the situation described and feminine identity. (pp. 163–64)

When women feel excluded from direct participation in society, they see themselves as subject to a consensus or judgment made and enforced by the men on whose protection and support they depend and by whose names they are known. A divorced middle-aged woman, mother of adolescent daughters, resident of a sophisticated university community, tells the story as follows:

> As a woman, I feel I never understood that I was a person, that I can make decisions and I have a right to make decisions. I always felt that that belonged to my father or my husband in some way or church which was always represented by a male clergyman. They were the three men in my life: father, husband, and clergyman, and they had much more to say about what I should or shouldn't do. They were really authority figures which I accepted. I didn't rebel against that. It only has lately occurred to me that I never even rebelled against it, and my girls are much more conscious of this, not in the militant sense, but just in the recognizing sense. . . . I still let things happen to me rather than make them happen, than to make choices, although I know all about choices. I know the procedures and the steps and all. [Do you have any clues about why this might be true?] Well, I think in one sense, there is less responsibility involved. Because if you make a dumb decision, you have to take the rap. If it happens to you, well, you can complain about it. I think that if you don't grow up feeling that you ever had any choices, you don't either have the sense that you have emotional responsibility. With this sense of choice comes this sense of responsibility.

The essence of the moral decision is the exercise of choice and the willingness to accept responsibility for that choice. To the extent that women perceive themselves as having no choice, they correspondingly excuse themselves from the responsibility that decision entails. Childlike in the vulnerability of their dependence and consequent fear of abandonment, they claim to wish only to please but in return for their goodness they expect to be loved and cared for. This, then, is an "altruism" always at risk, for it presupposes an innocence constantly in danger of being compromised by an awareness of the trade-off that has been made. Asked to describe herself, a Radcliffe senior responds:

> I have heard of the onion skin theory. I see myself as an onion, as a block of different layers, the external layers for people that I don't know that well, the agreeable, the social, and as you go inward there are more sides for people I know that I show. I am not sure about the innermost, whether there is a core, or whether I have just picked up everything as I was growing up, these different influences. I think I have a neutral attitude towards myself, but I do think in terms of good and bad. . . . Good—I try

> to be considerate and thoughtful of other people and I try to be
> fair in situations and be tolerant. I use the words but I try and
> work them out practically. . . . Bad things—I am not sure if they
> are bad, if they are altruistic or I am doing them basically for
> approval of other people. [Which things are these?] The values I
> have when I try to act them out. They deal mostly with interper-
> sonal type relations. . . . If I were doing it for approval, it would
> be a very tenuous thing. If I didn't get the right feedback, there
> might go all my values.

Ibsen's play, *A Doll's House* (1879/1965), depicts the explosion of just such a world through the eruption of a moral dilemma that calls into question the notion of goodness that lies at its center. Nora, the "squirrel wife," living with her husband as she had lived with her father, puts into action this conception of goodness as sacrifice and, with the best of intentions, takes the law into her own hands. The crisis that ensues, most painfully for her in the repudiation of that goodness by the very person who was its recipient and beneficiary, causes her to reject the suicide that she had initially seen as its ultimate expression and choose instead to seek new and firmer answers to the adolescent questions of identity and belief.

The availability of choice and with it the onus of responsibility has now invaded the most private sector of the woman's domain and threatens a similar explosion. For centuries, women's sexuality anchored them in passivity, in a receptive rather than active stance, where the events of conception and childbirth could be controlled only by a withholding in which their own sexual needs were either denied or sacrificed. That such a sacrifice entailed a cost to their intelligence as well was seen by Freud (1908/1959) when he tied the "undoubted intellectual inferiority of so many women" to "the inhibition of thought necessitated by sexual suppression" (p. 199). The strategies of withholding and denial that women have employed in the politics of sexual relations appear similar to their evasion or withholding of judgment in the moral realm. The hesitance expressed in the previous examples to impose even a belief in the value of human life on others, like the reluctance to claim one's sexuality, bespeaks a self uncertain of its strength, unwilling to deal with consequence, and thus avoiding confrontation.

Thus women have traditionally deferred to the judgment of men, although often while intimating a sensibility of their own which is at variance with that judgment. Maggie Tulliver, in *The Mill on the Floss* (Eliot, 1860/1965), responds to the accusations that ensue from the discovery of her secretly continued relationship with Phillip Wakeham by acceding to her brother's moral judgment while at the same time asserting a different set of standards by which she attests her own superiority:

I don't want to defend myself. . . . I know I've been wrong—
often continually. But yet, sometimes when I have done wrong, it
has been because I have feelings that you would be the better for
if you had them. If *you* were in fault ever, if you had done
anything very wrong, I should be sorry for the pain it brought
you; I should not want punishment to be heaped on you (p. 188).

An eloquent defense, Kohlberg would argue, of a Stage Three moral
position, an assertion of the age-old split between thinking and feeling,
justice and mercy, that underlies many of the clichés and stereotypes
concerning the difference between the sexes. But considered from another
point of view, it is a moment of confrontation, replacing a former evasion,
between two modes of judging, two differing constructions of the moral
domain—one traditionally associated with masculinity and the public
world of social power, the other with femininity and the privacy of
domestic interchange. While the developmental ordering of these two
points of view has been to consider the masculine as the more adequate
and thus as replacing the feminine as the individual moves toward higher
stages, their reconciliation remains unclear.

The Development of Women's Moral Judgment

Recent evidence for a divergence in moral development between men and
women comes from the research of Haan (Note 1) and Holstein (1976)
whose findings lead them to question the possibility of a "sex-related bias"
in Kohlberg's scoring system. This system is based on Kohlberg's six-stage
description of moral development. Kohlberg's stages divide into three
levels, which he designates as preconventional, conventional, and postconventional, thus denoting the major shifts in moral perspective around a
center of moral understanding that equates justice with the maintenance
of existing social systems. While the preconventional conception of justice
is based on the needs of the self, the conventional judgment derives from
an understanding of society. This understanding is in turn superseded by
a postconventional or principled conception of justice where the good is
formulated in universal terms. The quarrel with Kohlberg's stage scoring
does not pertain to the structural differentiation of his levels but rather to
questions of stage and sequence. Kohlberg's stages begin with an obedience and punishment orientation (Stage One), and go from there in
invariant order to instrumental hedonism (Stage Two), interpersonal
concordance (Stage Three), law and order (Stage Four), social contract
(Stage Five), and universal ethical principles (Stage Six).

The bias that Haan and Holstein question in this scoring system has to do with the subordination of the interpersonal to the societal definition of the good in the transition from Stage Three to Stage Four. This is the transition that has repeatedly been found to be problematic for women. In 1969, Kohlberg and Kramer identified Stage Three as the characteristic mode of women's moral judgments, claiming that, since women's lives were interpersonally based, this stage was not only "functional" for them but also adequate for resolving the moral conflicts that they faced. Turiel (1973) reported that while girls reached Stage Three sooner than did boys, their judgments tended to remain at that stage while the boys' development continued further along Kohlberg's scale. Gilligan, Kohlberg, Lerner, and Belenky (1971) found a similar association between sex and moral-judgment stage in a study of high-school students, with the girls' responses being scored predominantly at Stage Three while the boys' responses were more often scored at Stage Four.

This repeated finding of developmental inferiority in women may, however, have more to do with the standard by which development has been measured than with the quality of women's thinking per se. Haan's data (Note 1) on the Berkeley Free Speech Movement and Holstein's (1976) three-year longitudinal study of adolescents and their parents indicate that the moral judgments of women differ from those of men in the greater extent to which women's judgments are tied to feelings of empathy and compassion and are concerned more with the resolution of "real-life" as opposed to hypothetical dilemmas (Note 1, p. 34). However, as long as the categories by which development is assessed are derived within a male perspective from male research data, divergence from the masculine standard can be seen only as a failure of development. As a result, the thinking of women is often classified with that of children. The systematic exclusion from consideration of alternative criteria that might better encompass the development of women indicates not only the limitations of a theory framed by men and validated by research samples disproportionately male and adolescent but also the effects of the diffidence prevalent among women, their reluctance to speak publicly in their own voice, given the constraints imposed on them by the politics of differential power between the sexes.

In order to go beyond the question, "How much like men do women think, how capable are they of engaging in the abstract and hypothetical construction of reality?" it is necessary to identify and define in formal terms developmental criteria that encompass the categories of women's thinking. Such criteria would include the progressive differentiations, comprehensiveness, and adequacy that characterize higher-stage resolution of the "more frequently occurring, real-life moral dilemmas of interpersonal, empathic, fellow feeling concerns" (Haan, Note 1, p. 34), which have long been the center of women's moral judgments and experience. To ascertain whether the feminine construction of the moral domain relies on a language different from that of men, but one which deserves equal credence in the definition of what constitutes development, it is necessary first to find the places where women have the power to choose and thus are willing to speak in their own voice.

When birth control and abortion provide women with effective means for controlling their fertility, the dilemma of choice enters the center of women's lives. Then the relationships that have traditionally defined women's identities and framed their moral judgments no longer flow inevitably from their reproductive capacity but become matters of decision over which they have control. Released from the passivity and reticence of a sexuality that binds them in dependence, it becomes possible for women to question with Freud what it is that they want and to assert their own answers to that question. However, while society may affirm publicly the woman's right to choose for herself, the exercise of such choice brings her privately into conflict with the conventions of femininity, particularly the moral equation of goodness with self-sacrifice. While independent asser-tion in judgment and action is considered the hallmark of adulthood and constitutes as well the standard of masculine development, it is rather in their care and concern for others that women have both judged themselves and been judged.

The conflict between self and other thus constitutes the central moral problem for women, posing a dilemma whose resolution requires a reconciliation between femininity and adulthood. In the absence of such a reconciliation, the moral problem cannot be resolved. The "good woman" masks assertion in evasion, denying responsibility by claiming only to meet the needs of others, while the "bad woman" forgoes or renounces the commitments that bind her in self-deception and betrayal. It is precisely this dilemma—the conflict between compassion and autonomy, between virtue and power—which the feminine voice struggles to resolve in its effort to reclaim the self and to solve the moral problem in such a way that no one is hurt.

When a woman considers whether to continue or abort a pregnancy, she contemplates a decision that affects both self and others and engages directly the critical moral issue of hurting. Since the choice is ultimately hers and therefore one for which she is responsible, it raises precisely those questions of judgment that have been most problematic for women. Now she is asked whether she wishes to interrupt that stream of life which has for centuries immersed her in the passivity of dependence while at the same time imposing on her the responsibility for care. Thus the abortion decision brings to the core of feminine apprehension, to what Joan Didion

(1972) calls "the irreconcilable difference of it—that sense of living one's deepest life underwater, that dark involvement with blood and birth and death" (p. 14), the adult questions of responsibility and choice.

How women deal with such choices has been the subject of my research, designed to clarify, through considering the ways in which women construct and resolve the abortion decision, the nature and development of women's moral judgment. Twenty-nine women, diverse in age, race, and social class, were referred by abortion and pregnancy counseling services and participated in the study for a variety of reasons. Some came to gain further clarification with respect to a decision about which they were in conflict, some in response to a counselor's concern about repeated abortions, and others out of an interest in and/or willingness to contribute to ongoing research. Although the pregnancies occurred under a variety of circumstances in the lives of these women, certain commonalities could be discerned. The adolescents often failed to use birth control because they denied or discredited their capacity to bear children. Some of the older women attributed the pregnancy to the omission of contraceptive measures in circumstances where intercourse had not been anticipated. Since the pregnancies often coincided with efforts on the part of the women to end a relationship, they may be seen as a manifestation of ambivalence or as a way of putting the relationship to the ultimate test of commitment. For these women, the pregnancy appeared to be a way of testing truth, making the baby an ally in the search for male support and protection or, that failing, a companion victim of his rejection. There were, finally, some women who became pregnant either as a result of a failure of birth control or intentionally as part of a joint decision that later was reconsidered. Of the twenty-nine women, four decided to have the baby, one miscarried, twenty-one chose abortion, and three remained in doubt about the decision.

In the initial part of the interview, the women were asked to discuss the decision that confronted them, how they were dealing with it, the alternatives they were considering, their reasons for and against each option, the people involved, the conflicts entailed, and the ways in which making this decision affected their self-concepts and their relationships with others. Then, in the second part of the interview, moral judgment was assessed in the hypothetical mode by presenting for resolution three of Kohlberg's standard research dilemmas.

While the structural progression from a preconventional through a conventional to a postconventional moral perspective can readily be discerned in the women's responses to both actual and hypothetical dilemmas, the conventions that shape women's moral judgments differ from those that apply to men. The construction of the abortion dilemma, in particular, reveals the existence of a distinct moral language whose evolution informs the sequence of women's development. This is the language of selfishness and responsibility, which defines the moral problem as one of obligation to exercise care and avoid hurt. The infliction of hurt is considered selfish and immoral in its reflection of unconcern, while the expression of care is seen as the fulfillment of moral responsibility. The reiterative use of the language of selfishness and responsibility and the underlying moral orientation it reflects sets the women apart from the men whom Kohlberg studied and may be seen as the critical reason for their failure to develop within the constraints of his system.

In the developmental sequence that follows, women's moral judgments proceed from an initial focus on the self at the *first level* to the discovery, in the transition to the *second level*, of the concept of responsibility as the basis for a new equilibrium between self and others. The elaboration of this concept of responsibility and its fusion with a maternal concept of morality, which seeks to ensure protection for the dependent and unequal, characterizes the *second level* of judgment. At this level the good is equated with caring for others. However, when the conventions of feminine goodness legitimize only others as the recipients of moral care, the logical inequality between self and other and the psychological violence that it engenders create the disequilibrium that initiates the *second* transition. The relationship between self and others is then reconsidered in an effort to sort out the confusion between conformity and care inherent in the conventional definition of feminine goodness and to establish a new equilibrium, which dissipates the tension between selfishness and responsibility. At the *third level*, the self becomes the arbiter of an independent judgment that now subsumes both conventions and individual needs under the moral principle of nonviolence. Judgment remains psychological in its concern with the intention and consequences of action, but it now becomes universal in its condemnation of exploitation and hurt.

LEVEL I: ORIENTATION TO INDIVIDUAL SURVIVAL

In its initial and simplest construction, the abortion decision centers on the self. The concern is pragmatic, and the issue is individual survival. At this level, "should" is undifferentiated from "would," and others influence the decision only through their power to affect its consequences. An eighteen-year-old, asked what she thought when she found herself pregnant, replies: "I really didn't think anything except that I didn't want it. [Why was that?] I didn't want it, I wasn't ready for it, and next year will be my last year and I want to go to school."

Asked if there was a right decision, she says, "There is no right decision. [Why?] I didn't want it." For her the question of right decision would emerge only if her own needs were in conflict; then she would have to decide which needs should take precedence. This was the dilemma of another eighteen-year-old, who saw having a baby as a way of increasing her freedom by providing "the perfect chance to get married and move away from home," but also as restricting her freedom "to do a lot of things."

At this first level, the self, which is the sole object of concern, is constrained by lack of power; the wish "to do a lot of things" is constantly belied by the limitations of what, in fact, is being done. Relationships are, for the most part, disappointing: "The only thing you are ever going to get out of going with a guy is to get hurt." As a result, women may in some instances deliberately choose isolation to protect themselves against hurt. When asked how she would describe herself to herself, a nineteen-year-old, who held herself responsible for the accidental death of a younger brother, answers as follows:

> I really don't know. I never thought about it. I don't know. I
> know basically the outline of a character. I am very independent.
> I don't really want to have to ask anybody for anything and I am
> a loner in life. I prefer to be by myself than around anybody else.
> I manage to keep my friends at a limited number with the point
> that I have very few friends. I don't know what else there is. I am
> a loner and I enjoy it. Here today and gone tomorrow.

The primacy of the concern with survival is explicitly acknowledged by a sixteen-year-old delinquent in response to Kohlberg's Heinz dilemma, which asks if it is right for a desperate husband to steal an outrageously overpriced drug to save the life of his dying wife:

> I think survival is one of the first things in life and that people
> fight for. I think it is the most important thing, more important
> than stealing. Stealing might be wrong, but if you have to steal to
> survive yourself or even kill, that is what you should do . . .
> Preservation of oneself, I think, is the most important thing; it
> comes before anything in life.

THE FIRST TRANSITION: FROM SELFISHNESS TO RESPONSIBILITY

In the transition which follows and criticizes this level of judgment, the words selfishness and responsibility first appear. Their reference initially is to the self in a redefinition of the self-interest which has thus far served as the basis for judgment. The transitional issue is one of attachment or connection to others. The pregnancy catches up the issue not only by representing an immediate, literal connection, but also by affirming, in the most concrete and physical way, the capacity to assume adult feminine roles. However, while having a baby seems at first to offer respite from the loneliness of adolescence and to solve conflicts over dependence and independence, in reality the continuation of an adolescent pregnancy generally compounds these problems, increasing social isolation and precluding further steps toward independence.

To be a mother in the societal as well as the physical sense requires the assumption of parental responsibility for the care and protection of a child. However, in order to be able to care for another, one must first be able to care responsibly for oneself. The growth from childhood to adulthood, conceived as a move from selfishness to responsibility, is articulated explicitly in these terms by a seventeen-year-old who describes her response to her pregnancy as follows:

> I started feeling really good about being pregnant instead of
> feeling really bad, because I wasn't looking at the situation
> realistically. I was looking at it from my own sort of selfish needs
> because I was lonely and felt lonely and stuff . . . Things weren't
> really going good for me, so I was looking at it that I could have
> a baby that I could take care of or something that was part of
> me, and that made me feel good . . . but I wasn't looking at the
> realistic side . . . about the responsibility I would have to take on
> . . . I came to this decision that I was going to have an abortion
> [because] I realized how much responsibility goes with having a
> child. Like you have to be there, you can't be out of the house all
> the time which is one thing I like to do . . . and I decided that I
> have to take on responsibility for myself and I have to work out
> a lot of things.

Stating her former mode of judgment, the wish to have a baby as a way of combating loneliness and feeling connected, she now criticizes that judgment as both "selfish" and "unrealistic." The contradiction between wishes for a baby and for the freedom to be "out of the house all the time"—that is, for connection and also for independence—is resolved in terms of a new priority, as the criterion for judgment changes. The dilemma now assumes moral definition as the emergent conflict between wish and necessity is seen as a disparity between "would" and "should." In this construction the "selfishness" of willful decision is counterposed to the "responsibility" of moral choice:

> What I want to do is to have the baby; but what I feel I should do
> which is what I need to do, is have an abortion right now,
> because sometimes what you want isn't right. Sometimes what is

necessary comes before what you want, because it might not always lead to the right thing.

While the pregnancy itself confirms femininity—"I started feeling really good; it sort of made me feel, like being pregnant, I started feeling like a woman"—the abortion decision becomes an opportunity for the adult exercise of responsible choice.

> [How would you describe yourself to yourself?] I am looking at myself differently in the way that I have had a really heavy decision put upon me, and I have never really had too many hard decisions in my life, and I have made it. It has taken some responsibility to do this. I have changed in that way, that I have made a hard decision. And that has been good. Because before, I would not have looked at it realistically, in my opinion. I would have gone by what I wanted to do, and I wanted it, and even if it wasn't right. So I see myself as I'm becoming more mature in ways of making decisions and taking care of myself, doing something for myself. I think it is going to help me in other ways, if I have other decisions to make put upon me, which would take some responsibility. And I would know that I could make them.

In the epiphany of this cognitive reconstruction, the old becomes transformed in terms of the new. The wish to "do something for myself" remains, but the terms of its fulfillment change as the decision affirms both femininity and adulthood in its integration of responsibility and care. Morality, says another adolescent, "is the way you think about yourself . . . sooner or later you have to make up your mind to start taking care of yourself. Abortion, if you do it for the right reasons, is helping yourself to start over and do different things."

Since this transition signals an enhancement in self-worth, it requires a conception of self which includes the possibility for doing "the right thing," the ability to see in oneself the potential for social acceptance. When such confidence is seriously in doubt, the transitional questions may be raised but development is impeded. The failure to make this first transition, despite an understanding of the issues involved, is illustrated by a woman in her late twenties. Her struggle with the conflict between selfishness and responsibility pervades but fails to resolve her dilemma of whether or not to have a third abortion.

> I think you have to think about the people who are involved, including yourself. You have responsibilities to yourself . . . and to make a right, whatever that is, decision in this depends on your knowledge and awareness of the responsibilities that you have and whether you can survive with a child and what it will

do to your relationship with the father or how it will affect him emotionally.

Rejecting the idea of selling the baby and making "a lot of money in a black market kind of thing . . . because mostly I operate on principles and it would just rub me the wrong way to think I would be selling my own child," she struggles with a concept of responsibility which repeatedly turns back on the question of her own survival. Transition seems blocked by a self-image which is insistently contradictory:

> [How would you describe yourself to yourself?] I see myself as impulsive, practical—that is a contradiction—and moral and amoral, a contradiction. Actually the only thing that is consistent and not contradictory is the fact that I am very lazy which everyone has always told me is really a symptom of something else which I have never been able to put my finger on exactly. It has taken me a long time to like myself. In fact there are times when I don't, which I think is healthy to a point and sometimes I think I like myself too much and I probably evade myself too much, which avoids responsibility to myself and to other people who like me. I am pretty unfaithful to myself . . . I have a hard time even thinking that I am a human being, simply because so much rotten stuff goes on and people are so crummy and insensitive.

Seeing herself as avoiding responsibility, she can find no basis upon which to resolve the pregnancy dilemma. Instead, her inability to arrive at any clear sense of decision only contributes further to her overall sense of failure. Criticizing her parents for having betrayed her during adolescence by coercing her to have an abortion she did not want, she now betrays herself and criticizes that as well. In this light, it is less surprising that she considered selling her child, since she felt herself to have, in effect, been sold by her parents for the sake of maintaining their social status.

THE SECOND LEVEL: GOODNESS AS SELF-SACRIFICE

The transition from selfishness to responsibility is a move toward social participation. Whereas at the first level, morality is seen as a matter of sanctions imposed by a society of which one is more subject than citizen, at the second level, moral judgment comes to rely on shared norms and expectations. The woman at this level validates her claim to social membership through the adoption of societal values. Consensual judgment becomes paramount and goodness the overriding concern as survival is now seen to depend on acceptance by others.

Here the conventional feminine voice emerges with great clarity, defining the self and proclaiming its worth on the basis of the ability to care for and protect others. The woman now constructs the world perfused with the assumptions about feminine goodness reflected in the stereotypes of the Broverman et al. (1972) studies. There the attributes considered desirable for women all presume an other, a recipient of the "tact, gentleness and easy expression of feeling" which allow the woman to respond sensitively while evoking in return the care which meets her own "very strong need for security" (p. 63). The strength of this position lies in its capacity for caring; its limitation is the restriction it imposes on direct expression. Both qualities are elucidated by a nineteen-year-old who contrasts her reluctance to criticize with her boyfriend's straightforwardness:

> I never want to hurt anyone, and I tell them in a very nice way, and I have respect for their own opinions, and they can do the things the way that they want, and he usually tells people right off the bat. . . . He does a lot of things out in public which I do in private. . . . it is better, the other [his] way, but I just could never do it.

While her judgment clearly exists, it is not expressed, at least not in public. Concern for the feelings of others imposes a deference which she nevertheless criticizes in an awareness that, under the name of consideration, a vulnerability and a duplicity are concealed.

At the second level of judgment, it is specifically over the issue of hurting that conflict arises with respect to the abortion decision. When no option exists that can be construed as being in the best interest of everyone, when responsibilities conflict and decision entails the sacrifice of somebody's needs, then the woman confronts the seemingly impossible task of choosing the victim. A nineteen-year-old, fearing the consequences for herself of a second abortion but facing the opposition of both her family and her lover to the continuation of the pregnancy, describes the dilemma as follows:

> I don't know what choices are open to me; it is either to have it or the abortion; these are the choices open to me. It is just that either way I don't . . . I think what confuses me is it is a choice of either hurting myself or hurting other people around me. What is more important? If there could be a happy medium, it would be fine, but there isn't. It is either hurting someone on this side or hurting myself.

While the feminine identification of goodness with self-sacrifice seems clearly to dictate the "right" resolution of this dilemma, the stakes may be high for the woman herself, and the sacrifice of the fetus, in any event, compromises the altruism of an abortion motivated by a concern for others. Since femininity itself is one conflict in an abortion intended as an expression of love and care, this is a resolution which readily explodes in its own contradiction.

"I don't think anyone should have to choose between two things that they love," says a twenty-five-year-old woman who assumed responsibility not only for her lover but also for his wife and children in having an abortion she did not want:

> I just wanted the child and I really don't believe in abortions.
> Who can say when life begins. I think that life begins at concep-
> tion and . . . I felt like there were changes happening in my body
> and I felt very protective . . . [but] I felt a responsibility, my
> responsibility if anything ever happened to her [his wife]. He
> made me feel that I had to make a choice and there was only one
> choice to make and that was to have an abortion and I could
> always have children another time and he made me feel if I didn't
> have it that it would drive us apart.

The abortion decision was, in her mind, a choice not to choose with respect to the pregnancy—"That was my choice, I had to do it." Instead, it was a decision to subordinate the pregnancy to the continuation of a relationship that she saw as encompassing her life—"Since I met him, he has been my life. I do everything for him; my life sort of revolves around him." Since she wanted to have the baby and also to continue the relationship, either choice could be construed as selfish. Furthermore, since both alternatives entailed hurting someone, neither could be considered moral. Faced with a decision which, in her own terms, was untenable, she sought to avoid responsibility for the choice she made, construing the decision as a sacrifice of her own needs to those of her lover. However, this public sacrifice in the name of responsibility engendered a private resentment that erupted in anger, compromising the very relationship that it had been intended to sustain.

> Afterwards we went through a bad time because I hate to say it
> and I was wrong, but I blamed him. I gave in to him. But when it
> came down to it, I made the decision. I could have said, 'I am
> going to have this child whether you want me to or not,' and I
> just didn't do it.

Pregnant again by the same man, she recognizes in retrospect that the choice in fact had been hers, as she returns once again to what now appears to have been missed opportunity for growth. Seeking, this time, to make rather than abdicate the decision, she sees the issue as one of "strength" as she struggles to free herself from the powerlessness of her own dependence:

> I think that right now I think of myself as someone who can become a lot stronger. Because of the circumstances, I just go along like with the tide. I never really had anything of my own before . . . [this time] I hope to come on strong and make a big decision, whether it is right or wrong.

Because the morality of self-sacrifice had justified the previous abortion, she now must suspend that judgment if she is to claim her own voice and accept responsibility for choice.

She thereby calls into question the underlying assumption of Level Two, which leads the woman to consider herself responsible for the actions of others, while holding others responsible for the choices she makes. This notion of reciprocity, backwards in its assumptions about control, disguises assertion as response. By reversing responsibility, it generates a series of indirect actions, which leave everyone feeling manipulated and betrayed. The logic of this position is confused in that the morality of mutual care is embedded in the psychology of dependence. Assertion becomes personally dangerous in its risk of criticism and abandonment, as well as potentially immoral in its power to hurt. This confusion is captured by Kohlberg's (1969) definition of Stage Three moral judgment, which joins the need for approval with the wish to care for and help others.

When thus caught between the passivity of dependence and the activity of care, the woman becomes suspended in an immobility of both judgment and action. "If I were drowning, I couldn't reach out a hand to save myself, so unwilling am I to set myself up against fate" (p. 7), begins the central character of Margaret Drabble's novel, *The Waterfall* (1971), in an effort to absolve herself of responsibility as she at the same time relinquishes control. Facing the same moral conflict which George Eliot depicted in *The Mill on the Floss*, Drabble's heroine proceeds to relive Maggie Tulliver's dilemma but turns inward in her search for the way in which to retell that story. What is initially suspended and then called into question is the judgment which "had in the past made it seem better to renounce myself than them" (Drabble, p. 50).

THE SECOND TRANSITION: FROM GOODNESS TO TRUTH

The second transition begins with the reconsideration of the relationship between self and other, as the woman starts to scrutinize the logic of self-sacrifice in the service of a morality of care. In the interview data, this transition is announced by the reappearance of the word selfish. Retrieving the judgmental initiative, the woman begins to ask whether it is selfish or responsible, moral or immoral, to include her own needs within the compass of her care and concern. This question leads her to reexamine the concept of responsibility, juxtaposing the outward concern with what other people think with a new inner judgment.

In separating the voice of the self from those of others, the woman asks if it is possible to be responsible to herself as well as to others and thus to reconcile the disparity between hurt and care. The exercise of such responsibility, however, requires a new kind of judgment whose first demand is for honesty. To be responsible, it is necessary first to acknowledge what it is that one is doing. The criterion for judgment thus shifts from "goodness" to "truth" as the morality of action comes to be assessed not on the basis of its appearance in the eyes of others, but in terms of the realities of its intention and consequence.

A twenty-four-year-old married Catholic woman, pregnant again two months following the birth of her first child, identifies her dilemma as one of choice: "You have to now decide; because it is now available, you have to make a decision. And if it wasn't available, there was no choice open; you just do what you have to do." In the absence of legal abortion, a morality of self-sacrifice was necessary in order to insure protection and care for the dependent child. However, when such sacrifice becomes optional, the entire problem is recast.

The abortion decision is framed by this woman first in terms of her responsibilities to others: having a second child at this time would be contrary to medical advice and would strain both the emotional and financial resources of the family. However, there is, she says, a third reason for having an abortion, "sort of an emotional reason. I don't know if it is selfish or not, but it would really be tying myself down and right now I am not ready to be tied down with two."

Against this combination of selfish and responsible reasons for abortion is her Catholic belief that

> . . . it is taking a life, and it is. Even though it is not formed, it is
> the potential, and to me it is still taking a life. But I have to think
> of mine, my son's and my husband's, to think about, and at first
> I think that I thought it was for selfish reasons, but it is not. I
> believe that too, some of it is selfish. I don't want another one
> right now; I am not ready for it.

The dilemma arises over the issue of justification for taking a life: "I can't cover it over, because I believe this and if I do try to cover it over, I know that I am going to be in a mess. It will be denying what I am really doing." Asking "Am I doing the right thing; is it moral?," she counterposes to her belief against abortion her concern with the consequences of continuing the pregnancy. While concluding that "I can't be so morally strict as to hurt three other people with a decision just because of my moral beliefs," the issue of goodness still remains criticial to her resolution of the dilemma:

> The moral factor is there. To me it is taking a life, and I am going to take that upon myself, that decision upon myself and I have feelings about it, and talked to a priest . . . but he said it is there and it will be from now on, and it is up to the person if they can live with the idea and still believe they are good.

The criteria for goodness, however, move inward as the ability to have an abortion and still consider herself good comes to hinge on the issue of selfishness with which she struggles to come to terms. Asked if acting morally is acting according to what is best for the self or whether it is a matter of self-sacrifice, she replies:

> I don't know if I really understand the question. . . . Like in my situation where I want to have the abortion and if I didn't it would be self-sacrificing, I am really in the middle of both those ways . . . but I think that my morality is strong and if these reasons—financial, physical reality and also for the whole family involved—were not here, that I wouldn't have to do it, and then it would be a self-sacrifice.

The importance of clarifying her own participation in the decision is evident in her attempt to ascertain her feelings in order to determine whether or not she was "putting them under" in deciding to end the pregnancy. Whereas in the first transition, from selfishness to responsibility, women made lists in order to bring to their consideration needs other than their own, now, in the second transition, it is the needs of the self which have to be deliberately uncovered. Confronting the reality of her own wish for an abortion, she now must deal with the problem of selfishness and the qualification that she feels it imposes on the "goodness" of her decision. The primacy of this concern is apparent in her description of herself:

> I think in a way I am selfish for one thing, and very emotional, very . . . and I think that I am a very real person and an understanding person and I can handle life situations fairly well, so I am basing a lot on my ability to do the things that I feel are right and best for me and whoever I am involved with. I think I was very fair to myself about the decision, and I really think that I have been truthful, not hiding anything, bringing out all the feelings involved. I feel it is a good decision and an honest one, a real decision.

Thus she strives to encompass the needs of both self and others, to be responsible to others and thus to be "good" but also to be responsible to herself and thus to be "honest" and "real."

While from one point of view, attention to one's own needs is considered selfish, when looked at from a different perspective, it is a matter of honesty and fairness. This is the essence of the transitional shift toward a new conception of goodness which turns inward in an acknowledgement of the self and an acceptance of responsibility for decision. While outward justification, the concern with "good reasons," remains critical for this particular woman: "I still think abortion is wrong, and it will be unless the situation can justify what you are doing." But the search for justification has produced a change in her thinking, "not drastically, but a little bit." She realizes that in continuing the pregnancy she would punish not only herself but also her husband, toward whom she had begun to feel "turned off and irritated." This leads her to consider the consequences self-sacrifice can have both for the self and for others. "God, " she says, "can punish, but He can also forgive." What remains in question is whether her claim to forgiveness is compromised by a decision that not only meets the needs of others, but that also is "right and best for me."

The concern with selfishness and its equation with immorality recur in an interview with another Catholic woman whose arrival for an abortion was punctuated by the statement, "I have always thought abortion was a fancy word for murder." Initially explaining this murder as one of lesser degree—"I am doing it because I have to do it. I am not doing it the least bit because I want to," she judges it "not quite as bad. You can rationalize that it is not quite the same." Since "keeping the child for lots and lots of reasons was just sort of impractical and out," she considers her options to be either abortion or adoption. However, having previously given up one child for adoption, she says: "I knew that psychologically there was no way that I could hack another adoption. It took me about four-and-a half years to get my head on straight; there was just no way I was going to go through it again." The decision thus reduces in her eyes to a choice between murdering the fetus or damaging herself. The choice is further complicated by the fact that by continuing the pregnancy she would hurt not only herself but also her parents, with whom she lived. In the face of these manifold moral contradictions, the psychological demand for honesty that arises in counseling finally allows decision:

> On my own, I was doing it not so much for myself; I was doing it
> for my parents. I was doing it because the doctor told me to do
> it, but I had never resolved in my mind that I was doing it for me.
> Because it goes right back to the fact that I never believed in
> abortions. . . . Actually, I had to sit down and admit, no, I really

> don't want to go the mother route now. I honestly don't feel that
> I want to be a mother, and that is not really such a bad thing to
> say after all. But that is not how I felt up until talking to
> Maureen [her counselor]. It was just a horrible way to feel, so I
> wasn't going to feel it, and I just blocked it right out.

As long as her consideration remains "moral," abortion can be justified only as an act of sacrifice, a submission to necessity where the absence of choice precludes responsibility. In this way, she can avoid self-condemnation, since, "When you get into moral stuff then you are getting into self-respect and that stuff, and at least if I do something that I feel is morally wrong, then I tend to lose some of my self-respect as a person." Her evasion of responsibility, critical to maintaining the innocence necessary for self-respect, contradicts the reality of her own participation in the abortion decision. The dishonesty in her plea of victimization creates the conflict that generates the need for a more inclusive understanding. She must now resolve the emerging contradiciton in her thinking between the two uses of the term right: "I am saying that abortion is morally wrong, but the situation is right, and I am going to do it." But the thing is that eventually they are going to have to go together, and I am going to have to put them together somehow." Asked how this could be done, she replies:

> I would have to change morally wrong to morally right. [How?] I
> have no idea. I don't think you can take something that you feel
> is morally wrong because the situation makes it right and put the
> two together. They are not together, they are opposite. They
> don't go together. Something is wrong, but all of a sudden
> because you are doing it, it is right.

This discrepancy recalls a similar conflict she faced over the question of euthanasia, also considered by her to be morally wrong until she "took care of a couple of patients who had flat EEGs and saw the job that it was doing on their families." Recalling that experience, she says:

> You really don't know your blacks and whites until you really
> get into them and are being confronted with it. If you stop and
> think about my feelings on euthanasia until I got into it, and
> then my feelings about abortion until I got into it, I thought both
> of them were murder. Right and wrong and no middle but there
> is a gray.

In discovering the gray and questioning the moral judgments which formerly she considered to be absolute, she confronts the moral crisis of the second transition. Now the conventions which in the past had guided her moral judgment became subject to a new criticism, as she questions not only the justification for hurting others in the name of morality, but also the "rightness" of hurting herself. However, to sustain such criticism in the face of conventions that equate goodness with self-sacrifice, the woman must verify her capacity for independent judgment and the legitimacy of her own point of view.

Once again transition hinges on self-concept. When uncertainty about her own worth prevents a woman from claiming equality, self-assertion falls prey to the old criticism of selfishness. Then the morality that condones self-destruction in the name of responsible care is not repudiated as inadequate but rather is abandoned in the face of its threat to survival. Moral obligation, rather than expanding to include the self, is rejected completely as the failure of conventional reciprocity leaves the woman unwilling any longer to protect others at what is now seen to be her own expense. In the absence of morality, survival, however "selfish" or "immoral," returns as the paramount concern.

A musician in her late twenties illustrates this transitional impasse. Having led an independent life which centered on her work, she considered herself "fairly strong-willed, fairly in control, fairly rational and objective" until she became involved in an intense love affair and discovered in her capacity to love "an entirely new dimension" in herself. Admitting in retrospect to "tremendous naiveté and idealism," she had entertained "some vague ideas that some day I would like a child to concretize our relationship ... having always associated having a child with all the creative aspects of my life." Abjuring, with her lover, the use of contraceptives because, "as the relationship was sort of an ideal relationship in our minds, we liked the idea of not using foreign objects or anything artificial," she saw herself as having relinquished control, becoming instead "just simply vague and allowing events to just carry me along." Just as she began in her own thinking to confront "the realities of that situation"— the possibility of pregnancy and the fact that her lover was married—she found herself pregnant. "Caught" between her wish to end a relationship that "seemed more and more defeating" and her wish for a baby, which "would be a connection that would last a long time," she is paralyzed by her inability to resolve the dilemma which her ambivalence creates.

The pregnancy poses a conflict between her "moral" belief that "once a certain life has begun, it shouldn't be stopped artificially" and her "amazing" discovery that to have the baby she would "need much more [support] than I thought." Despite her moral conviction that she "should" have the child, she doubts that she could psychologically deal with "having the child alone and taking the responsibility for it." Thus a conflict erupts between what she considers to be her moral obligation to protect life and her inability to do so under the circumstances of this pregnancy. Seeing it as "my decision and my responsibility for making the decision whether to have or have not the child," she struggles to find a viable basis on which to resolve the dilemma.

Capable of arguing either for or against abortion "with a philosophical logic," she says, on the one hand, that in an overpopulated world one should have children only under ideal conditions for care but, on the other, that one should end a life only when it is impossible to sustain it. She describes her impasse in response to the question of whether there is a difference between what she wants to do and what she thinks she should do:

> Yes, and there always has. I have always been confronted with that precise situation in a lot of my choices, and I have been trying to figure out what are the things that make me believe that these are things I should do as opposed to what I feel I want to do. [In this situation?] It is not that clear cut. I both want the child and feel I should have it, and I also think I should have the abortion and want it, but I would say it is my stronger feeling, and that I don't have enough confidence in my work yet and that is really where it is all hinged, I think . . . [the abortion] would solve the problem and I know I can't handle the pregnancy.

Characterizing this solution as "emotional and pragmatic" and attributing it to her lack of confidence in her work, she contrasts it with the "better thought out and more logical and more correct" resolution of her lover who thinks that she should have the child and raise it without either his presence or financial support. Confronted with this reflected image of herself as ultimately giving and good, as self-sustaining in her own creativity and thus able to meet the needs of others while imposing no demands of her own in return, she questions not the image itself but her own adequacy in filling it. Concluding that she is not yet capable of doing so, she is reduced in her own eyes to what she sees as a selfish and highly compromised fight

> for my survival. But in one way or another, I am going to suffer. Maybe I am going to suffer mentally and emotionally having the abortion, or I would suffer what I think is possibly something worse. So I suppose it is the lesser of two evils. I think it is a matter of choosing which one I know that I can survive through. It is really. I think it is selfish, I suppose, because it does have to do with that. I just realized that. I guess it does have to do with whether I would survive or not. [Why is this selfish?] Well, you know, it is. Because I am concerned with my survival first, as opposed to the survival of the relationship or the survival of the child, another human being . . . I guess I am setting priorities,

and I guess I am setting my needs to survive first. . . . I guess I see
it in negative terms a lot . . . but I do think of other positive
things; that I am still going to have some life left, maybe. I don't
know.

In the face of this failure of reciprocity of care, in the disappointment of
abandonment where connection was sought, survival is seen to hinge on
her work which is "where I derive the meaning of what I am. That's the
known factor." While uncertainty about her work makes this survival
precarious, the choice for abortion is also distressing in that she considers
it to be "highly introverted—that in this one respect, having an abortion
would be going a step backward; going outside to love someone else and
having a child would be a step forward." The sense of retrenchment that
the severing of connection signifies is apparent in her anticipation of the
cost which abortion would entail:

Probably what I will do is I will cut off my feelings, and when
they will return or what would happen to them after that, I don't
know. So that I don't feel anything at all, and I would probably
just be very cold and go through it very coldly. . . . The more you
do that to yourself, the more difficult it becomes to love again or
to trust again or to feel again. . . . Each time I move away from
that, it becomes easier, not more difficult, but easier to avoid
committing myself to a relationship. And I am really concerned
about cutting off that whole feeling aspect.

Caught between selfishness and responsibility, unable to find in the
circumstances of this choice a way of caring which does not at the same
time destroy, she confronts a dilemma which reduces to a conflict between
morality and survival. Adulthood and femininity fly apart in the failure of
this attempt at integration as the choice to work becomes a decision not
only to renounce this particular relationship and child but also to obliterate the vulnerability that love and care engender.

THE THIRD LEVEL: THE MORALITY OF NONVIOLENCE

In contrast, a twenty-five-year-old woman, facing a similar disappointment, finds a way to reconcile the initially disparate concepts of selfishness
and responsibility through a transformed understanding of self and a
corresponding redefinition of morality. Examining the assumptions underlying the conventions of feminine self-abnegation and moral self-sacrifice, she comes to reject these conventions as immoral in their power to

hurt. By elevating nonviolence—the injunction against hurting—to a principle governing all moral judgment and action, she is able to assert a moral equality between self and other. Care then becomes a universal obligation, the self-chosen ethic of a postconventional judgment that reconstructs the dilemma in a way that allows the assumption of responsibility for choice.

In this woman's life, the current pregnancy brings to the surface the unfinished business of an earlier pregnancy and of the relationship in which both pregnancies occurred. The first pregnancy was discovered after her lover had left and was terminated by an abortion experienced as a purging expression of her anger at having been rejected. Remembering the abortion only as a relief, she nevertheless describes that time in her life as one in which she "hit rock bottom." Having hoped then to "take control of my life," she instead resumed the relationship when the man reappeared. Now, two years later, having once again "left my diaphragm in the drawer," she again becomes pregnant. Although initially "ecstatic" at the news, her elation dissipates when her lover tells her that he will leave if she chooses to have the child. Under these circumstances, she considers a second abortion but is unable to keep the repeated appointments she makes because of her reluctance to accept the responsibility for that choice. While the first abortion seemed an "honest mistake," she says that a second would make her feel "like a walking slaughter-house." Since she would need financial support to raise the child, her initial strategy was to take the matter to "the welfare people" in the hope that they would refuse to provide the necessary funds and thus resolve her dilemma:

> In that way, you know, the responsibility would be off my
> shoulders, and I could say, it's not my fault, you know, the state
> denied me the money that I would need to do it. But it turned out
> that it was possible to do it, and so I was, you know, right back
> where I started. And I had an appointment for an abortion, and
> I kept calling and cancelling it and then remaking the appoint-
> ment and cancelling it, and I just couldn't make up my mind.

Confronting the need to choose between the two evils of hurting herself or ending the incipient life of the child, she finds, in a reconstruction of the dilemma itself, a basis for a new priority that allows decision. In doing so, she comes to see the conflict as arising from a faulty construction of reality. Her thinking recapitulates the developmental sequence, as she considers but rejects as inadequate the components of earlier-stage resolutions. An expanded conception of responsibility now reshapes moral judgment and guides resolution of the dilemma, whose pros and cons she considers as follows:

Well, the pros for having the baby are all the admiration that you
would get from, you know, being a single woman, alone, martyr,
struggling, having the adoring love of this beautiful Gerber baby
. . . just more of a home life than I have had in a long time, and
that basically was it, which is pretty fantasyland; it is not very
realistic. . . . Cons against having the baby: it was going to
hasten what is looking to be the inevitable end of the relationship
with the man I am presently with. . . . I was going to have to go
on welfare, my parents were going to hate me for the rest of my
life, I was going to lose a really good job that I have, I would lose
a lot of independence . . . solitude . . . and I would have to be put
in a position of asking help from a lot of people a lot of the time.
Cons against having the abortion is having to face up to the guilt
. . . and pros for having the abortion are I would be able to
handle my deteriorating relation with S. with a lot more capability and a lot more responsibility for him and for myself . . . and I
would not have to go through the realization that for the next
twenty-five years of my life I would be punishing myself for
being foolish enough to get pregnant again and forcing myself to
bring up a kid just because I did this. Having to face the guilt of a
second abortion seemed like, not exactly, well, exactly the lesser
of the two evils but also the one that would pay off for me
personally in the long run because by looking at why I am
pregnant again and subsequently have decided to have a second
abortion, I have to face up to some things about myself.

lthough she doesn't "feel good about having a seond abortion," she
evertheless concludes,

I would not be doing myself or the child or the world any kind of
favor having this child . . . I don't need to pay off my imaginary
debts to the world through this child, and I don't think that it is
right to bring a child into the world and use it for that purpose.

Asked to describe herself, she indicates how closely her transformed
ioral understanding is tied to a changing self-concept:

I have been thinking about that a lot lately, and it comes up
different than what my usual subconscious perception of myself
is. Usually paying off some sort of debt, going around serving
people who are not really worthy of my attentions because
somewhere in my life I think I got the impression that my needs
are really secondary to other people's, and that if I feel, if I make
any demands on other people to fulfill my needs, I'd feel guilty

for it and submerge my own in favor of other people's, which later backfires on me, and I feel a great deal of resentment for other people that I am doing things for, which causes friction and the eventual deterioration of the relationship. And then I start all over again. How would I describe myself to myself? Pretty frustrated and a lot angrier than I admit, a lot more aggressive than I admit.

Reflecting on the virtues which comprise the conventional definition of the feminine self, a definition which she hears articulated in her mother's voice, she says, "I am beginning to think that all these virtues are really not getting me anywhere. I have begun to notice." Tied to this recognition is an acknowledgement of her power and worth, both previously excluded from the image she projected:

I am suddenly beginning to realize that the things that I like to do, the things I am interested in, and the things that I believe and the kind of person I am is not so bad that I have to constantly be sitting on the shelf and letting it gather dust. I am a lot more worthwhile than what my past actions have led other people to believe.

Her notion of a "good person," which previously was limited to her mother's example of hard work, patience and self-sacrifice, now changes to include the value that she herself places on directness and honesty. Although she believes that this new self-assertion will lead her "to feel a lot better about myself" she recognizes that it will also expose her to criticism:

Other people may say, "Boy, she's aggressive, and I don't like that," but at least, you know, they will know that they don't like that. They are not going to say, "I like the way she manipulates herself to fit right around me." . . . What I want to do is just be a more self-determined person and a more singular person.

While within her old framework abortion had seemed a way of "copping out" instead of being a "responsible person [who] pays for his mistakes and pays and pays and is always there when she says she will be there and even when she doesn't say she will be there is there," now, her "conception of what I think is right for myself and my conception of self-worth is changing." She can consider this emergent self "also a good person," as her concept of goodness expands to encompass "the feeling of self-worth; you are not going to sell yourself short and you are not going to make yourself do things that, you know, are really stupid and that you don't want to do." This reorientation centers on the awareness that:

> I have a responsibility to myself, and you know, for once I am
> beginning to realize that that really matters to me . . . instead of
> doing what I want for myself and feeling guilty over how selfish I
> am, you realize that that is a very usual way for people to live . . .
> doing what you want to do because you feel that your wants and
> your needs are important, if to no one else, then to you, and
> that's reason enough to do something that you want to do.

Once obligation extends to include the self as well as others, the disparity between selfishness and responsibility is reconciled. Although the conflict between self and other remains, the moral problem is restructured in an awareness that the occurrence of the dilemma itself precludes non-violent resolution. The abortion decision is now seen to be a "serious" choice affecting both self and others: "This is a life that I have taken, a conscious decision to terminate, and that is just very heavy, a very heavy thing." While accepting the necessity of abortion as a highly compromised resolution, she turns her attention to the pregnancy itself, which she now considers to denote a failure of responsibility, a failure to care for and protect both self and other.

As in the first transition, although now in different terms, the conflict precipitated by the pregnancy catches up the issues critical to development. These issues now concern the worth of the self in relation to others, the claiming of the power to choose, and the acceptance of responsibility for choice. By provoking a confrontation with these issues, the crisis can become "a very auspicious time; you can use the pregnancy as sort of a learning, teeing-off point, which makes it useful in a way." This possibility for growth inherent in a crisis which allows confrontation with a construction of reality whose acceptance previously had impeded development was first identified by Coles (1964) in his study of the children of Little Rock. This same sense of possibility is expressed by the women who see, in their resolution of the abortion dilemma, a reconstructed understanding which creates the opportunity for "a new beginning," a chance "to take control of my life."

For this woman, the first step in taking control was to end the relationship in which she had considered herself "reduced to a nonentity," but to do so in a responsible way. Recognizing hurt as the inevitable concomitant of rejection, she strives to minimize that hurt "by dealing with [his] needs as best I can without compromising my own . . . that's a big point for me, because the thing in my life to this point has been always compromising, and I am not willing to do that any more." Instead, she seeks to act in a "decent, human kind of way . . . one that leaves maybe a slightly shook but not totally destroyed person." Thus the "nonentity" confronts her power to destroy which formerly had impeded any assertion, as she considers the possibility for a new kind of action that leaves both self and other intact.

The moral concern remains a concern with hurting as she considers Kohlberg's Heinz dilemma in terms of the question, "who is going to be hurt more, the druggist who loses some money or the person who loses their life?" The right to property and right to life are weighed not in the abstract, in terms of their logical priority, but rather in the particular, in terms of the actual consequences that the violation of these rights would have in the lives of the people involved. Thinking remains contextual and admixed with feelings of care, as the moral imperative to avoid hurt begins to be informed by a psychological understanding of the meaning of non-violence.

Thus, release from the intimidation of inequality finally allows the expression of a judgment that previously had been withheld. What women then enunciate is not a new morality, but a moral conception disentangled from the constraints that formerly had confused its perception and impeded its articulation. The willingness to express and take responsibility for judgment stems from the recognition of the psychological and moral necessity for an equation of worth between self and other. Responsibility for care then includes both self and other, and the obligation not to hurt, freed from conventional constraints, is reconstructed as a universal guide to moral choice.

The reality of hurt centers the judgment of a twenty-nine-year-old woman, married and the mother of a preschool child, as she struggles with the dilemma posed by a second pregnancy whose timing conflicts with her completion of an advanced degree. Saying that "I cannot deliberately do something that is bad or would hurt another person because I can't live with having done that," she nevertheless confronts a situation in which hurt has become inevitable. Seeking that solution which would best protect both herself and others, she indicates, in her definition of morality, the ineluctable sense of connection which infuses and colors all of her thinking:

> [Morality is] doing what is appropriate and what is just within your circumstances, but ideally it is not going to affect—I was going to say, ideally it wouldn't negatively affect another person, but that is ridiculous, because decisions are always going to affect another person. But you see, what I am trying to say is that it is the person that is the center of the decision making, of that decision making about what's right and what's wrong.

The person who is the center of this decision making begins by denying, but then goes on to acknowledge, the conflicting nature both of her own needs and of her various responsibilities. Seeing the pregnancy as a manifestation of the inner conflict bewtween her wish, on the one hand, "to be a college president" and, on the other, "to be making pottery and flowers and having kids and staying at home," she struggles with contradition between femininity and adulthood. Considering abortion as the "better" choice—because "in the end, meaning this time next year or this time two weeks from now, it will be less of a personal strain on us individually and on us as a family for me not to be pregnant at this time," she concludes that the decision has

> got to be, first of all, something that the woman can live with—a decision that the woman can live with, one way or another, or at least try to live with, and that it be based on where she is at and other people, significant people in her life, are at.

At the beginning of the interview she had presented the dilemma in its conventional feminine construction, as a conflict between her own wish to have a baby and the wish of others for her to complete her education. On the basis of this construction she deemed it "selfish" to continue the pregnancy because it was something "I want to do." However, as she begins to examine her thinking, she comes to abandon as false this conceptualization of the problem, acknowledging the truth of her own internal conflict and elaborating the tension which she feels between her femininity and the adulthood of her work life. She describes herself as "going in two directions" and values that part of herself which is "incredibly passionate and sensitive"—her capacity to recognize and meet, often with anticipation, the needs of others. Seeing her "compassion" as "something I don't want to lose" she regards it as endangered by her pursuit of professional advancement. Thus the self-deception of her initial presentation, its attempt to sustain the fiction of her own innocence, stems from her fear that to say that *she* does not want to have another baby at this time would be

> an acknowledgement to me that I am an ambitious person and that I want to have power and responsibility for others and that I want to live a life that extends from 9 to 5 every day and into the evenings and on weekends, because that is what the power and responsibility means. It means that my family would necessarily come second . . . there would be such an incredible conflict about which is tops, and I don't want that for myself.

Asked about her concept of "an ambitious person" she says that to be ambitious means to be

> power hungry [and] insensitive. [Why insensitive?] Because people are stomped on in the process. A person on the way up

stomps on people, whether it is family or other colleagues or
clientele, on the way up. [Inevitably?] Not always, but I have
seen it so often in my limited years of working that it is scary to
me. It is scary because I don't want to change like that.

Because the acquisition of adult power is seen to entail the loss of
feminine sensitivity and compassion, the conflict between femininity and
adulthood becomes construed as a moral problem. The discovery of the
principle of nonviolence begins to direct attention to the moral dilemma
itself and initiates the search for a resolution that can encompass both
femininity and adulthood.

Developmental Theory Reconsidered

The developmental conception delineated at the outset, which has so
consistently found the development of women to be either aberrant or
incomplete, has been limited insofar as it has been predominantly a male
conception, giving lip-service, a place on the chart, to the interdependence
of intimacy and care but constantly stressing, at their expense, the importance and value of autonomous judgment and action. To admit to this
conception the truth of the feminine perspective is to recognize for both
sexes the central importance in adult life of the connection between self
and other, the universality of the need for compassion and care. The
concept of the separate self and of the moral principle uncompromised by
the constraints of reality is an adolescent ideal, the elaborately wrought
philosophy of a Stephen Daedalus, whose flight we know to be in jeopardy.
Erikson (1964), in contrasting the ideological morality of the adolescent
with the ethics of adult care, attempts to grapple with this problem of
integration, but is impeded by the limitations of his own previous developmental conception. When his developmental stages chart a path where
the sole precursor to the intimacy of adult relationships is the trust
established in infancy and all intervening experience is marked only as
steps toward greater independence, then separation itself becomes the
model and the measure of growth. The observation that, for women,
identity has as much to do with connection as with separation led Erikson
into trouble largely because of his failure to integrate this insight into the
mainstream of his developmental theory (Erikson, 1968).

The morality of responsibility which woman describe stands apart from
the morality of rights which underlies Kohlberg's conception of the
highest stages of moral judgment. Kohlberg (Note 3) sees the progression
toward these stages as resulting from the generalization of the self-centered
adolescent rejection of societal morality into a principled conception of

individual natural rights. To illustrate this progression, he cites as an example of integrated Stage Five judgment, "possibly moving to Stage Six," the following response of a twenty-five-year-old subject from his male longitudinal sample:

> [What does the word morality mean to you?] Nobody in the world knows the answer. I think it is recognizing the right of the individual, the rights of other individuals, not interfering with those rights. Act as fairly as you would have them treat you. I think it is basically to preserve the human being's right to existence. I think that is the most important. Secondly, the human being's right to do as he pleases, again without interfering with somebody else's rights. (p. 29)

Another version of the same conception is evident in the following interview response of a male college senior whose moral judgment also was scored by Kohlberg (Note 4) as at Stage Five or Six:

> [Morality] is a prescription, it is a thing to follow, and the idea of having a concept of morality is to try to figure out what it is that people can do in order to make life with each other livable, make for a kind of balance, a kind of equilibrium, a harmony in which everybody feels he has a place and an equal share in things, and it's doing that—doing that is kind of contributing to a state of affairs that go beyond the individual in the absence of which, the individual has no chance for self-fulfillment of any kind. Fairness; morality is kind of essential, it seems to me, for creating the kind of environment, interaction between people, that is prerequisite to this fulfillment of most individual goals and so on. If you want other people to not interfere with your pursuit of whatever you are into, you have to play the game.

In contrast, a woman in her late twenties responds to a similar question by defining a morality not of rights but of responsibility:

> [What makes something a moral issue?] Some sense of trying to uncover a right path in which to live, and always in my mind is that the world is full of real and recognizable trouble, and is it heading for some sort of doom and is it right to bring children into this world when we currently have an overpopulation problem, and is it right to spend money on a pair of shoes when I have a pair of shoes and other people are shoeless . . . It is part of a self-critical view, part of saying, how am I spending my time and in what sense am I working? I think I have a real drive to, I have a real maternal drive to take care of someone. To take care

of my mother, to take care of children, to take care of other
people's children, to take care of my own children, to take care
of the world. I think that goes back to your other question, and
when I am dealing with moral issues, I am sort of saying to
myself constantly, are you taking care of all the things that you
think are important and in what ways are you wasting yourself
and wasting those issues?

While the postconventional nature of this woman's perspective seems
clear, her judgments of Kohlberg's hypothetical moral dilemmas do not
meet his criteria for scoring at the principled level. Kohlberg regards this
as a disparity between normative and metaethical judgments which he sees
as indicative of the transition between conventional and principled thinking. From another perspective, however, this judgment represents a
different moral conception, disentangled from societal conventions and
raised to the principled level. In this conception, moral judgment is
oriented toward issues of responsibility. The way in which the responsibility orientation guides moral decision at the postconventional level is
described by the following woman in her thirties:

[Is there a right way to make moral decisions?] The only way I
know is to try to be as awake as possible, to try to know the
range of what you feel, to try to consider all that's involved, to be
as aware as you can be to what's going on, as conscious as you
can of where you're walking. [Are there principles that guide
you?] The principle would have something to do with responsibility, responsibility and caring about yourself and others . . .
But it's not that on the one hand you choose to be responsible
and on the other hand you choose to be irresponsible— both
ways you can be responsible. That's why there's not just a
principle that once you take hold of you settle—the principle put
into practice here is still going to leave you with conflict.

The moral imperative that emerges repeatedly in the women's interviews
is an injunction to care, a responsibility to discern and alleviate the "real
and recognizable trouble" of this world. For the men Kohlberg studied,
the moral imperative appeared rather as an injunction to respect the rights
of others and thus to protect from interference the right to life and self-
fulfillment. Women's insistence on care is at first self-critical rather than
self-protective, while men initially conceive obligation to others negatively
in terms of noninterference. Development for both sexes then would seem
to entail an integration of rights and responsibilities through the discovery
of the complementarity of these disparate views. For the women I have
studied, this integration between rights and responsibilities appears to

take place through a principled understanding of equity and reciprocity. This understanding tempers the self-destructive potential of a self-critical morality by asserting the equal right of all persons to care. For the men in Kohlberg's sample as well as for those in a longitudinal study of Harvard undergraduates (Gilligan & Murphy, Note 5) it appears to be the recognition through experience of the need for a more active responsibility in taking care that corrects the potential indifference of a morality of noninterference and turns attention from the logic to the consequences of choice. In the development of a postconventional ethic understanding, women come to see the violence generated by inequitable relationships, while men come to realize the limitations of a conception of justice blinded to the real inequities of human life.

Kohlberg's dilemmas, in the hypothetical abstraction of their presentation, divest the moral actors from the history and psychology of their individual lives and separate the moral problem from the social contingencies of its possible occurrence. In doing so, the dilemmas are useful for the distillation and refinement of the "objective principles of justice" toward which Kohlberg's stages strive. However, the reconstruction of the dilemma in its contextual particularity allows the understanding of cause and consequence which engages the compassion and tolerance considered by previous theorists to qualify the feminine sense of justice. Only when substance is given to the skeletal lives of hypothetical people is it possible to consider the social injustices which their moral problems may reflect and to imagine the individual suffering their occurrence may signify or their resolution engender.

The proclivity of women to reconstruct hypothetical dilemmas in terms of the real, to request or supply the information missing about the nature of the people and the places where they live, shifts their judgment away from the hierarchical ordering of principles and the formal procedures of decision making that are critical for scoring at Kohlberg's highest stages. This insistence on the particular signifies an orientation to the dilemma and to moral problems in general that differs from any of Kohlberg's stage descriptions. Given the constraints of Kohlberg's system and the biases in his research sample, this different orientation can only be construed as a failure in development. While several of the women in the research sample clearly articulated what Kohlberg regarded as a postconventional metaethical position, none of them were considered by Kohlberg to be principled in their normative moral judgments of his hypothetical moral dilemmas (Note 4). Instead, the women's judgments pointed toward an identification of the violence inherent in the dilemma itself which was seen to compromise the justice of any of its possible resolutions. This construction of the dilemma led the women to recast the moral judgment from a consideration of the good to a choice between evils.

The woman whose judgment of the abortion dilemma concluded the developmental sequence presented in the preceding section saw Kohlberg's Heinz dilemma in these terms and judged Heinz's action in terms of a choice between selfishness and sacrifice. For Heinz to steal the drug, given the circumstances of his life (which she inferred from his inability to pay two thousand dollars), he would have "to do something which is not in his best interest, in that he is going to get sent away, and that is a supreme sacrifice, a sacrifice which I would say a person truly in love might be willing to make." However, not to steal the drug "would be selfish on his part . . . he would just have to feel guilty about not allowing her a chance to live longer." Heinz's decision to steal is considered not in terms of the logical priority of life over property which justifies its rightness, but rather in terms of the actual consequences that stealing would have for a man of limited means and little social power.

Considered in the light of its probable outcomes—his wife dead, or Heinz in jail, brutalized by the violence of that experience and his life compromised by a record of felony—the dilemma itself changes. Its resolution has less to do with the relative weights of life and property in an abstract moral conception than with the collision it has produced between two lives, formerly conjoined but now in opposition, where the continuation of one life can now occur only at the expense of the other. Given this construction, it becomes clear why consideration revolves around the issue of sacrifice and why guilt becomes the inevitable concomitant of either resolution.

Demonstrating the reticence noted in the first section about making moral judgments, this woman explains her reluctance to judge in terms of her belief

> that everybody's existence is so different that I kind of say to myself, that might be something that I wouldn't do, but I can't say that it is right or wrong for that person. I can only deal with what is appropriate for me to do when I am faced with specific problems.

Asked if she would apply to others her own injunction against hurting, she says:

> See, I can't say that it is wrong. I can't say that it is right or that it's wrong because I don't know what the person did that the other person did something to hurt him . . . so it is not right that the person got hurt, but it is right that the person who just lost the job has got to get that anger up and out. It doesn't put any bread on his table, but it is released. I don't mean to be copping out. I really am trying to see how to answer these questions for you.

Her difficulty in answering Kohlberg's questions, her sense of strain with the construction which they impose on the dilemma, stems from their divergence from her own frame of reference:

> I don't even think I use the words right and wrong anymore, and I know I don't use the word moral, because I am not sure I know what it means. . . . We are talking about an unjust society, we are talking about a whole lot of things that are not right, that are truly wrong, to use the word that I don't use very often, and I have no control to change that. If I could change it, I certainly would, but I can only make my small contribution from day to day, and if I don't intentionally hurt somebody, that is my contribution to a better society. And so a chunk of that contribution is also not to pass judgment on other people, particularly when I don't know the circumstances of why they are doing certain things.

The reluctance to judge remains a reluctance to hurt, but one that stems now not from a sense of personal vulnerability but rather from a recognition of the limitations of judgment itself. The deference of the conventional feminine perspective can thus be seen to continue at the postconventional level, not as moral relativism but rather as part of a reconstructed moral understanding. Moral judgment is renounced in an awareness of the psychological and social determinism of all human behavior at the same time as moral concern is reaffirmed in recognition of the reality of human pain and suffering:

> I have a real thing about hurting people and always have, and that gets a little complicated at times, because, for example, you don't want to hurt your child. I don't want to hurt my child but if I don't hurt her sometimes, then that's hurting her more, you see, and so that was a terrible dilemma for me.

Moral dilemmas are terrible in that they entail hurt; she sees Heinz's decision as "the result of anguish, who am I hurting, why do I have to hurt them." While the morality of Heinz's theft is not in question, given the circumstances which necessitated it, what is at issue is his willingness to substitute himself for his wife and become, in her stead, the victim of exploitation by a society which breeds and legitimizes the druggist's irresponsibility and whose injustice is thus manifest in the very occurrence of the dilemma.

The same sense that the wrong questions are being asked is evident in the response of another woman who justified Heinz's action on a similar basis, saying "I don't think that exploitation should really be a right." When women begin to make direct moral statements, the issues they repeatedly address are those of exploitation and hurt. In doing so, they raise the issue of nonviolence in precisely the same psychological context that brought Erikson (1969) to pause in his consideration of the truth of Gandhi's life.

In the pivotal letter, around which the judgment of his book turns, Erikson confronts the contradiction between the philosophy of nonviolence that informed Gandhi's dealing with the British and the psychology of violence that marred his relationships with his family and with the children of the ashram. It was this contradiction, Erikson confesses,

> which almost brought *me* to the point where I felt unable to continue writing *this* book because I seemed to sense the presence of a kind of untruth in the very protestation of truth; of something unclean when all the words spelled out an unreal purity; and, above all, of displaced violence where nonviolence was the professed issue. (p.231)

In an effort to untangle the relationship between the spiritual truth of Satyagraha and the truth of his own psychoanalytic understanding, Erikson reminds Gandhi that "Truth, you once said, 'excludes the use of violence because man is not capable of knowing the absolute truth and therefore is not competent to punish' " (p.241). The affinity between Satyagraha and psychoanalysis lies in their shared commitment to seeing life as an "experiment in truth," in their being

> somehow joined in a universal "therapeutics," committed to the Hippocratic principle that one can test truth (or the healing power inherent in a sick situation) only by action which avoids harm—or better, by action which maximizes mutuality and minimizes the violence caused by unilateral coercion or threat. (p.247)

Erikson takes Gandhi to task for his failure to acknowledge the relativity of truth. This failure is manifest in the coercion of Gandhi's claim to exclusive possession of the truth, his "unwillingness to learn from *anybody anything* except what was approved by the 'inner voice' " (p. 236). This claim led Gandhi, in the guise of love, to impose his truth on others without awareness or regard for the extent to which he thereby did violence to their integrity.

The moral dilemma, arising inevitably out of a conflict of truths, is by definition a "sick situation" in that its either/or formulation leaves no room for an outcome that does not do violence. The resolution of such dilemmas, however, lies not in the self-deception of rationalized violence—"I was" said Gandhi, "a cruelly kind husband. I regarded myself as her teacher and so harassed her out of my blind love for her" (p.

233)—but rather in the replacement of the underlying antagonism with a mutuality of respect and care.

Gandhi, whom Kohlberg has mentioned as exemplifying Stage Six moral judgment and whom Erikson sought as a model of an adult ethical sensibility, instead is criticized by a judgment that refuses to look away from or condone the infliction of harm. In denying the validity of his wife's reluctance to open her home to strangers and in his blindness to the different reality of adolescent sexuality and temptation, Gandhi compromised in his everyday life the ethic of nonviolence to which in principle and in public he was so steadfastly committed.

The blind willingness to sacrifice people to truth, however, has always been the danger of an ethics abstracted from life. This willingness links Gandhi to the biblical Abraham, who prepared to sacrifice the life of his son in order to demonstrate the integrity and supremacy of his faith. Both men, in the limitations of their fatherhood, stand in implicit contrast to the woman who comes before Solomon and verifies her motherhood by relinquishing truth in order to save the life of her child. It is the ethics of an adulthood that has become principled at the expense of care that Erikson comes to criticize in his assessment of Gandhi's life.

This same criticism is dramatized explicitly as a contrast between the sexes in *The Merchant of Venice* (1598/1912), where Shakespeare goes through an extraordinary complication of sexual identity (dressing a male actor as a female character who in turn poses as a male judge) in order to bring into the masculine citadel of justice the feminine plea for mercy. The limitation of the contractual conception of justice is illustrated through the absurdity of its literal execution, while the "need to make exceptions all the time" is demonstrated contrapuntally in the matter of the rings. Portia, in calling for mercy, argues for that resolution in which no one is hurt, and as the men are forgiven for their failure to keep both their rings and their word, Antonio in turn foregoes his "right" to ruin Shylock.

The research findings that have been reported in this essay suggest that women impose a distinctive construction on moral problems, seeing moral dilemmas in terms of conflicting responsibilities. This construction was found to develop through a sequence of three levels and two transitions, each level representing a more complex understanding of the relationship between self and other and each transition involving a critical reinterpretation of the moral conflict between selfishness and responsibility. The development of women's moral judgment appears to proceed from an initial concern with survival, to a focus on goodness, and finally to a principled understanding of nonviolence as the most adequate guide to the just resolution of moral conflicts.

In counterposing to Kohlberg's longitudinal research on the development of hypothetical moral judgment in men a cross-sectional study of women's responses to actual dilemmas of moral conflict and choice, this essay precludes the possibility of generalization in either direction and leaves to further research the task of sorting out the different variables of occasion and sex. Longitudinal studies of women's moral judgments are necessary in order to validate the claims of stage and sequence presented here. Similarly, the contrast drawn between the moral judgments of men and women awaits for its confirmation a more systematic comparison of the responses of both sexes. Kohlberg's research on moral development has confounded the variables of age, sex, type of decision, and type of dilemma by presenting a single configuration (the responses of adolescent males to hypothetical dilemmas of conflicting rights) as the basis for a universal stage sequence. This paper underscores the need for systematic treatment of these variables and points toward their study as a critical task for future moral development research.

For the present, my aim has been to demonstrate the centrality of the concepts of responsibility and care in women's constructions of the moral domain, to indicate the close tie in women's thinking between conceptions of the self and conceptions of morality, and, finally, to argue the need for an expanded developmental theory that would include, rather than rule out from developmental consideration, the difference in the feminine voice. Such an inclusion seems essential, not only for explaining the development of women but also for understanding in both sexes the characteristics and precursors of an adult moral conception.

Reference Notes

1. Haan, N. *Activism as moral protest: Moral judgments of hypothetical dilemmas and an actual situation of civil disobedience.* Unpublished manuscript, University of California at Berkeley, 1971.
2. Turiel, E. *A comparative analysis of moral knowledge and moral judgment in males and females.* Unpublished manuscript, Harvard University, 1973.
3. Kohlberg, L. *Continuities and discontinuities in childhood and adult moral development revisited.* Unpublished paper, Harvard University, 1973.
4. Kohlberg, L. Personal communication, August, 1976.
5. Gilligan, C., & Murphy, M. *The philosopher and the "dilemma of the fact": Moral development in late adolescence and adulthood.* Unpublished manuscript, Harvard University, 1977.

References

Broverman, I., Vogel, S., Broverman, D., Clarkson, F., & Rosenkrantz, P. Sex-role stereotypes: A current appraisal. *Journal of Social Issues,* 1972, 28, 59–78.

Coles, R. *Children of crisis.* Boston: Little, Brown, 1964.

Didion, J. The women's movement. *New York Times Book Review,* July 30, 1972, pp. 1–2; 14.

Drabble, M. *The waterfall.* Hammondsworth, Eng.: Penguin Books, 1969.

Eliot, G. *The mill on the floss.* New York: New American Library, 1965. (Originally published, 1860.)

Erikson, E. H. *Insight and responsibility.* New York: W. W. Norton, 1964.

Erikson, E. H. *Identity: Youth and crisis.* New York: W. W. Norton, 1968.

Erikson, E. H. *Gandhi's truth.* New York: W. W. Norton, 1969.

Freud, S. "Civilized" sexual morality and modern nervous illness. In J. Strachey (Ed.), *The standard edition of the complete psychological works of Sigmund Freud* (Vol. 9). London: Hogarth Press, 1959. (Originally published, 1908.)

Freud, S. Some psychical consequences of the anatomical distinction between the sexes. In J. Strachey (Ed.), *The standard edition of the complete psychological works of Sigmund Freud* (Vol. 19). London: Hogarth Press, 1961. (Originally published, 1925.)

Gilligan, C., Kohlberg, L., Lerner, J., & Belenky, M. Moral reasoning about sexual dilemmas: The development of an interview and scoring system. *Technical Report of the President's Commission on Obscenity and Pornography* (Vol. 1) [415 060–137]. Washington, D.C.: U.S. Government Printing Office, 1971.

Haan, N. Hypothetical and actual moral reasoning in a situation of civil disobedience. *Journal of Personality and Social Psychology,* 1975, 32, 255–70.

Holstein, C. Development of moral judgment: A longitudinal study of males and females. *Child Development,* 1976, 47, 51–61.

Horner, M. Toward an understanding of achievement-related conflicts in women. *Journal of Social Issues,* 1972, 29, 157–74.

Ibsen, H. *A doll's house.* In *Ibsen plays.* Hammondsworth, Eng.: Penguin Books, 1965. (Originally published, 1879.)

Kohlberg, L. From is to ought: How to commit the naturalistic fallacy and get away with it in the study of moral development. In T. Mischel (Ed.), *Cognitive development and epistemology.* New York: Academic Press, 1971.

Kohlberg, L., & Gilligan, C. The adolescent as a philosopher: The discovery of the self in a postconventional world. *Daedalus,* 1971, 100, 1051–56.

Kohlberg, L., & Kramer, R. Continuities and discontinuities in childhood and adult moral development. *Human Development,* 1969, 12, 93–120.

Piaget, J. *The moral judgment of the child.* New York: The Free Press, 1965. (Originally published, 1932.)

Shakespeare, W. *The merchant of Venice.* In *The comedies of Shakespeare.* London: Oxford University Press, 1912. (Originally published, 1598.)

Ruth Messinger

Women in Power and Politics

My perspectives on women in power and politics are influenced by my professional career as a social worker, my substantial involvement in community issue organizations, and my two years in elected office. My thinking has been shaped by the contrast between jobs and community projects in which women were the dominant force, and the world of government and politics where that is not the case.

I want to share how I see the situation for women in the political arena, emphasizing the psychological aspects of their role, but first let me identify and review some of the findings of two valuable studies on women in politics. The Eagleton Institute at Rutgers University has completed a statistical profile identifying who the women are who hold elected office, what offices they hold, what their perceptions are of their jobs, what differences they and others see between them and male elected officials, and how they see their futures.[1] The Women's Education Fund has put out a short but informative booklet, *The Woman Elected Official*.[2] It reports on a conference with nineteen women elected officials who discussed their experiences in the world of politics and identified aspects of that experience which were different from those of men. I have organized many of their findings and several of my own into the matrix appended to this article, but would like to discuss some of them in more detail here.

Women hold 10 percent of all elected positions in the country, including seats on school boards. Unlike men, who enter politics through law, 47 percent of all women elected officials have backgrounds in teaching, social work, secretarial or homemaker service. Their backgrounds and their socialization influence how women elected officials do their jobs.

Women are more politically ambitious than their male colleagues, more likely to seek an additional term in their current office, and more eager to hold other offices in the future, although they in fact advance more slowly.

Women in politics work harder and spend more time researching their work. They may emphasize issues of community and constituent service by their own choice or that of their constituents. They are considered available and cooperative in working on local problems. It is, however, more difficult for women elected officials to focus on one or two issues to the exclusion of others, partly because their attention is in demand and partly because they proceed with the notion, not unfamiliar to women, that they ought to be able to do everything.

Women in politics are highly visible. They get asked to talk about everything, speak on every panel and join every board, partly because they are good and partly because individuals planning meetings or holding a conference are uneasy if they do not have female representation. Unfortunately, women who accept these invitations often find that while they may have achieved visibility, they still have to make their own way, overcoming the stereotypes of others about the role they will play. Often it is either assumed that they will join quietly, be a "token" and not "rock the boat," or it is assumed they will pitch in and do the work of several people. These two polar stereotypes not only plague women as they move in public life, but often describe the actual roles that are available and that they therefore end up playing, thus reinforcing the stereotype.

In the progressive legislative caucus that I have helped to create on the New York City Council, for example, work is done by both men and women, but more of the women are in regular attendance and there is some assumption, shared by all members of the group, including the women, that the women will help hold the group together and pick up on some of the extra work responsibilities.

Women in politics are stereotyped as being "honest" and "uncorrupt," as "peace makers," and as "naive." These stereotypes can be used to their advantage. Women enjoy a higher degree of public trust. They have the opportunity to serve as mediators. They can "get away with" asking questions on complicated matters of which others, too, would like to be able to expand their understanding.

In politics, women are additionally stereotyped as being "not loyal," "unwilling to go along," not playing by the existing "rules of the game." Some women find that they are therefore excluded from important informal discussion or decision-making sessions, the concern being that they will say or do the wrong thing, discuss the session publicly, and hurt others' reputations. Out of this and similar concerns women have less easy access to the power brokers. There is an advantage here, too, for when women are not approached by the power brokers, they secure more space from the worst pressures of government in which to pursue their own thinking and make their own choices.

Women are stereotyped as "caretakers" and expected to do for others. Their assertive behavior is often criticized to the extent that they may find playing such a role not worth the hassle.

The women surveyed by the Eagleton Institute research teams believed they were lacking in skills necessary to good government service, particularly in the areas of budget, taxes, and finance. The fact as I see it is that nobody in politics knows anything about these areas; it is just that the men involved don't recognize this, or recognize this and don't admit it.

Women in politics work somewhat differently from men, partly because they lack certain connections and have to create new ones, and partly because their styles are different.

Women enter politics with more limited support systems. They need to develop professional and personal networks, learning how to reach out to those who will be helpful and supportive to them, becoming more willing to ask for help and not assume that it will be seen as a sign of weakness or an admission of failure. They need to change some of their more conventional styles of working with others, learning how to work better with people they don't like and learning how to "let go" of people who have worked with them and want to move on. It is to women's advantage that they have natural abilities in developing relationships that are something more than totally instrumental, but it is possible for them to put too much emphasis on such aspects of their work.

Women elected officials are the victims of multiple demands on their time. They are asked to give service, represent their geographic constituency, make appearances, learn local issues, and represent the women's movement. In addition demands are imposed on them from their families and in their personal lives, demands more substantial than those experienced by men, and demands which they, much more than men in similar circumstances, think they have to meet. Women need to establish some sort of balance between and among these demands, and need to discover or create special resources to help them deal with those to which they must respond. I know, personally, that I need the perspective of some others on a pretty regular basis to help me sort out what is and what is not essential.

As much of the above suggests, women in political positions do not as easily have or get power. That is not to say that they should not or cannot. It is, in fact, my contention that we not only need more women in elected office but that we need more of those women to discover strategies for increasing their power. If, however, we want those women not to suffer in the process, and if we want women who have power to function in ways that continue to reflect some of the unique aspects of how they were socialized and how they view the world, then we must consider some of the special psychological consequences for women who pursue power and help them deal with these.

Women who advance in the political arena experience both isolation and psychological dissonance. They are moving ahead on their own path, often in ways different from those for which they have been socialized, and trying to make their impact on the world in which they find themselves. At the same time as they have to learn the rules of the game and play it as well as anybody, they also have to work to change the rules of the game and make it a better platform for their talents. They are involved with how to get power and use it, with changing its nature, and with coping with the stresses of doing this.

Women have to fight on three fronts a war that men only have to fight on one. Men have a set of tasks that are incumbent on them if they want to pursue success in the external world. Women who are pursuing that same set of tasks have also to cope with the emotional and psychological upheaval of finding themselves doing those things and then have to come to grips with the reactions of others in their lives to what they are doing.

Those women who develop roles for themselves that involve the exercise of power, women whose roles are more traditionally male, experience a great deal of psychological dissonance. For them it is like walking past a mirror on the street, catching sight of one's self and saying, "Wait a minute, is that me?" As the role expands, the questions abound. "Who am I to be doing this? How much of this can I do? Can I do it differently? Is it changing me or can I change it?"

Women can become comfortable with being this new person, but will have to deal with the same questions from others, others who are genuinely curious or are trying to use the questions as a form of control. Their questions may be charged, either because they are overtly hostile or because they reflect the concern and anxiety of someone whose opinion is important to the woman in question, usually someone who feels threatened.

Women need to be aware of these questions and this dissonance. Those who fail to acknowledge it will find that it overwhelms them. Either it will become so uncomfortable that it will be rejected and the woman involved will fall back into a more comfortable role inside the existing power structure, letting others clamber ahead on her shoulders, doing tasks without goals; or she will deny it and barrel ahead, becoming as much like men as she can as quickly as she can.

Women need not only to recognize and acknowledge this dissonance, but to create coping strategies. They need support structures at work and outside work, particularly in the form of other women with whom they can discuss these pressures and talk openly about their futures. They need mentors. They need to be able to ask for help and to accept it when it is offered. Women need to expand the number of people with whom they can work and the ways in which they can work with them. They need to learn how to delegate responsibility and authority. They need, also, to learn how to take better charge of their own time and, at times, make themselves inaccessible.

Women need to know what frightens them and develop strategies for combating these sources of anxiety over time. Probably, they need to know more and work harder to achieve the positions and power that come more easily to men. As my daughter's T-shirt says, "Fortunately, this is not difficult."

What are ways in which women can change the rules of the game? Women can make politics more collaborative. It is strange that although politics ultimately involves creating majorities around issues and shared work by those making up that majority, much of the "hows" is egocentric. Women can help to create a different climate, for exchange beyond the mere trading of roles, for dividing up responsibility and working together.

Special attention must be given to the question of who could be in such a working group, what that group's purposes might be, and how it could expand the legislative or public relations aspects of its members' world. As an example, our legislative Study Group is effective partly because it is composed of the brightest, most hard working members of the Council, and partly because it often challenges the Council leadership, but also because it is an independent center for political power. We meet to discuss the Council calendar and to plan how to work together in Council meetings. In addition, we often share with each other work we are doing and occasionally invite all or some of the other members of our group to be part of a press conference on that work.

Women can use their status in new ways if they do not keep all know-how and power to themselves. They can teach constituents how to make their own service complaints or involve them in planning for their own communities. We try in my office to handle simple complaints while the constituent is there to see how we proceed. Also, we solicit Block Watchers, individuals who monitor city services on the street where they live, phoning in complaints to city agencies on behalf of my office, keeping track of such things as whether sanitation pickups are missed, repairs are delayed, or crime is on the increase. These individuals have a list of key city phone numbers and forms to keep track of what they do. They help their street get services, facilitate the work of my office, and grow in the process.

Similarly, women elected officials can use their special organizing and process skills to work with more than one constituent at a time and leave behind an organized group that will continue to take action on its own behalf. We urge any single tenant with a complaint to convene a tenant meeting, which we will attend, to share information and make recommendations.

It is possible to work in new ways with community groups that have special issue interests. Rather than meeting with them and representing their interests in government, the official can work with them side by side, bringing them into direct contact with the decision-makers.

Women can, as well, work with power within the more standard confines of their jobs. They can play tough, hold out for their goals, and refuse to back down. They can negotiate for support from colleagues. They must operate both with respect for the system and with a willingness to challenge it.

I have established some space in which I can negotiate for amendments to legislation that improve it even though everyone knows I am not going to vote for the main piece of legislation. I "get away" with this because I don't do it all the time and because when I do, I'm informed about what I'm doing.

Elected officials can try to influence how a vote goes. They can use the more conventional methods of politics, including trade-offs, threats, or just plain argument. It is also possible to urge colleagues to a new voting position through discussion, or through helping to launch in that person's district a group involved in the effort, waking up new constituencies and pressuring the representative.

One way to get power is to act as if one had it. Calls to people in city agencies, at least in New York City, are responded to in part by how one (or one's staff) sounds, by what indication is given of what kind of response is expected. Knowing what the agency does and how it operates can easily advance one's cause.

These have been some examples of how women develop power in the political arena. Women have much to offer themselves and the world in that sphere. Many more of them should be involved. They must remember that they have a natural constituency, women. To the extent that they speak to that constituency about its problems without ignoring others, to the extent that they reach out to all women and do not allow this movement to become divided over issues of class, they have a leg up on securing a voter majority.

Women's greatest contributions will be made not only when more of them are involved, but when they understand the problems that power creates for women in this society, determine to work with those problems and grow beyond them, and commit themselves to using their strengths, both as discrete individuals and as women, to change the way things are done.

Women in Politics

Key Factors	Positive Aspects	Negative Aspects
Hard Work Accessibility Issue Orientation	community service backgrounds; emphasis on accessibility and responsiveness to community needs; strong issue focus, less party discipline; more willing to take strong stands on tough issues	• work very hard • put in very long hours • "do homework" • "men get away with doing less . . ." • find it hard to focus
Visibility	easy access to media; more public exposure early opportunity for special positions in gov't/other assns.	• live in "goldfish bowl"; blunders more visible • must be "credit to their sex" • chosen for "balance"; not always given full share of leadership
Stereotypes	"honest," "uncorrupt"; enjoy public confidence "peace makers"; mediators for party or legislative disputes "naive" about technical and procedural matters; can ask questions and get to bottom of issues	• "naive loners"; not seen as *serious* politicians or team members; don't understand "how things are done" • "not loyal"; untrustworthy as allies; • won't "go along"; excluded from decision-making groups and positions • "care taker"; expected to do for; assertive behavior criticized
Skill Development	special talents in process area	• feel weak in budget, tax, finance • problems handling time, delegating work, building team, setting personal goals • too easily focus on process
Contacts, Information Resources	strength from peers, constituents, service recipients	• fewer mentors and contacts in business, financial, political worlds • problem tapping men's networks and systems, must proceed anew each time; find it difficult to get information or assistance • need to learn more about how to work with those they don't "like"

Multiple Demands	(none)	• must balance demands among constituents, local concerns, and role as a women's leader • risk designation as special-interest politician • job is time-consuming and emotionally draining
Power	confident of service they give constituents, and of re-election for that reason	• stereotyped to service, not power • given little time for establishing networks, trading support, because they have multiple demands, high visibility • seen as tokens without perquisites of power and as not trustworthy, so not wise to approach • working to get and use power creates internal dissonance
Personal Strategies	must begin to be more strategic about own future planning must become comfortable with idea of self-advancement must learn to "beat one's own drum" must cultivate mentors and develop own political mechanisms, networks must deal with emotional and social consequences of change must focus on personal and psychological, recognize and cope with dissonance, "aloneness" must learn how to ask for help must become mentors for others must figure out how to get and use power, how to play game and how to change it, how to cope with the consequences	

Source: *The Woman Elected Official: A Report of a National Needs Assessment Conference.*
The National Woman's Education Fund.
Additions courtesy of Judy Wenning, Ruth Messinger.
Matrix design by Ruth Messinger.

Notes

1. *Women in Public Office: A Biographical Directory and Statistical Analysis*, compiled by the Center for the American Woman and Politics, Eagleton Institute of Politics, 2nd ed. (Metuchen, N.J.: Scarecrow Press, 1978).
2. *The Woman Elected Official: A Report of a National Needs Assessment Conference* (Washington, D.C.: The Women's Education Fund, 1978).

Elizabeth Janeway

Women and the Uses of Power

The word "power" awakens suspicion, or at least ambivalence, in many people, especially women. So it should. We face a situation today in which it appears that an effort to achieve *within* the system—that is, a reach for status and/or authority—brings a grave risk of cooptation *by* the system. In addition, women who attempt to move up the ladder have very realistically to expect hostility and resentment, as if the old promise that there's room at the top applied only to cocks, and not to hens, who are supposed to roost on a rung further down. When we put these two reactions together, we get some very sensible questions. Suppose I do make a breakthrough; what will I get that's worth the hassle? Won't I have to commit myself to masculine goals and techniques for doing my work that I both dislike and resent, personally and in principle? How can a woman get anywhere without following Henry Higgins's suggestion and being more like a man? Do I want to pay that price in order to lay my hands on power? In fact, do I really want to lay my hands on it at all?

I don't intend to try to answer those questions as stated, because I think that they are based on an inaccurate understanding of the situation, and, to a degree, function as social controls. The reasons I've described are perfectly justified, on the overt evidence. But let us try, instead, to begin further back, and question both the inevitability of cooptation *and* the assumption that traditional masculine ideas about power are uniquely correct.

When confronted with a dilemma, the only useful approach is to widen the context in which the unanswerable question poses itself. To do that, we must look at the axioms underlying the situation as it is presented. I have been trying to do this recently, in the course of writing a book that considers definitions of power as currently accepted, and rewriting them.[1] The definitions we get now are badly deficient. Let me illustrate by quoting briefly from the texts of two standard dictionaries. The Oxford English Dictionary divides its definitions into parts. Part I deals with power "as a property or quality," and begins with "the ability to do something." That's fine: here we have power as an effective act, often creative, toward a chosen end. No quarrel with that. But halfway through, this section mutates into definitions of power as "possession of control or command over others; dominion; government; sway; authority; political ascendancy." Part II considers power not as possession but as possessor, with the personal usage of "ruler, governor" preceding the institutionalized "state or nation." "Spiritual power, divinity," follow, and next comes "a force of armed men." Webster's Third has been criticized for being representative of current popular usages rather than prescriptive of proper ones. But if that's true, it only makes its concepts more valuable as a way of understanding what the system has on its mind. Webster doesn't begin with "ability," but opts at once for "dominion, control."

"A position of ascendancy," it continues, and the first time it gets to ability what we have is "ability to compel obedience." Before we reach "capability of acting," in fact, we note "a military force or its equipment," and the "ability to wage war." The aggressive aspects of power are much to the fore. "Physical might" checks in before we come to "vigor, intensity," and when "strength, solidity" appear, the illustrative quotation implies menacing strength. Both compendiums of popular wisdom then tail off into technical uses—mathematical, mechanical, and so on.

Reading these definitions, it's easy to see why we're ambivalent about power, for what we get is a mix of good, bad, good, bad—and no apparent way to separate the one from the other. There is no way to tell when *my* ability to act becomes a bar compelling *you* to obedience instead of acting on your own. I won't belabor that point, but I will try to develop it. What's wrong with these definitions is that they are *static*. As a result, they prevent us from seeing power as a process of interaction between human beings, or groups of human beings; a moving, dynamic relationship which always includes at least two members. Each member wants something from the other, and each has some ability to grant or withhold what is asked.

Yes, one member is very often stronger than the other; but not absolutely strong, to the point where the second member has no capacity for bargaining at all. I know that there are extreme situations which approach that point, where the weaker member is indeed weak. But though extreme situations—slavery, tyranny, dictatorships—supply a test of my alternative definition and the theories I've based on it, I believe it survives. We don't, however, live in these circumstances most of the time, and so I shan't go now into the possible uses of power in these cases—though I'll be happy to discuss them later, if it's wanted.

In the main, the two members of the power relationship—we can call them the powerful and the weak, or the governors and governed, rulers and ruled, leaders and followers—do not interact at the ultimate level of total dominance and utter subordination. Now, why not? For if the dictionaries were right on their definitions, definitions which are derived from normative male experience and thinking, all of life would be lived in a state of totalitarian terror. It would be 1984, now and forever. And it isn't. So something else has to be operating in this political process. I suggest that it is the powers of the weak which check the urge to domination of our rulers. Let me briefly lay out the understanding I've developed of these powers and of the appropriate ways to use them (appropriate to them, I mean, not appropriate to the "feminine role").

The powers of the weak are strictly pragmatic—that is, outside of extreme conditions of terror, based both on what the powerful want and on what the weak are capable of doing, *without* having to risk either martyrdom or cooptation. What the powerful want is clearest if we put it first into macropolitical terms: they want to be recognized as exerting legitimate authority. In Thomas Jefferson's familiar words, they want the consent of the governed to the governance they enforce. If they have that, the job of governing is much easier. They do not have to proceed by threat, by maintaining expensive police forces or other bodies of armed men, and by limiting their options to those which won't provoke rebellion or assassination. Far from being able to do anything they want, tyrants become—fairly rapidly, too—the prisoners of rigid hierarchical structures whose first business always has to be the need to hold down a potentially rebellious populace.

In the different situation where legitimate authority is granted to rulers with some ease, the constitutional state is still a state and does have to maintain some police, some structure with which to implement policies. But there can be a great deal more flexibility, more room for maneuver, and more opportunity to initiate new programs as they are required by changing circumstances in the outer world. Rulers and ruled agreed that they share a fair number of common interests, that their purposes run together a good deal of the time, and that they are not polarized into utterly different segments. There is both respect and reciprocity within this relationship.

I believe that it isn't too hard to extrapolate from macropolitics to the social and personal. Kate Millett, whose *Sexual Politics* appeared just ten years ago,[2] gave us a helpful steer, and of course other new and rediscovered works—*Three Guineas*, for instance—easily come to mind.[3] To me, the situation of women in a patriarchal society is paradigmatic of the situation of the weak and the governed. We have been labeled "other," we have been denied access to control of our lives, and we have been described as secondary, for longer than any particular minority group (though all these things have been used to define and distance minority groups, as well). Our greatest value has been declared to lie in service to a society whose norms do not reflect the experience of our lives. If ever there was a case of taxation of energy and talent without representation, we are it.

And yet—here we are. Still. In the recent past, we have improved our situation somewhat. I think we have to ascribe this to our grasp on the powers of the weak.

I see these powers as falling into three stages. The first is distrust and disbelief—a fundamental questioning of the masculine definitions and the social mythology they serve, which puts forward both an explanation of why the world works as it does, and prescribes proper behavior for living here successfully—or at least, for living. In my opinion, every single woman who has ever lived—including Phyllis Schlafly—harbors some smidgeon of this mistrust. If Phyllis Schlafly doesn't, tell me why she is out campaigning against the women's movement. If she really trusted me, she'd be sitting home dusting her Belleek. No. Distrust, which is where we begin, I believe to be universal in women.

But of course we have to go on from this starting point. If you stop at distrust, doubt, and questioning, you may end by turning your doubts against yourself. Betty Friedan made that point seventeen years ago, and Adrienne Rich has illuminated it both in prose and in poetry. Any group of the weak that wants to do more than sulk, drop out, and cop out must go to work to overcome the isolation where doubt can turn inward. And of course, quite simply, this is done by forming a group. That's the second power of the weak—bonding. Through it, individuals validate the truth, and the value, of their individual experience. They can believe, then, that their doubts are real; and on the base of a revision of their understanding of the world and its orthodox social mythology, they can imagine a program for action—and begin to act. And this is the third power of the weak: action. *Joint* action.

Every time I start trying to put down these ideas, I am overcome by their almost infantile ring. I feel as if I were talking, and thinking, baby talk. And then I tell myself, well, yes, you are. But the great and wonderful thing about the powers of the weak is that they are so natural, ordinary, everyday, handy for use. We know all about them. We act on them easily. What we have to do now is *revalue* them, and stop looking at them, and ourselves, according to the definitions of the powerful. We must understand that we *are* important in the world, in our position of difference and doubt, that we are right and wise to doubt the operations of patriarchal society, and that we know one hell of a lot about the world—if we will just take a look at it objectively and stop valuing our knowledge less than we do male social mythology. The second and third stages of using our powers, in which we come together and compare notes, and discover that we can intervene effectively in the world of action by acting—these work backwards to the first stage. They add to the distrust of male structures a positive trust of our ability to be *right* when we distrust them.

There are two things to say about effective action. First, it follows coming together. That is, our individual reactions, which can be idiosyncratic as well as insightful, are brought to a first test by sharing them with other women and other experiences. Single action that does not go through such sharing and bonding can—I don't say it has to, but it very easily can—be deflected from the individual woman's intention, even if the goals sought are those we'd agree on as being good. This is where cooptation can come in. Single actors, who have not experienced and understood and brought home to themselves their membership in the group of the governed who are female, are extremely liable to cooptation. They get yanked off course. They find they have no real, thought-through, dependable alternative to accepting masculine aims, masculine methods, masculine values, and they turn into the unhappy tokens, or the Queen Bees. I don't say that is their fault; I do say it is their misfortune.

A second thing to remember about effective action: it requires some kind of support system, and that means some sort of structure. Now, right here, where we begin to think about forming coherent, continuing organizations, we run into another justified anxiety: won't any structure necessarily turn into a power structure?

Well, it may; but not necessarily. The way to prevent that, I think, is to hang onto our own natural powers and refuse to accept the methods recommended by the powerful, along with their definitions. We want to build into the structure we make occasions when it's loosened up or even turned around; when those who have taken on the job of making quick decisions and reacting toward sudden pressures from outside—and we have to have people who do that—move out of this position, maybe for some time, maybe just for the duration of discussions and questioning and the voicing of doubts and creative suggestions from the rest of us. If standard practices have started to develop—well, let's review them from time to time and see whether they are a good idea; within what limits they are useful; and whether others may not be useful, too, and perhaps even better. The one thing we *don't* want to do is set up a hierarchical structure with one right way to operate. But so long as we provide some fail-safe mechanisms to prevent that outcome *by using the first two powers of the weak*, I believe we can create and maintain a satisfactory system. We want to remember that life and politics aren't static, and don't run on eternal principles, and that the weak—whether the weak in any immediate situation is us or them, me or you—know a lot, and can furnish untapped sources of evolutionary potential. Then I think we can go ahead without assuming that we are bound to be either coopted or corrupted. Of course, we may be. But the great thing about understanding and using the powers of the weak is that they are *ours*. They do not belong to the powerful. We can act for ourselves. And so we don't have to sit around and worry about the ethics and the morals of the powerful—which are usually beyond our control. Of course, it's nice to have moral and ethical leaders and gover-nors—but in my opinion, that's a bonus. What can keep people acting morally and thinking ethically is *us*—the governed folk who will damn well withdraw our consent if our rulers get too big for their britches.

I haven't got into individual uses of power, because those are always best understood in terms of a particular individual relationship. But I believe that the powers of the weak work here, too. Now, you are not going to save a marriage, shall we say, by conclave. But what can happen, and probably will, is that understanding the social and political aspects of a personal situation can give you a better grip on what you do about it. How many women, throughout history, have put up with horrible situa-tions because they couldn't see any alternative to them? Because they couldn't reach a support group, or share their problems, and discover that others had them, too? I'm thinking of those pretty extreme situations of battered wives or castrated Victorian daughters. Middle-classwise, things are not that extreme today, at least overtly. But the massive inattention that the academic establishment evinces toward women faculty and stu-dents, and particularly toward Women's Studies as a discipline, tells us a lot about where the heads of our eminent professors and philosophers are located. It is those heads which lay down the definitions, and validate the practices that support these definitions, of proper female roles and accept-able behavior between the sexes. Both in your professional lives and in your private lives, you know that we still have to deal very often with power situations on a one-on-one basis, more than do members of minority groups, overall. That means that our experience of living as governed is more *intense*, as well as more *central*, than that of the other groups that make up this majority of human kind. I don't think myself that it makes it essentially different, but that's more a matter for philo-sophic discussion than action.

In one-to-one situations, the experience of bonding has often to be extended. That second power of the weak is not just useful in itself, it also increases the knowledge women have about possible action in the world as it is. Even more vital, it raises self-confidence and the capacity—the power—to value oneself adequately. A sense of control over life grows with a sense of possibilities, and having your roots in soil that's enriched by the presence of others is strengthening.

In conclusion—three points. I want to apologize again for the "baby-talk" style of what I've been saying. It's due to an effort to cover a lot of ground, not to a lack of respect for you who are here. Second, I've addressed immediate uses of power for limited goals; but I believe that powers of the weak can be extended both for resistance to extreme conditions, and for dramatic, even revolutionary, aims. Third, I haven't mentioned the pertinence of this topic to our overall theme of difference;

but I'm not only talking about different uses of power, and different definitions of it. I am also talking about very different ways of envisaging the world—a common interest that supplements contest and confrontation; and a sense of community that can defuse polarization.

Discussion

Q. I'm wondering whether ultimately our only success will be separatist success or whether in fact we will eventually be able to transform male institutions.

A. I think it's a major question. Historically speaking, we have records of women moving toward separatism. For instance, English feminists during the nineteenth century very much had to remove themselves from attempting to do anything in any established structures. There were separate girls' schools and separate colleges and there was a whole process in which women necessarily undertook an exploration of the situation of their selfhood by themselves. I think it's entirely possible that we will have to do that. But I don't think we can lay out one right way to do this, or any one solution—and I didn't mean to; I'm sorry if I did; it was because I was trying to go fast. I do think that these are the three powers we can use, and we may have to use them in different situations in different ways.

Q. I think the problem historically has been that when the presence of women begins to make an impact, men separate out. Women have been the censors of society and before making their dirty jokes, before smoking, men have turned to the women for permission. When that becomes oppressive, the men have gone to their men's clubs and dining rooms and they have separated into their male structures. The problem that we seem to be facing now is, there are many places, despite laws of equal access, that men can go into their own separate spaces and totally ignore what it is that women have to say. The construct of the consent of the governed is unworkable, as long as men have the power to move on and up into their separate spheres. Women still don't have that power; we don't have the spaces, we don't have the technology, we don't have the money. As a result, our growth seems very bound, and limited. I think that if some few women are involved in a corporation, if women are involved in academia, in any area, it's because women have not yet become so much of a problem that men need to separate out. Men become separatist when women get in the way.

A. I don't think you want to be paranoid! I think that certainly, there are tendencies toward this as a quick male reaction. But I don't think it's the only reaction, and I do think that there are common, human interests, and that some men are intelligent enough to perceive them. These men want women's talent and energy and intelligence enough to accept some bargaining relationships. I think we can bargain more, in different places, and harder than we have.

Q. There was a case, a couple of years ago, in New York City involving the law firm of Sullivan and Cromwell, one of the most powerful in the country, which had started to let a couple of young women in, because they were under all kinds of pressure. One young woman lawyer employee had to sue to get Sullivan and Cromwell to agree that not only would they go on recruiting, hiring, and paying women from the law schools on the same basis as the men, but that they would cease having all of the firm's "social functions" from which women were excluded. I want to throw out two thoughts—because I've been dealing with the concept of power in my work as a political scientist. One of the things that made me start rethinking power was the female groups I belong to in which I discovered that everybody tried to stay away from power. The groups had no focus, they had no nucleus, and they had no center, because as soon as a woman became sufficiently assertive to arrive at the center, she thought, Oh, my goodness, I'm grabbing for power, and she retreated like mad. And I thought, that really picks up on a theme that runs throughout Western politics, which is that power is a relationship between two people, one of them superior, and the other inferior. If we were to substitute for "power" the word "leadership," I think we might begin seeing our way clear to something new. Leadership is also a relationship between people, but it means that the leader is being followed, because the leader is answering the needs of the follower. Once the leader stops answering the needs of the follower, the follower will stop following. There is nothing wrong with exercising leadership, as long as it is accountable, in the sense of meeting the needs of the other people in the group. That in itself is not bad. My second thought is that it does seem to me that at this moment in American history the only group that we can perceive as being anywhere on the left of the political spectrum, that has the power and the coherence to organize effectively, is women. If you look at what's going on in American politics, there is no other organized group on the left. Of course politics is dominated by men, but it doesn't have to go on being dominated by them. I don't think the women's movement needs to become powerful in the male sense; it can become a political movement in which leadership is exercised. I think maybe we should start rethinking in those terms.

A. Well, I don't mind whether we call it leaders and followers, or rulers and ruled, but I think that the ability of the followers to communicate their needs to their leaders, and make this stick, will be effectuated by using the powers of the weak. Otherwise, I think you're going to have the kind of leadership that James McGregor Burns describes in his book, which is a synonym for pedagogy.[4] In his vision, there is a transforming leader, who sets the goals, for his followers (naturally it's "he"), who gets them off the ground, and raises them to their true worth. All of the energy comes out of him. I think we ought to be careful not to imagine this as a proper way of using power. But I think the effectiveness of the relationship remains in the hands of what is a dyadic relationship. I don't know that it will be, in that future which we may be able to invent. One of the things that we need to invent is a way not to polarize. We have been polarized on the basis of the division of labor by sex, for as long as anybody remembers. And the contest in the middle has preempted our sense of the unity of humankind around it. Once we can begin to play down the inevitable necessity of conflict, and of solving problems by coming to decisions by debating and disputing them, we will be able to get more variety into each group, male *and* female.

Q. I find a conflict in what you're saying. You said that most reasonable men would want to include women, and would be willing to bargain with them. My question is, why? Patriarchy exists, because men don't want to give up power. That's the basic conflict.

A. Well, one thing is the state of the external world. First, some men are sick of power. They're terrified of it. And second, not all men are the same. Let us not homogenize.

Q. But what we are talking about here is those men who are in control of power now, and we're trying to say something about how we can change this. To say there are a few men who are different doesn't really address itself to that conflict in your position.

A. I'm sorry, I think it does. I said at the beginning that if the reality of power were total dominance and total submission, we would be living in a condition of 1984 forever and a day, and we're not. If we had nothing but a patriarchal structure, in which all men not only aspired to power, but adored it when they got it, and beat us over the head in order to enforce their wishes, I would agree with you. But that isn't the case. Look at the world! It's not good, but it isn't that bad! And I think we have to explain why it isn't.

Q. Explain why it isn't that bad? I don't understand. It seems to me that women are having a very hard time getting some power in this society.

A. But we are not having as bad a time as some women in extreme conditions of patriarchy, where you cannot go out without a veil over your face.

Q. I'm not trying to polarize either and say we're as bad off as . . . ; I'm saying, in this society it is very difficult for women to get ahead, because it is a patriarchal society, as you have said yourself, and because men are not particularly interested in giving up power. On the one hand, you presented us with what patriarchy means, that men are in control; on the other hand, you seemed to be surprised, or think it was extreme, for the women who mentioned something about the separatist nature of men; that men are in control of places where women can't go. Yet it's true for industry, on the whole, and it's true in religion; those are places where men are making the rules and there aren't any women allowed.

A. When you started to make your point, you spoke a good deal more extremely than you did when you finished your point, and perhaps I spoke more extremely than I meant to, too. I certainly did not dispute the need and the value of a separatist understanding, in which women go off to investigate their situation, share it with each other, and discover new ways to reach new purposes. What I was trying to say was that there already exists in the world as it is a situation which is not as extreme as it would be if there were nothing but patriarchal domination. We are not in a good situation; patriarchy exists. But something else exists, which works to limit it, and I don't want to believe that it is simply the ethics and the morals of our noble leaders. To me, it seems to be the fact that we who are the weaker member of a relationship still have sufficient power to modify the relationship by what we do.

Q. Do you suggest we do that within the patriarchal structure?

A. I think if we're going to do it at all we start within the patriarchal structure, because that's what's there. I don't say we're going to end with it. I particularly didn't want to say where I thought we were going. I did, I think, say that wherever we wanted to go, it seemed to me we were going to have to use the powers that were naturally ours and easily available to us, the powers of the weak.

Q. I want to address a couple of points that have been made already. One of them has to do with what was said about leadership. I don't think that by exchanging the word leadership for power we're going to accomplish anything. I'd like to share with you a study that I did on leaderhsip between men and women. First we paired male and female, and then female and female, the same women in two situations. And in the situation, the pair, who didn't know each other, were forced to decide who was going to be the leader for a particular task. What we found was that women were far less likely to assume leadership in the cross-sex pair than when they were paired with other women. And this was despite the fact that they were equally likely to *make* the decision. The usual decision-making conversation started like this: either the man or the woman saying, what would *you* like to do? And then either the man or the woman would decide, and it was equally likely, in both cases, that the man should be the leader. So the women had equal access to the leadership opportunities, but they gave them away to the men. It was an interview situation, in which they were going to decide who was the guilty party of two suspects. It didn't call for specific "male" or "female" abilities. The crucial two points were that the women were equally likely to make the decision, and the women gave it away. Also, we did a personality test on these people and we looked at dominance on the C.P.I., for those of you who know it—the California Psychological Inventory—and neither sex was more dominant than the other sex. So it wasn't personality, and it wasn't decision-making, it was apparently just the norm that two young people—and these were college-age people—who didn't know each other were conforming to what everybody says they're supposed to do. It's the "right" thing to do. And if you stick your neck out and say, no, *you* do the secretarial task, then you're doing precisely that, you're sticking your neck out, and you're risking being different, being rejected. I'd like to pick up on one of the points that you brought out: there is a price and a cost to assuming power. It's risky; you stick your neck out; you risk failure, and you risk assuming responsibility. And I think that as women many of us—either because we've been socialized to say, hey, it's easier not to assume this power, it's easier to let someone else do it, or because it's just the norm—resist power, and run away from it.

A. We also tend to think that it has to be immoral, instead of just being ambiguous and amoral. That affects everybody, but women most, because of their socialization to carry the moral values of the culture.

Q. I was recently told about a study which showed that once women got into a field that was thought to be solely male-oriented, male-dominated, where the power was held by men, and there were enough women in it, the prestige and the power in that field fell off. How do women become a powerful force, if after striving and fighting to get into a certain position, all of a sudden the power in that position disappears?

A. I think what we're all suggesting is that this is a total situation. I know that I began by saying "within the system," and starting where we are, and doing what we can. But the more we talk about the practicalities of it, the more what you and other people have raised becomes clear; that we can make progress, and we can change things, and at the same time, because we're contained within a situation, the change in one area will be affected by that in another. But just the same, I do not want to devalue or belittle the changes that are taking place, and they *are*. Let me just give you an example from my field. Two hundred years ago there were very few women writers. It was quite odd to do this; there were some, and they were beginning, but it was still difficult to make a living doing it. After two hundred years, we can make a living doing it. But how many of us won Pulitzer prizes this year, for instance? And how many are taught in the academic canon outside of Women's Studies? In other words, there are different sides and different aspects even to the change of a growing ability to live by your pen if you're female. You're still not regarded as saying what's so important that you have to be taught as part of literature. But it is better to be able to live by your pen than not.

Q. Isn't the real question how few women publishers there are? I mean, there aren't very many more than there were two hundred years ago.

A. Oh, I think male publishers will publish a woman who sells! A male editor picked up *The Women's Room*.[5] There are quite a lot of women editors in publishing, but very few who control the money.

Q. I'm the most worried about a power that nobody's mentioned today, and that's nuclear power, which was invented by men, and which men are lying about right and left. There aren't enough women scientists to be able to weed through the truth of what's going on. It may be that all these things we're talking about are complete luxuries because in twenty or thirty years nobody will be here. I'd like to see women mobilize and organize, using the three precepts that you gave, to stop this. I have not met a woman who is in favor of going on with nuclear energy.

A. Obviously this is a field where we can not only undertake a task that seems vital, but we can also establish something in the process: that what women and feminists care about are not just problems that are defined as women's issues.

Q. I am sitting here thinking that one of the problems of a centralized power structure is that there's a weakness in the power, which is that not many men and not many women are happy as they move up the ladder. I'll just take that as a given. I was trying to think about the idea of process, in kind of a long-range view of things. It seems to me that one of the things we have to look at most closely is, what kind of targets we want and what view we have of power. Is there such a thing as a decentralized power, whether it be power to generate energy for homes, or the power to generate changes in our lives? One of the basic principles of the women's movement is decentralization. In some ways that has minimized our effect, in the view of the majority press, because we seem to be a bunch of people who disagree with each other and contradict each other. There's lots of controversy and disagreement, and that immediately is taken to mean that we're not together.

A. It's a very important point. The only time I've seen that strongly made and well made, incidentally, was by a man! It's Gene Sharpe, in his *The Politics of Non-Violent Action*.[6] One of the strengths of a nonviolent political group is that it tends to decentralize, rather than to centralize, itself. This is partly in response to the need to act in different locales and in different situations. But also, it essentially undercuts the idea of a forceful leader ruling by force and challenges definitions of power. If you don't know that book, you might find it interesting.

Q. As someone who spent three years in a Wall Street law firm, I must say that even if you do amass numbers up to a dozen or even twenty, the changes brought about on the women are much more significant than the changes on the system. You don't change the system, and the only way you manage to stay there is to adopt the values and, in many ways, all of the trappings of the system, because that's what makes you successful there. And it has nothing to do with your being a woman. Now it's true that you do gain some support from the other women, and you do manage to hold on to some things that you consider vital to your personal identity, but I think you have to give up an enormous amount of yourself to succeed. Some women are going to do that, and they'll adopt the values and the trappings of the system they're trying to work up in. The impact on them is really enormous. But I do think that women can recognize this, and we can develop our own institutional approaches to problems. I just came from the national Women and the Law conference. There were 1,500 or 2,000 women from all over the country that came together in Texas. We've come up with very different kinds of strategies and ways to work together to solve problems. We have an enormous amount of power ourselves to do these things and we don't necessarily have to work within the structures that exist. That in itself is a very significant way of exercising the power that we have.

A. I agree with you, and I'm sorry . . . you've taught me not to sound too optimistic, or to speak too fast! I have to remember that. But you are in fact illustrating the use of powers of the weak, disagreeing and dissenting from the ways things are done and beginning to form groups which will confront the general disagreement with the structures, definitions and rules, and work out strategies.

Q. I guess what I'm suggesting is that distrust and bonding are two important steps that can be put into action outside of the structure.

A. Certainly! They can be put into action any place. And undoubtedly they will be. There will be the creation of new settings, which may very well be single-sex, or may very well be a new kind of withdrawal on the model of blacks creating a Black Power concept (I don't know enough about this to do more than mention it in passing). We do know that this has taken place in women's history and probably will again, and can be very strengthening. There are things that we desperately need to know that we can tell ourselves only when we're together.

Q. I'd just like to add that there are a lot of men who are very willing to cooperate and also interested in developing new strategies.

A. Yes, there are different areas and different levels, I think, at which both of those things can take place; they work best when they work together, that's all.

Q. It's how they work together that's the crucial issue here. When you talk about polarization, that we need to move toward the middle, I agree, but it's at what point we move toward the middle that's crucial. I'd like to use Women's Studies as an example, because that is the area I teach in. I feel that the strength women academics have shown in planning Women's

Studies is a good model for us, because that's where new forms of leadership were exercised and practiced. I think practice is essential here, because if we move toward that center before we're practiced, we're going to be in trouble. We're going to be coopted again, and that's my concern. In the university, we still remain apart. We remain apart as programs, some of us as departments, and we don't want to move too quickly toward that middle because I think we're going to get lost again. Our strength has been in being separate. However, I don't suggest that as a permanent position. It's just that I don't think we should move toward the center too quickly. We should not be too optimistic, or maybe unrealistic, not see the illusions within some of what you say is progress. There are illusions in that progress that we really have to look at. But there's certainly hope. I think we've created all sorts of new models that we can use and that are powerful, especially since the majority of the student population in the 1980s in the university will be women.

Q. I'd like to point out that the concept of bonding is certainly not confined to the weak. That has been a very powerful feature of the male power structure throughout history. So to say that those women in Texas are an example of a bonding of the powerless, I think, is really a polarization which is a disservice to everybody. What troubles me about a lot of what I've heard here is that something that's really a function of time and space is not an absolute, that is, whether we should be separate or together, becomes a kind of excuse for polarization again, which is a feature of the old system. I think at this point in our lives, wherever we are throughout the universe, the female principle has been brought into play as part of the cosmic evolution of the planet. The male principle, based on Newtonian mechanics and the separation of subject and object and supposedly objective relationships, and the tiny, the limited parameters of science, have led us to a mindless technology, which is like Frankenstein and is on the verge of devouring us. It is only through the introduction of the female principle, which is concern for process, concern for the life force, concern for values, that there is a possible solution. This is something that men are aware of, too, although we're all at different stages, and some men in some places are not, just as some women in some places are not. But this is going on as a general evolutionary process, and we need only join the parade. This doesn't mean that we always have to decide, well, are we feminists or are we scholars? It's no longer either/or, but both/and. We have to recognize that we can draw on the strengths that are now available to us in various parts of the world. We are now on spaceship earth, it's very clear. Everything we do everywhere affects us. But our conception of what the future is will change the future. So in that sense, the previous speaker was right when she said we have to look ahead, because our very intentionality defines what we discover.

Let me give you an example: I have a friend in Washington who is the Assistant Secretary of Commerce; her name is Elsa Porter, and she is the only woman who has ever had charge of the budget. Now that's hard-line stuff: $9 billion, 39,000 employees. And she has totally turned around the whole concept of that department about what they're doing, that government is for the people in it and not the reverse. Now it sounds simplistic! But what she has done is to institute human growth seminars. The whole concept is not the model of the hierarchical triangle, where the leader or ruler is at the top, and everyone else is on varying degrees of the scale below. Rather, she is a facilitator at the center. The other people have access to the entire process, and their place in it is respected. Everybody's input is respected, and you don't have to be at a certain level in order to be validated, which is also important. It's the old business of, do you have to be successful in man's terms, the old terms? Well you don't *have* to be *anything*, anymore, if you can have a structure which will allow everybody to have an input. This can make the kind of organic change which will save us from blowing ourselves up.

A. I'm afraid it still sounds utopian to me. I'm still concerned with how we effect this.

Q. You're absolutely right; only I'm saying that there *are* little sparks of hope here and there. The State Department is so impressed by the results that she has achieved that they are sending people around to find out how she does it. So I don't think we should feel that we're a beleaguered minority who have no support anywhere. I believe that, as Audre Lorde says, we have to explore our dreams and then go out and find everybody else who's dreaming the same way.

Q_2. What you're talking about is influence, not power. When your friend can cut the military budget, then she can really make a difference in our lives. I have found, from the study of history, as have all of us—it's available to everybody—that no class has ever given up power without a struggle. I think we were very optimistic about what happened in Iran. It seemed as though people—powerless people—could take power. But it ended up with a kind of a bloodbath, because the revolutionaries had to destroy the class that they just put out of power. Now, it is true that the weak do have powers, and everything that we're doing is to strengthen our consciousness, but in the end, what is it? Do we take power? Do we share power? Nobody gives it away. How do we get it? I think the reason that women can rise in the corporations and that there's a certain amount of democracy in America is because the class in power is a very strong class, with very firm power, and it can share it to a very large extent. But when you get close to taking it away, your friend's seminars are not going to help.

Q. It's not a question of a seminar. But what I'm saying is, we have to link up with all the other people, including males and all the minorities, who see things the way we do.

Q₂. I say this not to be pessimistic, but to understand the difference between influence and power. We have had women writers, but they have not had the power to influence thought and movement. As Ann Douglas says, they have really sentimentalized [women's position], and their writing has been an aid to the party in power, the class in power, and the sex in power.[7]

A. Some women writers have actually done things to create change. First you change perceptions, and then you change the way people apply those perceptions in daily life. I would say that Rachel Carson has had a great deal to do with changing our perceptions of how we ought to deal with the physical environment; Jane Jacobs has had an effective influence on how we think about urban problems.

Q. Rachel Carson was ignored for years after her book came out.

A. I don't think she was. The *New Yorker* ran the whole damn thing, and it was picked up and discussed.

Q. It's a question of who's the target, who do you want to reach.

A. I agree with you, but I think there may be a number of targets you want to reach, depending on different situations. I don't think we have to say that there is only one target or only one goal or only one ideology. In fact, I think we begin to lock ourselves into inflexible positions if we think too much [about this].

Q. I don't see anything wrong with polarization; it's part of the dialectical process. I don't see anything wrong with conflict. If we're trying to create a politics of power that doesn't have conflict in it, we're crazy, because conflict exists in life, it exists in experience. We can't go through this whole thing of being nice to one another, because the world that we live in isn't nice, we're not nice as people all the time, and we're in conflict internally, as the world is in conflict externally. I think we have to build that into our power system.

Q₂. Power involves conflict of interest; that's what power is all about.

A. That's why I say that we need negotiation between different people with different ideas and different values; of course you have conflict. There's no way to get around it. But there are things that cut across. Also, I think there is a difference between conflict and polarization. Polarization carries conflict to extremes, can become lethal, can knock out any sense of humankind as an entity—we hope!—containing all of us. I do not at all turn away from the idea of conflict, but I do not think that it fits every situation in which a decision is going to be made.

Q. It's just very troubling to me to defuse polarization, or to defuse the intensity of conflict. That's what energizes the weak to become stronger and to unbind themselves. They—we—are bound terribly. We are bound by socialization, we're scared to death, we hide behind all the things we've been doing.

A. Let me suggest that the power of the weak, distrust and dissidence, sets up a situation in which we immediately experience a sense of conflict with the structure, within our heads at least.

Q. The conflict is real! Men don't have to fight for the Equal Rights Amendment. I'm embarrassed that I have to ask for the independence that was declared so many years ago. Is it going to take another thousand years, and we'll wait very politely, while the church fights us, and the military fight us? I'm also embarrassed that I cannot be free to use my body as I wish, whether it be expressively, or with reference to reproduction, or anything else. To me this is so basic, when the freedom of mind, and options that I was promised in the Constitution, and the freedom of my body, which I was promised when I was made, I suppose, isn't there! The men have a perfect grip on it. I think we have to address this, not with violence, but with emphasis, and passion.

Q$_2$. What power means as a term, whether it's male, female, feminine, nonfeminine, doesn't interest me that much. First, power, it seems to me, is the capacity to get people to make decisions that are compatible with your own interests. Second, I think it's very important to distinguish between power and authority—Max Weber's old distinctions. There's a legitimate, institutionalized structure which may or may not have power. But power can also exist outside of the institutionalized structure. You've got, therefore, a basic dichotomy between culture and ideology, on the one hand, and the structural reality, which is action and behavior, on the other. I'm hearing a confusion here between power and authority, legitimate and nonlegitimate. When I talk about power, I talk almost exclusively about something that's *illegitimate* until it moves into a central position in the society, that is, when it becomes legitimized by meeting the people's interests.

A. Aren't you saying that we are in fact in the process of redefining these terms, which is something that we have to do? It seems to me we do that by our activity, and redefine as we go.

Q. But it *has* to be illegitimate activity, because if we're part of the institutional structure we are buying into the system and being controlled by it.

A. I think you can do illegitimate things perfectly well within the structure!

Q. But how many decisions can you get that are compatible with your own interests by doing that?

A. I don't know. But again, I don't in my own mind want to make the polarization, between within the structure or revolution against the structure. I think the activity can be either or both. It can turn out to have an unintended, larger effect than was thought at the time. I also think that there are many revolutions, but perhaps the biggest ones are those which take place almost without our knowing it, which are based more on active intervention than on being thoroughly thought out ahead of time. So I'm just trying to keep it open, really, not to cut you back or to debate.

Q. I think these are very important distinctions. You play around with the term power, and we almost always confuse it with the established authority, the structure, the government; and that's not really where power is at.

A. That's why—whether I've been doing it the right way or not here—I want to get us thinking about *ourselves* as possible participants, and how to go about doing that.

Notes

1. Elizabeth Janeway, *Powers of the Weak* (New York: Alfred A. Knopf, 1980).
2. New York: Doubleday, 1970.
3. Virginia Woolf, *Three Guineas* (New York: Harcourt, Brace & World, 1963; orig. pub. 1938).
4. James McGregor Burns, *Leadership* (New York: Harper & Row, 1978).
5. By Marilyn French (New York: Summmit Books, 1977).
6. Gene Sharpe, *The Politics of Non-Violent Action* (Boston: P. Sargent, 1973).
7. Ann Douglas, *The Feminization of American Culture* (New York: Avon Books, 1977).

Notes on Contributors

Jessica Benjamin is a psychoanalytic psychotherapist in New York City. She has been formally trained both as a psychoanalyst and as a sociologist and has written widely about psychoanalysis, feminism, and social theory. Her forthcoming book is an analysis of the psychology of sexual domination.

Carolyn Burke has translated and published articles on recent French feminist theorists, as well as on the female modernist writers. She is completing a biography on the poet/painter Mina Loy.

Nancy Julia Chodorow is associate professor of sociology at the University of California, Santa Cruz, and associate research sociologist at the Institute of Personality Assessment and Research, University of California, Berkeley. She is the author of *The Reproduction of Mothering: Psychoanalysis and the Sociology of Gender*, which won the Jessie Bernard Award of the American Sociological Association, and of numerous articles. She is currently working on a study of early women psychoanalysts.

Clare Coss is co-artistic director of the Women's Experimental Theater and coauthor of *The Daughters Cycle*. Playwright, poet, and psychotherapist, she has had her work produced at the Theatre for the New City, the New Federal Theatre, the Interart Theatre, and the Berkshire Theatre Festival, and has published in *Aphra, Chrysalis, Sinister Wisdom, Feminary*, and *Works*, among other journals. She has taught at Hunter College and the State University of New York at Stony Brook.

Rachel Blau DuPlessis is the author of *Writing Beyond the Ending: Narrative Strategies of Twentieth-Century Women Writers* (Indiana University Press, 1985), and of *Wells* (Montemora, 1980) and *Gypsy/Moth* (Coincidence, 1984), two collections of poems. She is completing a study of H. D. for Harvester Press.

Hester Eisenstein, editor of this volume, is Assistant Director of Equal Opportunity in Public Employment in the state government of New South Wales (Sydney). Before moving to Australia in 1980 she taught history at Yale University and was Coordinator of the Experimental Studies Program at

Barnard College, where she also taught Women's Studies. A former member of the Scholar and the Feminist planning committee, and chair of the Columbia University Seminar on Women and Society, she is the author of *Contemporary Feminist Thought* (Boston: G. K. Hall & Co., 1983).

Tucker Pamella Farley teaches Women's Studies, American Literature, and writing at Brooklyn College, City University of New York. A founding member of the National Women's Studies Association Coordinating Council and coordinator of the Lesbian Caucus, she codeveloped and facilitated "Political, Cultural and Sexual Realities of Lesbian Experience" at Maiden-Rock, Women's Learning Institute, and taught "Reclaiming Herstory: The Lesbian Literary Tradition" at Barnard College, and "Beyond the Mirror: Realities of Female Experience" at the New York School for Marxist Education. Coauthor of *Power, Oppression and the Politics of Culture: A Lesbian-Feminist Perspective* (New York: Goodman, 1978), she is also the author of articles on Virginia Woolf.

Josette Féral is assistant professor at the University of Toronto. She has published in French, American, and Canadian journals on feminism in France, feminine writing, and psychoanalysis and women; she is involved in feminist issues and is currently working on the question of feminist discourse.

Jane Flax teaches political theory at Howard University and is a psychotherapist in private practice. Her writing has appeared in *Quest, Feminist Studies, Politics and Society, Journal of Politics*, and *Journal of Philosophy*. She is currently working on a book, *Freud's Children: Psychoanalysis, Feminism and Critical Theory in the Post-Modern West*.

Jane Gallop teaches French and Women's Studies at Miami University. She is the author of *Intersections: A Reading of Sade with Bataille, Blanchot, and Klossowski* (1981), *The Daughter's Seduction: Feminism and Psychoanalysis* (1982), and *Reading Lacan* (1985). She is currently at work on feminist criticism and literary theory.

Carol Gilligan is associate professor at the Laboratory of Human Development at the Harvard Graduate School of Education.

Carolyn G. Heilbrun, the author of *Christopher Isherwood, The Garnett Family, Toward a Recognition of Androgyny,* and *Reinventing Womanhood*, is professor of English literature at Columbia University. She has been a Guggenheim Fellow, a fellow of the Radcliffe Institute, and recipient of a fellowship from both the Rockefeller Foundation and the National Endowment for the Humanities. She lives in New York City and was President of the Modern Language Association in 1984.

Elizabeth Janeway is the author of numerous books, including, most recently, *Powers of the Weak, Cross Sections,* and *Man's World, Woman's*

Place: A Study in Social Mythology. Her discussion of women's literature appears in the *Harvard Guide to Contemporary American Writing*, and her critical articles have been published by many journals.

Alice Jardine, associate editor of this volume and academic coordinator of the conference on which it is based, is assistant professor of Romance Languages and Literatures at Harvard University. She is the author of *Gynesis: Configurations of Woman and Modernity* (Cornell, 1985), and cotranslator of Julia Kristeva's *Desire in Language: Semiotic Approaches to Literature and Art* (Columbia, 1980).

Audre Lorde is teaching poetry at Hunter College of the City University of New York. She is the author of *The Black Unicorn* (W. W. Norton & Co., 1978), *Sister Outsider* and *Zami* (The Crossing Press, 1983), and is completing her first novel, *I've Been Standing on This Streetcorner a Hell of a Long Time.*

Christiane Makward (D. Lit. Sorbonne) is associate professor of French at Pennsylvania State University. She has taught in West Africa, Quebec, and at the University of Wisconsin. Her publications include articles in *Sub-Stance, La Revue des Sciences Humaines, Poétique,* and *Women and Literature.* She is a founding editor of *BREFF* and the general editor of *Ecrits de Femmes*, an updated edition of which will be published shortly by Des Femmes. She is currently completing a drama anthology in translation and researching unpublished materials in Switzerland for an essay on Corinna Bille.

Sally McConnell-Ginet is associate professor of Linguistics at Cornell University. She has written several articles on women and language and is co-editor, with anthropologist Ruth Borker and literary scholar Nelly Furman, of *Women and Language in Literature and Society* (New York: Praeger, 1980).

Ruth Messinger is a member of the New York City Council and a community activist. She has been a feminist all her life, and she defines every issue as a feminist issue.

Barbara Omolade is an activist in the women's movement and in the liberation struggles of black people. She is a member of the staff of the City College, Center for Worker Education and is also a member of the board of the Sisterhood of Black Single Mothers and a consultant to the Medgar Evers College, Center for Women's Development, one of the few women centers in the country which is devoted to women of color. She teaches and writes about black women and is author of a forthcoming book, *Birth: A Black Womanist Vision.*

Quandra Prettyman is an Associate in English at Barnard College. Her poems have appeared in several anthologies, including *The Poetry of Black Amer-*

ica. She prepared a contemporary English version of passages from William Heale's "An Apologie for Women, or An Opposition to Mr. Dr. G. . . . that it was lawfull for husbands to beat their wives" (1609) for Maria Roy, ed., *Battered Women: A Psychosociological Study of Domestic Violence* (New York: Van Nostrand Reinhold, 1977).

Naomi Schor is professor of French Studies at Brown University. She is the author of *Zola's Crowds* and *Breaking the Chain: Women, Theory, and French Realist Fiction*. She also coedited *Flaubert and Postmodernism*.

Sondra Segal is co-artistic director and performer with the Women's Experimental Theater and coauthor of *The Daughters Cycle*. Ms. Segal has been creating and performing feminist theater since 1972. She is involved in an ongoing research and development of feminist acting theory and has conducted workshops and been guest instructor at universities on the East Coast.

Roberta Sklar is co-artistic director of the Women's Experimental Theater and coauthor of *The Daughters Cycle*. Formerly codirector of the Open Theater and recipient of the New York Drama Critics Award (1972), she has devoted her creative work to the development of feminist theater through writing, directing, and the teaching of acting for women.

Domna C. Stanton is professor of French and Women's Studies at the University of Michigan, Ann Arbor. The associate editor of *Signs: Journal of Women in Culture and Society* from 1975–1980, she is the author of *The Aristocrat as Art: A Comparative Study of the "Honnête Homme" and the Dandy* (1980) and of articles on seventeenth-century French literature, women writers, and critical theory. Stanton is also the editor of *The Female Autograph* (1984), a collection of critical essays and archival pieces on women's autobiographies, memoirs, and letters. Her anthology of French poetry, part of a four-volume series entitled *The Feminist Poets*, is scheduled for publication in 1985.

Index

Master-slave relationship. *See* Hegel,
Georg Wilhelm Friedrich
Matriarchal society, 271
Matrilineage: in Women's Experi-
mental Theater, 193, 195, 198–201,
231–34
Mehlman, Jeffrey, 116
Men: and formation of gender iden-
tity, 12–15, 44–45; and violence
against women, 42; moral develop-
ment of, 274–316
Merchant of Venice, The (William
Shakespeare), 315
Merleau-Ponty, Maurice, 21
Metzger, Deena: quoted, 132, 137
Middle Ages, the (Europe), 147–48,
247–49
Miller, Casey, 91
Miller, Henry, 131, 140
Miller, Jean Baker, xviii, 132
Miller, June, 131
Miller, Nancy K., xxv
Millett, Kate, xv, 81, 329
Mill on the Floss, The (George Eliot),
282, 294
"Minoan" ruins. *See* Freud, Sigmund
Mitchell, Juliet, xvii, 5
Modernists: and women writers, 150
Montgomery Bus Boycott. *See* Bus
Boycott, Montgomery (Alabama)
Montrelay, Michèle, 96, 98
Moral development: in men and
women, 274–316
Morris, Jan: transsexual, 262–63
Mother: as other, 7, 11; as source of
nurturance, 36; primary significance
of, 269. *See also* Mother-daughter
relationship; Motherhood; Mother-
ing
Mother-daughter relationship: and
gender identity, 13–14, 22–23; in
case-study of K., 31–35; psychody-
namics of, 35–37; in family, 193–95
Motherhood: in Julia Kristeva, 113;
in Adrienne Rich, 132
Mothering: and feminism, xviii, 107,
113–114, 157; identified with nurtur-

ance, 41; distorted in culture, 64–65;
reduced significance of, 104
Mouvement de libération des femmes
(France), 107
Ms.: as used in United States, 91; in
linguistic perspective, 159
Ms. Magazine, 99
Muller, Marcel, 174
Mulvey, Laura, 108
Murphy, M., 311

Name-of-the-Father. *See* Lacan,
Jacques
National Association for the Ad-
vancement of Colored People, 253
National Women's Suffrage Associa-
tion, 253
Nature, 27–28. *See also* Human na-
ture
Négritude: and black writing, 150
New Left, the (United States), 157
New York City Council, 319, 322
New Yorker, The, 243, 342
Nin, Anaïs: quoted, 131, 140; men-
tioned, 128
1950s, aesthetic of, 145
Nitzberg, Debbie, 193
*Nom d'Oedipe: Chant du Corps Inter-
dit, Le* (Hélène Cixous), 77
Nom-du-Père (Name-of-the-Father).
See Lacan, Jacques
Nonhegemonic: position of women,
147–51
Nonviolence: in women's moral de-
velopment, 301–308
Nuclear power: and women's move-
ment, 338
Nurturance: and autonomy, 36; and
mothering, 41, 64–65; and women,
132

Objectivity: as psychological distortion, xix; as philosophical issue, 20;
and male development, 45; and
women's writing, 146; and feminist
scholarship, 158–59
Object-relations theory: and develop-